I TATTI STUDIES IN
ITALIAN RENAISSANCE HISTORY

Sponsored by Villa I Tatti
Harvard University Center for Italian Renaissance Studies
Florence, Italy

The

AVIGNON PAPACY
CONTESTED

An Intellectual History
from Dante to Catherine of Siena

Unn Falkeid

Harvard University Press

Cambridge, Massachusetts
London, England
2017

Library of Congress Cataloging-in-Publication Data
Names: Falkeid, Unn, author.
Title: The Avignon papacy contested : an intellectual history from Dante to
Catherine of Siena / Unn Falkeid.
Other titles: I Tatti studies in Italian Renaissance history.
Description: Cambridge, Massachusetts : Harvard University Press, 2017. |
Series: I Tatti studies in Italian Renaissance history | Includes bibliographical
references and index.
Identifiers: LCCN 2017001898 | ISBN 9780674971844 (alk. paper)
Subjects: LCSH: Papacy—History—1309-1378. | Popes—Temporal power. |
Catholic Church—Public opinion—History—To 1500. | Europe—Intellectual life.
Classification: LCC BX1300 .F35 2017 | DDC 262/.1309023—dc23
LC record available at https://lccn.loc.gov/2017001898

To my mother and my father

CONTENTS

THE
AVIGNON PAPACY
CONTESTED

INTRODUCTION

nder the cover of darkness on the night between 26 and 27 May 1328, a small group of Franciscan friars left the city of Avignon in Provence and fled southward. Among the group were Michael of Cesena, the minister-general of the Franciscan order and professor of theology; Bonagrazia da Bergamo, professor of canon law and the official representative of the Minors at the papal curia in Avignon; Henry of Thalheim, provincial minister of Upper Germany; and the two theologians Franceso di Marchia d'Ascoli and William of Ockham, educated at Paris and Oxford, respectively. Breaking their vow to the pope in Avignon, they left the city secretly, without permission. The armed guards, dispatched to pursue them the following morning, could not find them in time. At the very last moment the fugitives managed to escape, and soon after they arrived at the port of Aigues Mortes, from where a ship brought them to the safety of the open sea. Then, on board a galley from Genoa, they wended their way toward the Italian peninsula. At the beginning of June, they arrived in the Tuscan city of Pisa, where they awaited the emperor of the Holy Roman Empire, Ludwig of Bavaria, and his court from Rome.[1]

Why did such an eminent group, comprising the head and the leading friars and theologians of the Franciscan order in Europe, need to flee Avignon? What was at stake, and what did they expect from the emperor? There are no simple answers to such questions, but the immediate reason was the painful conflict over apostolic poverty that had broken out in the 1320s between the papacy in Avignon and the Franciscan order. The underlying causes, however, were far more complex, closely connected to the ongoing centralization of the church in the fourteenth century and the subsequently increasing temporal power of the pope. The pope's authority was encapsulated in the expression of his claimed supremacy—his "fullness of power" (*plenitudo potestatis*)—over secular rulers, a notion that roused bitter resistance in various groups of people all over Europe.

The conflicts escalated under the reign of Pope John XXII. He had rejected the validity of Ludwig's election in 1314 as the new emperor after the death of Henry VII. Nevertheless, Ludwig entered Rome in April 1328 intending to be crowned emperor of the Holy Roman Empire, even without

1

the pope's support. Then, two months after the coronation ceremonies in Italy, he returned to Germany, with a short stop in Pisa, where the group of refugees waited hoping to receive imperial protection and sustenance. And Ludwig did not disappoint them; he took the friars under his wing, and they joined him on his way back to Munich, on the other side of the Alps.

Two of the protagonists in this book were among Ludwig's court. The first was William of Ockham (ca. 1287–ca. 1347), a top theologian and logician, who in 1324 had been summoned from Oxford to the pope in Avignon to answer charges of heresy. Up to this point, none of his many works had shown any trace of attacking political or ecclesiastical rulers, but suddenly Ockham found himself in the eye of the storm, with the result that his life and authorship took a completely new direction. The second was Marsilius of Padua (ca. 1275–ca. 1342), whose huge political treatise *Defensor pacis* (The defender of peace) was condemned as heretical in 1327. Marsilius had already sought refuge at Ludwig's court in Germany, and in 1328 he followed the emperor to Rome, as both his personal physician and his political adviser.

The other four protagonists in this book are Dante Alighieri (1265–1321), Francis Petrarch (1304–1374), Birgitta of Sweden (1303–1373), and Catherine of Siena (1347–1380). Two of these six great thinkers were branded heretics (Marsilius and Ockham), two were later canonized (Birgitta and Catherine), and two became leading models for future generations of humanists (Dante and Petrarch). What they all had in common was an intensely critical view of the growing secular power of the Avignon papacy. Despite their dissimilar backgrounds, and despite the different, though profoundly innovative, solutions they came to offer for the political and ecclesiastical crisis of their time, they shared a mutual resistance to the rapid development of the papal monarchy in Provence.

THE AVIGNON PAPACY CONTESTED

From 1309 to 1377, the pope and the Roman curia resided in the city of Avignon in Provence in southern France. In this period the church underwent an extraordinary process of centralization. The rearmament of papal power was not novel, but it took a radical new turn in the fourteenth century. Ecclesiastical domination had its roots in Pope Gregory VII's series of reforms from the eleventh century, which were designed to free the church from lay control and increase the central, administrative power of the papacy.[2] These reforms ended in a conflict with the German emperors, known as the Investiture Controversy (1075–1122). Since Gregory's time, the popes had assumed moral leadership of Christendom, strongly supported by the canonists of the thirteenth century who defended the pope's supremacy. Over time, this idea of supremacy had repercussions both for the internal structure of the church and for the church's relationship with secular rulers, emperors, and national kings alike. In the twelfth and thirteenth centuries, papal power had been consolidated by the Crusades, taxation systems, and the European universities, from which the popes could articulate, expand, and govern theological doctrines. In addition, there were the new orders of mendicant friars, the foot soldiers of the church, through which the papacy was able to watch over the spiritual lives of urban citizens. The result of this series of factors was that the pope could influence every aspect of Christian life.[3]

Although this process of centralization had been taking place for quite some time, it intensified strongly in the fourteenth century. In an attempt to prevent secular states from appropriating church revenues without the pope's permission, Pope Boniface VIII issued the bull *Clericis laicos* (1296), which stated that lay rulers had no jurisdiction over clerics or their property. By this time, kings obviously had more power than the pope, and the confrontation between Pope Boniface and secular European rulers was, as the historian Barbara Rosenwein has described it, "one sign of the dawning new principles of national sovereignty."[4] The salvos were especially intense between the pope and King Philip IV of France, known as Philip the Fair. Thus, in 1302, Boniface tried to put an end to the conflict by boldly confronting his opponent with his bull *Unam Sanctam* (1302), which has probably become the most famous of all papal documents of the Middle Ages:

> Urged by faith, we are obliged to believe and to maintain that the Church is one, holy, catholic, and also apostolic. We believe in her firmly and we confess with simplicity that outside of her there is neither salvation nor the remission of sins . . . and she represents one sole mystical body whose Head is Christ and the head of Christ is God. . . . Therefore, of the one and only Church there is one body and one head, not two heads like a monster; that is, Christ and the Vicar of Christ, Peter and the successor of Peter. . . . We are informed by the texts of the gospels that in this Church and in its power are two swords; namely, the spiritual and the temporal. . . . Certainly the one who denies that the temporal sword is in the power of Peter has not listened well to the word of the Lord commanding: *"Put up thy sword into thy scabbard"* [Mt 26:52]. Both, therefore, are in the power of the Church, that is to say, the spiritual and the material sword, but the former is to be administered *for* the Church but the latter *by* the Church; the former in the hands of the priest; the

latter by the hands of kings and soldiers, but at the will and sufferance of the priest.[5]

The unique feature of this constitution is that it represents, as Joëlle Rollo-Koster has recently argued, the most extreme assertion of the pontiff's political and juridical primacy over secular rulers that had ever been promulgated.[6] It proposed a severely hierocratic interpretation of papal power, with no independence for secular rulers: as the successor of Peter, Christ had appointed the pope the leader of Christianity, with full power on earth, both spiritual and temporal. The church is moreover portrayed as a mystical body (*corpus mysticum*), with a strong emphasis on the corporeal and juridical senses of the expression, and the pope as the head of this body, giving him the right to judge, depose, and concede power to secular rulers, although he could not be judged by any other human being.[7]

The reactions to this extraordinary claim to sovereignty were immediate. In September 1303, under the command of King Philip's counselor Guillaume de Nogaret, who was accompanied by the notorious Sciarra Colonna from Rome, a band of 1,600 men attacked the pope's palace in Anagni, the Caetanis' fort southeast of Rome, and imprisoned the pope. They intended to take the pope to France and charge him with heresy there. After three days in captivity, however, the pope was rescued by his townspeople, but died a few weeks later, presumably from the shock he suffered.

The "Outrage at Anagni," as historians have usually dubbed it, represents a radical shift in ecclesiastical history. Forced by King Philip, Boniface's successor, Pope Benedict XI, who died on his way to Perugia less than a year after his election, annulled the *Unam Sanctam*. Nevertheless, the bull created the foundation for the popes' claim to sovereignty in the coming decades. In 1305, the canon lawyer and archbishop of Bordeaux, Bertrand de Got, was elected the new pope. Taking the name Pope Clement V, he moved to Poitiers in France, where he was crowned with the tiara in the presence of King Philip. Soon after, he settled in Avignon. Under the governance of the following six popes who resided in Avignon—seven including Clement V—the papacy grew considerably in authority and wealth.

The fate of Pope Boniface haunted his successors, reminding them of the pope's profound vulnerability, and the fear of similar events came to influence their political activities in the decades to come. Still, the reaction to the threats emanating from the increasing power of national kings and secular rulers was not to give way, but rather to adapt, astutely and carefully, to the new situation. This took place in the form of a comprehensive reorganization of the church, which strengthened the pope's authority in temporal and spiritual matters. Within a short time, the papal curia was turned into the most powerful and prosperous court in Europe, rousing mixed reactions. Different groups, both within and outside the church, harshly criticized the burgeoning power of the papacy. Besides the emperor, the critics consisted of the Italian *signori* who supported the emperor's control over the *regnum italicum,* thereby creating their own jurisdiction of authority with no papal intervention. The city-states in northern Italy, on the other hand, were usually torn between their imperial and papal sympathies, as reflected in the bloody conflicts between the Guelphs, the party traditionally sympathetic to the papacy, and the Ghibellines, who supported the emperor.

As the historian Arthur Stephen McGrade has described it, a literary war broke out, which engaged intellectuals all over Europe, and which rivaled in length and bitterness any previous contest between the papacy and secular rulers.[8] That the structural changes took place in Avignon and not in Rome, where the tomb of Saint Peter, Christ's vicar, was to be found, was in itself a provocation for many Christians. Jerusalem was lost to the Muslims in 1187, in 1291 the last Christian stronghold in the Holy Land, the port of Acre, was overrun, and now even the Holy See was in exile. Moreover, the swift increase in French dominance within the Sacred College of Cardinals produced bitter reactions. Despite the fact that the pope showed his strength and independence toward secular rulers, there is no doubt that there were strong bonds between the papal curia and the French crown during the papacy's seventy-year stay in Avignon. Nepotism flourished and the Italian members of the curia were reduced to a minority, seriously provoking the growing number of Italian immigrants—the many notaries, merchants, artisans, and traders—in the city. In short, a dense and multifaceted critique of the papacy's residency in Avignon arose—it rose from every corner of Europe, and from a mixed group of people, with various social and intellectual backgrounds, and with different intentions and arguments.

The purpose of this book is to investigate six of the most prominent critics of the Avignon papacy whose texts came to have a compelling actuality. Dante Alighieri, Marsilius of Padua, William of Ockham, Francis Petrarch, Birgitta of Sweden, and Catherine of Siena fiercely contested the claimed supremacy of the pope as articulated in Boniface's *Unam Sanctam.* They questioned the legitimacy of the pope's secular power while appealing for a profound reformation of the church, the *Ecclesia Romana.* While Dante's conviction, expressed in his *Commedia,* his political letters, and his treatise *Monarchia,* was that only a secular monarch, the emperor, with unlimited temporal power could create peace and thus bring citizens universal liberty, Marsilius emphasized in his *Defensor pacis* the unrestricted power and freedom of citizens to elect their ruler. In their political tracts, however, both Dante and Marsilius strongly delimited the pope's power to religious affairs. William of Ockham was the Franciscan friar who more than anyone else stressed the heretical core of the pope's theocratic claims to supremacy. At the same time, Ockham transformed Franciscan discourses on poverty into a question of subjective rights and individual freedom. With Petrarch, a new turn appeared in the debate. Influenced by the Franciscan Spirituals' rhetoric, as well as by Dante's *Monarchia* and political letters, he continually depicted Avignon as an infernal city that had perverted the authority of both divine and natural laws, in contrast to Rome, whose authorial legitimacy was grounded in the glorious culture of the classical past. In Birgitta of Sweden's numerous visions and in Catherine of Siena's book *Dialogo,* as well as her letters, Rome is defended as the spiritual capital of Christendom, a Christian interpretation of the revived classical idea of Rome as *caput mundi.* Both women's eager attempts to convince the pope to return were thus strongly connected to notions of the thorough reform of the ecclesiastical institution, and the belief that the legitimacy of the pope's power was to be found in Rome, not in Avignon.

Each chapter of the book offers a case study showing how the six figures tried to cope with the precarious situation that the Avignon papacy had created. Dante, Marsilius, Ockham, Petrarch, Birgitta, and Catherine did not only come to have a decisive influence on the political events of their time; as well as being significant political agents, their literary works dominated the agenda of the contemporary political and intellectual debates, with far-reaching effects for the political discourses of early modern Europe. Intriguingly, all six authors were connected to one another, by textual transmissions, by more or less implicit references to each other, or by a common network of acquaintances, collaborators, and friends. Read together, their works reflect the broad and multifaceted scale of political resistance to the Avignon papacy, as well as offering us a survey of the period from the papacy's settlement in Provence in 1309 until the pontiff's return to Rome in 1377.

Which questions did these authors raise? Which solutions did they seek, and which strategies and arguments did they deploy? In short, they all provide important insights into the productive exchanges between different intellectual cultures of fourteenth-century Europe, of which the Avignon papacy constituted both the pulsating heart and the contested authority.

METHODOLOGICAL REFLECTIONS

In the introduction of her book *Avignon and Its Papacy (1309–1417)*, the French American historian Joëlle Rollo-Koster offers a valuable and updated review of the scholarship on the history of the popes' dwelling in southern France, which, in fact, has been surprisingly scarce. As she argues, "Surveys of papal Avignon have been close to nonexistent."[9] Still, she presents a comprehensive review of the scholarly tradition from Étienne Baluze's *Vitae paparum avenionensium* (1693), via the antiquarian and historical investigations that followed in the wake of the opening of the Vatican Archives in 1881, such as those of Léopold Duhamel and Robert Brun, to Patrick Zutshi's concise but expedient chapter in *The New Cambridge Medieval History* (2000).[10] We will not repeat Rollo-Koster's helpful summary here, but rather briefly mention the studies that have been important for this present book.

The work that remains the richest and most useful synthesis of the Avignon papacy, with a special focus on papal administration and finances, is *The Popes at Avignon (1305–1378)* by Guillaume Mollat, originally published in French in 1912.[11] The book paved the way for a new generation of scholars, among whom Yves Renouard and his study *La Papauté à Avignon* from 1954 are of major interest.[12] The originality and strength of Renouard's perspective is his emphasis on the many connections between Avignon and Italy— economic as well as political and cultural exchanges. Another book worth mentioning is the more popular but highly sympathetic and readable *The Popes of Avignon: A Century of Exile* (2008), by the British writer, art critic, and journalist Edwin Mullin.[13] A narrower, yet powerful, study is Diana Wood's biography of Clement VI from 1989, which gives us a fascinating glimpse of the ideas of an intelligent and ambitious pope, as well as of his actions in connection with some prime issues during his pontificate.[14] Yet another insightful book is the study of the ecclesiastical crisis of *trecento* edited by Diego Quaglioni in the voluminous Italian series *Storia della chiesa* (1994).[15] The most recent examination of the Avignon papacy is the already cited book by Rollo-Koster (2015). Thanks to the author's familiarity with the archives and sites of the late medieval Avignon, the book offers a broad approach to the multifaceted interaction between the papal court and the social scenery, the "urban fabric," as she calls it, of the city.

These mentioned historical studies have been invaluable for the contextual framework of this book. Another scholarly tradition that has been of great significance is the many surveys of the political philosophy of the fourteenth century, such as *The Foundation of Modern Political Thought* by Quentin Skinner, *A History of Political Thought: From the Middle Ages to the*

Renaissance by Janet Coleman, and *The Ideas of Power in the Late Middle Ages* by Joseph Canning.[16] Notwithstanding their centrality for our assessment of the political and intellectual climate of the fourteenth century, a weakness with these studies is that none of them has been primarily concerned with the context of Avignon. One exception is the work of Jürgen Miethke, who in his book *De potestate papæ: Die päpstliche Amtskompetenz im Widerstreit der politischen Theorie von Thomas von Aquin bis Wilhelm von Ockham* offers the Avignon papacy considerably more space.[17] Still, Miethke's selection of authorial voices in the intellectual debates is as incomplete as in the studies by Skinner, Coleman, and Canning.

The most prevalent studies of late medieval political thought completely exclude figures such as Francis Petrarch, Birgitta of Sweden, and Catherine of Siena, despite their indisputable contributions to the contemporary intellectual polemics. The reason is probably that they fall outside our modern and somewhat narrow-minded definitions of what a political "thinker" or "philosopher" is. However, the danger with such restricted conceptions is that as readers we anachronistically lose sight of details that may give us more balanced and reliable pictures of the past, indeed, even alter our understanding of a whole period. Especially the two women, Birgitta and Catherine, have fallen prey to such limited considerations, with the result that they more or less are wiped out of the historical-political scenery. But as the readers of this book hopefully will discover, these and similar conclusions are deeply wrong. Both Birgitta and Catherine played decisive roles and were among the major voices in the political debates of the fourteenth century.

The present book has no pretentions of giving a detailed historical or socioeconomic account, based on documentary and archival studies, of the Avignonese era. The primary sources for the following investigation consist of some major political, literary, and visionary texts produced during the period, which contested the legitimacy of the temporal power of the pope while calling for profound reform of the church. The term "literature" is to be taken in a broad sense, as writings or a body of written work—including political treatises, letters, visions, rhymed epistles, sermons, and orations—and not only imaginative works of fiction, which to a certain degree has become the modern, restricted meaning of the word. The methodological approach applied in this book is to read these writings with a view toward the historical setting of the Avignon papacy, and thus explore the connection between rhetoric, modes of thinking, and the historical context.

The main argument is that the particular situation created by the Avignon papacy and by the cultural exchanges that took place within the borders of what turned out to be a European cosmopolitan city drove the intellectual and political debates in new and unexpected directions. It has been essential to incorporate figures who are not represented as often in intellectual histories or in histories of political ideas, but who were nonetheless of immense significance in the political and ecclesiastical debates of fourteenth-century Europe. By examining Francis Petrarch and his passionate nostalgia for classical Rome, and the prophetic voices of the two most influential women of the period, Birgitta of Sweden and Catherine of Siena, alongside authors who more frequently appear in histories of political thought, such as Dante Alighieri, Marsilius of Padua, and William of Ockham, the book aims to contribute a more nuanced and vibrant interpretation of the shifting discussions about power and politics in fourteenth-century Europe. Per se, each of these six figures has hardly ever been explored in terms of the historical backdrop of the Avignon papacy, and even more seldom are they brought together by comparative readings, for which such a common historical context opens. Thus, in addition to enriching the more traditional historical versions of the Avignon papacy, the book aspires to bring new and fresh perspectives on the singular texts that are explored, as well as on the actual authors' genuine responses to the seventy-year-long exile of the pope and his curia.

PRESENTATION OF THE CHAPTERS

Each of the protagonists has been the subject of long traditions of scholarly investigation, of which the most important will be singled out and discussed more thoroughly in the respective chapters. The principal contribution in this book will be to provide an exploration of Dante, Ockham, Marsilius of Padua, Petrarch, Birgitta of Sweden, and Catherine of Siena together in light of the specific setting they shared, which so intensely preoccupied their minds and which became the point of departure for their political and literary commitments.

Chapter 1 offers a new reading of *Paradiso* VI from Dante's *Commedia*.[18] In this canto, one of the most politically charged in Dante's fictional journey through the three realms of the afterlife, Dante the pilgrim meets Justinian, the sixth-century emperor who created the body of Roman or civil law, the *Corpus Iuris Civilis*. Justinian's long monologue strongly defends the Roman Empire and is not so very different from the justification we find in Dante's political treatise, *Monarchia* (On the monarchy). The two texts were written at the same time, probably in 1317–1318, as a response to Pope John XXII's attack on the validity of the posts of imperial vicars that had been awarded by Emperor Henry VII to several northern Italian *signori,* including Dante's patron, Cangrande della Scala.

Dante was deeply disappointed by Henry VII's failed attempt to regain imperial control over Italy, and his defeat and death in 1313 only consolidated the power of Pope Clement V in Avignon and paved the way for his notorious successor, Pope John XXII. Thus, in the *Monarchia* Dante invokes a monarch capable of bringing peace not only to a war-torn Italy but also to a Europe ravaged by war and discord. The main reason for the problems was the temporal power of the pope due to Constantine the Great's presumed donation of the western empire to Pope Sylvester early in the fourth century. For Dante, the Donation of Constantine was profoundly wrong.[19] His solution was to strictly divide jurisdiction between secular and ecclesiastical authority, with no interference between the two realms. Indeed, a complete transfer of secular power to the emperor was a precondition for establishing peace: jurisdiction over terrestrial matters belonged to the emperor alone, according to Dante, whereas spiritual matters in terms of humans' eternal happiness were under the jurisdiction of the pope.

Chapter 2 consists of a comparative analysis of Dante's *Inferno* VI and *Monarchia,* and Marsilius of Padua's treatise *Defensor pacis.*[20] When Ludwig of Bavaria, Henry VII's successor, went to Rome in 1328 to be crowned, Marsilius accompanied the emperor as his personal physician and as one of his main advisers. A few years earlier, Marsilius had published his extensive treatise *Defensor pacis* (1324), in which he strongly criticized the Avignon papacy. The emperor and his adviser later applied the ideology of the treatise to their undertakings in Rome. Of importance is that the emperor's supporters also referred to Dante's *Monarchia,* leading Pope John XXII to deem both Dante's and Marsilius's works to be heretical. Despite the shared fate of these two books and both authors' attacks on the Avignon papacy, Dante and Marsilius differed greatly in their interpretations of legitimate authority. Whereas Dante emphasized the divine origin of both secular and ecclesiastical power, Marsilius founded the idea of legitimacy on the sovereignty of the people. To Marsilius, the body of citizens represented the will of the whole and the government rested on the ultimate authority of them.

Whereas Chapters 1 and 2 focus on two figures whose initial political training and intellectual education took place within the walls of the Italian city-states, in Chapter 3 we will turn to William of Ockham, who was a Franciscan friar from Oxford.[21] After carving out a career as a philosopher who made important contributions to logic, he became involved in the controversies of apostolic poverty in Avignon. He was imprisoned by the pope but managed to escape and joined Ludwig of Bavaria and his court, which included Marsilius of Padua, on their way back to Germany. He spent the rest of his life there in a Franciscan monastery, where he wrote a series of political tractates, including *Breviloquium de principatu tyrannico* (A short discourse on tyrannical government), the main text of Chapter 3 of this study.

In contrast to many of Ockham's other political works, the *Breviloquium* (1342) is a deeply personal text and its main focus is on the fundamental liberty granted to all human beings by both divine and natural rights. Ockham's argument, which is a wide-ranging attack on the doctrine of papal absolutism, is derived from the disputes about apostolic poverty that fifteen years earlier had condemned the celebrated theologian and scholar as a heretic. Although Pope John XXII rejected the division between ownership (*dominium*) and the use (*usus*) of things, this division constituted the heart of Franciscan spirituality—the friars' voluntary rejection of any *dominium* in order to live under what Ockham described as prelapsarian freedom. Ockham argued that the Franciscans had renounced all worldly rights, including the right to sue in court and to own property. Nonetheless, there was a right that was universal to all men and that consisted of the right to use external things. This was a natural right and liberty, conferred by God and nature, since it was necessary to maintain life.

Chapter 4 turns to Francis Petrarch, the "father of humanism" or "l'initiateur de la Renaissance," as Pierre de Nolhac once so famously called him because of his efforts to transform the cultural agenda through a revival of antiquity.[22] The portrayal of Petrarch as just such a seminal, humanist figure has been modified today by a stronger focus on the contextual realities of his works, as well as more nuanced studies of the early humanist movements.[23] Nevertheless, there has been, and still is, a tendency to undervalue the impact of the city of Avignon, which in many respects shaped Petrarch's role as the most celebrated intellectual of his time.

Petrarch's works are full of ambiguities, not all of which are easy to grasp. The exiled author, or the *peregrinus ubique*—the pilgrim everywhere—as he liked to describe himself,[24] constantly challenged his many interlocutors while he swiftly shifted positions and loyalties. In Chapter 4 we will examine a letter to Cola di Rienzo (*Lettere disperse* 8) in which Petrarch stepped decisively into contemporary politics. His fervent defense of Cola's revolution in Rome in 1347 and the subsequent establishment of the Roman Republic were followed by the author's increasingly harsh condemnation of the Avignon papacy, in which he applied a biblical and apocalyptic rhetoric common among the Spirituals: classical ideals (the restoration of Rome) and eschatological desires (the dawn of a new age) merged, according to Petrarch, in the figure of Cola.

In 1350, the year of Rome's great Jubilee, of which Petrarch had been one of the main promoters, and four years before the melodramatic execution of Cola at the Capitoline Hill, Birgitta of Sweden entered Rome.[25] Except for her frequent trips around Italy, her journey to Cyprus and even to Jerusalem, Rome became her residence for the last twenty-three years of her life, and from here she started a campaign to return the papacy from Avignon. No one fought with more fervor and constancy for the sake of Rome than Birgitta. Unfazed by their high station, she wrote letters, compiled in her vast collection of *Revelaciones,* to Popes Clement VI, Innocent VI, Urban V, and Gregory XI in which she described in a most apocalyptic manner the wretched state of the city, claiming that its princes were like feral robbers, its buildings were dilapidated, its churches were abandoned, and its canons, priests, and deacons openly kept mistresses in their homes. According to Birgitta, it was high time to restore Rome, as well as the Catholic faith, and only the return of the pope could dispel the evils present in the city.

Chapter 5 consists of an analysis of the way in which Birgitta came to model her activities on the figure of the widow who was speaking for the sake of Rome. In a letter obliquely addressed to Pope Clement VI (*Rev.* IV, 78), she presents herself as a widow—which she was in real life after her husband, with whom she had had eight children, passed away. The actual letter is written just after her arrival in Rome, and the text describes a vision she presumably received in the basilica of Santa Maria Maggiore on the top of the Esquiline Hill. However, the miserable state of the church, as Birgitta depicts it, soon turns into a profound critique of the current state of the *Ecclesia Romana.* As such, the *topos* of the widow has profound political connotations. It reflects the personification of the widowed Rome already adopted by Dante and Petrarch, and later used by Cola di Rienzo in his powerful ideological propaganda during the revolution in Rome in 1347.

Catherine of Siena is often depicted as an overwrought woman whose thinking was befuddled by a strained, individual mysticism.[26] However, in the last chapter of this book, Chapter 6, we will discuss how her writings and her personal engagement seem in fact to have a compelling actuality. As the first female author in Italian, she entered the political-historical stage with a surprising vibrancy and strength. Her insistence on using the *volgare* (the vernacular) in her book *Dialogo della divina provvidenza* not only challenged the Latin discourses of contemporary humanists and ecclesiastical authority; it also strengthened her critique of the Avignon papacy and the theological disagreements that had torn the church apart. The important discussions in her book about the mystical body of the church subtly reject the theocratic ideas of *Unam Sanctam,* Pope Boniface VIII's bull from 1302, which in many ways initiated the fourteenth-century conflicts and brought the pope and his curia to Avignon. Recalling Thomas Aquinas's interpretation of the concept of *corpus mysticum* from the period before the papacy settled in France, Catherine's response to the problem of the Avignon papacy was most diplomatic: she defended the historical and institutional role of the church while calling for profound reform, thus contributing in her own way to a conflict that had preoccupied humanists, lawyers, and theologians for almost a century.

To summarize, through this series of case studies, *The Avignon Papacy Contested* offers an in-depth analysis of some of the most authoritative voices of the fourteenth century who responded, each in their own individual and original manner, to the Avignon papacy. Dante, Marsilius, Ockham, Petrarch, Birgitta, and Catherine were all concerned with the pope's claims to absolute jurisdiction and the papacy's swift increase in prosperity and secular power. Although addressing these problems with different arguments, images, and motivations, we will see how their works in many ways are surprisingly and intriguingly linked to each other, by internal references and textual transmissions, by common networks of friends and acquaintances, or by the historical realities in which they were written. Of greatest importance is that Dante's *Paradiso* VI and his *Monarchia*, Marsilius's *Defensor pacis*, Ockham's *Breviloquium*, Petrarch's letter to Cola di Rienzo, Birgitta's *Revelaciones*, and Catherine's *Dialogo* both reflect and set the agenda for the political debates of the fourteenth century. Concurrently, the production of each text follows the development of the papacy, from its settlement in Avignon to its return to Rome. When considered together, they open a window onto a highly dramatic century in European intellectual history.

A BRIEF OUTLINE OF THE AVIGNON PAPACY

As we have seen, each chapter of this book focuses on some specific texts, and explores through systematic analyses how they address the questions of the legitimacy of power and the reformation of the church. To historically locate these texts, it may be helpful, though, to have a certain familiarity with the principal events of the papacy's residency in southern France. Why did the popes choose to go to Avignon, and then to stay there for such a long period? Did the popes ever plan to return? What effects did the exile have on ecclesiastical and secular politics in Italy and Europe, and, finally, how did the culture of the city change with the presence of the papacy?

The answers to these questions can only be brief and superficial, and they are indebted to the important works by the historians of the Avignon papacy, such as Mollat, Renouard, and Rollo-Koster. The main reason mentioned by all three of them why Clement V chose Avignon was the impossibility of returning to Rome after the outrage at Anagni. The unstable situation in Rome, riven with the continuous feuding between the Roman barons, such as the Caetani, the Colonna, and the Orsini, made the city a most unsafe place for the pope. Comtat Venaissin in Provence, however, was one of the papal territories outside Rome, and the only transalpine state. Still, Clement preferred the city of Avignon, which was close to, though not within the borders of, Comtat Venaissin. Avignon was a vassal of King Charles of Naples, who, for his part, held his Italian lands from the pope. Thus, under the protection of King Charles and his successor, King Robert of Naples, who was loyal toward the pope, the papacy enjoyed a certain proximity to Rome, the bishopric of the pope.

During the first decades of the fourteenth century, the political conditions in Italy were in general extremely difficult. The republics were in decline and the city-states were at constant war with each other. Perhaps no one offered a more illustrative report of the deplorable situation than Dante in his *Commedia*. When the two pilgrims, Virgil and Dante, meet the Mantuan poet Sordello in *Purgatorio* VI (76–114), he issues his famous vituperation of Italy:

> Ahi serva Italia, di dolore ostello,
> nave sanza nocchiere in gran tempesta,
> non donna di provincie, ma bordello!
> Quell' anima gentil fu così presta,
> sol per lo dolce suon de la sua terra,
> di fare al cittadin suo quivi festa:
> e ora in te non stanno sanza guerra
> li vivi tuoi, e l'un l'altro si rode
> di quei ch'un muro e una fosse serra.
> Cerca, misera, intorno da le prode
> Le tue marine, e poi ti guarda in seno,
> s'alcuna parte in te di pace gode.
> Vieni a veder Montecchi e Cappelletti,
> Monaldi e Filippeschi, uom sanza cura:
> color già tristi, e questi con sospetti!
> Vien, crudel, vieni, e vidi la pressura
> d'i tuoi gentili, e cura lor magagne;
> e vedrai Santafior com' è oscura!
> Vieni a veder la tua Roma che piagne
> vedova e sola, e dì e notte chiama:
> "Cesare mio, perché non m'accompagne?"

[Ah, servile Italy, hostel of grief, ship without pilot in great tempest, no mistress of provinces, but brothel! So eager was that noble soul, only at the sweet name of his city, to give glad welcome there to his fellow-citizen—and now in you your living abide not without war, and of those whom wall and one moat shut in, one gnaws at the other! Search, wretched one, round the shores of your seas, and then look within your bosom, if any part of you enjoys peace! Come to see Montecchi and Cappelletti, Monaldi and Filippeschi, you man without care, those already wretched and these in dread. Come, cruel one, and see the distress of your nobles, and heal their hurts; and you will see Santafiora, how forlorn it is. Come see your Rome that weeps, widowed and alone, crying day and night, "My Caesar, why do you abandon me?"][27]

In this mighty apostrophe, hurled out with a prophetic intensity, Dante presents Italy as enslaved ("serva Italia") and cast into the most violent of conflicts. The queen of the provinces ("donna di provincie"), as the Roman emperor Justinian once called Italy, has now been reduced to a brothel. The pain is all-encompassing and percolates down to every single citizen: the quotation does not only refer to the chaotic situation that existed between the Italian city-states, including the Papal States, but also to what was unfolding within the shelter of the city walls, where concord and peace have been replaced with self-devouring fights between families, such as the ongoing feuds between the Montecchi and the Capuletti—later the Montagues and Capulets of Shakespeare's *Romeo and Juliet*. The darkness that has descended on Italy because of all these calamities is finally followed by the image of Rome, depicted as the widow, left by her husband.

This seventy-five-line invective, of which only a part is quoted here, clearly shows that, in Dante's opinion, Italy was in such a tragic state because it was a country abandoned. Both lords—pope and emperor, connected in the rhetorical hendiadys as the widow's husband—were absent. Even though the citizens did have the correct instrument, Roman law, to assuage the conflict, there was no leader to enforce it. From the perspectives of the popes, however, settling in Rome was impossible. When Pope John XXII was newly elected in 1316, his intention was supposedly to return the papacy to Italy, but during his reign the situation in Italy worsened.

None of the seven Papal States in Italy outside of Rome was sufficiently politically stable for the papacy to settle there. Many of them were in the hands of opportunist warlords or constantly threatened by powerful neighbors, above all by the mighty Visconti family in Milan, who through the Ghibelline alliance sought to extend their territory. Pope John XXII tried to defeat the Ghibellines by supporting their enemy, the Guelph alliance, but the Ghibellines received help from Ludwig of Bavaria, the newly elected emperor of the Holy Roman Empire. Thus, when Ludwig of Bavaria entered Rome to be crowned emperor in 1328, accompanied by, among others, Marsilius of Padua, the papacy's return was made more unfeasible than ever before. Although Pope John did at one point try to reestablish papal authority in the Papal States and go to Bologna, this attempt was unsuccessful, and by his death in 1334, any hope of return to Rome had been dispelled.

In addition, there was the papacy's attempt to bring peace between England and France, a question that particularly interested Birgitta of Sweden. The conflict between the two states, which strengthened the national identities of citizens in both countries, gradually escalated and ended in the Hundred Years' War (1337–1453). However, without the support of the French and English, any crusade on Jerusalem, long the papacy's intention, would be impossible. Yet another reason to choose Avignon was the city's attractive location. Avignon offered tranquility and peace, a population without any tradition of self-government, in contrast to the Roman citizens, and a far better climate than the hot, unhealthy, and malaria-ridden summers in Lazio. Furthermore, in the late Middle Ages, the center of gravity of Christendom moved northward, and Avignon was strategically situated between the political and economic powers of northern and southern Europe.

In short, Avignon made it far easier for the popes to govern the Christian world, with its bridge over the river Rhône, the valley's borders between the Holy Roman Empire and the kingdom of France, and the ports of the lower Rhône from Marseille to Montpellier. As Renouard has described it, during the reign of Pope John, all the advantages of the city were revealed. While Avignon became a crossroads between the majority of the Christian population in northern Europe and the holy sites and ancient centers of the south, divisions of important Florentine companies turned the city into the trading and banking center of Provence.[28]

Throughout the government of Pope John's two successors, Benedict XII and Clement VI, plans to return to Rome were put aside, while the city of Avignon reached the peak of its power and success. When Pope John died in December 1334, the conclave elected the Cistercian monk and bishop of Pamiers Jacques Fournier, who had been the zealous hunter of heretics under the previous pope, and whose efforts are carefully recorded in Emmanuel Le Roy Ladurie's bestselling book *Montaillou*.[29] Benedict was a dogmatic and austere theologian. He remained a monk even as a pope and, as such, he tried to act most uprightly. On the one hand, he attacked nepotism, on the other, his wish to reduce abuses led to his personal in-

volvement in the nomination of ecclesiastical benefices, which often demonstrated his fairness.[30] This took place, though, alongside the increasing
centralization process around the pope and his personal decisions.

As with the previous two popes, it was Benedict's initial intention to
bring the papacy back to Rome. So he told his electors, and one of the first
things he commissioned was the reconstruction of the basilicas of Saint
Peter and the Lateran. Like his forerunners, though, he was not able to sta-
bilize the situation in Italy and this, combined with the strong resistance of
the French majority of the papal court to the idea of leaving Avignon, made
him change his mind. He decided to stay in Provence, and as soon as this
decision was made, he initiated the reconstruction and transformation of
the episcopal residence, turning it into a new papal palace. Then, in 1339,
when the pope was already residing in his own fortress, demonstrating that
he was no longer a guest, the papal archives were brought from Assisi,
which underscored that the stay in Avignon was meant to be permanent.

The modest Pope Benedict was succeeded in 1342 by the extravagant
Pierre Roger, who took the name Clement VI, and who, in contrast to his
forerunner, brought Rome's splendor and grandeur to Avignon. "My predecessors did not know how to be popes," he famously announced, while
transforming the city into an *altera Roma*.[31] Again nepotism flourished.
The papal court swelled, and in the new offices Clement placed many of
his relatives and friends from the Limousin district. Boosting Avignonese
self-confidence by making his court the political, intellectual, and artistic
capital of Europe, he generously spent the prosperity amassed by his parsi-
monious predecessor. Many of the sites in Avignon were given new names
so they might reflect their Roman prototypes, and he built a second palace,
close to his predecessor's, which from the outside had the same somber,
monastic look, but which inside was adapted to the pope's intention
of making his court the most splendid and the most ceremonious in the
world. For instance, he had the walls decorated with exquisite frescoes of
secular and aristocratic motifs, such as in the famous Chambre du Cerf, or
the Stag Room, which reveals a taste for the Gothic style, usually described
as a new naturalism.[32] Furthermore, by purchasing the city from Queen
Joanna of Naples, while ensuring that the new emperor of the Holy Roman
Empire, Charles IV, renounced his feudal rights to the city, the pope became the single ruler of Avignon and of Comtat Venaissin.

Clement VI was an impressive pope, a humanist, as Diana Wood has
described him, or perhaps more correctly, a medieval polymath, as Ronald
Musto has preferred to call him.[33] His interests were encyclopedic in
scope, stretching from astronomy, geography, liturgy, and law, to philosophy, medicine, and classical learning. He acted as a patron for artists and

intellectuals, such as Petrarch, and he enriched the papal library, established by Pope John XXII, with Cicero, Pliny, Macrobius, and other classics, as well as with books in Arabic and Hebrew. He behaved courageously during the Black Death, protecting the Jewish population from scapegoating and accusations of responsibility for the plague. And his involvement in Cola di Rienzo's revolution in Rome in 1347 reveals his political prudence, as well as his actual interest in the city of Rome. Still, Clement never managed to establish peace in the Papal States, and he expressed no desire to move the papacy to Rome, despite increasing attempts to convince him to return. As a consolation, however, he proclaimed the year 1350 as a Holy Jubilee, a year of special grace for the pilgrims who visited Rome and its basilicas, only fifty years after the last Jubilee in 1300. The Jubilee turned out to be an economic blessing for Rome. Furthermore, it gained a profound, spiritual sense after the dreadful outbreak of the Black Death at the end of the 1340s. Pilgrims from all over tormented Europe flocked to the Eternal City, among them Birgitta of Sweden and her company of friends, confessors, and relatives.

THE RETURN TO ROME

It was not until Clement's successor, Pope Innocent VI, and his efforts to regain authority in the Papal States in Italy that the papacy could consider the possibility of returning. Innocent, elected in December 1352, was an elderly man in poor health whom the Sacred College of Cardinals probably thought would be easy to control after his flamboyant and unruly predecessor. But the cardinals were wrong, although Innocent did not have the resources to follow in the footsteps of Clement. The treasury was more or less empty, while the political turmoil in Europe, above all the war between England and France, escalated. However, Innocent decided to focus on the Papal States, charging the Spanish nobleman and cardinal Gil Álvarez Carrillo de Albornoz with reestablishing the power of the pope. As Renouard has described it, Albornoz was at once soldier, peacemaker, and lawyer—and he was amazingly successful in his task.[34] He started in Rome, that is, from the south, and paved his way northward. The most difficult job was the battles with the Visconti in Romagna. But with help from Emperor Charles IV, who since his first meeting with the young Pierre Roger (later Pope Clement VI) was on good terms with the papacy, the Spanish cardinal defeated Bernabò, the leader of the Visconti clan, in 1361.

Innocent was not able to return to Rome before he died in 1362, and perhaps this had never been his intention. In the meantime, while Albornoz was fighting in Italy, Provence was attacked by free legions of mercenaries, made unemployed by the temporary truce between England and France, and thus without any commitments or income. The continuous plundering and assaults by the violent and frustrated mercenary companies destabilized Provence and turned Avignon into an unsafe place, a fact that obviously made it easier for Innocent's successor, Urban V, to think about a return to Italy, although the majority of cardinals were still against the idea. After Albornoz's interventions, the political situation in the Papal States dramatically improved—even Rome was more peaceful than ever before. In 1363 Albornoz had codified the Roman Statutes, which excluded the nobility from public office, thereby establishing civil order.[35]

In October 1368, both Pope Urban V and Emperor Charles IV entered Rome, followed by a series of solemn ceremonies, which Birgitta of Sweden experienced. The man in charge in Avignon was Philippe de Cabassole, the former bishop of Cavaillon, who was then appointed vicar-general of the city.[36] Incidentally, Philippe had been one of Petrarch's best friends and his neighbor in Vaucluse, where the bishop's castle towered atop the steep cliff behind Petrarch's more modest house by the Sorgue River. They had spent much time together, and Petrarch even dedicated his treatise *De vita solitaria* to the bishop.[37] Only a year after Urban's transfer, though, the talented Philippe left Avignon in order to help the pope in Rome, but without much success. The pope's stay in the Eternal City was short-lived. Doubtless to the great pleasure of the disloyal French cardinals, the pope's Italian journey was a fiasco, and after just three years he returned to Avignon in 1370, where he soon died.

When Cardinal Pierre Roger de Beaufort, the nephew—some have even argued the illegitimate son—of Pope Clement VI, was offered the tiara in December 1370, he became the last of the seven Avignonese popes. He took the name Gregory XI. As a former student of the famous jurist Baldo degli Ubaldi in Perugia, he had lived in Italy for many years, and he knew Italian politics and the peninsula well. Despite his young age—he was only forty-two years old when he was elected—he was reportedly a profoundly cultured man, learned, humble, and calm. Even Coluccio Salutati, the Florentine humanist, praised his moral and scholarly qualities.[38] Indeed, the unusual thing about Salutati's praise was that it came from a man who belonged to the pope's group of enemies. During the 1370s Florence, traditionally a papal ally, had taken a leading role in the coalition with the Italian city-states and their war against the Papal States, known as the War of the Eight Saints (1375–1378). In fact, the Florentines' aggression was one of the main hindrances, and a reason why it took so long for Pope Gregory to be able to return to Rome. The Florentines were against the possible presence of the papacy in Italy. As F. Thomas Luongo has explored in his book *Saintly Politics of Catherine of Siena* (2006), the young Catherine of Siena came to play a key role in the political negotiations between Florence and the papacy.[39]

Another hindrance for Pope Gregory was a lack of means. After the expensive wars of Cardinal Albornoz, the treasury was empty, and the papacy even had to borrow money. Furthermore, turning the will of the people that surrounded the pope in Avignon would be a massive task. The majority of the curia, most of them natives of southern France, and a large number of the cardinals, were against the transferal.[40] Still, in September 1376, Gregory left Provence. As Rollo-Koster has explained, part of his success was that he did not make his forerunner's mistake. Instead of halving the government of the church, he left it in Avignon, and then, once he was safely settled in Rome, he transferred the whole administration to the city.[41]

The return was not easy. The Roman people, used to freedom and self-governance, and now even more excited by the ideas of communal liberty after the war between the Papal States and the Italian cities, were hesitant about Gregory's arrival. The economic prospects of the papacy's return were optimistic, though, but Florentine merchants in the city fueled the inhabitants' irritation with the pope. Moreover, nationalistic sentiments between the French flank of the curia and Roman citizens emerged. Accordingly, when Gregory died on the night between 26 and 27 March 1378, confined in Castel Sant'Angelo, where he had sought refuge from the rebellious Roman mob, he left the Christian world more or less plunged into political anarchy, a fact that came to form the beginning of the Great Schism of the Western Church.

SUCCESS AND RESISTANCE

The residence of the papacy in Avignon led to the swift consolidation and concentration of the internal government of the church. As well as being French, all seven popes during the Avignon papacy had also been successful lawyers or had at least received legal training. This had a profound effect on the papacy, which during its seventy-year-long stay in Provence reached its peak of power. In short, the popes' juridical focus was on a permanent strengthening and expansion of their rule and administration.

It was especially within three areas that the popes bolstered their authority. The first was the nomination of benefices, the appointment of clergy to ecclesiastical offices. Above all Pope John XXII developed, with great caution, the art of nomination so it would not excite too much protest, while the appointments increased the pope's own power. The strategy was to make priests, ministers, deacons, and bishops indebted to the pope by direct appointments, a process that was easily accepted by secular rulers throughout Christendom, except in the countries where the papacy openly favored a particular party, like the Guelphs in Italy, or the enemies of Emperor Ludwig of Bavaria in Germany.[42] The second area through which the pope multiplied his authority was the imposition of papal taxes. Here too Pope John did an effective job by creating an intricate, centralized fiscal system, which, together with spoils from the newly banned Templars, rapidly developed the papal curia into a court that outshone all the secular courts in Europe in power and wealth. The third field of government where the Avignon popes made significant progress was the waxing monarchical structure of the church. As Renouard has underlined, the papacy had both the oligarchy and democracy to struggle with.[43] Still, we see the same tendency within the church as within various European states during the fourteenth and the fifteenth centuries, namely, a general political tendency toward absolutism. In an ecclesiastical context this absolutism was reflected in the pope's theocratic claim to "plenitude of power" (*plenitudo potestatis*) in both spiritual and temporal matters. Notably, the power of the Sacred College of Cardinals was a constant threat to the popes, and it was the cardinals who caused the Great Western Schism after Gregory XI's return to Rome. Out of the Great Schism grew the conciliar movement as well, which demanded the supremacy of the Ecumenical Council over the pope, and which also came to represent a severe challenge to the pope's authority.

The effect of this extraordinary process of centralization, especially under the government of Pope John XXII, was a concentration of mammon and temporal power, which undoubtedly gave Avignon, the religious capital of Christendom, an air of secular lavishness. Mollat has given us a vivid portrait of the extravagant living and the splendor of the feasts at the papal court. The papal palace showed, as he writes, "a strange mixture of sumptuousness and simplicity."[44] The windows were covered with wax linen instead of glass, and the furniture was often modest. The halls and official rooms, on the other hand, were elegantly decorated with fine tapestries from Spain and Flanders, or even with hangings of silk, taffeta, or serge, if they not were covered with the beautiful frescoes such as in the Chambre du Cerf. Plates of gold and silver were in use, and there were knives and forks with handles of ivory and jasper, expensive clothes, and furs in great quantities, especially for the women at the court. We have lists of the requirements for banquets such as the dinner Pope John XXII offered as a celebration of the marriage of his great niece on 22 November 1324: the list contains 4,012 loaves of bread, 9 oxen, 55 sheep, 8 pigs, 4 wild boars, a large quantity of various kinds of fish, 200 capons, 690 chickens, 270 rabbits, 40 plovers, 37 ducks, 50 pigeons, 4 cranes, 2 pheasants, 2 peacocks, 292 small birds, about 3 hundredweights of cheese, 3,000 eggs, 11 barrels of wine, and a mere 2,000 apples, pears, and other fruit.[45] One can only imagine the great number of servants, cooks, and kitchen assistants who were required to organize such vast volumes of food and drink!

Concerning the fate of Avignon in a broader setting, the city's fortune altered dramatically after the arrival of the papacy. Avignon had originally been a rather poor city, but soon it became a hub for all kinds of trades and services. Italian, and in particular Florentine, banking houses proliferated there, and rich merchants from the Italian cities established their own businesses in town. Soon Avignon was turned into an economic, political, and cultural center. It grew in extent, and became far more important than Rome.

The fortune of Avignon also brought along a cultural boom. Employed by the papacy, notaries, theologians, physicians, and lawyers from all over Europe settled in the city, and Avignon became a meeting point for a lively exchange of ideas and manuscripts, creating the environment where early forms of humanism would flourish. The papacy came into possession of remarkable collections of antique manuscripts and was an important center for book markets.[46] The papal library established in Avignon grew significantly during that period, bearing witness to a keen interest in classical studies. Furthermore, the city was vastly enriched and architects, artists, and craftsmen were summoned to build and decorate new houses, palaces, and churches, such as the celebrated Gothic painter Simone Martini, who also painted a portrait of Petrarch's Lady Laura during his stay.[47] Moreover, the city became a center for the innovative polyphonic music of the fourteenth century—the *Ars nova*—named after the famous treatise *Ars nova notandi* by Philippe de Vitry, who served at the papal court for some time.[48]

Despite this fabulous economic and cultural boom, though, the political situation was tense—and growing tenser. As we have already seen, different groups, both within and outside the church, severely criticized the burgeoning power of the papacy, such as Emperor Ludwig of Bavaria and his supporters in Germany; the Italian *signori,* primarily the Visconti, in the *regnum italicum;* and the city-states in northern Italy, usually torn between imperial and papal sympathies. In addition came the attacks from the mendicant friars, the Spirituals, the Beguines, and other companies of religious laypeople condemned by the church, as well as the critique by growing groups of early humanists and educated people in the European cities. The political, cultural, and religious situation in which many different parties and alliances were intertwined and played active roles was generally so intricate that it is not easy for modern readers to unravel the interlocking images, arguments, and sympathies within the debates. A renewed interest in classical learning and in the revival of the golden age of antiquity was, for instance, often entangled with a deep desire for spiritual *renovatio.* Rome declined considerably during the fourteenth century, although the symbolic significance of the city remained undisputed. The defense of Rome as *caput mundi*—the head of the world as it once had been—was economically, ideologically, and theologically motivated. Likewise, secular rulers often cloaked their language in religious terms, whereas the pope's defenders used secular rhetoric belonging to the Aristotelian body politic.

Of greatest importance for this book is the way in which invaluable texts arose from these conflicts, texts that came to chart early modern notions of the legitimacy of power and the profound desire to reform the *Ecclesia Romana,* such as Dante's *Monarchia,* Marsilius's *Defensor pacis,* Ockham's *Breviloquium,* Petrarch's political letters, Birgitta's revelations, and Catherine's *Dialogo.* All six authors stand out as crucial in the debates of the fourteenth century, and they all took part in the conflicts stemming from the Avignon papacy. More importantly, their works offered inventive solutions to the contemporary crisis. As the analyses and discussions in this book will show, their texts do not only reflect the intellectual climate. Rather than reading their literary works as mere symptoms mirroring the larger picture of the political reality, we will approach these texts as works aimed at transforming the political-religious agenda of the papacy. The texts responded to, interpreted, and contested the contemporary language of power, sometimes even covertly, for instance in subtle discussions about humility and powerlessness. Notwithstanding the authors' different origins and ways of life, they were related through their mutual focus on Avignon. Their texts thus also serve as highly important commentaries on the events during this period.

CHAPTER 1

THE EAGLE'S FLIGHT: DANTE'S *PARADISO* VI AND THE *MONARCHIA*

Protect me as the most precious part of the eye;
hide me under the shadow of your wings.

Psalm 17:8

hen Dante Alighieri entered the political stage with his treatise *Monarchia* (On the monarchy), there was already a rich tradition of polemical texts that had been produced by the precarious situation between the pope and secular rulers at the beginning of the fourteenth century. Although conflicts between the papacy and secular governments returned to haunt the high Middle Ages, a balance between temporal and spiritual power, based on the Gelasian principle known as the two powers or two swords, had long served as the model for governance and also the common political theory.[1] The idea, articulated in a letter from 494 written by Pope Gelasius I and addressed to the Eastern emperor Anastasius (*Epistula* 12, *Ad Imperatorem Anastasium*), was that emperors and kings, popes and bishops, had distinct spheres of authority. In accordance with Saint Paul's recognition of the divine origin of political authority (Rom 13:1–2), both powers were divinely ordained and, as such, they ought to display a mutual respect for each other's boundaries of responsibility. Whereas the secular ruler was supposed to establish and preserve public order, the priest aimed at the salvation of souls. Yet despite this independence from one another, the separation was not absolute, according to Gelasius; while the priest depended on the secular ruler and should obey him in matters concerning the state, the secular ruler depended on the priest in spiritual matters and received the sacraments from him.

Early canon law (Gratian's *Decretum*) affirmed the view advocating a Gelasian moderation between the two powers, which found support among the most outstanding theologians in the second half of the thirteenth century, such as Albert the Great and Thomas Aquinas. Despite the increasing and recurrent tendencies of both secular and spiritual leaders to claim superiority over the other, both Albert and Thomas, as the historian Sophia Menache has described it, "supported Gelasius's tenets as the ideal means of neutralizing the more radical positions in both papalistic and anti-papalistic camps."[2] Nevertheless, by the end of the thirteenth century, this balance was greatly disturbed, resulting in repercussions that sent political discourses in completely new directions.

When Pope Boniface VIII issued the bull *Unam Sanctam* in 1302, in which he pronounced the ultimate subordination of temporal to sacerdotal power, this was meant as a final response to the long and increasingly harsh dispute with King Philip IV of France. Like the monarchies of England and Germany, the French monarchy was undergoing a process of secular, national autonomy. Philip IV of France and Edward I of England claimed sovereignty over their subjects, both clerical and lay. This claim included royal taxation of the clergy to finance the persistent wars between France and England. There was also growing disapproval of the legal immunity of the clerics. According to canon law, only ecclesiastical courts could try the priesthood. To Pope Boniface VIII, the rumblings of discontent from the French and English monarchs, royal taxation of the priesthood, and the attacks on clerical immunity jeopardized the liberty of the church; his response, enunciated in the bull *Unam Sanctam,* was to maintain the subordination of the temporal rulers under his jurisdiction. He was obviously aware of the risk of the fragmentation of the Western world due to the wars between the European royal houses, and in an attempt to establish peace and save the universality of the church, he encouraged the monarchs to—rather than fighting each other—regain control over the Holy Land, which had fallen to the Muslims in 1291. Boniface was, however, unsuccessful in this task—the national kings had become too powerful to allow their vassals to enlist in a crusade without their permission, as Yves Renourd has explained it, and France and England were too occupied by their own conflicts with each other to think about a crusade.[3]

Boniface's theocratic pretensions—the extreme papalist interpretation of the Gelasian theory in his *Unam Sanctam*—drew considerable support from the new generation of canon lawyers, the decretalists—also called the hierocrats—who eagerly defended the sovereignty of the pope. But the bull also roused strong reactions. Indeed, Boniface's attack on King Philip provoked one of the most extensive propaganda campaigns of the Middle

Ages.[4] The conflict with the French king resulted in a stream of pamphlets and treatises both for and against the sovereignty of the pope; these included *De ecclesiastica potestate* (On ecclesiastical power) by Giles of Rome, *De regimine christiano* (On Christian rulership) by James of Viterbo, *De potestate regia et papali* (On royal and papal power) by John of Paris, and *De ortu, progressu et fine Romani imperii* (On the rise and end of the Roman Empire) by Engelbert of Admont. Dante's *Monarchia* was written some years later than these treatises, probably at the end of 1318, long after Boniface had been defeated and his heirs had moved to Avignon.[5] Furthermore, unlike his forerunners, Dante represented a new type of intellectual and political thinker who was neither cleric nor lawyer—in fact, his authority did not derive from a particular group or institution. But, like many others of his time, he was engaged in the government of his city, Florence, from which he was expelled in 1302, the same year that Boniface VIII issued the *Unam Sanctam*—an event that only spurred on Dante's political commitment, albeit in new directions.

The *Monarchia* presents a strong defense of the unlimited jurisdiction of the *sacrum imperium* in temporal matters, and at the basis of this defense is the universality of Roman law. The treatise has been read as a defender of secular governments and a promoter of early modern notions of the separation of church and state;[6] as an advocate of Avveroist politics;[7] or as a reactionary treatise in the way it returns to the nostalgic ideas of restoring the classical past, the Roman Empire, as it existed under Emperor Augustus.[8] Ernst Kantorowicz once suggested in his now classic reading of Dante's *Monarchia* that the poet brought in radically new and original perspectives unprecedented in the history of political thought, such as the notion of the universality of the *civilitas humana,* which included pagans as well as Muslims and Christian inhabitants.[9] Albert Russell Ascoli, who has analyzed the treatise from a literary-rhetorical point of view, offers another vital and thought-provoking interpretation. As he argues, although institutional power is at the very center of *Monarchia*—"specifically, it is concerned with defining the exercise of legal power through transpersonal institutions"— Dante is simultaneously, although discreetly, carving out spaces for a personalized authority, the "aporia dantesca," as Ascoli calls it, as a necessary supplement to both the emperor's and the pope's authority.[10]

Despite its indebtedness to earlier work on *Monarchia,* the present chapter offers a reading of Dante's political treatise from yet another angle. Through the lens of Emperor Justinian's long speech in *Paradiso* VI, we will explore how Dante not only argued for the divine origins and separate powers of church and state, but also used Justinian as a key to criticize canon law and Roman law alike. As such, Dante, through the figure of Justinian, suggested limits to a positivist view of secular powers, which he seemingly defended so strongly in his *Monarchia*.

Monarchia was written more or less contemporaneously with *Paradiso,* the third canticle of *Commedia,* and in the sixth canto of *Paradiso* the wanderer Dante meets just such an ideal universal ruler that the author invokes in *Monarchia*. By the end of the previous canto, *Paradiso* V, a crowd comes toward Dante and Beatrice that is described as a thousand radiances from a veil of intense light. Among this crowd is Justinian (ca. 482–565), the Byzantine emperor who codified the *Corpus Iuris Civilis,* the uniform compilation of Roman law, which still forms the foundation of our civil rights today. Dante can hardly make out who he is, but, encouraged by Beatrice, he addresses the emperor, who then responds. Interestingly, Justinian's long answer in the following canto, *Paradiso* VI, repeats but also challenges many of the arguments that are presented in *Monarchia*. As such, the poetic language of the poem transforms the plain and logical language of the political tractate into an elusive complexity.

In the following we will examine the underlying discussions of lust and political power in Justinian's speech and explore how they are connected to Dante's arguments in *Monarchia*. As we will see, in the tangled web of the political polemics, theological depth, and poetic subtlety of the emperor's response, the harmonic model of the universal empire, examined in *Monarchia,* is disturbed by a most troubling story that not only casts a shadow over the vision of the *sacrum imperium* but also conceals the idea of the divine origin of Roman law.

DANTE'S VICTORIES AND DISAPPOINTMENTS

Dante came from a Guelph family, which may not mean that much because, according to the historian John Najemy, most Florentines at that time were Guelphs.[11] In the Battle of Montaperti in 1260, the Florentine Guelphs had suffered a disastrous defeat against the Ghibelline city of Siena, led by Farinata degli Uberti, who was a banished Florentine Ghibelline aristocrat. The violent confrontations are recalled by Dante in his meeting with Farinata in *Inferno* X where this ambiguous hero recounts how he came to change his mind: when the Ghibellines planned to destroy Florence like the Romans had once crushed Carthage, he started to defend his native city.

Not many years after the defeat of Montaperti, the Guelphs regained control, so when Dante started his political career in the mid-1290s, Florence was again a Guelph city. By then Dante was married to Gemma Donati, who bore him four children, and he was already an admired poet, celebrated above all for his *Vita nuova* (1295), the beautiful collection of poems and prose that follows Dante's life from his birth and early childhood, to his first meeting with the Florentine girl Beatrice, to her death in 1290. In public life Dante came to hold several important posts, and he reached the peak of his political career in 1300 when he served from 15 June to 15 August as one of the six priors of the city. What then went wrong is unclear. In his *Vita di Dante*, the Florentine historian and humanist Leonardo Bruni (1369–1444) refers to a now lost epistle where Dante reportedly explained that the cause and origin of all his woes and misfortunes were the decisions taken during his period as prior.[12]

The Guelphs for a period had been divided into two bitterly opposed factions known as the Blacks and the Whites; whereas the Blacks followed the traditionally Guelph line supporting the papacy, the Whites were critical of papal interventions. The Whites opposed above all Pope Boniface VIII's influence. Which sympathies Dante personally had is unsure, but during his priorate, the priors decided to repatriate those White leaders who had been banished from the city, such as Dante's friend Guido Cavalacanti. When the Blacks, heavily supported by the papacy, took control of the city in November 1301, Dante in the following months was one of the citizens who were condemned and permanently expelled—an episode that marks the beginning of his long years of exile that lasted until his death in 1321. It was only after his banishment from Florence, however, that he joined the conspiracy of White Guelphs who were planning the military seizure of Florence. Accordingly, as Najemy has convincingly argued, it is largely the first years after his exile that have caused historians to label Dante as White.[13] Of greater importance, though, is that Dante now came to refuse not only Florence, depicting his hometown as the prototype for the corrupt, violent societies in *Inferno*, but even "the whole idea of the city as the proper and natural form of political association."[14] The only figure who could break the sinister spirals of violence within the city walls, and bring peace to the war-ridden Italian peninsula and to Europe, increasingly threatened by national fragmentations, was a monarch, a prince, whose jurisdiction was universal.

When Henry VII of Luxemburg was elected emperor by the Germans in 1308, Dante was full of enthusiasm. With the intention of restoring the Holy Roman Empire, Henry traveled to Rome to be crowned by Pope Clement V in 1312. Dante hailed his Italian expedition with a fervent epistle (*Epistole* VII, dated 17 April 1311), describing the event as a new messianic beginning— "like the rising of the long-awaited Sun, a new hope of a better age shone upon Italy."[15] However, because of harsh political conflicts—King Philip the Fair's strong pressure on Pope Clement—and a chaotic series of obstacles, the coronation was a fiasco. Henry had to flee Rome, and soon thereafter, in

August 1313, when he was about to intensify the war against King Robert of Naples and his papal supporters, the Guelph league, he fell seriously ill and died of malaria in Buonconvento, outside Siena.

Dante's high esteem of Henry is made clear by the prominent place he gives him in the *Commedia*. Even at the final moment of the poem, he recalls Henry's glory by referring to his future seat (the emperor is not yet dead in the fictive date of the journey) among the blessed. As Beatrice explains, after his death, Henry will shine among the joyous blessed in the eternal Rose of Paradise (*Par.* XXX, 133–138):

> E 'n quell gran seggio a che tu li occhi tieni
> per la corona che già v'è posta,
> prima che tu a queste nozze ceni,
> sederà l'alma, che fia giù agosta,
> de l'alto Arrigo, ch'a drizzare Italia
> verrà in prima che'ella sia disposta.

[And in the great chair whereon you fix your eyes because of the crown that already is set above it, before you sup at these nuptials shall sit the soul, which on earth will be imperial, of the lofty Henry, who will come to set Italy straight before she is ready.]

Henry's unsuccessful attempt to regain imperial control over Italy was obviously a great disappointment to Dante, and his *Monarchia* is usually considered to have been conceived after this experience. Evoking a universal monarch or emperor who could establish peace in both Italy and Europe, he developed and intensified his arguments from the quoted letter to Henry. In general, the treatise offers harsh criticism of the secular powers of the church—the papacy's *cupiditas*, that corrupting lust for power—which, according to Dante, had only increased with the close ties between the Avignon papacy and the French monarchy.[16]

Most scholars agree today that *Monarchia* was written in the later period of Dante's stay in Verona, where he lived from 1312 to 1318 under the protection of his patron, Cangrande della Scala, the leader of the Ghibelline faction in northern Italy, or perhaps even later, after he had moved to Ravenna, where he remained until his death.[17] We may assume that the mighty image of Justinian in *Paradiso* VI is inspired by the poet's contemplation of the emperor configured in the golden mosaics of San Vitale in Ravenna. A passage in *Monarchia*, however, refers perhaps to some contemporary events: "It has happened that sometimes those to whom the honor of heralding has been granted fall into disagreements."[18] The passage is indeed very vague, and, as Ascoli has argued, Dante excludes practically all references to contemporary historical realities in order to avoid being accused of any partisanship in contemporary conflicts.[19] Still, it is not unlikely that the passage quoted refers to the bitter controversy that ensued after the election of Ludwig of Bavaria in 1314 as Henry VII's successor to the imperial crown.[20] Like his predecessor, Pope John XXII refused to recognize the validity of the German election—a refusal that came to affect those who were bestowed office even by the previous emperor. In 1317 Pope John issued the bull *Si fratrum,* claiming that it was the pope's task to appoint the imperial vicars during an interregnum, which involved Dante's patron in Verona as well. In this respect, *Monarchia* may have been written as a defense of Cangrande della Scala.

Even though the possible reference in *Monarchia* to contemporary events is most elusive—Dante's arguments would obviously appear more powerful if they expressed universal truths that transcended time and place—there is no doubt that the conflicts around Pope John XXII occupied his mind while he was working on *Monarchia* and the last canticle of his *Commedia.* As Nick Havely has suggested, Pope John is indirectly but recognizably configured both in *Paradiso* XVIII (130-136) and in *Paradiso* XXVII (58-59).[21] Even the *trecento* commentator, Benvenuto da Imola, identified John XXII as one of the popes referred to in *Paradiso* XXVII.[22] Both passages indicate the storms surrounding the question of Franciscan poverty, Pope John's condemnation of Petrus Joannis Olivi's eschatology, and the attempts to gain control over the disobedient Spirituals.[23] As Havely argues, if the reference in *Paradiso* XVIII is more oblique, in *Paradiso* XXVII Saint Peter's outburst against his current successor clearly covers events that fall beyond the *Commedia*'s fictional date (*Par.* XXVII, 55-60):

> In vesta di pastor lupi rapaci
> si veggion di qua sù per tutti i paschi:
> o diffesa di Dio, perché pur giaci?
> Del sangue nostro Caorsini e Guaschi
> s'apparecchian di bere: o buon principio,
> a che vil fine conviene che tu caschi!

[Rapacious wolves, in shepherd's garb, are seen from here above in all the pastures; O defense of God, wherefore dost thou yet lie still? Cahorsines and Gascons make ready to drink our blood. O good beginning, to what vile ending must you fall!]

The *Caorsini* and *Guaschi* in this quotation are clear references to the Gascon pope, Clement V, and the Cahorsin pope, John XXII. Furthermore, the image of these popes drinking blood reveals Dante's profound influence by the Spirituals' apocalyptic discourse, probably inspired by Olivi and Ubertino da Casale, whose preaching he may have listened to in the late 1280s. Between 1285 and 1289 Olivi and Ubertino were both in Florence for some years, so we may assume that Dante at least heard about their thoughts when he, as he states in his *Convivio* (The banquet), started to frequent the "schools of the religious," the Dominican Santa Maria Novella and the Franciscan Santa Croce in Florence, in the early 1290s (*Conv.* II, 12, 27). In any case, there is no doubt as to the influence of medieval Franciscanism and the debates about poverty on Dante's poetic masterwork, and, as we will see, traces of the same discussion are clearly present in the *Monarchia* too.

TIME REVERSED

Paradiso, the third realm of the afterlife described in Dante's *Commedia*, which Dante the pilgrim reaches after his journey through *Inferno* and *Purgatorio*, consists of nine spheres—seven planets (the Moon, Mercury, Venus, the Sun, Mars, Jupiter, and Saturn), the Fixed Stars, and the Primum Mobile. From the Primum Mobile Dante ascends from the physical world to Empyreum, the immaterial residence of God, the angels, and the holy souls. In each sphere the wanderer, and the readers with him, encounters different souls marked by the spheres to which they belong, and in the heaven of Mercury (*Par.* VI–VII) we meet the Ambitious, who are celebrated for their love of glory and earthly fame. The main subject of the two cantos of Mercury is a discussion of two kinds of love—the lust for power and the desire to serve—which, according to Augustine, dominated the earthly city and the city of God, respectively. In book XIV, chapter 28 of his *De civitate Dei* (The city of god), Augustine writes, "We see then that the two cities were created by two kinds of love: the earthly city was created by self-love reaching the point of contempt for God, the Heavenly City by the love of God carried as far as contempt of self. . . . In the former, the lust for domination lords it over its princes as over the nations it subjugates; in the other both those put in authority and those subject to them, serve one another in love, the rulers by their counsel, the subjects by obedience."[24]

In *Paradiso* VI, the two categories of love described by Augustine are so disguised that we have to read carefully to discover them. One is concealed under the veil of logic, whereas the other shines in the light of wisdom. Both, however, are connected to power, or, more precisely, to the legitimate right to judge and avenge injustice, and the crux is the political situation in Europe. In fact, in the sixth canto, Europe is mentioned for the first time in the *Commedia,* and after that the European question grows in force and importance in Dante's poetic universe, above all in the heaven of Jupiter (*Par.* IX and XX), which, with its profound discussions of justice across the three known continents of the earth, is closely connected to Mercury.[25]

The whole of canto six consists of Justinian's speech, emerging as a prophetic comment on the political situation in Italy, as well as in Europe. The canto opens with Justinian's answer to Dante's first question at the end of the previous canto: Who is this worthy spirit who nests himself in his own light? (*Par.* V, 124–129):

> Io veggio ben sì come tu t'annidi
> nel prorio lume, e che de li occhi il traggi,
> perch' e' corusca sì come tu ridi;
> ma non so chi tu se', né perché aggi,
> anima degna, il grado de la spera
> che si vela a' mortai con altrui raggi.

> [I see well how you do nest yourself in your own light, and that you dart it from your eyes, because it sparkles when you smile; but I know not who you are, nor why, O worthy spirit, you have your rank in the sphere that is veiled to mortals by another's rays.]

The emperor's answer is the longest speech in the *Commedia* and shows the special significance given to Justinian by Dante. The response is intricate and reflects the heaven in which the pilgrim now finds himself (*Par.* VI, 1–9):

> Poscia che Constantin l'aquila volse
> contr'al corso del ciel, ch'ella seguio
> dietro a l'antico che Lavinia tolse,
> cento e cent' anni e più l'uccel di Dio
> ne lo stremo d'Europa si ritenne,
> vicino a' monti de' quai prima uscìo;
> e sotto l'ombra de le sacre penne
> governò 'l mondo lì di mano in mano,
> e, sì canhiando, in su la mia pervenne.

> [After Constantine turned back the Eagle counter to the course of the heavens which it had followed behind the ancient who took Lavinia

to wife, a hundred and a hundred years and more the bird of God abode
on Europe's limit, near to the mountains from which it first had issued;
and there it governed the world beneath the shadow of its sacred wings,
from hand to hand, until by succeeding change it came into mine.]

Justinian recounts that the eagle, the sacred emblem of the Roman Empire, came into his hands about two hundred years later than the Roman
emperor Constantine the Great's *translatio imperii* and his donation of the
western empire to Pope Sylvester.[26] As we shall also see in *Monarchia,* Justinian describes the donation as a transgression, a violation of the economy
of history: God's bird, following Aeneas (Lavinia's future husband) from the
burning Troy, moved along the course of the heavens, from sunrise toward
sunset, and consequently across the course of time. Turning the eagle back,
as Constantine did when he moved eastward, could therefore only mean reversing time, and thus delaying or hindering the necessary end of history
and Judgment Day.

CONVERSION OF AN EMPEROR

From the very first line and throughout the canto, the eagle's movements are
emphasized—toward the west and toward the east, southward and northward—and in this way the old Roman Empire is circumscribed or delineated
under the shadows of its wings. That its movements, the constant circling of
the eagle, have an important role in the heaven of Mercury should not be
surprising. Mercury, with his winged feet, is the swift messenger of the gods,
and, as Cicero writes in *De natura deorum,* the law is one of the things that
Mercury brought from heaven to humans.[27] However, within the ancient
classification of the many properties attributed to Mercury, at least two
others are of importance to Justinian's speech. Mercury is the god of commerce, and Justinian's speech, as Beatrice's explanation reveals in the following canto, deals with the accounts of history, with the balance between
debit and credit, with corruption, restitution, sacrifice, and revenge. Mercury is also the god of dialectics. As Dante writes in *Convivio,* his unfinished
collection of long poems furnished with allegorical commentaries,

> The heaven of Mercury may be compared to Dialectics because of
> two properties: for Mercury is the smallest star of heaven, because the
> magnitude of its diameter is not more than 232 miles, according to Al-
> fraganus, who says it is 1/28th of the diameter of the earth, which is

6500 miles; the other property is that in its passage it is veiled by the rays of the sun more than any other star. These two properties are found in Dialectics, for Dialectics is less in substance than any other science, for it is entirely constituted by and contained within that text alone which is found in the Old Art and in the New; and its passage is veiled more than that of any science, in that it proceeds by a more sophistical and polemical mode of argument than any other.[28]

This quotation shows that it is dialectics above all that Dante relates to Mercury. Therefore, dialectics, which in the Middle Ages was compatible with logic, penetrates the speech of Justinian, as is clear from his very first appearance (*Par.* VI, 10–21):

> Cesare fui e son Iustinïano,
> che, per voler del primo amor ch'i' sento,
> d'entro le leggi trassi il troppo e 'l vano.
> E prima ch'io a l'ovra fossi attento,
> una natura in Cristo esser, non più,
> credea, e di tal fede era contento;
> ma 'l benedetto Agapito, che fue
> sommo pastore, a la fede sincera
> mi dirizzò con le parole sue.
> Io li credetti; e ciò che 'n sua fede era,
> vegg' io or chiaro sì, come tu vedi
> ogne contradizione e falsa e vera.

> [I was Caesar, and am Justinian, who, by will of the Primal Love which I feel, removed from among the laws what was superfluous and vain. And before I had put my mind to this work, one nature and no more I held to be in Christ, and with that faith I was content; but the blessed Agapetus, who was the supreme pastor, directed me to the true faith by his words. I believed him, and what he held by faith I now see as clearly as you see that every contradiction is both false and true.]

In this passage, logic is connected to justice. Evidently, the name of Justinian reflects the emperor's just or rightful character (*iustus*), and, in accordance with the will of God, Justinian has brought justice to the law by cutting away contradictions and repetitions, or the superfluous from the established. The objective of logic is precisely this: to distinguish the true from the false in contradictions. As Isidore of Seville explains in his *Etymologiae:* "Dialectic [*dialectica*] is the discipline devised for investigating the causes of things. It is a branch of philosophy, and is called logic [*logica*], that is, the rational [*rationalis*] power of defining, questioning, and discussing. Dialectic teaches, with regard to many types of questions, how the true and the false may be distinguished by disputation."[29]

Justinian's conversion is described as a similar logical process: Under the spiritual guidance of Pope Agapetus, he can now clearly see that every contradiction is both false and true, a paraphrasing of what Peter of Spain wrote in *Summulae logicales:* "If one [of two contradictories] is true, by contradictory of opposites, the remaining one is false, and vice versa."[30] The same passage of Peter of Spain is also used by Dante in *Monarchia* when he defends the legal existence of the Roman Empire: "I therefore affirm that if the Roman Empire did not exist *de iure,* then Christ by his birth approved something unjust; the consequent is false; ergo, the contradictory of the antecedent is true. For contradictory propositions can be understood mutually from each other since they have diametrically opposed meanings."[31]

As we shall soon see, in *Monarchia* Dante uses dialectics as an effective weapon against his enemies, above all against the decretalists, or the canon lawyers, who defended the temporal power of the pope through logical arguments. But as Joseph Canning has noted, the jurists argued in an entirely circular way in terms of legal texts, and Dante's approach was to disprove, polemically, the papal positions on the grounds that their arguments were illogical or inapposite.[32] One may wonder, however, why Dante described the dialectic (*Dialettica*) as "veiled more than that of any science, in that it proceeds by a more sophistical and polemical mode of argument than any other."[33] What does the logic veil or mask, according to Dante?

Despite its logical argumentation, Justinian's self-presentation includes a strong critique of logic: the conversion from heresy to orthodoxy involves the emperor accepting a fundamental logical paradox, namely, the double nature of Christ. Logic, for its part, requires the heresy of Monophysitism, the Christological position that posited the impossibility that Christ could be both man and God.[34] In the Middle Ages it was widely believed that the young Justinian professed Monophysitism.[35] In the speech of the converted Justinian, however, Dante radically proposes a necessary break between logical and theological truths. Because of faith, Justinian was forced to turn his back on Monophysitism, and consequently on the course of logic. Even more striking, however, is the way in which the story, which immediately follows, unmasks that not only beneath the logical arguments, but also beneath the prosaic rhetoric of economy, lurks one of the most dangerous temptations for human beings—power.

ABUSING SIGNS

After answering Dante's first question, Justinian turns to his second one: Why does he possess his rank in the sphere that is veiled to mortals by the rays of another sphere? Before he can answer properly, however, Justinian explains that he is obliged to give Dante some additional information so he can discern or judge better. The information he provides is an account of Roman history, a *res gestae* from the very beginning up until Dante's own days. Justinian does this to remind the pilgrim and his contemporaries about the duties that rest on them, because the speech is nothing less than a commentary on the contemporary political situation in Italy and Europe, marred by violent wars and discord. *Paradiso* VI is thus closely connected to the sixth songs of both *Inferno* and *Purgatorio*. Whereas *Inferno* VI treats the state of Florence—"la città partita" (*Inf.* VI, 61: "the divided city")—and *Purgatorio* VI, the state of Italy—"di dolore ostello" (*Purg.* VI, 76: "Italy, hostel of grief")—in *Paradiso* VI we turn to Europe. The pilgrim, and the readers with him, is in other words now invited to gaze more widely or more universally on the world.[36]

It is a heroic history, extending over almost half the canto, which unfolds under the wings of the eagle, and Justinian speaks in an elevated and rhetorical way, apt for an emperor: "See what great virtue made it worthy of reference, beginning from the hour when Pallas died to give it sway" (*Par.* VI, 34-36: "Vedi quanta virtù l'ha fatto degno/di reverenza; e cominciò da l'ora/che Pallante morì per darli regno"). A providential plan followed the eagle's movements—from Aeneas's flight from Troy until his marriage to Lavinia; from the sacrifice of Pallas, the son of King Evander, to the foundation of Alba Longa; from the triumph of Scipio and Pompey up to the power of Caesar and so forth. Justinian explains that he recounts this story so "you may see with how much reason they move against the sacred standard, both those that take it for their own and those that oppose it" (*Par.* VI, 31-33: "perché tu veggi con quanta ragione/si move contr' al sacrosanto segno/e chi 'l s'appropria e chi a lui s'oppone"), and he ends the story with a prophetic vision of Dante's own time, hurled out most bitterly (*Par.* VI, 97-111):

> Omai puoi giudicar di quei cotali
> ch'io accusai di sopra e di lor falli,
> che son cagion di tutti vostri mali.
> L'uno al pubblico segno i gigli gialli
> oppone, e l'altro appropria quello a parte,
> sì ch'è forte a veder chi più si falli.

> Faccian li Ghibellin, faccian lor arte
> sott' altro segno, ché mal segue quello
> sempre chi la giustizia e lui diparte;
> e non l'abbatta esto Carlo novello
> coi Guelfi suoi, ma tema de li artigli
> ch'a più alto leon trasser lo vello.
> Molte fïate già pianser li figli
> per la colpa del padre, e non si creda
> che Dio trasmuti l'armi per suoi gigli!

[Now you may judge of such as I accused but now, and of their offenses, which are the cause of all your ills. The one opposes to the public standard the yellow lilies, and the other claims it for a party, so that it is hard to see which offends the most. Let the Ghibellines, let them practice their art under another ensign, for this one he ever follows ill who cleaves justice from it. And let not this new Charles strike it down with his Guelphs, but let him fear talons which have stripped the hide from a greater lion. Many a time ere now the sons have wept for the sin of the father; and let him not believe that God will change arms for his lilies.]

The roots of contemporary evils are the deceits and offenses of the Ghibellines and the Guelphs. They do not understand the sign that is ordained by God to preserve the order of the world, according to Justinian. Thus, the eagle, the sacred emblem of the empire, is abused in partial or fractional situations to promote self-interest. In addition to being an allusion to the conflicts in Florence, Justinian's prophecy shows how the city's struggles have ramifications for European families and royal houses as well. While the Guelphs oppose the universal banner of the golden lilies, which is the emblem of the French monarchy, the Ghibellines have appropriated the eagle as their own sign and for their own purposes. Let the Ghibellines act under another sign, Justinian declares, and let not the Guelphs, who support Charles II of Naples (Charles of Anjou), believe that God will exchange the emblem of the eagle for that of the lilies.

The quotation gives us a glimpse of the bewildering array of loyalties, deceits, and shifting sympathies between various parties in contemporary European politics. Still, Justinian's mission is clear enough: the maltreatment of the emblem of the eagle indicates a fractioning, retrieved by the expression "appropria quello a parte" (v. 101; "claims it for a party"), which paints a picture of the ongoing fragmentation of Europe and thus the obstruction of the universality of Roman law.

IN THE SERVICE OF HUMANKIND

In Dante's *Monarchia* we find a similar defense of the universal monarchy. The treatise is a polemic against the canon lawyers who argued for the idea of the *plenitudo potestatis* of the pope, and, as such, the text introduces a defense of the empire or of the temporal monarchy alluded to in the title, which Dante explains at the outset of the text: "Temporal monarchy, then, which they call 'empire,' is the one single principality placed over all men in time, or among and over those things that are measured by time."[37] Dante's defense does not, in other words, include every state ruled by a king. *Monarchia* instead refers to the empire, or, as we shall soon discover, to the universal Roman Empire. However, in contrast to previous defenders of the empire, such as Engelbert of Admont in his *De ortu, progressu et fine Romani imperii,* Dante chooses to fight his enemies with their own weapons: he confronts the discussions with philosophical, theological, and juridical arguments, all ensconced within the strict rules of the scholastic, logical syllogism. As such, *Monarchia* mirrors the dominant philosophical-theological discourses of the day, as Ascoli has argued.[38] What is also clear, as Giuseppe Mazzotta has suggested, is that Dante applies logic rhetorically to alter the existing political game, because logic may be, as he argues, not so much a tool for knowing the contingent configurations of reality as a rhetorical weapon to control and manipulate it.[39] Dante is thus wielding his polemics under the cover of a dry, discarnate, scholastic argumentation, which gives the impression of being governed by "the light of human reason," as presented at the beginning of the second part of *Monarchia* (*Mn.* II, 1, 7–8).

The treatise is divided into three books ordered according to the three questions that, immediately after the definition of the temporal monarchy, Dante states he will discuss: "Indeed three principal problems are to be investigated in its regard: first, there is some doubt and question whether it [the universal monarchy] is necessary for the well-being of the world; second, whether the Roman people appropriated the office of monarchy to itself *de jure;* third, whether the authority of monarchy depends directly upon God or on some other minister or vicar of God."[40] The essential scope for Dante's examination is thus the definition of legitimate authority, where it lay, and whence it originated, as well as the fundamental mission of the temporal monarchy. He addresses the questions in new and original ways that nonetheless allow for a dialogue or a peaceful balance between the two powers.

The crux of the *Monarchia* is the unique position of the Roman Empire in the providential history of man. As for the question of the necessity of the universal monarchy for the well-being of the world, Dante establishes a principle on which all of his arguments depend, namely, the principle of universal peace. As he explains, "In the tranquillity of peace, mankind is able to attend without hindrance or difficulty to its proper functioning, which is a functioning almost divine. . . . Accordingly, it is clear that universal peace is the most important of all things that are ordained for our beatitude."[41]

Although following the Aristotelian notion of citizens' happiness as the aim of the state, Dante's happiness is not reserved only for a city, a state, or certain social groups or classes. Dante's quest is universal happiness, or beatitude for the entire *civilitas humana,* which reflects the fundamental Catholic idea of salvation not only for a selected people but for the whole of humanity.[42] As Dante explains, universal peace is a prerequisite for achieving such happiness. Universal beatitude, the perfect state for humankind, depends on peace or a concordance of every single will, and in attaining this, a prince is needed, one prince over all, whose will can be the master and guide of all others (*Mn.* I, 15, 9). This may sound like a defense of tyranny, but the just emperor depicted in *Monarchia* is far from the tyrants we meet in the lower part of *Inferno,* in the bloody streams of Phlegethon, who have made their own will their law (*Inf.* XII, 46–48). The defense of the seeming omnipotence of the emperor in *Monarchia* is instead a marking of the *limits* of the emperor's power. What is at stake is the prevention of uninhibited displays of power.

Such perfect harmony and tranquility throughout the world had once existed, according to Dante, during the government of Emperor Augustus, or Divus Augustus, as Dante calls him (*Mn.* I, 16, 1). He supports his argument by referring to Saint Paul, Saint Luke, and Roman historians and poets who all bore witness to the greatness of Rome. The underlying image that is evoked, however, is Suetonius's account in *De vita caesarum* of the exemplary life of Divus Augustus. Suetonius describes the "divine" emperor as a most humble and hardworking servant for his people who, despite being the mighty ruler of all nations, "always felt horrified and insulted when called 'My Lord' [*dominus*] . . . he would not let even his adopted children, or grandchildren, use the obsequious word (though it might be only in jest), either when talking to him or about him."[43]

In Dante's *Monarchia,* the key to the just emperor is this very humility described by Suetonius. As he argues, humanity is at its best when it is most free, and the essence of freedom is *libertas arbitrii,* the "free judgment of the will" (*Mn.* I, 12). However, such judgment is free only when it wholly governs the appetite and is in no way prejudiced by it. Only through this principle of liberty can human beings achieve the state of supreme happiness. A good emperor is a just emperor, a man whose judgment is free of any subjection to appetite or *cupiditas,* which is evil love, in contrast to *car-

itas. As Dante writes, "Where, then, there is nothing to be desired, cupidity is impossible; for when their objects have been destroyed, the passions cannot exist."[44] Thus, when cupidity is removed, there remains nothing contrary to justice, to the free and unselfish judgment of the will. The question is, though, how an emperor can be free of any cupidity. Dante's highly original solution is that the emperor has no occasion for cupidity because his jurisdiction is universal. Since his dominion is worldwide, for him there is nothing more to desire.

CUPIDITY GONE ASTRAY

Striking in Dante's reasoning is that he argues from a Franciscan point of view.[45] Perhaps even more striking is the way in which he turns the Franciscan argument around by connecting it to the Augustinian theory of desire. In his staking out of the limits of ecclesiastical power in the third book of *Monarchia*, Dante obviously agrees with the Franciscans: priests ought to live in accordance with the apostolic ideal of poverty. But when it comes to the monarch, he carefully modifies this and even turns upside-down their renunciation of temporal things. By having dominion over *all* goods, as well as the rights, ownership, and use of them, the monarch could gain the same liberty. By eliminating every temporal anxiety, he could reach the highest perfection as the humble servant of his people. In the fourth book of *Convivio*, in which Dante explains how the pilgrim's cupidity at a certain point is fulfilled or even erased when all his desires are met, we encounter the same conversion of the desire. Retrieving the Augustinian restless heart (*Confessiones*, bk. 1), the human soul always has new objects of desire before its eyes in the guise of a pyramid, until it finally reaches the apex of the ultimate object of all desires, which is God.[46] In *Monarchia* this is how the emperor's cupidity is transformed into charity. In dominating all things, and thus becoming a universal ruler, he is free from cupidity. There is, in other words, "nothing for the monarch to desire, for his jurisdiction is bounded only by the ocean."[47] And since cupidity is the opposite of charity, and the universal monarch is free of the former, he should possess the latter to the highest degree, which is rightly ordered love. Humankind would thereby gain peace and universal freedom, because the universal monarch, free of any cupidity, would exist only for the sake of the people (*Mn.* I, 12, 10–12).

According to Dante, this kind of universal monarchy, the willingness to serve rather than dominate humanity, did exist during the Pax Romana of Divus Augustus, a topic he returns to in book II of *Monarchia*, where he examines whether the Roman people appropriated the office of monarchy for themselves de jure. The greatness of Rome is now evoked by a quotation from Virgil's *Aeneid* (*Mn.* II, 6, 9), where Aeneas, during his descent into Hades, glimpsed the future events of the coming empire pointed out by his father, Anchises. Justinian's long account in *Paradiso* VI is in many ways an echo of Anchises's archive of heroic accomplishments: "Others, I doubt not, shall beat out the breathing bronze with softer lines; shall from marble draw forth the features of life; shall plead their causes better; with the rod shall trace the paths of heaven and tell the rising of the stars; remember thou, O Roman, to rule the nations with thy sway—these shall be thine arts—to crown Peace with Law, to spare the humble, and tame in war the proud."[48] By this quotation of Aeneas's vision of the sacred mission of Rome, where the lust for domination was transformed into a desire to serve, Dante recalls the providential role of the Roman Empire. What has gone wrong, then? By the end of book I, after the discussion of the just monarch and the necessity of his existence for universal peace, Dante exclaims in a highly rhetorical manner, not very different from the majestic words of Justinian, "O humankind! By how many tempests and misfortunes, by how many shipwrecks must you be tossed while you, having turned into a beast with many heads, strain in such conflicting directions?"[49] The image of the beast recalls the description of the monster atop the Mount of Purgatory (*Purg.* XXXII, 148–160), which again reflects the apocalyptic language employed by the Spirituals, such as Olivi and Ubertino.[50]

In the Earthly Paradise of Purgatory (*Purg.* XXX), Dante meets an allegorical procession, led by a Griffin, the symbol of Christ. When the procession is resting in a wood, its chariot—the symbol of the church—is transformed into a seven-headed, ten-horned monster. A whore, which is obviously an allusion to the Avignon papacy, then takes a seat on the chariot, fornicating with a giant, the symbol of the French king. Moreover, the image of the many-headed beast is also a direct comment on the bull *Unam Sanctam,* in which Boniface declared that the church had only one body and one head, not two heads like a monster. This was the core of the hierocrats' argument: the total subjection of temporal power to the spiritual because spiritual things surpassed all other things in dignity. The pope, the head of the church, was appointed by God, and all nations and authorities should therefore obey him.

According to Dante, the main cause of the fall of the Roman Empire was the Donation of Constantine, a document that the hierocrats, or the papal defenders, used as the source for the temporal power of the church (*Mn.* III, 10). According to the donation, Constantine should, out of gratitude for being cured of leprosy by Pope Sylvester, have transferred the authority over Rome and over the western lands of the empire to the pope. Even though it was not exposed as a forgery until later, many people in Dante's time, including the canon lawyers, regarded the document as a feeble, flawed basis for papal authority.[51] However, even though Dante may have considered it to be a weak, suspect document, it was highly useful for him in order to demonstrate and discuss the greed of the church. Furthermore, the donation revealed the false hierarchy of textual authorities from which the papalists, or the canon lawyers, enjoyed primacy over the church fathers and Holy Scripture.

The donation is fiercely attacked by Dante: Constantine did not have permission to give away the empire's lands, he argues, because the empire was universal and, as such, founded on human right: "The empire's foundation is human right."[52] In addition, the Roman Empire was blessed by God's will: it participated in the redemption of man's original sin by preparing the way for the spreading of the gospel of Christ, affirmed by the birth and death of Christ under Roman governors (*Mn.* II, 10, 4). In other words, the Donation of Constantine was unjust. However, the church had also broken a fundamental command by accepting the donation, according to Dante: because Christ had forbidden it to possess temporal goods, the church was not fit to accept Constantine's gift. Just as the emperor should possess everything, the pope should possess nothing in accordance with the biblical requirement for apostolic poverty, as expressed in Matthew (Mt 10:9), which Dante also quotes: "Take no gold, nor silver, nor copper in your belts, no bag for your journey, and so on" (*Mn.* III, 10, 14). Dante claims that it was actually because of the Donation of Constantine that the Roman Empire had once started to fail in its sacred mission to guide men to universal freedom, first envisioned by Aeneas and later confirmed by Christ. The restoration of the empire would therefore involve the restoration of the church to its original form. Only by the total removal of the pope from temporal political jurisdiction could universal freedom be achieved. In this way, the early humanists' myth of a renaissance—the rebirth of Roman culture—was strongly connected in *Monarchia* to the Franciscan myth of the purification or rebirth of the Roman Church.

Dante's main thesis in book III is that the church and the empire are equal in that both institutions are willed by God. Neither the pope nor the emperor is a vicar of Christ in the sense of possessing fullness of power, though the decretalists had started to claim that the pope was indeed just such a vicar. Rather, both institutions are expressions of God's will, according to Dante, and the source from which their authority springs is the one, supreme authority of God. Hence, both institutions are governed by men who do not have the power to question or reexamine the will of God. Even in the realm of the spirit, then, the pope was not omnipotent; he did not have any *plenitudo potestatis* (*Mn.* III, 8), either politically or spiritually, because the ultimate authority for him, as for the emperor, was God. There is, in other words, a strict limit on power that the emperor and the pope share equally, and it is this limit or boundary that is imperative for Dante to clarify. What the two institutions did not share, however, was jurisdiction over terrestrial matters; these should belong to the emperor alone.

According to Dante, the universal emperor alone should rule the *civilitas humana* on earth, whereas the pope should guide men to the heavenly city. This is explained by the Thomistic idea of the twofold goal and the twofold happiness of man: Because of man's dual nature, composed of the corruptible body and the incorruptible soul, Providence has set before him two goals to attain: "the blessedness of this life . . . and the blessedness of eternal life."[53] Because of man's cupidity, these dual goals require equally dual, aiding guides: the emperor through philosophy and the pope through revelation: "On this account it was necessary for man to have a dual guide for his dual end; namely, the Supreme Pontiff who would lead mankind to eternal life according to those things that have been revealed, and the emperor, who would direct mankind to temporal felicity according to philosophical teaching."[54]

The wise ruler evoked in *Monarchia* had already been foreshadowed in *Convivio* (IV, 6). In both contexts it seemed urgent for Dante to refute the papacy's claim of sovereignty—a claim that was based on unjust documents and supported by false syllogisms and inapposite conclusions invalid for the exercising of earthly power. The pope should be a guide to the next life, the emperor to this life, and any switching between these two roles could only produce such multiheaded monsters as Dante the pilgrim meets in the Earthly Paradise, and which lead to nothing but strife and confusion.

THE VENGEANCE OF THE CROSS

Dante's subtle rejection of Augustine's condemnation of Rome and of the *libido dominandi* (lust for domination) that haunted its rulers as described in *De civitate Dei* has led many readers to suggest that Dante glorified the old Roman Empire.[55] According to Charles Davis, Dante's political theory rests on memory and desire—a memory of the golden age under Emperor Augustus and a desire for a new Augustus.[56] As Mazzotta has argued, though, Dante agrees in many ways with Augustine: beneath the Virgilian ideology of the greatness and eternity of Rome, violence and cupidity are concealed.[57] Despite Dante's apparent break in *Monarchia* (II, 2, 2-6) with the position of Augustine, though without mentioning his name, Justinian's speech in *Paradiso* VI demonstrates that the old Roman history consists of a series of events compelled by the force of arms.

A careful reading of Justinian's speech reveals a story based on violence—from the sacrifice of Pallas and all the victims of the city, from the rape of the Sabines, ordained under the government of Romulus, to Lucretia's suicide, and so on. Each story evokes as much suffering and death as heroic virtues. However, in the midst of this history of violence, and in the very middle of the canto (*Par.* VI, 80-82), God intervenes by correcting the pride of man, which is the greedy perspective of logic that cannot accept paradoxes. The consequence of God's intervention in history—or, as Justinian explained at the beginning of the canto, the effect of the logical paradox that God took the flesh and thus the suffering of a human being—is the redemption of the earthly city. Hence, the incarnation restores the equilibrium, the economic balance of sacrifice and forgiveness, between the Creator and his creation. As such, the restoration of man's sinfulness evokes one of the main characteristics of Mercury—the god of commerce. Furthermore, it recalls Justinian's own conversion from Monophysitism to the truth of the double nature of Christ, which qualified the emperor in providing true justice to the *Corpus Iuris Civilis*.

A subtle emblem seems to be unfolding in the course of Justinian's speech. The eagle's flight from east to west and the intervention of God in the middle of the canto create the imaginative sign of a cross, which on this occasion represents the point of transformation of human reason and human desire. A key argument in the emperor's discourse is that only *after* his conversion was he able to organize Roman law, which means that the justice of the law may be ensured only after experiencing the incarnation. This is confirmed and elaborated on by Beatrice in the next canto, where she explains that the cross represents vengeance for human error (*Par.* VII, 34-42):

> Or drizza il viso a quell ch'or si ragiona:
> questa natura al suo fattore unita
> qual fu creata, fu sincera e buona;
> ma per sé stessa pur fu ella sbandita
> di paradise, però che si torse
> de via di verità e da sua vita.
> La pena dunque che la croce prose
> s'a la natura assunta si misura,
> nulla già mai sì giustamente morse.

[Turn your sight now to that which now I say: this nature, which was thus united to its Maker, was, when it was created, pure and good; but by its own self it had been banished from Paradise, because it turned aside from the way of the truth and its proper life. The penalty therefore which the Cross inflicted, if it be measured by the nature assumed— none ever so justly stung.]

According to Beatrice's explanation, turning away from God led humankind astray for many centuries, and the sacrifice on the cross was the penalty for their error. However, the sacrifice of God, which the suffering and death of Christ configured, has paradoxically given the human race the right to avenge; this not only defends Tito's vengeance on the city of Jerusalem that crucified Christ, "the vengeance on the vengeance for the ancient sin" (*Par.* VI, 92–93: "vendetta . . . de la vendetta del peccato antico"); as an extension, Beatrice's explanation also subtly touches on the universality of Roman law: Christ's sacrifice preserves the law of Justinian as well. Just as God redeemed the whole of humanity by making himself a scapegoat, Roman law encompasses every single human being. Confirmed by the sacrifice of Christ and the accompanying human right to retrieve balance through vengeance, this universality, as Dante depicts it, is the divine spark of *Corpus Iuris Civilis*. Moreover, this universality distinguishes Roman law from ancient law, and also from contemporary national laws, which by definition are always condemned to be partial. Like Christ is the rock of the church, the universal empire is founded on human right (*ius humanum*), and, as such, the empire has a decisive role in the economy of history, according to Dante: "Therefore, such governing powers are remedies for the infirmity of sin."[58]

Although not in accordance with the mature Augustine, who by necessity had to reject Roman ideology, Dante's providential view of history was in many ways a traditional one within late medieval historiography, at least since the time of Bonaventure and his defense in *Hexaemeron* of the fallen time within the history of salvation.[59] However, Dante's defense of the monarchy is imbued with contemporary political experiences, rather than being mere nostalgia for a distant and glorious past. We must not forget that the actual political context for Dante was Florence and Italy, riven by wars that drew families, cities, and the whole community into cruel, destructive conflicts. The justification for the universal monarchy may therefore be interpreted as a wish to renew the universality of Roman law rather than the empire itself; this body of law should aim to advance peace and encompass the whole of humanity. For these reasons, Roman law reflected the justice of God (*Par.* VI, 88–90):

> ché la viva giustizia che mi spira,
> li concedette, in mano a quell ch'i' dico,
> gloria di far vendetta a la sua ira.

[because the living Justice which inspires me granted to it, in his hand of whom I speak, the glory of doing vengeance for its own wrath.]

The idea here is that Justinian is the mouthpiece for divine Justice. God's justice once permitted the vengeance of the vengeance that paved the way for the possibility of human salvation, a paradox that, as we have seen, Beatrice carefully unfolds in *Paradiso* VII. According to Justinian, the same divine, living Justice is to be found in the body of Roman law.

A JARRING DISSONANCE

Justinian concludes his historical presentation by explaining that Mercury, "questa picciola stella" (*Par.* VI, 112), inhabits spirits who have not ascended farther because they have chiefly pursued honor and fame while on earth: they have yearned for horizontal glory—glory among human beings—instead of directing their desire toward heaven. However, from a divine viewpoint their reward is well pondered, Justinian explains. From the perspective of true Love, they are now able to discern the balance between reward and merit, and the concord that their different voices create reflects the living Justice that is active in them (*Par.* VI, 118–123):

> Ma nel commensurar d'i nostri gaggi
> col merto è parte di nostro letizia,
> perché non li vedem minor né maggi.
> Quindi addolcisce la viva giustizia
> in noi l'affetto sì, che non si puote
> torcer già mai ad alcuna nequizia.

[But in the equal measure of our rewards with our desert is part of our joy, because we see them neither less nor greater. Hereby the living Justice makes our affection so sweet within us that it can never be bent aside to any evil. Diverse voices make sweet music, so diverse ranks in our life render sweet harmony among these wheels.]

The spirits of Mercury sing a polyphony, a *concordia discors,* which connects the east to the west and earth to heaven. Ironically, canon law had already adopted this musical metaphor, which alludes to the new polyphonic music of the *trecento,* the Ars Nova.[60] The complete title of Gratian's law, the *Decretum Gratiani,* was in fact *Concordia discordantium canonum.* That Justinian is one of the voices in such a heavenly choir reveals that, for Dante, it is Roman law, and not canon law, that is the rightful administrator of earthly justice. It is through Roman law that the justice of God resonates. This is also confirmed in *Monarchia,* where he strongly dismisses the power of the decretalists.[61]

In the third book of *Monarchia,* where he discusses the three major groups of opponents of the emperor—the pope and the bishops, the supporters of the Guelph party, and the decretalists—he describes the last group thus: "There is also a third category whom they call decretalists, who are ignorant and unskilled in any knowledge of theology and philosophy, basing their whole cause upon their decretals (which I truly consider to be worthy of veneration) and placing their hopes (I believe) in the supremacy of these decretals, denigrate the empire. And no wonder, since once I heard a certain member of this group state and impudently maintain that the 'traditions' of the Church were the foundation of the faith."[62] Here Dante turns the hierocrats' argument upside-down by arguing that the tradition of the church, consisting of decretals, papal edicts, and so forth, are of secondary importance compared to the biblical texts and the church fathers, an opinion that he shared with other critics of the contemporary popes, such as William of Ockham, to whom we will return in Chapter 3. A similarly bitter attack is expressed in the ninth canto of *Paradiso* (*Par.* IX, 133–138):

> Per questo l'Evangelico e i dotto magni
> son derelitti, e solo ai Decretali
> si studia, sì che pare a' lor vivagni.
> A questo intende il papa e' i cardinali;
> non vanno i lor pensieri a Nazarette,
> là dove Gabrïello aperse l'ali.

[For this the Gospel and the great Doctors are deserted, and only the Decretals are studied, as may be seen by their margins. Thereon the Pope and Cardinals are intent. Their thoughts go not to Nazareth whither Gabriel spread his wings.]

According to Dante, the universal empire was not only the best form of government—it was even "necessary for the well-being of the world," as he stated in *Monarchia* (I, 2, 3). In *Paradiso* VI Justinian's long response to Dante's request manifests itself, as we have seen, as a strong defense of the universal empire, vindicated by the body of Roman law, the *Corpus Iuris Civilis*. However, through a more nuanced reading of the canto, we can see that the universal dream discussed in Dante's political tractate and repeated by Justinian in *Paradiso* VI is fading. Toward the end of the emperor's speech, an aesthetic perspective accentuates his arguments: the song of the blessed accompanies his idea of a global concord that reflects the divine order. Yet a dissonance interrupts the polyphonic beauty that the song creates, a dissonance that cannot be understood other than as a reminder, both to Dante the pilgrim and to the whole of humanity. On this occasion, as well as in many other passages in the *Commedia,* the poem challenges the far more straightforward arguments in *Monarchia.* The poetic text, in other words, allows for ambiguities, or, maybe better, an opaque realism that is deemed to disappear in the political tractate's reductive language of logic.

Justinian's speech ends most enigmatically: "Within this same pearl shines too the light of Romeo, whose great and noble work was ill rewarded" (*Par.* VI, 127–129: "E dentro a la presente margarita / luce la luce di Romeo, di cui fu l'ovra grande e bella mal gradita"). Romeo, or Romieu de Villeneuve, was a servant or an eager minister of Ramon Berenguer IV, Count of Provence (1198–1245); he arranged for his four daughters to marry various European kings—Margaret married Louis IX of France; Eleanor married Henry III of England; Sancha married Henry's brother, Richard of Cornwell; and Beatrice, his youngest daughter, married Charles of Anjou. Romeo's ambitious cultural program—the establishment of peace and family bonds through marriages between powers and nations in conflict—evokes the marriage of Aeneas and Lavinia as the foundation of Rome at the beginning of the canto. The story also recalls Justinian's radical nuptial law, which enabled him to marry his own mistress, Theodora, in 525.

The tragedy conveyed in this story is that Romeo's desire to serve was not well received. The reward for Romeo's efforts was exile, and his destiny may thus allude to what Dante's ancestor Cacciaguida later on, in *Paradiso* XVII, foreshadows for the poet of *Commedia,* as many commentators have already noticed.[63] We may add, though, that Cacciaguida lives in the heaven of Mars, and Mars is, according to *Convivio,* the planet of music. The prophecy of Dante's exile creates in this canto a dissonance in the harmonic polyphony. The same is true of Romeo's destiny in *Paradiso* VI. Romeo's story is a warning about humans' fundamental status as pilgrims or as estranged, as depicted in the biblical story about Adam and Eve's expulsion from Paradise (Gn 3). A clear allusion in Dante's portrayal of Romeo is that every human being is a "Romeo, a man of low birth and a stranger" (*Par.* VI, 135: "Romeo, persona umile e peregrina"), condemned to eating bread by the sweat of his brow (Gn 3:19), in the same way as Romeo is condemned to "begging for his bread morsel by morsel" (*Par.* VI, 141: "Mendicando sua vita a frusto a fusto"). Cacciaguida passes a similar judgment on Dante, his younger relative, in the heaven of Mars (*Par.* XVII, 55–60):

> Tu lascerai ogne cose dileta
> più caramente; e questo è quello strale
> che l'arco de lo essilio pria saetta.
> Tu proverai sì come sa di sale
> lo pane altrui, e come è duro calle
> lo scendere e 'l salir per l'altrui scale.

[You shall leave everything beloved most dearly; and this is the arrow which the bow of exile shoots first. You shall come to know how salt is the taste of another's bread, and how hard the path to descend and mount by another man's stairs.]

Romeo's story, like Cacciaguida's prophecy of Dante's future exile, is a narrative about the human state as an existential banishment, which is a pervasive and fundamental notion in Dante's poetry. In addition, Romeo's destiny reveals the hidden traps of the belief that human beings, by virtue of logic, can penetrate the justice of God. Just when man thinks he knows God's will, he commits, according to Dante, the gravest of all sins—pride (*superbia*)—which is the very sin committed by Lucifer and his two acolytes, the murderers of Christ and of Caesar (*Inf.* XXXIV).

Romeo's light is hidden in the light of Mercury, just as the light of Mercury is hidden in the light of the sun—Mercury's passage is veiled by the rays of the sun more than by any other star. This may be interpreted as the impossibility of law, whether Roman or national, to bind the will of God to the economy of logic, to logic's account of credit and debit, of sin, remedy, sacrifice and vengeance. According to Dante, there is an economy that is superior to all human law, even to Roman law, despite its divine reflections. The story about Romeo has revealed its limits. Notwithstanding the harsh vengeance on earth, Romeo is rewarded in Paradise. In other words, the judgment of God is veiled, unpredictable and therefore free from human calculations—in the same way as the most valuable gift conferred by God to human nature is free will, *libertas arbitrii*. These two kinds of freedom, which mirror one another, have just been taught to Dante the pilgrim in the previous sphere, in the heaven of the Moon (*Par.* II–V), and above all during his meeting with Piccarda, the woman whose veil was forcefully torn by her brothers in order to marry her off (*Par.* III).

Dante's response to the contemporary crisis is, as we have seen, highly complex. On the one hand, while praising the apostolic poverty of the clergy, he condemns the increasing temporal power of the church. On the other hand, his defense of the legitimate authority of the universal empire conveys a warning against unlimited monarchical power. So as not to be transformed into a tyrant, the emperor must, like Divus Augustus, be a humble and hardworking servant for his people. As such, the missions of the pope and the emperor were related. They were both heads of institutions willed by God, their authority was to guide humanity to happiness—both earthly and divine—but they were also both subject to a superior power, the almightiness of God. Likewise, Dante's defense of the divine origin of Roman law contains the seeds of a profound admonition. As he argues in *Monarchia,* the emperor is supposed to direct humankind to temporal felicity according to philosophical teaching, whereas the emperor's weapon is Roman law, founded on humans' right to avenge injustice. However, as we have seen in the poetic language of *Paradiso* VI, Roman law also has its boundaries. Logic is always subject to a superior wisdom that is impossible for human reason to penetrate. Thus, true justice will forever be concealed in the will of God.

CHAPTER 2

MARSILIUS OF PADUA AND THE QUESTION OF LEGITIMACY

ven though Dante's political thoughts in many senses reactivated a long and broadly accepted tradition in the Middle Ages, rooted in the Gelasian theory of the two swords, later echoed in the Thomistic idea of the twofold goal and the twofold happiness of man, *Monarchia* faced strong opposition from the Avignon papacy. According to Giovanni Boccaccio, a great admirer and the first biographer of Dante, in the initial years after the poet's death his book was hardly known. However, as he writes in *Tratatello in laude di Dante* (A short treatise in praise of Dante), when the harsh conflict between Pope John XXII and Ludwig of Bavaria broke out in the 1320s, Dante's name and his work became notorious. The poet—though already dead—was charged with heresy, and his work and remains were sentenced to be burned:

> This book [the *Monarchia*] was condemned several years after the author's death by Messer Bertrand, Cardinal of Pouget, and papal legate in the parts of Lombardy, when Pope John XXII was in the chair. The reason was because Ludwig, Duke of Bavaria, chosen King of the Romans by the electors of Germany, came to Rome for his coronation, against the desire of Pope John, and, being in Rome, he made a minor friar Pope, who was called brother Piero della Corvara . . . and had himself crowned there by this Pope. His authority was questioned in many ways, and he and his followers, having come upon this book, began to make use of many of the arguments it contained, in support of his authority and of themselves. And so the book, scarcely known before, became very famous. Afterwards, when Ludwig had gone back to Germany, and his followers, especially the clergy, had come to ruin and were dispersed, the Cardinal

[of Pouget], with no one to contradict him, seized the book and condemned it publicly to the flames, as containing heresies.[1]

The treatise by the popular and almost sanctified Florentine poet was used, according to Boccaccio, to defend Ludwig's coronation as Holy Roman emperor and his election of an antipope in Rome in 1328. Pope John XXII responded with a strong condemnation of the book, and many copies were burned in public squares. The treatise remained on the church's index as late as 1881.[2] As for the poet's remains, the Franciscan friars in Rimini managed to hide them and save them from burning.

One of the men who accompanied Ludwig to Rome was Marsilius of Padua, the former rector of the University of Paris, and later a diplomat in the service of the mighty northern Italian *signori* and leaders of the Ghibelline League, Cangrande della Scala and Matteo Visconti, with whom Dante's name is also associated.[3] After a failed mission to offer Charles de la Marche, the future King Charles IV of France, leadership of the league, Marsilius returned to Paris, where in 1324 he published the large tractate *Defensor pacis* (The defender of peace). In 1325 he left Paris with his friend John of Jandum, who was long regarded as a coauthor of *Defensor pacis*, to join the court of the newly elected emperor Ludwig of Bavaria in Nuremburg. In 1327–1328 he followed Ludwig to Italy, probably as his personal physician, and during the coronation in Rome he became one of the emperor's closest counselors in political and spiritual matters.

Defensor pacis consisted of a profound critique of the Avignon papacy, and above all of Pope John XXII's claim to possess *plenitudo potestatis*. In the wake of Ludwig's coronation in Rome and the installment of an antipope, during which process Marsilius was a crucial figure, the book was deemed heretical. Dante's *Monarchia* and Marsilius's *Defensor pacis* thus suffered the same fate to a certain degree, in that both tractates were connected to the events in Rome, and arguments from both were used by the emperor's supporters. As Joan Ferrante has argued, it is most likely that Dante and Marsilius also knew of each other and of each other's ideas: they were both at Verona for some time during the second decade of the fourteenth century, both were under the patronage of Cangrande della Scala, and both were staunch defenders of the Holy Roman Empire.[4] Moreover, they were both in one way or another connected to the Franciscan Spiritual Ubertino da Casale—Dante in his youth in Florence, as we have seen in Chapter 1, and Marsilius around three decades later. Marsilius, however, did not only take Dante's argument to extremes. Despite the kinship or many similarities between *Defensor pacis* and *Monarchia*, Marsilius fundamentally opposed some of Dante's notions. This chapter offers a comparative reading of Dante's

Inferno VI and Marsilius's *Defensor pacis,* and what such comparative reading reveals are the fundamental differences between the two thinkers: whereas Dante adopts a critical stance toward the physiological metaphor of the social organism—the comparison of the civil community with the body of an animal—the same metaphor constitutes the core of Marsilius's intellectual universe. As Alan Gewirth once wrote, Marsilius went so far in his use of physiological analogies and metaphors, probably due to his medical background, that whereas those who subscribed to the traditional notion of body politics moralized biology, Marsilius biologized morals and politics.[5] Dante, on the other hand, seemed to be highly aware of the potential pitfalls of such naturalism.

WORN, TORN BODIES

In the sixth canto of Dante's *Inferno,* which represents an opposite world to the justice and peace that govern in the heaven of Mercury (*Par.* VI and VII), the two pilgrims, Dante and Virgil, meet a disgusting fellow called Ciacco. He is from Florence, and Dante starts discussing the situation of his hometown with him. We do not know who Ciacco was in the real world, but his name means "hog" or "pig," and in his piggishness he is an apt figure or mouthpiece for the rotten state of Florence. This is the first time Florence is mentioned in the *Commedia,* but it is not the last because nothing occupies Dante more than the political condition of the city from which he was exiled, as well as the situation of Italy and Europe in general.

The description of the depraved Florentines we meet in *Inferno* VI recalls Dante's letter to the German emperor Henry VII, in which he pleaded with the emperor to devote his attention to "the ill-omened beast" on the river Arno: "Florence is the name of this ill-omened beast. She is the viper who turns against the vitals of her mother; she is the sick sheep, which infects her master's flock with her disease. . . . With all the ferocity of a viper she strives to tear her mother to pieces, as she sharpens the horns of her rebellion against Rome, which made her in its own image and likeness."[6] The allusion here is to the rebuilding of Florence based on the model of Rome—"la bellissima e famossisima figlia di Roma," as Dante depicted Florence in his *Convivio* (*Conv.* I, 3, 4)—after the city's destruction by the Ostrogoth King Totila in the middle of the sixth century.[7]

In *Inferno* VI, the Florentines are compared to beasts in a similar way as in the letter to Henry VII. The wanderers are crossing the third circle, where the gluttons ("golosi") may be found, and it is guarded by Cerberus, a voracious monster with a worm's body (v. 22; "il gran vermo") who administers the putrefaction around him. The sinners wallow in the noisome mud, described as the most despicable (v. 48; "spiacente") of all punishments. The sinners, obviously Epicureans, who in their earthly life reveled in luxury and were entangled in bodily pleasures—their sins are examples of that incontinence ("incontinentia") that marks the upper regions of Hell (cf. *Inf.* XI, 82)—are now, according to the *contrappasso* system of punishment, rolling around in the gutter.

In his reading of the canto, Simone Marchesi has convincingly glossed Dante's description of the condemned people on a passage from Isidore of Seville's *Etymologiae*. As such, the meaning of Ciacco's name—hog—is connected to the Epicureans' way of life (*Etymologiae* VIII, 6, 15-17):[8] "Epicureans derive their name from Epicurus, some philosopher who loved vanity not wisdom, whom even the other philosophers called hog [*porcum*], since he was, as it were, rolling around in carnal filth. He maintained that pleasure is the highest good and said that the world is neither created nor governed by any kind of divine providence. . . . They maintain that God is idle, that everything is material and that the soul is nothing but body. On this basis Epicurus also said: 'I will not be after I will be dead.'"[9]

As Marchesi makes clear, Isidore based his descriptions of the Epicureans on other sources, such as Augustine (*Ennarationes in Psalmos* LXXIII, 25), Jerome (*Adversus Ioviniamum* II, 12), and Horace (*Epistulae* I, 4, 15-16), although it is the passage from Isidore's *Etymologiae* that comes closest to Dante's canto. Important in our context, however, is the way in which the gluttons' behavior is connected to the nonbelievers' materialistic view of life. The Epicureans' assertion of the mortality of the soul and the indifference of God to human destiny will be developed later in the *Commedia*, in *Inferno* X. The Epicureans in *Inferno* VI, however, are depicted as nonbelievers who indulge in the pleasures of the flesh. Nevertheless, the food, drinks, and bodily desires are not so much the subject of this canto as is the lust for power. The erotic desire discussed in the previous canto, when the pilgrims meet Francesca (*Inf.* V), is now transformed into an unslakable thirst for power.

When Dante realizes that Ciacco is a Florentine citizen, he asks him about the outcome of the conflicts within the torn city (*Inf.* VI, 57-63):

Io li rispuosi: "Ciacco, il tuo affanno
mi pesa sì, ch'a lagrimar mi 'nvita;
ma dimmi, se tu sai, a che verranno
li cittadin de la città partita;
s'alcun v'è giusto; e dimmi la cagione
per che l'ha tanta discordia assalita."

[I answered him, "Ciacco, your misery so weighs upon me that it bids me weep. But tell me, if you can, what the citizens of the divided city will come to; and if anyone in it is just; and tell me why such discord has assailed it."]

As discussed in Chapter 1, late thirteenth-century Florence suffered from inner conflicts between two competing parties—the Ghibellines, who supported the emperor, and the Guelphs, who supported the pope—which again splintered into several more factions. Dante's next question to Ciacco is thus whether there is a just person among all the citizens of Florence, and why no agreement has been arrived at.

Throughout the canto, parallels are drawn between the torn bodies and the divided city. The human body is discreetly dismembered, and body parts, such as eyes, beards, bellies, mouths, nails, faces, necks, brows, hearts, and flesh, are strung out in the text, with the effect of dismissing, and even ridiculing, any attempt to gather them into a harmonic unity. In the center we find Florence, ruled by injustice, or, as Ciacco says, it is "so full of envy that already the sack runs over" (*Inf.* VI, 49–50: "La tua città, ch'è piena / d'invidia sì che già trabocca il sacco"). Ciacco, however, presents himself as someone who stands outside the power struggles. His own "piggishness" is nothing compared to the greed of those who compete for political control over Florence, and he predicts a most cruel fate for the city (*Inf.* VI, 64–76):

> E quelli a me: "Dopo lunga tencione
> verranno al sangue, e la parte selvaggia
> caccerà l'altra con molta offensione.
> Poi appresso conviene che questa caggia
> infra tre soli, e che l'altra sormonti
> con la forza di tal che testé piaggia.
> Alte terrà lungo tempo le fronti,
> tenendo l'altra sotto gravi pesi,
> come che di ciò pianga o che n'aonti.
> Giusti son due, e non vi sono intesi;
> superbia, invidia e avarizia sono
> le tre faville c'hanno i cuori accesi."
> Qui puose fine al lagrimabil suono.

[And he to me, "After long contention they will come to blood, and the rustic party will drive out the other with much offense. Then, through the power of one who presently is temporizing, that party is destined to fall within three years, and the other to prevail, long holding its head high and keeping the other under heavy burdens, however it may lament and feel the shame. Two men are just, and are not heeded there. Pride, envy, and avarice are the three sparks that have inflamed their hearts." Here he ended his grievous words.]

The notion that connects the two subjects—the gluttons' depraved bodies in *Inferno* VI and the sick political body of Florence—has its origin, according to Giuseppe Mazzotta's compelling reading of the canto, in the classical story about Menenius Agrippa, as told by Livius in his *Ab urbe condita* (II, 32, 2–3). The story is, moreover, based on the Aesopic fables (206 and 286) that convey the idea about the *homonoia,* the public concord that unites the *polis.*[10] In order to heal the split between the patricians and plebeians, Menenius draws an analogy between food, the stomach, and the corporative organization of the state. The argument is that the organization is based on an organic, corporative model and that the harmony of the state is dependent on its functional diversity and cooperation. The belly supplies what is needed to each limb and distributes the blood, produced by digesting food, through the rich networks of veins. Thus, the order and stability of the city presuppose the profound interdependency of the citizens. Rather than an assembly of individual human beings, the political community is regarded as an entity or a unitary whole. What Ciacco's story reveals, however, is the deceptions linked to such an organic understanding of human society: a harmonic model that takes consensus and concord as natural starting points easily conceals human pride, envy, and avarice (v. 74, "superbia, invidia e avarizia"), which create nothing but discord.

POWER TO THE PEOPLE

Marsilius's solution to the problems of the Italian city-states was not to call for a strong ruler, a king or a prince of true virtues, which Dante and, later, Machiavelli and other political thinkers of Renaissance humanism suggested as the solution. Marsilius instead belonged to the scholastic tradition that, according to Quentin Skinner, stressed that government was effective whenever its institutions were strong, and corrupt whenever its machinery failed to function adequately.[11] Marsilius presented himself chiefly as a political analyst rather than a moralist. Instead of virtuous individuals, he evoked an efficient institution as the best means to promote the common good and rule of peace. This does not mean, however, that he reckoned on a society of nonbelievers. He accepted that the citizens of his perfect state would be Christians. Nonetheless, he presented a political structure where God was placed in the background as a remote rather than a direct cause (*DP* I, 9, 2).

Expressed in strictly secular terms, his model assumes that governments are established by human will, and subsequently ultimate authority is to be found in the people (*populus*) or the corporation of citizens (*universitas civium*), and not in God or his vicar. According to Marsilius, all coercive or compulsive power in this world belongs to human law and to its legislator, which is the corporation of the citizens, or the prevailing part (*pars valentior*) thereof: "Let us say, then, in accordance with both the truth and the counsel of Aristotle, *Politics* III chapter 6, that the 'legislator', i.e. the primary and proper efficient cause of the law, is the people or the universal body of citizens or else its prevailing part. . . . And in consequence of this I say that laws and anything else instituted by election must receive their necessary approval from the same primary authority and no other."[12]

It is not completely clear what Marsilius meant by the "prevailing part," and according to Gewirth this was not a common expression in medieval political philosophy before Marsilius, although it was used in William of Moerbeke's translation of Aristotle.[13] Marsilius, however, who employs the expression *pars valentior* throughout the *Defensor pacis,* explains that "prevailing part" implies that he is taking into consideration both the quantity and the quality of persons in the community to whom the law applies (*DP* I, 12, 3). Like Aristotle, he excludes young boys, women, strangers, and slaves from citizenship (*DP* I, 12, 4). However, the first principle in Marsilius's philosophy, fundamental to his entire argument, is that power belongs to the people: government rests on the ultimate authority of the whole corporation of the citizens, the *universitas civium*. The body of citizens, or the prevailing part thereof, represents the will of the whole, and when gathered together the corporation of citizens is called *legislator humanus*—the human legislator. This is the most authoritative forum for discussing all legal and political affairs, he argues, and its will must be "expressed in speech in a general assembly of the citizens."[14]

The full emphasis in Marsilius's thought is on the supreme will and consent of the citizens, who delegate power to what he calls the *principatus* or *pars principans,* the government that implements the laws. As he explains, when the *regnum* is well tempered, the *principatus* governs in accordance with the will and consent of the human legislator: "Polity, even if in one of its significations it is something common to every kind or type of regime or principate, nevertheless in another implies a certain specific type of tempered principate in which every citizen has some share in the principate or councillor function, in turn and according to his rank, means or condition, and also for the common advantage and according to the will or consent of those subject."[15]

Following the model of Aristotle, Marsilius implies that a well-tempered principate may be found under different regimes—in monarchies, aristocracies, or polities. When the common good is subjected to factional interests, however, we find corrupt or diseased versions, namely, tyranny, oligarchy, and democracy. As also suggested by Aristotle, Marsilius reminds his readers that different societies at different times and in different places have been inclined to different kinds of polities and governments. He stresses, however, that in a well-tempered principate it is the consent and will of the human legislator that establish the standard of the law. This standard regulates all civil acts (*DP* I, 10, 6). Its efficient driving force is the will and consent of the people—and, consequently, the worldly ruler who implements the laws, as well as the priesthood and the body of citizens, is also subject to it.

The people are seemingly given unlimited power in Marsilius's philosophy. Even the government or the ruler—the part of the community that effects the laws by exercising coercion—has its origin in the human legislator: "For from the soul of the universal body of the citizens or its prevailing part, one part is or should be formed first within it which is analogous to the heart. In this the soul instituted a certain virtue or form with the active potential or authority to institute the remaining parts of the city. And this part is the principate, the virtue of which is the authority to judge, command and execute sentences of what is advantageous or just in civil terms."[16]

In short, as Marsilius depicts it, legitimate power belongs entirely to the human legislator who appoints the task of ruling to the *principatus*. Though limited by dependence on the will of the people and by the laws of the human legislator, the aim of the *principatus* is to unify the political community, and, to this end, its power has to be full or undivided: "Now it is only this principate, sc. the supreme, that I say must necessarily be one in number, and not several, if the realm or city is to be rightly ordered."[17] Thus, the main reason for the discord and lack of tranquility in *regnum italicum*, which Marsilius sets out to reveal at the beginning of *Defensor pacis*, and which he says that Aristotle could never have known, was nothing but the profound deprivation of this legitimacy of the human legislator: the threat of discord and the reason for the strife in Italy were the universal jurisdiction that the church and the bishops of Rome increasingly and over the centuries had assumed for themselves.

THE "MODERNITY" OF MARSILIUS

The prominence of "people power" has given *Defensor pacis* the reputation of being an early expression of modern political theory and a precursor to the political ideas of Thomas Hobbes and John Locke. Scholars like Nicolai Rubenstein, Quentin Skinner, and Cary J. Nederman have continued Gewirth's portrayal of Marsilius's doctrine as a forerunner to "the monism of authority in which the modern conception of the sovereign state consists."[18] Despite his derision of the many bizarre and unhistorical readings of Marsilius—that he advocated religious toleration, totalitarianism, socialism, Marxism, democracy, and so forth—Gewirth did not completely resist the temptation of describing him as a "prophet of modern ideas and institutions." As he solemnly proclaimed, "Marsilianism can be described by the same epithets customarily assigned to the modern era: naturalism, secularism, movement away from hierarchic controls and towards a libertarian individualism mingled with egalitarian collectivism."[19] In a similar way, Rubenstein and Skinner have depicted Marsilius as a republican advocate of popular sovereignty. According to Skinner, Marsilius's aim was to confirm the idea of sovereignty already matured in the Italian city republics. As soon as the arguments were applied in the case of a *regnum* (Italy), as well as a *civitas* (the city), his republicanism could develop into a "recognisably modern theory of popular sovereignty in a secular state."[20] Nederman has gone even further in stressing the modernity of Marsilius; he uses *Defensor pacis* as a prism through which "the possibilities of politics in our time and place come into focus with special clarity." Marsilius, he continues, "may serve not merely as an inspiration but even as a guide to contemporary political theory."[21]

There are many reasons to question this enthusiasm for Marsilius's supposed modernity. By reading the tractate anachronistically only from our "modern" perspective, we may easily lose sight of its historical particularity. Joseph Canning has noticed that Marsilius's model fitted the whole range of existing forms of rulership—emperors, kings, and *signori*—and not only Italian city republics—which also becomes evident by the end of the treatise (*DP* III, 3).[22] Furthermore, Marsilius's philosophy is deeply rooted in medieval corporation theory. As Janet Coleman has argued, Marsilius is presenting a notion of free individuals in a multitude of free men whose corporate will regarding the common good is necessarily the *same* and can therefore be represented by the weightier part: "He [Marsilius] believes that a collected group of people, the multitude, can have their objective view on the common advantage represented by the voice of one man or several, that a representative can accurately mirror the collective will of a community, a will that is the product of rationally logical inference from experience."[23] This naïve trust in common agreement or consent, built around physiological, organic analogies of a self-ordering and self-equalizing system, can hardly be characterized as "modern." As we shall discuss, it also radically differs from Dante's far more skeptical view of human nature.

Another important matter that challenges any uncritical enthusiasm for Marsilius's modernity is that he expressed clear support for Ludwig of Bavaria and his claim to the imperial title.[24] In the introduction to her English translation of *Defensor pacis*, Annabel Brett has convincingly claimed that up until the middle of the second discourse, Marsilius's assertion is that priests had no temporal jurisdiction. After that he constructs his argumentation on the basis of the emperor's right to fullness of power, which is the only means to restore the tranquility desired.[25] In the opening of *Defensor pacis*, he appeals to Emperor Ludwig to fulfill his call for peace: "And so . . . I, a son of Antenor, acting . . . to recall the oppressors from the byway of error, and to spur on those who allow these things to happen when they should and can prevent them; and with an especial regard for you, most noble Ludwig, emperor of the Romans, as the minister of God who will give this work the ending it hopes for from outside."[26]

This passage reveals Marsilius's wish to intervene in contemporary political events. Addressing not only the emperor but even the entire corporation of citizens, the tractate ends with a clarion call to act: "Furthermore, both prince and subject, the primary elements of any civil order, can understand by this treatise what they must do in order to preserve the peace and their own liberty."[27] Through this initial support for the emperor, as well as the final exhortation to readers to wake up and react, *Defensor pacis* is immediately drawn away from the general, nonhistorical field of political theories that makes it seem alluringly modern, and into the center of the conflicts in its own time.

AN INFECTIOUS DISEASE

Scholars who have stressed the modern aspects of Marsilius's philosophy have mainly focused on the first part of *Defensor pacis*, on the seemingly nonhistorical speculations on the origin and nature of earthly power. They have thus underestimated or even ignored the actual events that framed the tractate and to which *Defensor pacis* in its entirety responds. The second discourse gradually unpacks the profound polemical character of the treatise and places it at the heart of the political controversies of the Avignon papacy. *Defensor pacis* consists of three discourses or parts called *Dictiones:* Whereas *Dictio* I offers a general political theory, mainly borrowed from Aristotle's *Politics,* and establishes the principles used to decide where legitimate authority does and does not lie, *Dictio* III consists of a summary of a few pages. In contrast, *Dictio* II is by far the longest part. It constitutes almost two-thirds of the tractate and its aim is to reject the secular power of the clergy.

By the end of the first discourse of *Dictio* II, just before he fires away in the second, Marsilius proclaims that it is the church's involvement in worldly affairs that is the principal cause of strife in Italy. The origin of the suffering is the bishops of Rome and their temporal ambitions:

> This wrong apprehension on the part of certain Roman bishops—and perhaps also their perverted inclination for principate, which they assert is due to them from the plenitude of power handed them (as they say) by Christ—is the singular cause that we have said is productive of intranquillity or discord in a city or realm. For being prone to creep up on every realm (as said in the proem), it has for a long time harassed the realm of Italy with its baneful action, and has kept and still keeps it from tranquillity or peace by preventing with all its might the accession or institution of its prince, sc. the Roman emperor, and his action in the said empire.[28]

The quotation conveys the idea that the papacy's intervention in secular matters did not threaten only Italy. The pope's actions were an infection that was easily transmitted to other countries in Europe as well, a claim that, because of its scope, necessitated urgent action.

As already stated by Dante, Marsilius reiterates that the root of these evils was the notorious Donation of Constantine. Although the motives for Constantine the Great's grant, as well as Pope Sylvester's acceptance, were good, scripture demonstrated that neither the Roman nor any other bishop, priest, or cleric could "claim or ascribe to himself any coercive principate or contentious jurisdiction, still less the supreme, over any cleric or layperson." Marsilius argues, like Dante did, that scripture attested that "on the counsel and example of Christ, they [the bishops] should refuse such principate if it is offered or granted to them by one who has authority to do so."[29] Christ himself chose to live in poverty, claiming, "My kingdom is not of this world" (Jn 18:36). He did not come into the world to have dominance over men, nor to be a temporal prince, but "rather to be subjected in respect of status of this present world."[30] Indeed, he wanted to and did exclude himself, and also his apostles and disciples, as well as their successors, the bishops and priests, from all coercive principate or worldly government (*DP* II, 4, 3). Marsilius's argument is clear enough: contrary to Christ's original intentions, the church had gone astray in developing into the powerful and hierarchical institution it had become in the fourteenth century.

George Garnett has emphasized the importance of the second discourse in *Defensor pacis*. As he makes clear, it was chiefly the discussions of papal power that roused the attention of Marsilius's contemporary readers and lent him notoriety. Furthermore, the second discourse reveals Marsilius's providential understanding of history, which is rooted in Christian convictions. According to Garnett, Marsilius integrated providential history, based on scripture, with the history of Rome.[31] Since the time of Christ's intervention, the Christian and Roman histories had been intertwined. As we have seen in Chapter 1, a similar argument was presented by Dante: the birth of Christ under the Roman emperor offered the empire de jure a providential role (*Mn.* II, 10, 4), and his crucifixion, as Beatrice explained, gave the legitimate authorities (or the human race) the paradoxical right to avenge Adam's original sin (*Par.* VI, 92–93: "vendetta . . . de la vendetta del peccato antico").

Dante, however, was more careful in his critique of the church than Marsilius was. As Dante famously concludes in the *Monarchia*, he admitted the divine origin of the institution, as well as the authority of the pope: "The truth of the last, of course, must not be understood so strictly that the Roman prince is not in a certain sense under the Roman pontiff, since the happiness of this mortal life is in some way ordered toward eternal happiness. Therefore, let Caesar [the emperor] show Peter [the pope] that reverence that a first-born son should show his father, so that, illuminated by the light of paternal grace, he may enlighten the globe of the earth more powerfully, for he presides over it solely by way of him who is the ruler of all things temporal and spiritual."[32]

As a response to the hierocrats' organic model, which argued that the pope was the sole head of the world, Dante recalls the medieval tradition that had sought to diversify the order. The twofold goal that Providence had set for mankind, and that reflects the dual nature of humans, required dual guides: the emperor, who, by philosophy, should lead mankind to temporal happiness; and the pope, who, guided by the Holy Spirit, should lead mankind to eternal happiness. However, despite Dante's affirmation of and deep respect for the reality of the worldly end, the preceding quotation suggests that the two beatitudes of man will converge at the source whence all things spring forth. In terms of the unity of God, the secular and the spiritual guides have the same goal, which means that the temporal order is subordinated to the eternal order, toward which the pope guides mankind.

ECCLESIA SPIRITUALIS VS. ECCLESIA CARNALIS

Marsilius's response to the pope's claim to possess fullness of power was quite different. To a certain degree he retained the decretalists' hierarchical structure, but reversed it: the human legislator possessed plenitude of power, and the prestige of the priesthood originated wholly from the authority of secular rulers. Marsilius accepted the twofold goals of men, but, in contrast to Dante, he did not see any convergence. The two ends were kept separate in that divine law had no coercive power in this life. Its dominion was the world hereafter. As he argued, the New Law, which was a perfect law of freedom (James 1:25), had replaced the old Mosaic law, which God had once ordained with coercive sanctions in this world. The evangelic law, however, had no coercive sanction in this world (*DP* II, 9, 3). It was applied only in the future life, in the world to come (*DP* II, 8, 5). The priests, he claimed, should live in accordance with apostolic poverty, renouncing all material goods and ambitions and teaching contempt for secular values. They might administer the sacrament and teach divine law, but their task was purely spiritual, to guide men to eternal life. The power to enforce divine as well as human law belonged to the secular ruler, in accordance with the principle Marsilius had established by the end of the first discourse: "The office of coercive principate over any individual person, of whatever rank, or any community or collective body, does not belong to the Roman or to any bishop, priest or spiritual minister in his capacity as such."[33] He thereby clearly expressed a positive view of human law, which meant that the laws were coercive only when the human legislator had established the norms as laws.[34]

In Marsilius's state, the clergy has no legal immunity. Like all other citizens, they are subject to secular rulers and the human legislator. In order to avoid any erosion of the unity and absolute power of the state, even the appointment of the clergy should be in the hands of the people, according to Marsilius. As for the church, he had a purely spiritual interpretation of it. With a reference to 1 Corinthians 1:2, he defines the term "church" as what "is said of the universal body of faithful believers who call upon the name of Christ."[35] The definition reduces the role of the church as a hierarchically organized institution or an organization with any worldly pretensions.[36] In Marsilius's opinion, the priests, as we have seen, should follow Christ's advice in refusing any temporal dominion, even if it were offered to them by the emperor, as was the case with the Donation of Constantine. As a voluntary gathering of faithful believers, the authority of the church belonged to the *universitas* or *congregatio fidelium*, the congregation itself or a general council that represented it. In this way the organization of the church reflected the organization of the civil community and the aim, of course, was to deprive the pope, his decretals, and canon law of authority.

The authority within the church, as a spiritual institution, pertains, according to Marsilius, to the universal body of believers, or its general council, who established the norms valid for the Church. Evidently, these norms had no coercive power in civil society, and the *universitas fidelium* was, like everyone else, subject to the laws established by the human legislator and implemented by the *principatus*. In the second discourse of *Defensor pacis*, there is no doubt that the *principatus* Marsilius is thinking of is the future emperor Ludwig of Bavaria.

In Marsilius's philosophy there is a clear link to the contemporary Franciscans, and above all to the most radical branch thereof, the Spirituals, such as Petrus Joannis Olivi and his successor, Ubertino da Casale. In his important work *Arbor Vitae Crucifixae* (Tree of life), Ubertino sought to fuse the utopian Joachim da Fiore's apocalyptic interpretations of history with the ethics of Franciscan poverty. The immanent growth of time, configured in the image of the Tree of History, entailed the dissolution of all institutions except for a third part of the Order of Saint Francis. Saint Francis, the seraphic saint, who reenacted the Passion in his own body, initiated the sixth *status* or stage of history. Through his renewal of the life of the Second person in the Trinity—"the great restorer of the life of Christ"—Saint Francis inaugurated, according to Ubertino, the seventh and last stage of history, in which the Holy Spirit would be poured out on the few chosen men—on the Spirituals and those who lived in voluntary apostolic poverty—as had once happened at Pentecost.[37] In this new epoch—the age of the Holy Spirit—when Antichrist and all "false prophets" would be destroyed, the spiritual church (*ecclesia spiritualis*) would replace the carnal church (*ecclesia carnalis*) and dissolve its rigid hierarchy of orders and ministries.

Ubertino and the Spiritual Franciscans considered themselves as living on the threshold of this new age, and the conflict with the Avignon papacy represented the final tremendous conflict with Antichrist.[38] Accused by Dante (*Par.* XII, 124–26) of going too far in his strict interpretation of the Franciscan rule, Ubertino was, however, first acknowledged by Pope John XXII when he in 1322 was called to Avignon to clarify his viewpoint in the controversy concerning the poverty of Christ and the Apostles. When the controversies escalated, however, he was accused of heresy, and, like many other Spirituals of his time, he sought refuge with Ludwig of Bavaria, whom he accompanied to Rome. In Rome he reached the peak of his crusade against the Avignon papacy when he, together with Marsilius, wrote the decree that justified the public deposition of John XXII on 18 April 1328.[39]

Besides biographical and historical events, Marsilius had several connections to the Franciscans. His spiritual understanding of the *ecclesia,* his wish to dissolve the institutional hierarchy of the contemporary church, his extreme otherworldly ideal for the priesthood, and his interpretation of the evangelic law as a law of freedom betray the eschatological or what Garnett has called Marsilius's "Christian-providential" understanding of history. Evidently inspired by the mystical theories of Ubertino and other Spirituals, Marsilius even describes Ludwig of Bavaria in apocalyptic terms.[40] Like the stone that was hewn from the mountain without hands and that fell and crushed the terrible statue of iron, clay, silver, and gold envisioned by Nebuchadnezzar (Dn 2:31–33), Ludwig, the king elected by the universal body of citizens, shall one day destroy the Roman pontiff and his curia, he argues (*DP* II, 24, 17).

There is no doubt that Marsilius's philosophy is framed by a providential understanding of time. Nevertheless, Garnett, who is among the most eager opponents of secular interpretations of Marsilius, seems to ignore the Spirituals' opening up to modern secular notions, or what may be considered the inherent kinship of their eschatological convictions with future Protestant as well as profane ideas. Much, for instance, has been written about the impact of Marsilius's work on the Great Western Schism and the conciliar movement of the fifteenth century, which were preparatory stages for the final division of the church in the sixteenth century.[41] Furthermore, of vital importance is the general interiorization of faith that we encounter in Marsilius's thought; the banishment of divine law to the spiritual realm of individual faith without any possibilities for worldly interventions laid the political community open to be grasped in purely secular terms. As Marjorie Reeves has argued in her insightful reading of *Defensor pacis,* to Marsilius the preservation of peace is a this-worldly, secular aim, wholly cut off from any eternal values.[42] It is also at this point we discover the profound contrast with Dante. While Dante stressed the divine origin of both the church and the empire, Marsilius does not divulge any religious piety for either of these institutions. The contemporary church is regarded largely as a human invention (*DP* II, 22, 10), and the source of temporal power was not God, according to Marsilius, but the people—the *universitas civium.*

THE CITY ANIMAL

Defensor pacis is a huge treatise, and stylistically it seems far removed from the forceful poetry that characterizes Dante's *Commedia.* In a typically scholastic manner, *Defensor pacis* is written in complex, meticulously constructed prose, which can be challenging for modern students to read. However, unlike most of his enemies—the decretalists and even the Avignon popes, who were all trained lawyers—Marsilius's professional background was not legal but medical. The metrical epistle *Ad Magistrum Marsilium Physicum Paduanum eius inconstantiam arguens* (To Marsilius of Padua, master, naturalist, reproaching him for his inconstancy), written by the poet, historian, and civic leader of Padua Albertino Mussato, is considered the most important source of information about Marsilius's life before he wrote *Defensor pacis*. According to this epistle, Marsilius asked Mussato whether to study law or medicine. Following Mussato's advice, Marsilius pursued medical studies with Peter of Abano, another fellow citizen and one of the leading medical authorities in a century when medicine as an academic discipline was constantly gaining repute.

As many have noticed, Marsilius's medical background profoundly influenced his philosophy, which is constructed on some fundamental biological principles. Most recently, Takashi Shogimen and Joel Kaye have explored the influence of Galen and medieval Galenism on *Defensor pacis*.[43] As Kaye argues, "beneath Marsilius' web of social and political agreement lies a sense of integration and cooperation that comes close to the Galen concept of 'health,' the integrated balance (*coaequlitas*) of parts within the whole."[44] To this one may add that it is also in the medical qualities of Marsilius's language that we may discover the roots of what makes Dante and Marsilius travel in such opposite directions despite the many factors that connected them.

Medieval political writings were replete with organic analogies, ushered in above all by the twelfth-century humanist John of Salisbury, who, in his *Policraticus* (The statesman's book), compared the structures and functions of the bodies natural and political, describing the *res publica* as a body animated by the granting of divine reward (V, 2). In *Policraticus* we also encounter Livy's classical fable defending the authority of the prince, who is both the head and the belly of the state (VI, 24). Marsilius, however, refers to Aristotle's *Politics*, which soon became a key text on university curricula after its rediscovery and translation in 1260; this also caused the increasing popularity of the expression *corpus politicum*.[45]

> Since, then, we are to describe the tranquillity and its opposite, let us suppose with Aristotle in the first and fifth books of his *Politics*, chapters 2 and 3 respectively, that the city is like a kind of animate or animal nature. For an animal which is in a good condition in respect of its nature is composed of certain proportionate parts arranged in respect of each other, all communicating the actions between themselves and

towards the whole; likewise too the city which is in a good condition and established in accordance with reason is made up of certain such parts. A city and its parts would therefore seem to be in the same relation to tranquillity as an animal and its parts to health.[46]

In his compelling reading of *Defensor pacis,* Kaye has argued that, despite the fact that Marsilius introduces his animal analogy by referring to the authority of Aristotle, yes, even despite the fact that Galen's name appears only once in the entire tractate, Marsilius provides in this quotation "a marvellously succinct description of the functioning Galenic body."[47] Aristotle never directly compared a *polis* to a living animal body, as Marsilius does here, although he suggested a vague analogy between the city and its parts and the human body and its parts.[48] In Marsilius's theory, however, the bond between the city and the body is strong, and he built many of his arguments on it.[49]

Marsilius's claim is that the correct proportions of the *corpus politicus* bring health (*DP* I, 2, 3). Marsilius draws his naturalistic model of *civitas* and the functioning of the various parts and orders from Galen's theory of the body's constant balancing of the different parts, the members and organs of the body, to produce a well-functioning whole:

> For they think that health is an animal's optimal condition according to nature, and likewise that tranquillity is the optimal condition of a city established according to reason. Now health—as the more expert physicians say when they describe it—is that good condition of an animal, in which each of its parts is enabled perfectly to perform the operations appropriate to its nature. If we follow this analogy, tranquillity will then be that good condition of a city or realm, in which each of its parts is enabled perfectly to perform the operations appropriate to it according to reason and the way it has been established.[50]

As we can see from the quotation, "tranquility" is health, and as such it is a physical expression of cooperation and peace. "Discord," on the other hand, is compared to sickness: "Into this darkness, then, have these wretched people been plunged as a result of this discord or strife among themselves. Like sickness in an animal it can be diagnosed as the indisposition of a civil regime."[51] This is what has happened in *regnum italicum,* according to Marsilius. The pope's intervention and claimed fullness of power have resulted in a sick or infected body politic, spreading rapidly throughout Europe (*DP* I, 19, 12).

The power of Marsilius's rhetoric is that it seems to be based on biological realities, and as such his arguments are imperative and indisputable. As Canning has argued, by equating the city with an animal body, Marsilius placed ultimate authority in the body of citizens, which—like an animal—did not require external justification. Both the animal and the city existed as a simple fact of life.[52] The argument that logically follows from such a proposition is that the city, like an animal, knows what is best for its own health and self-preservation: "Let us then lay this down as the fundamental principle of everything that we must demonstrate, a principle naturally held and believed and freely conceded by all: sc. that all men not deficient or otherwise impeded naturally desire a sufficient life, and by the same token shun and avoid those things that are harmful to them. Indeed, this principle is not only granted for man, but also for every kind of animal."[53] Despite the technical and logical reasoning, this is one of the weak points in Marsilius's philosophy: The assertion that the city or the state, like an animal, knows what is best for it is assumed as an axiom. The instinctive, natural desire of man is a biological fact, a self-equalizing system, on which he builds his entire political theory, and where the consent of the citizens emerges as a vital, unavoidable force.

NATURAL BALANCE

In Ciacco's story in *Inferno* VI, Dante created subtle links between the Epicureans' delight in material pleasures and a naturalistic, this-worldly view of human society governed by the lust for power rather than ordered by divine justice and peace. The corrupt bodies around Ciacco dissolve into dirt and mud, which their guardian, Cerberus, so eagerly devours—an allusion to the gluttony for which the sinners are condemned in this canto. The scene is horrific, the most loathsome in hell (*Inf.* VI, 48), and the associations with the situation in Florence seem clear. The horror portrayed signifies the self-cannibalization unfolding behind the shelter of the city walls by the end of thirteenth century, recalled by contemporary Florentine historians such as Dino Compagni and Giovanni Villani.[54] Their narratives convey the profound injustice, the lust for power, and the brutal conflicts at the heart of Florence.

In contrast to Dante's deep skepticism of human nature—the city riven by bloody power struggles due to the lack of a just prince—Marsilius presupposes the citizens' consent as a natural, given phenomenon. Proportionality or balance within the *corpus politicus* is presented as the main reason for peace and tranquility. Indeed, Marsilius also discussed the clash of man against man, or the threat of citizens' individual wills being in strife with each other. In fact, this dwelling on strife and man's inevitable conflicts pervades *Defensor pacis,* as Gewirth has noted.[55] Disagreements, disputes, violations, and crimes occur wherever humans are gathered together and cause what Marsilius calls "transient acts," which cross over into other agents, in contrast to "immanent acts," which remain within persons (*DP* I, 5, 4). However, as he argues, and which follows like a self-evident, fundamental principle just like the principle that all men naturally desire a sufficient life, "no one willingly harms or wants what is unjust for himself, therefore all or most of them [the citizens] want a law that is adapted to the common advantage of the citizens."[56] Consent and the human will, then, are placed within a biological-physiological framework, and they display the same power of necessity or inevitability as men's natural desires. From this foundation arises the law, the justice of the people's will, to which all citizens must submit.

It is at this fundamental point—the interpretation of human desire—that Dante and Marsilius differ so radically. Whereas for Marsilius human desire constitutes the source of legitimate power and law, for Dante this is the origin of discord, whether it emerges from the citizens, rulers, or clergy. Referring to Aristotle, Dante opens the *Monarchia* by declaring that the desire (*cupiditas*) to which all human beings are inclined is the main impediment to justice (*Mn.* I, 11). In the treatise he evokes a just prince, a prince whose desire is extinguished because he has universal jurisdiction. As universal monarch, the prince would desire nothing, thus becoming a true servant of his people. The people, under the shelter of peace, could then develop their specific human ends, which, according to Aristotle, were radically different from those of animals. The prince, guided by philosophy, and the pope by theology, would together raise citizens from the lower biological conditions of animals to the higher aims of a virtuous life, which was a necessary step toward eternal bliss.

Monarchia's ideal prince is of course a utopian figure in many senses, as indeed Dante himself discreetly suggested, as we have seen, in his depiction of Justinian in *Paradiso* VI: despite his glaring contrast with Ciacco and his avaricious fellow citizens, Justinian's justice has obvious limitations when confronted with the hidden wisdom of God. However, Dante's prince has a highly polemical purpose: whereas Ciacco mirrors the ruin of the political community just when the citizens were starting to consider the pleasures of this life to be the ultimate good, the wise prince raises the aim of the political community out of the mundane, temporal realm of men. The Epicureans of *Inferno* VI have cut off every such bond to the next world. In their opinion, the *corpus politicus* does not represent a step toward divine happiness. God is idle, and, as Ciacco's discourse reveals, power is sought for its own sake, end, and reason.

Dante's and Marsilius's ideas intersect at some points—they both agreed that the papacy's increasing secular control was the main cause of the strife in Italy; they also both supported the imperial party in the conflicts between the pope and the emperor that dominated the late Middle Ages and that flared up more aggressively than ever under the Avignon papacy. Nonetheless, their ideas took different directions. An essential shift of perspective divided them: While Dante emphasized the divine origin of the church and the empire—the power of both institutions was limited by the almightiness of God—Marsilius regarded them as purely human inventions. The proper location and the correct use of power were to be found in the human legislator alone. In contrast, Dante depicted Justinian's conversion as the reason for his being a just emperor. The conversion guaranteed true justice to his compilation of Roman law. Marsilius, on the other hand, configured his perfect state as a healthy animal organism without any divine intervention. Rooted in the biology of men, the aim of the state was not the future happiness or the eternal salvation of the citizens, but, as with all animals and living organisms, a sufficient life.

Marsilius treats the body politic without any reference to transcendental ends. Rather than being a doctrine rooted in the Aristotelian or Christian intellectual and moral values that characterize Dante's ideal political community, Marsilius's conception of justice has its origin in medieval physiological doctrines of bodily "complexion" or *temperamentum*—the proper temperament and balance between qualities and things. He applied his teacher Peter of Abano's medical vocabulary, gathered from Peter's eager studies and translations of Galen's texts, describing justice and human acts in the civil community. The effect was the autonomy of the political discourse, where the teleological subjection to spiritual powers was dispelled.

Like Peter of Abano, who in his treatise *Conciliator differentiarum philosophorum et praecipue medicorum* (Conciliator of the differences debated between philosophers and physicians) described justice as a relative concept of balanced complexion between elements and qualities, justice is, according to Marsilius, due to proportion.[57] It represents a standard, a law, created by the human legislator, in order to avenge or make commensurate violations of the law, and it is the *principatus* who will measure such actions according to the law (*DP* I, 15, 6). Justice, then, is reduced to a technical conception—a smooth functioning of the different parts of the state that is necessary for the "sufficient life" that is the ultimate aim of Marsilius's state. The comparison of the city with an animal body highlights the proportionality of the elements and cooperation between the parts of the body politic. The metaphor encompasses, as we have seen, the idea that the proportionality or balance between the parts brings health, while a lack of tranquility occurs, like when an animal falls ill, when the balance is disturbed.

Marsilius's change of perspective makes him appear appealingly modern. However, his theory is beset with pitfalls, which ultimately entrapped the author himself. As Marsilius depicts it, the human legislator cannot fail. In other words, there is no contradiction between ultimate power and the people's consent. A law is valid, even if it is unjust, as long as it has its origin in the human legislator (*DP* I, 10, 5).

Justice, in other words, is of secondary importance. In contrast to Dante's vision, the justice of a law does not reflect any cosmic order in Marsilius's philosophy. The law's validity is derived from the "true cognisance" (*vera cognitio*) of the human legislator alone, an argument that reveals the seeds of the despotism in Marsilius's theory.[58] One problem is that power is identified with the human will. Another problem is that power is transferred by the people to the *principatus,* whom they then have to obey. Although bound by the legislator's laws, the *princiaptus* had preeminent power over his subjects. As Canning has cautiously suggested, "The people had given the exercise of its powers away to the principate which it had in consequence to obey so long as the prescribed limits were observed."[59] It was this despotism that unfolded in the following months in Rome. During his short stay in the capital of the Holy Roman Empire, the physician helped transform the emperor into an almighty tyrant, to whom both clergy and laymen were subject.

DECLARATION OF WAR

To summarize so far, Marsilius turned the rhetoric of the pope and his supporters upside-down. As he argued, the fullness of power did not belong to the pope but to the people. There had earlier been published a series of treatises defending the pope's temporal power, such as Giles of Rome's *De ecclesiastica potestate,* James of Viterbo's *De regimine christiano,* or Henry of Cremon's *De potestate pape.* All these treatises, rooted in canon law, intricately argued for the ultimate authority of the clergy. By inverting their arguments, the *Defensor pacis* reveals its profoundly polemical character. Despite its diplomatic title, the book is an outright declaration of war on the papacy, and, as such, it reflects the Greek etymology of the word "polemics"—*polemikos* (warlike, belligerent) and *polemos* (war). Marsilius's solution to the contemporary crisis was the total elimination or removal of any kind of priestly authority. Acts of such removal were also what he initiated in Rome when he presented himself as the spiritual physician to a diseased Italy.

In a valuable contemporary source, Albertino Mussato's "Ludovico Bavarus," which offers a historical account of Ludwig's Italian expedition, Marsilius and the Spiritual Ubertino da Casale are depicted not only as the emperor's close counselors—they even appear, and Marsilius foremost, as the leading organizers of the events in Rome: "While the Romans, ignited with passionate zeal, their minds became more and more inclined towards establishing reform, especially after the sentence of excommunication by Pope John XXII had been delivered. Accordingly, the aforesaid counsellors and moreover authors of the processes [of Ludwig's], Marsilius and Ubertino, with great skill wrote and compiled edicts against his person and deeds, which were then promulgated by the Senate and people of Rome."[60]

This stay in Rome demonstrates that Marsilius put into action his doctrines from *Defensor pacis*. He also took advantage most brutally of the power he had received from the emperor, which horrified even Mussato, Marsilius's old friend and admirer from Guelphan Padua. In short, after his arrival in Rome in January 1328, Ludwig had himself crowned emperor of the Holy Roman Empire in a ceremony led, according to the Florentine historian Leonardo Bruni, by Sciarra Colonna.[61] Another contemporary historian, Giovanni Villani, claimed that it was the first time in history that an emperor had been crowned by neither pope nor papal legate.[62] Three bishops, previously removed by Pope John XXII, were responsible for the consecration and anointing, while a group of Roman feudal lords, including Sciarra Colonna, performed the coronation. Throughout the fourteenth century, the Colonna family had the reputation of being strongly critical of the papacy's stay in Avignon, and Sciarra Colonna was the man who, with the French king Philip IV's commander Guillaume de Nogaret and their band of 1,600 men in 1303, had attacked and imprisoned Pope Boniface VIII in Anagni. Of further interest is that Sciarra Colonna was the brother of Stefano Colonna the Elder—senator of Rome and the imperial vicar in Italy, and also Petrarch's great protector. Petrarch, who for several years was closely connected to the mighty Colonna family, dedicated, among other things, his majestic sonnet *Gloriosa columna* (*Rerum vulgarium fragmenta* 10) to Stefano Colonna.[63]

After the coronation in April 1328, Emperor Ludwig proclaimed in a decree called *Gloriosus Deus*, read before the basilica of Saint Peter's, the deposition of Pope John XXII, who was also charged with heresy.[64] As the quotation from Mussato shows, and likewise with other contemporary sources, Marsilius played a key role in the deposition. Ludwig was encouraged by Marsilius's doctrines and his many public speeches. Indeed, even John XXII stressed the centrality of Marsilius: the pope's reaction was that the deposition was an outright enactment or execution of Marsilius's heresy.[65] According to Mussato, the minds behind the decree that deposed the pope in Avignon were those of Marsilius and Ubertino. The decree was probably also the reason for Mussato's own change in his relationship with his friend from his youth. Marsilius acted cruelly: he apparently persecuted the Roman clergy, as well as their families and relatives, and, as Frank Godthardt describes it, "the impression is evoked of a man making ruthless use of his newly acquired power."[66]

The installment of an antipope, Nicholas V, followed the deposition of Pope John XXII, and to that role was elected the Franciscan monk Peter of Corbara, who governed a schismatic church limited to just some parts of the empire. In these events, too, the doctrines of *Defensor pacis* apparently had a remarkable influence, and Marsilius took a leading role. When Peter of Corbara resigned after about only one year, he confessed to Pope John XXII that Emperor Ludwig's politics in religious matters were governed by Marsilius's theories.[67] With the help of the Roman aristocracy, Marsilius had conquered and controlled the clergy under the rules of his new order, inspired by the strict apocalyptic theories of the Franciscan Spirituals.

In 1329 Marsilius returned with Ludwig to Germany, where he was kept under the emperor's protection. Despite Ludwig's many attempts at reconciliation with the popes in Avignon—first with John XXII, and later with Benedict XII and Clement VI—he never gave in to the papal demand to encourage Marsilius and the Franciscans at his court—including Ubertino da Casale, and, as we soon shall see, William of Ockham—to declare their obedience to the church. He refused to punish them, and Marsilius continued to have a certain influence on Ludwig's politics, although not as much as in Rome, until his death in 1343. Ludwig died in October 1347, only a few months after a new revolt in Rome was ignited, which once again reenacted the spiritual heritage of the apocalyptic Friars Minor of the thirteenth and fourteenth centuries.

CHAPTER 3

INDIVIDUAL FREEDOM
IN WILLIAM OF OCKHAM'S
BREVILOQUIUM

"'Hear these things, all peoples; give ear, all who live on earth,' 'for I am about to speak of matters which are great' and necessary to you. For I grieve and lament over the iniquities and injustices that have most wickedly been brought upon you all, to the whole world's cost, by him who boasts that he sits in Peter's chair and by some who preceded him in tyranny and wickedness. The anguish I feel is the greater because you do not take the trouble to inquire with careful attention how much such tyranny wickedly usurped over you is contrary to God's honor, dangerous to the Catholic faith, and opposed to the rights and liberties given to you by God and nature; and worse, you reject, hinder, and condemn those who wish to inform you of the truth."[1]

These are the opening words of William of Ockham's *Breviloquium de principatu tyrannico* (A short discourse on tyrannical government), a book written by one of the most outstanding and original authors in Western philosophy. Equally importantly, the book was written by a man who obviously intended to bear witness and to act: Time was running out and he could not postpone his protestation against the injustices he was experiencing. It was not only his responsibility but also his duty as a free human being to defend both his and his fellow men's rights, which then seemed seriously under threat. As he writes in the prologue, "I will in this short work try to attack with a free voice the errors of those who, not content with their own rights, do not fear, trusting in temporal power and favour, to reach out for others' rights, divine as well as human."[2]

Few people were more critical of the Avignonese papacy's theocratic claim to fullness of power than William of Ockham, and especially in this specific treatise. It is a great irony, though, that before he came to Provence, Ockham never uttered any doubt about the supreme authority of the pope. There are, in fact, no traces of any confrontation with contemporary secular or ecclesiastical rulers in his early writings. So why did he suddenly risk his academic career, even as a relatively young man and as one of the most brilliant of European intellectuals? Why did he risk his very life to express, or, as he writes, "speak freely" about, the circumstances that burdened his thoughts and weighed on his heart?

In the present chapter we will investigate the events that may have forced Ockham to make such radical statements as we encounter in *Breviloquium*, as well as his profound attacks on the doctrine of papal absolutism. As we will see, he confronted papal interventions in the Franciscan friars' voluntary poverty—interventions that Ockham found heretical—with the idea of a fundamental right conferred on all human beings. This was the right to a minimal use (*usus*) of external things—this right could not be prohibited, not even by the pope, because it was necessary to maintain life. As such, it was a right or a liberty granted both by God and by nature. Ockham identified this liberty with the human will, which he described as essential to live a virtuous life. Accordingly, it was this same liberty that gave him the right to protest against the injustice he witnessed.

As will be discussed toward the end of this chapter, the notion of universal freedom, a liberty shared by all human beings, was an idea Ockham had in common with other contemporary thinkers, such as Dante and Petrarch. However, in contrast to both these early Italian humanists, it is difficult to distinguish any thoughts about the problem of translating human will into actions in Ockham's political philosophy. How can a human being *will* what she or he has come to *know?* Can humans enjoy the same freedom as God, whose will and knowledge converge, according to Dante: "Vuolsi così colà dove si puote / ciò che si vuole" (*Inf.* III, 95–96: "Thus it is willed there where that can be done which is willed").

In the summer of 1324—four years before the flight from Avignon described in the introduction of this book—William of Ockham left England for the long and arduous journey to Provence. Apart from the sea crossing, he probably traveled on foot, which was most common among the mendicant friars in the Middle Ages. By that time he was about thirty-seven years old, a Franciscan friar partly educated at Oxford, and already with a wide reputation for his treatises on logic, theology, and physics. We do not know much about his birth and early life, but he probably entered the Franciscan order at a young age, which gave boys like himself from relatively modest conditions the possibility of geographic and social mobility. In the case of Ockham, this meant moving from a small village southeast of London to the English capital, and later to Oxford, where he studied theology, although he never gained a full master's degree.

It is traditionally thought that Ockham was called to Avignon to answer charges of having taught heresy. The accusations were supposedly brought forward by John Lutterell, a former chancellor of the University of Oxford who was expelled because of his unpopularity.[3] However, the circumstances around and the reasons for Ockham's arrival in Avignon have been questioned more recently. While some scholars have argued that Ockham came to Avignon because he had been appointed professor of philosophy at the city's Franciscan school,[4] others have suggested that he visited Avignon voluntarily, although he knew that an examination awaited him there at the papal court.[5] What did happen in Avignon, however, was that during the initial examinations of his works in 1324-1325, he was acquitted of the charges, despite the judge finding many of his articles erroneous. But this did not bring a stop to the accusations. As Arthur Stephen McGrade has argued, "We can only speculate as to whether John XXII's recent and continuing attacks on the Spiritual Franciscans were important in stimulating a second and harsher examination of the order's most brilliant theologian."[6] The second report was submitted to the pope in 1326, and it was still undergoing evaluation by Jacques Fournier, the future Pope Benedict XII, when Ockham escaped the city. He was thus not judged to be heretical before his flight, nor were his works ever condemned as such. But soon after they left Avignon, the entire group of Franciscan refugees was excommunicated.

THE FRANCISCANS AND THE PAPACY

To grasp the complexity of the controversy between the pope and the Franciscans, in which Ockham suddenly became so heavily involved, it is important to underscore that the Franciscans, as well as the Dominicans or the Order of Preachers—the other mendicant order that appeared more or less contemporaneously—had long received considerable papal support.[7] In accordance with Saint Francis's mystical marriage to "Lady Poverty" at the beginning of the thirteenth century, famously recorded in Giotto's fresco in the basilica of San Francesco in Assisi and in Dante's *Commedia* (*Par.* XI), the Franciscans refused ownership of any earthly belongings. In contrast to earlier medieval Christianity, where the monastery possessed property but the individual monks were poor, Saint Francis's revolutionary message was that not only the mendicant friars but even the Franciscan order itself, in a strict imitation of Christ, should possess nothing. As stated in his *Rule* from

1223, the friars, as well as the entire order, were "to appropriate nothing for themselves, neither house, nor place, nor anything else. As strangers and pilgrims (I Pet 2: 11) in this world, who serve God in poverty and humility, they should beg for alms trustingly."[8]

The popes recognized early on the positive impact of the mendicant friars.[9] The mendicant orders, and above all the Franciscans, took upon themselves the vocation of preaching and the curing of souls in the new cities all over Europe, where the traditional organizations of the church were inadequate or even entirely absent. In addition, the friars came to exert influence on the universities and diocese, and their work and their usually profound papal loyalty were well rewarded: The popes soon offered the Franciscans powerful positions in the ecclesiastical hierarchy, such as those of inquisitors, bishops, and cardinals, alongside the more modest duties they already performed, as teachers, pastors, and preachers. Even the responsibility for evangelizing in the non-Christian world was entrusted to the Franciscans.

However, not everyone applauded the power of the most well-placed friars, their wealth, and the increasing clericalization of the order in general. From the very beginning, there had been tensions within the order itself between those of Francis's followers who obeyed his strict demand for poverty, and those friars who took a more relaxed view of the issue. Whereas the mixed group of rigorists, later called the "Spirituals," emphasized absolute poverty, the majority of the order, usually termed the "Community," preferred to settle for a lower standard, thus accepting forms of compromise over the distinction between use (*usus*) and ownership (*dominium*).

Bonaventure, the minister-general of the order from 1257 to 1274, tried to quiet the quarrels by transforming the image of Francis into one of an ascetic and a mystic, where his poverty was, as André Vauchez has described it, "reduced to an interior virtue deprived of all human and social repercussions."[10] Indeed, Saint Francis's voluntary poverty was holy and an ideal, according to Bonaventure, but as an order the Franciscans had to adapt to the new historical circumstances. In his influential *Legenda major*, Bonaventure discussed the providential role of Saint Francis in the history of salvation, arguing that the growth and increasing assimilation of the Order of Friars Minor within the structures of the church were not signs of the order's decadence, as the critics maintained, but rather of its inherent divine grace. In other words, the friars' new authoritative roles were most useful in their Christian mission.

Bonaventure's reconciliation was to a certain degree affirmed by Pope Nicholas III, who in 1279 issued the bull *Exiit qui seminat*. The bull defended the Franciscans' ideal of poverty: their renunciation of the possession of common goods was in accordance with evangelic perfection. As such, the bull aimed to protect the Franciscans' right to use goods, whereas ownership of such goods belonged to the church. But the bull turned out to be a double-edged sword: although it protected the Franciscans' ideal vow of poverty, it also compromised the lifestyle the vow implied.

The growing power and prosperity of the order, as well as the idleness and the lavish lifestyle of a number of friars, justified by the hypocritical argument that the vow of poverty bound friars only to a lack of possessions, not to live moderately, provoked the Spirituals.[11] Violent conflicts between the *fraticelli,* as the Spirituals were often called, and the Community erupted during the 1290s when a group of dissidents sought the pope's permission to establish their own congregation outside the order. The newly elected pope Celestine V, famous for his ascetic simplicity, welcomed the Spirituals' eagerness to return to the ideal of the Umbrian *poverello,* and in 1294 he authorized them as the "Poor Hermits of Pope Celestine," appointing Cardinal Napoleone Orsini as their protector. The Spirituals' triumph, however, was short-lived. Celestine resigned only five months after his election, and was succeeded by Pope Boniface VIII, who immediately canceled Celestine's resolution. When he forced the rebellious *fraticelli* back under ecclesiastical control, some of them refused to obey, such as Angelo Clareno and Ubertino da Casale. Clement V, who was the first of the seven French popes who settled in Avignon, tried to reconcile the factions of the Community and the unruly Spirituals, though with only slight success. So when Pope John XXII finally ascended to the pinnacle of power in 1316, he proclaimed war not only on the *fraticelli:* soon the conflict came to involve the whole order.

At the beginning, it was the question of obedience that concerned John XXII. From Petrus Joannis Olivi—the most influential theologian of the Spirituals who was accused of heresy in 1282 by the Community—the Spirituals had inherited a theory of poverty that required disobedience if a superior insisted on a violation of the vow of *usus pauper,* even if he was a pope.[12] However, given his strong desire to centralize the church and strengthen the ecclesiastical hierarchy, Pope John soon came to attack the entire Franciscan order and what was regarded as its foundation—the fundamental claim of apostolic poverty. As conveyed with great aplomb by Umberto Eco in his popular novel *The Name of the Rose,* a series of painful actions took place.[13] With the help of Franciscan leaders—such as the minister-general Michael of Cesena, the inquisitor Michel Le Moine, and, later, the notorious Bernard Gui and Jacques Fournier, who also came to consider Ockham's work in Avignon—John placed the rebels in southern France and Italy under the supervision of the Community. Those who refused were accused of heresy and burned at the stake, while those who had powerful protectors, such as Ubertino, went free—in Ubertino's case because he was living with his patron, Cardinal Orsini, at the papal court in Avignon. Ubertino, however, left the Franciscan order at Pope John's command and transferred to the Benedictines, and in 1325, when he was accused of heresy, he fled the papal court, seeking the protection of Emperor Ludwig of Bavaria in Germany, from where he followed, together with Marsilius of Padua, the emperor to Rome, as we have seen in Chapter 2.

As the Spirituals' disobedience was closely connected to the Franciscan ideal of apostolic poverty, an ideal that, according to the bull from 1279, the *Exiit qui seminat,* all the members of the order theoretically shared (although many did not feel obliged to follow it), Pope John decided to reconsider the bull.[14] Then, in the constitution *Ad conditorem* (1322), he decreed that the papacy would not accept ownership of things given to the Franciscans; the Franciscan order itself would be the owner of them. It was his review of the bull *Exiit qui seminat*—notably a review of a decision taken by a previous pope—that provoked the moderate Franciscans. The members of the Community, such as Michael of Cesena and, soon after, William of Ockham, insisted on the irreformability of earlier papal decrees.[15] As Patrick Nold has suggested, though, in his well-balanced reading of the conflict, Pope John's refusal was not as harsh as many scholars have argued.[16] Rather, he took the *Rule* of Saint Francis most seriously. The core of Pope John's critique was his experience that the ideal of apostolic poverty had made the friars more *anxious* about material things, rather than liberating them from worldly cares. Thus, according to Nold, Pope John tried to be "a faithful, if literal, interpreter of the Franciscan *Rule* rather than an antagonist who sought to destroy it."[17]

Nonetheless, Pope John's attack practically destroyed the Franciscans' claim that as a unit or an order they possessed no property.[18] Indeed, the pope rejected the crux of their argument: the notion that the papacy could own something that the Franciscans had only permanent *use* of was incompatible with the principle of Roman law that ownership and usufruct could not be separated permanently. However, Pope John went even further: in another constitution, the famous *Cum inter nonnullos* (1323), he rejected the doctrine that Jesus and the Apostles owned nothing either individually or as a group. In other words, the pope not only refuted the ideal of Christian poverty, he also wounded the heart of the Franciscan order, on which both the Spirituals and the Community agreed. The consequences were serious: after the Spirituals' defeat, opposition to Pope John XXII continued among the Community and the more moderate Franciscans, who had usually exhibited profound papal loyalty. As McGrade has quite sarcastically argued, *Ad conditorem* turned the Franciscan friars into possessors, while *Cum inter nonnulos* seemingly turned them into heretics.[19]

THE WITNESS FROM OXFORD

It was amid such turbulence that Ockham was summoned to the papal court in Avignon. He did not belong to the Spiritual Franciscans, although it may seem that he, and many relatively moderate Franciscans with him, was forced into such radical positions by the politics of Pope John. As Ockham would later declare in *Epistola ad frates minors,* a letter to the Minor friars from 1334, he came to know Pope John's constitutions on apostolic poverty only some years after his arrival in Avignon.[20] He had simply not cared to study or possess them earlier, he explained, because he did not want to believe too readily that a person of such a high rank in the ecclesiastical hierarchy could pronounce and spread heresy. However, at the command of the head of the Franciscan order, Michael of Cesena, he was asked in Avignon to study the pope's constitutions, including *Ad conditorem* and *Cum inter nonnullos.* The task turned his life upside-down, resulting in him devoting the rest of it to struggling against papal absolutism. As he wrote in the same letter to the Minor friars, he deemed the bulls to be deeply wrong: "In these I found a great many things that were heretical, erroneous, silly, ridiculous, fantastic, insane, and defamatory, contrary and likewise plainly adverse to orthodox faith, good morals, natural reason, certain experience, and fraternal charity."[21] The outcome of Ockham's examination was, in other words, that he came to regard the pope as a heretic, and, as we may also read in the letter, it was the author's duty, his responsibility as a Christian, to protest and speak out. And this is just what he did do some years later, above all, as we soon shall see, in his *Breviloquium.*

After his flight from Avignon and for the remaining twenty years of his life, Ockham only wrote political texts fighting the idea of the pope's *plenitudo potestatis.* With the other Franciscan refugees, he followed Ludwig of Bavaria's return to Munich, where he spent most of the time in the Franciscan convent of the city.[22] Periodically he collaborated with the imperial court, as did Marsilius, and as a counselor he tried to influence the politics of the emperor. His truest weapon, however, was his political writing. An apocryphal story would have it that Ockham greeted the emperor with the following words: "I will defend you with my pen, if you will defend me with your sword."[23] However, his apology for Ludwig of Bavaria was not entirely clear. As McGrade has maintained, he probably had an important role in formulating Ludwig's claims at the historical national assemblies of Rhens and Frankfurt in 1338, which were obviously important for the dawning German national self-confidence. Still, he expressed a far stronger enthusiasm for King Edward III of England.[24]

What was at stake, however, and what Ockham apparently considered the main problem of his age, was the situation in Avignon and the heresy of Pope John and his successors. It would not be wrong to argue that Ockham was in fact trying to *save* the pope as the head of Christianity. According to Ockham, the Avignonese popes were not fulfilling the divine mission entrusted to them as vicars of Christ; instead, they seemed to deal only with politics, which ought to be the domain of temporal rulers alone. Thus, Ockham's political polemics were meant to correct the many errors performed in Avignon—not in practice as much as in theory.

Unlike his more impersonal political works, such as the *Opus nonaginta dierum* (Work of ninety days), the *Dialogus* (Dialogue), and the *Octo quaestiones de potestate papae* (Eight questions on the power of the pope), the tone in *Breviloquium* is highly personal. Hence, this work is presumably where Ockham reveals his own convictions. It was written as late as 1342, a few years before he died in 1347. Pope Clement VI complained that Ockham died unreconciled with the church. As the pope reportedly said, "I call God as my witness that I have never desired anything after the salvation of my soul as much as I have desired that man's salvation, so that he would return to the bosom of holy mother church."[25] What this remark demonstrates is at least a profound respect for Ockham, even as a political figure. He probably succumbed to the Black Death and was buried in the Franciscan convent of Munich.

What is strikingly new in *Breviloquium* compared to Ockham's more academic and less polemical works is that it is organized as a testimony supplied by a witness in a court of law. This device was obviously a deliberate choice by the author, as the court and the juridical rhetoric must have been most familiar to the lawyer-popes in Avignon. During the Avignon papacy, the popes surrounded themselves with canon lawyers; they brought actions against those who criticized the papacy, issuing charges of heresy and constantly producing new decretals. Ockham had been the one prosecuted for many years, but now it was his turn to bear witness against the pope. As he explains in the first book of *Breviloquium*, citing civil as well as canon law, on the stage of the court both parties have to accept the rules of the trial: "For what someone brings forwards in his own favour, he should also not reject when it is brought against him; thus also one who brings forward a witness in his favour, must accept that witness against himself. If the pope brings forward decretals in his own favour he should therefore accept them against himself, and the same must be said of the emperor if he brings forward laws in his own favour."[26]

The court of law as the framework for his polemic was effective not only in reaching his audience—the lawyers of Avignon, as well as the counselors and clerks of the many European royal houses. The setting was also an effective way to strip the pope and the canonists of their authority because the legal rhetoric demonstrates that most truths are arbitrary and therefore negotiable. In a highly polemical way, Ockham puts his opponents' arguments on display to then let them be revealed, as he says, in the light of the two indubitable authorities—right reason and Holy Scripture. Truths accessed through right reason or the scriptures are undeniable in that they cannot be corrected by logical demonstrations. As he declares by the end of the prologue, he himself is prepared to be corrected, but only to a certain degree: "Things certain through holy Scripture or evident reasoning, or in any other way, I do not submit to anyone's correction, since they must be believed, and not corrected."[27]

LIMITS OF POWER

Consisting of six books, and ending in the middle of a sentence because of the lack of manuscripts,[28] *Breviloquium* shifts from an investigation of papal power to the many aspects of liberty—the freedom of the Gospels, the fundamental liberty according to divine and natural law, and the Minor friars' voluntary rejection of any *dominium* in order to live under the prelapsarian freedom granted by God and nature.

In contrast to Marsilius, Ockham was not against the pope's *plenitudo potestatis*. In accordance with the Franciscan tradition he acknowledged papal authority, and he regarded the papacy as a divine institution. The fullness of power, however, consisted of the pope's duty to do everything necessary for Christians to gain eternal life. In his rich study, Takashi Shogimen discusses how Ockham even allowed for papal interference in temporal matters, though only in accidental cases, for instance when the temporal sphere became averse to the Christian faith or was converted to evil.[29] In general, however, spiritual power, like temporal power, was limited by the rights and liberties granted to mankind by God and nature, which were established before papal or any other official power. What had gone awry, as Ockham explains in *Breviloquium*, was the interpretation of that authority:

> Now just as sometimes from true principle correctly understood countless truths are inferred, so sometimes from a false principle, or a true one misunderstood, are inferred countless errors; a wise man has said that given one anomaly many follow, and elsewhere it is said that a small error in the beginning is a big one in the end. I believe that this has happened with the power of the pope. For since in certain writings which

many venerate as authoritative it is asserted that the pope has "fullness of power" on earth, some called supreme pontiffs, not knowing the true meaning of such words, have gone on, not only into errors, but even into the most blatant wrongs and iniquities.[30]

According to Ockham, the pope has lost the right tool to measure the limits of his power, that is, to accept what power he has and what power he does not have over others. The first part of *Breviloquium* thus consists of an examination of the perverted theory of *plenitudo potestatis* claimed by the popes in Avignon, and Ockham's main argument is that such a claim is contrary to divine and natural law.

Ockham distinguished, as Joseph Canning has discussed, between two parallel orders of human life: the natural one, relating to the condition of mankind in the Garden of Eden before the Fall; and the postlapsarian one of property and rulership instituted by God as a remedy for original sin.[31] The two orders, rooted in Augustine's doctrine of the two cities, offered two sets of legal systems: whereas *ius poli* (the right of heaven) consisted of divine and natural law, *ius fori* (the right of forum) was composed of positive law. In *Breviloquium* Ockham casts accusations at the canonists who argued that Christ had promised fullness of power to the pope in spiritual and earthly matters so the pope could do on earth everything without exception (*Brev.* II, 2). He also criticizes the assertion that the vicar of Christ should be obeyed in whatever is not wrong, and, finally, that the pope was not bound by positive law. Ockham suggests that the pope broke both divine and natural law due to such claims. Such an understanding of *plenitudo potestatis* was wrong: "In my opinion that assertion is not only false, and dangerous to the whole community of the faithful, but even heretical."[32]

Concerning divine law, the pope's claim was heretical chiefly because it conflicted with scripture. As Ockham argues, compared to the Law of Moses, Gospel law (*lex evangelica*) is a law of perfect freedom (*lex libertatis*), and he supports his arguments with a reference to James (1:25): "But the man who looks intently into the perfect law that gives freedom, and continues to do this, not forgetting what he has heard, but doing it—he will be blessed in what he does" (*Brev.* II, 3). As this and a number of other passages in the Gospels demonstrate, the Gospel law of freedom has replaced the old Mosaic law, or, as Ockham explains, "because the servitude of the Mosaic Law was unbearable, it was not to be imposed on believers."[33] Rather, as Saint Paul writes in the second letter to the Corinthians (2 Cor 3:17), "Where the Spirit of the Lord is, there is freedom." This was a tremendously important message for the recipients of Saint Paul's letter, Ockham argues, because Christians would not have been consoled if they had to be subject to even greater servitude by Saint Peter and his successors than by the Mosaic law. Thus, if the pope had such fullness of power as was under discussion, "Christ's law would involve a horrendous servitude, incomparably greater than that of the Old Law, for all Christians—emperors and kings and absolutely all their subjects—would be in the strictest sense of the term, the pope's slaves."[34]

Ockham's argument is that scripture reveals humanity's fundamental freedom. However, this freedom, which was given to all human beings by birth, was experienced even before the coming of Christ, he adds. The pope was not to be obeyed in everything, no more than "in many things children are not bound to obey their parents, since they are not slaves but free, or wives their husbands, since they are not maidservants but are judged to be entitled to equality in many things."[35] According to Ockham, human liberty is an absolute, individual right possessed also by non-Christians. In a prelapsarian condition, this freedom consisted of the right of use (*usus*) of worldly things to stay alive, while ownership (*dominium*) was a right given to humans after the Fall: "Lordship common to the whole human race is that which God gave Adam and his wife for themselves and all their posterity, power to manage and use temporal things to their own advantage. That power would have existed in the state of innocence without power to appropriate any temporal thing to any one person or to any one particular collectivity or to certain persons, but after the fall it exists together with such a power of appropriating temporal things. The other kind is exclusive lordship, called 'ownership' in the legal sciences and in writings which imitate that terminology."[36] Humanity's freedom thus consisted, by prelapsarian natural and divine law, in the right to use anything necessary to sustain life, even property that belonged to someone else. As Ockham wrote in *Opus nonaginta dierum*, using another's property—in extreme necessity—is a law of nature.[37]

THE GIFT OF REASON

A crucial question in *Breviloquium* is how human beings may come to know this fundamental freedom that is given to them by nature. Ockham demonstrates a profound confidence in the individual believer, as well as in the individual's cognitive capacities; he also maintains that the natural and divine laws are perceptible by human reason, which involves the reason applied to revelation as well. As we have seen, he establishes in the prologue two indubitable authorities—right reason and Holy Scripture. Right reason is a gift given to all human beings, believers as well as nonbelievers, that is further perfected by divine, scriptural revelation. In both cases the truth is accessible through knowledge and sense experiences rather than through authority and papal interpretations.

Janet Coleman has connected Ockham's discussion of freedom to his epistemology. For Ockham, she explains, all knowledge is the result of the cognition of individuals who are particular and contingent.[38] Reversing the trend of earlier scholastics, he asked not how the individual derives from an essence or a universal common nature, but how a world of individuals can ever be known in a nonindividual and general manner. Universality and commonality are not properties of things. Everything that exists in reality is unique and individual, and humans naturally have an immediate and intuitive knowledge through the sense experiences of the existence and presence of the individuals in the temporal world. To this one may add that with his roots in the Franciscan tradition, Ockham's nominalism, or his keen eye for individuals, is a conviction tightly connected to the vision of the founder of the order itself. Saint Francis's famous poem *Laudes Creaturum,* as well as his hagiographers' depictions of the naïve saint talking to the birds, reflects an intense respect for each individual being in the Creation of God. However, moving within the boundaries of this worldliness of the Franciscans, what is important in Ockham's philosophy is that we, as human beings, cannot logically demonstrate intuitive knowledge about our surroundings. We only experience this as a fact of life. Logic is not a part of life or reality; it is only the means by which we try to organize our experiences, and therefore no less a rhetorical tool than are speaking and writing.

One of the things that human beings come to know through right reason and sense experiences, and that is central to the protest against papal absolutism in *Breviloquium,* is humans' God-given, natural right, prior to the church's foundation, to freely use worldly things to survive. Through their natural, intuitive cognition, all people understand this original freedom given to them by birth. This knowledge, however, is perfected and reinforced by the reading of the scripture's *lex libertatis.*

Like most Franciscans, and above all like his confrere John Duns Scotus, Ockham emphasized God's omnipotence. Duns Scotus described the Creator's omnipotence as "that active power or potency whose scope extends to anything whatever that can be created."[39] As such, the freedom of God and the freedom of man reflect each other: the free will bestowed on men is conditioned by a loss of knowledge of the will of God. However, the pope's imitation of God's omnipotence in claiming fullness of power in secular and spiritual matters was heretical, according to Ockham, because it deprived the freedom of others, as well as opposing the omnipotence of God, that is, God's freedom to conceal his own will or to intervene in human affairs. The pope's interpretation of *plenitudo potestatis* was, in other words, an act of *superbia*—the sin of Lucifer himself. Therefore it was a Christian duty to react to such a claim:

> It must be said, therefore, that although the pope is Christ's vicar, it is nevertheless by no means true, as the flattering and heretical fables of some pope-worshippers suggest, that the whole power of Christ, according to either his divine or his human nature, has been granted to the pope. Rather, as was said before, the rights and liberties of others granted to them by God and nature are excepted from the pope's power, so that he cannot oppress the just and innocent against their will with heavy and burdensome ordinances, statutes, laws, or precepts going beyond the things that must be done of necessity, to which they are obliged by divine and natural law.[40]

Despite being Christ's vicar, the pope did not have the same power as the Lord. Divine and natural law marked the limits of this power. In the following chapters of *Breviloquium,* there is a discussion of the canonists' allegorical interpretation of certain scriptural quotations used to support the pope's version of absolute power. Ockham dismisses any such attempt by stressing the literal reading of the Gospels, a reading that he maintained was accessible to every Christian, based on Catholic faith and right reason, and that clearly revealed the fundamental liberty of man.

SOLA SCRIPTURA

Like Dante in his *Monarchia,* as we have seen in Chapter 1, Ockham dwells particularly on the hierocrats' allegorical interpretation of the biblical passages, "Here are two swords" (Lk 22:38), and the comparison of the sun and moon (Gn 1). The hierocrats read these biblical passages allegorically in order to support papal authority: while the first passage was regarded as proof that the pope had both temporal and spiritual power, the second, based on an allegorical understanding of the sun as pontifical power and the moon as kingly power, was interpreted as a confirmation that the empire derived from the pope (*Brev.* V, 3). Ockham, however, rejects these readings. There is no need to accept such mystical or allegorical interpretations, he argues, because "a mystical sense not explicit in sacred Scripture can never be adduced in this way, except in so far as it rests on another Scripture or on evident reason."[41] In other words, the teachings of those who lived after the writers of the scriptures were, in Ockham's opinion, not so authoritative as to be immune to critique. Mystical senses, which such "authorities" had drawn from the scriptures to support contentious points—for instance, claims that the pope was the source of legitimate imperial power—did not need to be accepted.

This principle has much in common with the later Protestants' *sola scriptura,* the doctrine that scripture either contains all knowledge within the text itself or can be arrived at by valid deductive reasoning, which is necessary for salvation. Nonscriptural authorities that govern Christian life and devotion—such as papal decretals, the hierocrats' allegorical interpretations or even biblical readings, and finally the works of the church fathers—are subordinate and must be corrected by the written word of God. In Ockham's view, there was thus no such thing as papal infallibility, a doctrine that became increasingly important during the Schism and later the Counter-Reformation, but that was not defined dogmatically until the first Vatican Council (1869–1870).[42] In *Breviloquium* Ockham rejects any such idea of infallibility: "For anyone who is orthodox is certain that the pope can sin against good morals and err against faith, and his teaching is therefore to be classed in every respect among the teachings of the bishops, which, according to Augustine, can be faulted by just judgement and without rashness. . . . No matter how much authority the pope has, the truth must always be preferred to him, especially a truth known to relate to divine law."[43]

The subordination of the pope, of the church fathers, and of the hierocrats' allegorical interpretations to the truths of scripture was necessary to control or regulate the papal greed for earthly power. Furthermore, the primacy of scripture was important in other cases of heterodoxy because not only Catholics but also heretics endeavored to expound on sacred scriptures mystically or allegorically in favor of their heresies and errors. One should therefore not lightly adhere to such mystical senses, much less accept them to support anything known to relate to divine law, according to Ockham.

Who, then, should judge whether the pope's assertion is true or false, Catholic or heretical? Here we come to the very core of Ockham's political thought, which is clearly bound to his vision of freedom, as well as to his nominalist philosophy:

> To this I answer that judgement by way of simple knowledge and outward assertion, as a doctor judges medical matters or any craftsman matters relating to his craft, belongs to anyone who knows the truth with certainty, whether he knows it by faith alone, if it is the sort of truth that relates to faith, or by evident argument or certain experience, if it can be known that way. Accordingly, if the pope defined something,

made an assertion or even offered an opinion against things every Christian is bound to believe explicitly, it would be for anyone to judge in this way that on this occasion the pope erred.[44]

The truth, according to Ockham, and which this quotation also reveals, is not based on authority but on knowledge and experience. It is a practical question, a method similar to those applied by doctors or craftsmen performing their skills. In the same way, every Christian should be able to discern the truth about faith by applying his or her reason—the gift given to all human beings—to the scripture. Witnesses who had experienced Christ's years on earth had transmitted the truths in the Gospels. Likewise, every Christian by faith could read and interpret the infallible words of God. According to Ockham, then, one did not need to be a theologian or a canon lawyer to access biblical truths. Anyone sane and literate could determine the correct meaning of the sacred text.

As Canning has noted, this was an application of Ockham's nominalism or epistemological theory whereby knowledge was based on signs signifying concepts derived from individual experience.[45] It was probably not as radical an emphasis on common sense as that we encounter in later thinkers like Lorenzo Valla, but Ockham's notion of truth was profoundly democratic, accessible to all, or to all sane and literate people, through experience and knowledge.[46] Using right reason, then, the heresies of John XXII would be obvious to everyone: "So also, the error of John XXII, that in things consumable by use, use of fact cannot be separated from lordship or ownership, is so obvious even to the simple that even the simple should judge that he errs."[47] Thus, in accordance with his epistemological ideas, in *Breviloquium* Ockham speaks out on behalf of the simplest human being defending his or her right against papal authority.

A POLITICAL THINKER?

A central topic in *Breviloquium* is the legitimacy of the Holy Roman Empire, which Ockham connects to the questions of individual freedom and property. As mentioned earlier, Ockham elaborated a theory of ownership as a right created after the Fall. In a prelapsarian condition man was free to use temporal things to survive, which, as a divine law, also continued after the Fall. However, after the sin, God granted to humankind, whether Christian or non-Christian, the power to appropriate material goods, in addition to using them, and to set up rulers with legal jurisdiction: "This twofold power, to appropriate temporal things and to establish rulers with jurisdiction,

God gave without intermediary not only to believers but also to unbelievers, in such a way that it falls under precept and is reckoned among purely moral matters. It therefore obliges everyone, believer and unbeliever alike."[48]

The purpose of this distinction—between *usus* and *dominium*—was obviously an attempt to respond to Pope John XXII, whom Ockham quotes frequently in the third book of *Breviloquium*. By claiming that all lordship over temporal things was introduced by divine law—"Sacred Scripture clearly says . . . that it was indeed by divine law, not human, that lordship was brought in"[49]—Pope John refused to accept the Franciscan friars' wish to live in poverty outside the legal structures of *dominium*. Ockham emphasized the monstrousness of this assertion. As the administrator of divine law, which the pope claimed the church was, it should follow that "there is outside the Church no true lordship of temporal things, or any ordinate granted power, but permitted power only."[50]

This is how Ockham exposed the greedy heart of the idea of *plenitudo potestatis*: If lordship over temporal things was determined by divine rather than positive law, the church would have rightful dominium over everything in the world. Ockham's argument, though, is that property and jurisdiction were first introduced by human, positive law for utilitarian purposes. God had bestowed on human beings the freedom to create their own arrangements, in terms of property, laws, civil communities, and governments, so they could organize their lives and control the avarice and desire that beset them after the Fall. Accordingly, human institutions were, in contrast to Marsilius's notion of the human legislator or in the context of the church, the congregation of believers, also fallible and always susceptible to change. Actual property and jurisdiction came with human laws, meaning laws that are conventional and changeable and not divine (*Brev.* III, 9).

It has been suggested that Ockham's work, because of this resistance to absolutism, is a contribution to political thought within the tradition of constitutional theory.[51] However, modern scholarship has in general been beset by a harsh dispute, summarized by Shogimen, about whether Ockham can be considered a political thinker at all.[52] As Shogimen argues, historians of European political thought usually consider him to be one of the giants of the late Middle Ages, along with Dante, Marsilius, and John Wycliffe. Nonetheless, in recent decades scholarship has shifted from a portrayal of Ockham as a radical critic of the papacy and defender of secular power to a portrayal of him as an antipolitical thinker, suggested above all by Canning.[53]

Coleman may be right in arguing that the depiction of Ockham as a nonpolitical or even antipolitical writer is anachronistic, or, as she writes, it is "to adopt a twentieth-century view of secular intentions behind [mediaeval] political expression."[54] Canning, for his part, stresses the Franciscan origin and context as fundamental conditions for Ockham's writings after his encounter with the Avignon papacy. The point of departure for Ockham's polemics was a defense of the Franciscan friars' right to live under prelapsarian divine and natural law. For Ockham, it was more important to defend voluntary poverty, the friars' desire to withdraw from and forsake the world of power in terms of possessions and rules over others, which the Augustinian *ius poli*—the right of heaven—allowed them, rather than draw up a coherent political theory such as we have seen in Marsilius's *Defensor pacis*. To summarize Canning's point, Ockham expressed a scale of values that minimized the significance of politics, law, and power: "For him the most authentic human life was one of Christian poverty outside (and above) the world of property, law and politics—he espoused the way of powerlessness as opposed to power."[55]

Yet, there is no doubt that Ockham was drawn into the contemporary conflicts connected to the Avignon papacy, and that he discussed questions regarding the government of the church, which in many ways constituted the core of the general political debates of the fourteenth century. Furthermore, of greatest importance is that he developed a body of systematic political ideas about power, and this he did above all in his late works such as *Breviloquium.*

Ockham's intricate reasoning suggests that he proposed a different interpretation of legitimate power from that proposed by the pope's defenders, the hierocrats, who claimed that rulership derived from God through the pope. According to the hierocrats, such as Giles of Rome and Augustinus Triumphus, there was no legitimate jurisdiction outside the church. All power derived, or, perhaps more precisely, descended from above, through the pope—the true *caput* of the church. As Giles of Rome described it, the power of the pope offered measure, weight, and number to all other authority without itself being measured, weighed, or numbered.[56] Moreover, Ockham's interpretation of power departs from the dualists' approach. Dante maintained that both the emperor's and the pope's power came directly from God. Dante's aim was, as we have seen in Chapter 1 of this book, to incorporate the temporal and spiritual jurisdictions within a dualistic institutional synthesis, with God as the direct origin for both orders' authority. Ockham expressed a similar idea of the supreme God. Omnipotent as he was, God could intervene at will in human affairs. However, the standard would be a divinity *withdrawn* from human affairs. As such, one might describe Ockham's notion of secular power as "desacralized," as McGrade has done, as he regarded law and government as purely instrumental, and not as the animating force in society.[57]

Ockham's solution also differed radically from the naturalism of Marsilius, which in many ways might be described, as we have seen in Chapter 2, as the antithesis of the hierocrats' ideas. Rather than deriving from God through the pope, Marsilius argued that the power of secular rulers ascended from the active will of the people. The legitimacy of power was based on the body of the citizens, which represented the will of the whole. In contrast to the hierocrats, the dualists such as Dante, and Marsilius's notions of popular sovereignty, the core of Ockham's political thought was the defense of individual freedom, articulated through his strong resistance to ecclesiastical as well as secular absolutism. An obvious effect of his attempts to separate or extend the distance between secular and spiritual government was an emphasis on the reduced juridical power of the pope, but also the limits of the secular rulers. As we have seen, and as he clearly argued in his *Breviloquium,* natural and divine law constituted the *limits* of both the pope's and the emperor's power while concurrently protecting the fundamental liberty of each human being.

MOBILIZED WILL

Yet there is another challenge in Ockham's political thought, a challenge that is striking by its absence from *Breviloquium* and that is rarely discussed by scholars of Ockham. As we have seen, the humans are granted liberty both by God and by nature. In other texts Ockham identifies freedom with the spontaneous will.[58] Liberty, thus, is indistinguishable from volition itself, and, as Ockham argues, free will is necessary to be virtuous. Humans cannot be compelled to be good. Moral actions have to follow the route of the free will. What is equally important, as we have seen, is that humanity's liberty is evident through right reason to all human beings and intelligible by experience. Ockham thus displays an essential trust in human knowledge. He allows for the individual believer's access to the truth, and, consequently, the simple, unlearned woman's or man's right to determine the correct meaning of the scripture and to speak out freely when she or he witnesses things that go against faith or contradict the truth—the fundamental liberty of humanity. Indeed, this was what Ockham himself did with Pope John XXII's claim to *plenitudo potestatis.* In *Breviloquium,* though, there is little reflection on what may move the human will to act. How do human beings solve the dilemma of the divided will, once expressed by Saint Paul in a letter to the Romans? "For I do not do the good I want to do, but the evil I do not want to do—this I keep on doing" (Rom 7:19). Or, to put it otherwise: How can human beings will or effect what they have come to know? In what way do we mobilize the will, or how may knowledge about what is good and true be translated into action—which in many ways marks the beginning of a moral life?

In contrast to contemporary thinkers, such as Dante and Petrarch, who recurrently discussed the discrepancy between will and knowledge, there are hardly any similar discussions in Ockham's *Breviloquium.* In Dante's *Commedia,* problems regarding the will—how the will betrays reason in refusing to submit itself to known facts, how it is weak, slow, and divided—are something that the pilgrim repeatedly faces in his wanderings through the three realms of the afterlife. In the generation after Dante, Petrarch retrieved his Italian ancestor's complex reflections on the will. The notion of the weak or divided will, elaborated in Augustinian theology, as well as in Franciscan visions of man, became a recurrent topic in Petrarch's literary work. In his famous invective *De sui ipsius et multorum ignorantia* (On his own ignorance and that of many others), he presents the tensions between knowledge and will as a dispute between two different cultures—on the one hand, the philosophers' studies of logic, and on the other, the humanists' studies of rhetoric and classical poetry.

The invective was written as an answer to four scholastic philosophers, or Aristotelians, as Petrarch calls them, who claimed that Petrarch, despite being a good man, did not possess any rigorous philosophical knowledge. He was obviously a loyal friend, but an illiterate person, according to the philosophers. Petrarch's answer is a redefinition of the concept of knowledge by calling attention to the limits of Aristotelian epistemology. He claims that he has read all of Aristotle's books on ethics, admitting that they have made him more learned, but never a better person: "I see how brilliantly he [Aristotle] defines and distinguishes virtue, and how shrewdly he analyzes it together with the properties of vice and virtue. Having learned this, I know slightly more than I did before. But my mind is the same as it was; my will is the same; and I am the same."[59] The problem, as Petrarch defines it, is that Aristotle may teach what virtue is, but his books lack the necessary stimulation, the ardent words, which move humans to act virtuously: "For it is one thing to know, and another to love; one thing to understand, and another to will. I don't deny that he [Aristotle] teaches us the nature of virtue. But reading him offers us none of those exhortations, or only a very few, that goad and inflame our minds to love virtue and hate vice. . . . What good is there in knowing what virtue is, if this knowledge doesn't make us love it?"[60]

As Petrarch develops his arguments, true knowledge is connected to ethics and rhetoric. By virtue of his redefinition of knowledge, he melds wisdom with humility. This he does even at the beginning of the text by referring to the Augustinian conception of "pietas est sapientia" (piety is wisdom).[61] Instead of rejecting the insinuation of his lack of knowledge, Petrarch explains that, indeed, he recognizes his own ignorance in pain and silence: "When I reflect how far I am from learning all that my avid mind seeks to know, I sadly and silently acknowledge my ignorance."[62] The relief is, he continues, that he is not alone in being ignorant; rather, ignorance is what all human beings have in common. Because human knowledge is deemed always to be limited and partial, ignorance is a more distinctive human feature than is wisdom. The will, however, which is set in motion by rhetoric, may help humanity toward the ultimate goal of immortality and eternal happiness. Words, music, and images—the fundamental components of rhetoric—move the will, through their capacity to incite love, toward the beauty of virtue.[63]

Petrarch and Ockham have apparently much in common. Nevertheless, similar reflections on the value of art and poetry as we meet in Petrarch's literary corpus cannot be found in Ockham's work. Ironically, Petrarch was, as Giovanni Boccaccio wrote in a letter from 1339, a *monarcha* or a king of logic, thanks to William of Ockham—a comparison that expresses a profound respect both for Petrarch's philosophical learning and for the extensive reputation of Ockham several years before his death.[64] Petrarch grew up in Avignon, and he was strongly influenced by thoughts about poverty and the Franciscans' diatribe against the Avignon papacy. We do not know, though, if the humanist at the papal court and the Franciscan friar from Oxford ever met, but like Ockham, Petrarch soon became—whether he liked it or not—deeply involved in the political debates of his time. And, as he came to portray himself, he was the new Virgil whose song would ignite the love of Rome.

CHAPTER 4

PETRARCH, COLA DI RIENZO, AND THE BATTLE OF ROME

n the middle of the fourteenth century, a new argument made its mark on the political debates about the Avignon papacy. The critique of the papacy's stay in southern France was from now on increasingly coupled with an ardent defense of Rome. Whereas the popes up until the time of Pope John XXII had regarded their stay in Avignon as temporary, with Benedict XII there was a change in attitude; this was demonstrated by the construction of an enormous papal palace at the end of the 1330s and the transferal of the papal archives from Assisi to Provence. By virtue of these events, the stay suddenly appeared to be permanent. Moreover, thanks to the next pope, Clement VI, who flaunted his splendor and ostentatious lifestyle, accompanied by an extensive program to transform Avignon into an *altera Roma,* a return to Rome seemed to be more or less completely forgotten. A consequence of these events was that a growing group of opponents started to juxtapose Avignon with Rome as *caput mundi*—and the most outstanding of this new generation of critics was Francis Petrarch. He never really questioned the sovereignty of the pope, but, as he claimed, the legitimacy of both papal and imperial power was to be found in the city of Rome, not elsewhere. Only Rome could provide the Holy See and the throne of the Holy Roman Empire with the much-needed renewal.

According to Petrarch, Rome and not Avignon was the true institutional, political, and cultural center of the world. Throughout his life he worked with eagerness, political as well as cultural, to restore the ancient glory of Rome—and for a brief moment his visions seemed to materialize in the figure of Cola di Rienzo. During the revolution in Rome in 1347, Cola took the title of tribune of Rome with the aim of reinstating the classical Republic. For that occasion Petrarch wrote a panegyric letter addressed both to Cola and to the Roman citizens. The text constitutes the eighth letter of

95

Petrarch's *Lettere disperse*—the group of scattered letters that were never included in the poet's major epistolary collections. In the present chapter we will examine Petrarch's ideological battle over Rome, as expressed in this letter (*Disperse* 8).[1] It is usually regarded as an exalted panegyric written by a man who soon grew disappointed in and even ashamed of his political hero.[2] Nonetheless, *Disperse* 8 represents one of the clearest expressions of Petrarch's grandiose visions of Rome. It is closely connected to his other texts concerning the role of Rome, such as *Collatio laureationis,* the oration Petrarch gave at the Capitoline Hill when he was crowned with laurels in 1341, or his letter to Giovanni Colonna (*Fam.* VI, 2), which recalls the poet's first visit to the city in 1336–1337.[3] Above all, *Disperse* 8 testifies to the new defense of Rome that took place in the fourteenth century, and, as we will see, the defense was rooted in both classical and biblical sources, which were fundamental to the period's idea of rebirth and restoration. In other words, in the fourteenth century's notions of restoring Rome as *caput mundi,* both classical and Christian traditions merged into a powerful unity.

AVIGNON VERSUS ROME

Petrarch is the one person of the six main figures explored in this book who knew Avignon from the inside of the bastion of power. In his famous autobiographical "Letter to Posterity" (*Sen.* XVII, 1), he presents himself as born in exile ("in exilio natus sum"), obviously in competition with Dante, whom his father, Ser Petracco, probably knew well.[4] Like Dante, Ser Petracco belonged to the White Guelph party that supported the emperor, and for that reason he was expelled from Florence the same year as Dante (1302). This did not involve any serious confrontation with the papacy, however. Rather than seeking refuge with mighty Italian *signori* or tyrants, Ser Petracco gained employment at the papal court in Avignon and the family settled in Carpentras, fifteen miles from the city, in 1312, when Petrarch was eight years old. Avignon grew swiftly in these years and went from being a rather modest center to one that soon surpassed even Rome in size and in its international blend of people. Sharing his fate with an increasing number of the city's inhabitants, Petrarch grew up in the city or nearby as the eldest son of exiled parents, and as a young man he followed in his father's footsteps by entering papal service.

Much has been written about the irony that Petrarch, who earned his keep from the papal curia for a number of years, could display such ambiguity toward his employer. In the already quoted "Letter to Posterity," he described not only his own status but also that of the church as "exiled":

"Avignon, where the Roman Pontiff holds, and has long held, the Church of Christ in shameful exile."[5] Over the years he spent in the city he articulated a violent diatribe against the Avignon papacy. One must remember, however, that the Italian flank of the curia with which Petrarch was linked was not the most loyal to the French popes. After studying in Montpellier and Bologna, where he developed a deep friendship with Giacomo Colonna (later the bishop of Lombez), Petrarch entered the service of Cardinal Giovanni Colonna, Giacomo's brother, in 1330. The two brothers were the sons of the powerful Stefano Colonna the Elder, the senator of Rome and the imperial vicar in Italy; they were also the nephews of the more notorious Sciarra Colonna, who, as we have seen, was involved both in the Outrage at Anagni in 1303 and later in the coronation of Emperor Ludwig in Rome in 1328. Petrarch expressed in one of his *Epystole* (*Epystola* I, 2) a clear critique of the coronation. The epistle, in which a personified Rome is the speaking voice (v. 19: "Roma vocor"), describes the coronation and the election of the antipope Nicholas V as a violation and a forced marriage.[6] Nonetheless, his status as an exiled Italian, whether voluntary or not, seemed to be accompanied by a profound skepticism of the Avignon papacy. For the Italians, more than for any other immigrants, the wish to return the pope to Rome became part of an intense desire to restore the city to its glorious past. Rome should once again be the *caput mundi,* the capital of the world, as it had once been. As Petrarch wrote in one of his latest texts, the invective *Invectiva contra eum qui maledixit Italie* (Invective against a detractor of Italy), Rome was truly "the capital of the world, the queen of the cities, the seat of the empire, the citadel of the Catholic faith, and the source of all remarkable models of virtue."[7]

A central point in this new defense of Rome was the ideological purification of the city. Since early Christianity, Rome had been torn between the bright vision of the eternal city and the dark vision of sin, deterioration, and death. The Christians' attack was largely based on Saint Augustine's powerful condemnation of the classical city, which regarded it as the Babylon between the seven hills, as foreseen in the book of Revelation.[8] The Spiritual Franciscans of the late thirteenth century, such as Petrus Joannis Olivi and Ubertino da Casale, applied a similar apocalyptic rhetoric in their critique of the papacy in Rome. Influenced by Joachim da Fiore, the pope was described as *meretrix,* the Babylonian whore, and as Antichrist, who needed to be conquered before the dawn of the new age.[9]

In his critique of the papacy, Petrarch clearly adopted the Franciscan apocalyptic rhetoric. But as the papacy now was located in Avignon, he transferred with ease the hell, the reversed world of sin and obscenity, from Rome. In his *Sine nomine,* the collection of anonymous letters written in the 1350s when Petrarch was about to leave Avignon for good, Avignon is described as the "newest" or the third Babylon, successor to those of Assyria and Egypt. She is the foulest of all cities, "where every street crawls with worms,"[10] "the whore with whom the kings of the earth have committed fornication,"[11] "the mother of harlots and abominations of the earth,"[12] and "the woman drunken with the blood of the saints, and with the blood of the martyrs of Jesus."[13] Of greatest importance, however, is that Petrarch's blaming of Avignon is balanced by a veneration of Rome. Avignon was Babylon, the prefiguration of sin, discord, and slavery, with the underlying notion that Rome was the New Jerusalem, the city of virtue, concord, and freedom. In short, with the dislocation of the papacy to Avignon, Rome was gradually purified of such violent associations, which characterized the early Franciscans' configurations of the city.

In the letter to Cola di Rienzo (*Disperse* 8), written in the wake of the uprising in Rome during Pentecost in 1347, the defense of Rome as the New Jerusalem merged with an intense celebration of the classical city, and, as we shall soon see, Petrarch came to be regarded as the mind behind Cola's attempt to restore the ancient glory of Rome. Before we return to *Disperse* 8, though, it may be useful to paint a picture of the contemporary political situation, which places the letter in a highly dramatic chapter in Rome's history.

ROME IN MOURNING

In a valuable source from the middle of the fourteenth century known as *Cronica*, written by an unknown Roman author, therefore referred to as Anonimo Romano, an event in Rome's history is vividly depicted. Early in the morning on the Sunday of Pentecost in 1347, a throng of armed men left the church of Sant'Angelo in Pescheria, close to the ancient fish market along the Tiber, where they had kept vigil throughout the night listening to masses.[14] The group was led by Cola di Rienzo, described as "de vasso lenaio," a man of lowly or humble lineage, a Roman plebeian, son of a tavern keeper and a cleaning woman. Parading before him he had three men from his conspiracy, each bearing a banner. According to the author, the first banner was enormous, red, and emblazoned with gold letters. On it was an image of the ancient goddess of Rome sitting on her throne, flanked on either side by a lion, and with "lo munno," the orb of the world, and "la palma," the palm of victory, in her hands. "Questo era lo confallone della libertate"—"this was the banner of liberty," Anonimo Romano explains.[15] The second banner was white and bore an image of Saint Paul with his sword and a crown of justice. On the third banner Saint Peter was depicted with his keys to concord and peace. In addition, there came a fourth con-spirator, bearing the banner of Saint George, the knight who rescued the church, the *Ecclesia Romana*, by slaying the apocalyptic dragon.[16]

The procession following the banner bearers, which soon grew to one hundred armed supporters and was even joined by the papal vicar in Rome, marched through the city and ascended the Senators' Palace at the Capito-line Hill, encouraged by the chants and praise of the mass of people in the streets. From the top of the hill Cola gave a speech "della miseria e della servitude dello puopolo de Roma" (on the misery and the servitude of the people of Rome), followed by a reading of a list of ordinances that proclaimed the foundation of the *buono stato*—the good state. Cola declared himself tribune of Rome, intending to revive the Roman Republic and restore the glory—the liberty and peace—of the ancient city.

This story of Cola's triumph is immediately, and antithetically, pre-ceded by Anonimo Romano's lamentation of the state of Rome:

> Meanwhile the city of Rome was in agony. It had no rulers; men fought every day; robbers were everywhere; nuns were insulted; there was no refuge; little girls were assaulted and led away to dishonor; wives were taken from their husbands in their very beds; farmhands going out to work were robbed, and where? in the very gates of Rome; pilgrims, who had come to the holy churches for the good of their souls, were not pro-tected, but were murdered and robbed; even the priests were criminals. Everywhere lust, everywhere evil, no justice, no law; there was no longer any escape; everyone was dying; the man who was strongest with the sword was most in the right. A person's only hope was to defend himself with the help of his relatives and friends; every day groups of armed men were formed.[17]

The misery of Rome is presented as the backdrop to Cola's revolution, and it gives us a glimpse of Anonimo Romano's enthusiasm for Cola. The city was in deep trouble, and Cola seemed to embody its long-awaited savior. The Pentecost revolt, however, was well prepared. Already in the spring of 1342, the Romans had sent a delegation of eighteen men to Avignon with a plea to the newly elected Pope Clement VI that he should return to Rome. The delegation also asked the pope to declare a Jubilee to take place in Rome in 1350 in order to improve the city's poor economic situation, caused by the loss of the rich papal court when it moved to Avignon, and by the con-stant feuds between the city's mighty barons, mostly the Orsini family and the Colonna family.[18] The delegation was led by Stefano Colonna the

Younger, whom Petrarch had befriended the year before when he won his crown of laurels on the Capitoline Hill.

As a Roman citizen, an honor that was bestowed on his winning the laurel crown, Petrarch, who was now back in Avignon, supported the delegation by composing a metrical epistle addressed to Clement VI (*Epystola* II, 5) in which he reaffirmed the appeal for the pope's return. Through the rhetorical device of the *personificatio* of the widowed Jerusalem from the book of Lamentations, Petrarch let Rome herself present the case to the pope: at the pontiff's feet the city deplores her circumstances, urging her spouse to hear her complaints and return home, lest his bride suffer a widowed old age.[19]

Configurations of Rome as the widowed Jerusalem had been adopted earlier in the Middle Ages. Bernard of Clairvaux, for instance, powerfully used the image in his letter to the Roman people (*Epistola* 243) after the uprisings in 1145 when Pope Eugene III was driven from Rome into exile in Viterbo.[20] In the letter, Rome appears as the widow: "Open your eyes, you miserable people, and see the desolation that is even now upon you. How the finest colour has changed in brief time [Lam 4:1]: the mistress of the world and the prince of the provinces has become a widow [Lam 1:1]."[21]

The imagery of the widow was founded on the opening lines of the book of Lamentations (Lam 1:1):

> How deserted lies the city,
> once so full of people!
> How like a widow is she,
> who once was great among the nations!

Some lines later a personified Jerusalem raises her voice (Lam 1:12):

> "Is it nothing to you, all you who pass by?
> Look around and see.
> Is any suffering like my suffering
> that was inflicted on me,
> that the Lord brought on me
> in the day of his fierce anger?"[22]

In the Franciscan tradition of the thirteenth century, these verses were often transferred to the suffering of Christ on the cross, such as in Bonaventure's *Vitis Mystica*, or in John Peckam's and later Petrus Joannis Olivi's commentaries on the Lamentations.[23] The image of the widowed Rome was moreover reinforced by the losses of Jerusalem and by the final loss of the Holy Land in 1291. However, only when the representation of the widowed Rome was connected to the papacy's stay in Avignon was the rich potential of the image rediscovered.[24] Dante constructed two of his political letters around the image of Rome as both bride and widow waiting for her husband to return in the tradition of the Lamentations: we find the image in his *Epistola* V to the princes and people of Italy, and in *Epistola* XI to Italian cardinals.[25] Moreover, as we have seen in the introduction, the same image was used in *Purgatorio* VI, where Dante hurls out his long vituperation of the deplorable situation in Italy (*Purg.* VI, 112–114):

> Vieni a veder la tua Roma che piagne
> vedova e sola, e dì e notte chiama:
> "Cesare mio, perché non m'accompagne?"

[Come see your Rome that weeps, widowed and alone, crying day and night, "My Caesar, why do you abandon me?"]

As we can see from these verses, Dante's configuration of a Rome mourning even has Christological allusions in the way it dramatically echoes the suffering Man's last cry on the cross: "My God, my God, why have you forsaken me?" (Mt 27:46; Mk 15:34). An irony, though, is that the dialectic imagery of widowed sorrow and nuptial joy was used by Pope Clement VI as one of his favorite motifs—the bridegroom who comes to meet his bride, the city of Rome. Clement, however, twisted this argument by putting more emphasis on the pope's role as the universal pastor of the *Ecclesia Romana* than on the bishop of Rome, thereby discreetly underlining that his presence was not that urgent.[26] Clement's argument was simply that *ubi papa, ibi Roma*—where the pope is, there is Rome. In contrast to this idea, Petrarch strongly stressed the function of the pope as husband of the church, and the city of Rome as the mother of all nations. As the lamenting Rome declares in his epistle to Clement (*Epystola* II, 5, 277–279),

> Sic ego conspiciens quorum sumus ambo parentes
> Meque, laresque meos solabor prole frequenti
> Perdita possessis mulcens, et tristia laetis.

[Thus I seeing those to whom we both are parents will console myself and my household goods with abundant offspring, sweetening what is lost with what is found, sorrows with joy.][27]

The epistle offers an appeal to the pope. To support the plea for a new Jubilee, which was the mission of the Roman delegation, Rome ends her moving appeal to the pontiff as follows: if her spouse cannot return, the many pilgrims who may gather in the city for such a papal Jubilee will comfort her and mix the sorrow of the yearning mother for what she has lost with the joy of abundant offspring.

In using such a figure of a lamenting widow, Petrarch's letter did not only evoke a traditional medieval and Franciscan interpretation of nuptial imagery; the figure anticipates above all the ambitious political propaganda that was to be realized in Rome in subsequent years.

A REVOLUTION LOADED WITH SYMBOLS

The delegation from Rome did not manage to convince Clement to return. However, after a revolt in Rome only a few months later, when the people overthrew the newly appointed senators Bertoldo Orsini and Stefano Colonna the Younger, and placed governance in the hands of a group called the Thirteen Good Men, a new delegation was sent to Avignon. Its mission was to inform the pope about the events in Rome and once again plead for his return. The leader chosen for this embassy was the young Cola, who had already established himself as the principal activist for Rome's revival. Cola had a reputation of being an extraordinary orator, the best in Rome, and, as Anonimo Romano presents him, he was also familiar with the classical legacy and classical culture:

> From his youth he was nourished on the milk of eloquence: a good grammarian, an excellent speaker, and a good scholar. Lord, what a fast reader he was! He was well acquainted with Livy, Seneca, Cicero, and Valerius Maximus; he loved to describe the great deeds of Julius Caesar. Every day he would gaze at the marble engravings which lie about in Rome. He alone knew how to read the ancient inscriptions. He translated all the ancient writings; he interpreted those marble shapes perfectly. Lord! How often he would say, "Where are those good Romans? Where is their high justice? If only I could live in such times!"[28]

In Anonimo Romano's description, there is no doubt about Cola's classical learning, despite his plebeian origins, and in an audience with the pope in Avignon he used his intellectual talents and gifts for speaking. As we can read in his letters to the Roman people from Avignon, he presented the city's case in an ardent vocabulary of renewal and resurrection, of the emergence of a golden age after a long and dark period.[29] He referred to Virgil's fourth *Eclogue,* which in the Middle Ages was interpreted as the prophecy of a new Christian era, as well as the prophecy of the Tiburtine Sibyl echoed in the legend of the Franciscan church of Aracoeli. According to the legend, the church, atop the Capitoline Hill next to the Senators' Palace, was built over the Augustan altar of *Ara primogeniti Dei,* where the Sibyl prophesied to Augustus the coming of Christ. In addition, Cola's language was replete with biblical references that set the rebirth of Rome within a grand apocalyptic framework, where the city appeared as a bride dressed for her husband and as the New Jerusalem (Apoc. 21:2).

Yet despite Cola's eloquence, the pope did not approve the new government of the Thirteen Good Men, above all because of the harsh resistance by Cardinal Giovanni Colonna, who supported his relatives, the overthrown barons in Rome. The government was annulled, and the pope, restoring the bonds with the Colonna faction in Avignon, appointed two barons, Matteo Orsini and Paolo Conti, as his new vicars and senators.[30] The pope, however, was so moved by Cola's speech, according to Anonimo Romano, that he fell in love with him and wanted to see him daily.[31] In addition, we may assume that the pope, who was an astute politician, wanted to have a certain degree of control over the mighty families and the Italian flank of the curia, because even though he was far from Rome, he was still the city's rightful lord, as the emperor also was. Cola was, in other words, a useful tool in order to keep at bay the powerful Roman barons and their relatives in Avignon. Cola was probably also given aid by Petrarch, who during the former's stay in Avignon had developed an intense friendship with the young rebel, a friendship that came to have radical consequences for his own contact with the Colonna family.

In June 1344, Cola finally returned to Rome appointed as Pope Clement VI's protégé and the new notary of the Chamber of Rome, a position traditionally held by the city's senators; this only enflamed the already tense situation.[32] The position of notary, however, was a humble one, and the barons still ruled the city. Over the coming weeks, months, and years, Cola gradually built his own power base, modestly and carefully, behind the shifting governments and constant battles between Rome's mighty families. He took his time and prepared the revolution well, for example by using visual arts as a medium to convey his program and win public sympathy for his ideas. Most astonishing was his commissioning of an enormous panel painting on the façade of the Senators' Palace on the Capitoline Hill, which, with the church of Aracoeli, was the most conspicuous landmark in Rome. Anonimo Romano also vividly described these paintings, now lost:

> Cola further admonished the rulers and the people with an image which he had painted on the Palace of the Campidoglio [Capitol] in

front of the market. On the outer wall above the Chamber he had a picture painted of a tremendous sea, with horrible waves, storming vio-
lently. In its midst a ship was foundering, without rudder or sail. In the
endangered ship was a widow woman, dressed in black, bound in a belt
of mourning, her gown ripped from her breast, her hair torn, as if she
would weep. She was kneeling, her hands piously crossed over her breast,
as if praying to be saved from her danger. The inscription said, "This is
Rome." Around the ship in the lower part of the water were four sunken
ships, their sails fallen, masts broken, rudders lost. In each was a woman,
sunken and dead. The first was named Babylon, the second Carthage,
the third Troy, and the fourth Jerusalem. The inscription said, "Because
of injustice these cities were endangered and fell." Among the dead
women these words were written: "Once you held high dominion over
all; now here we await your fall."[33]

As we may well understand from this scene, employing biblical as well as
classical tropes, Cola's message was strong and clear: rescuing Rome was
of the utmost urgency. The widowed Rome—placed in a boat surrounded
by a horrible storm—was about to sink, joining failed empires like Babylon, Carthage, Troy, and Jerusalem. So when Cola marched through the
streets with his banners and army that early Sunday morning of Pentecost
in 1347 and ascended the Capitoline Hill, he was celebrated as the savior,
the long-awaited liberator and restorer of the sacred and glorious Roman
Empire, prophesied by the Sybil and ordained by God himself.

A BALANCED GREETING

Cola's revolution was met with enthusiasm, above all by the many *literati* of
the time. One of them was Barbato da Sulmona, who once belonged to the
circle of artists and religious reformers around King Robert of Naples. A few
weeks after the revolution, Barbato published his allegoric epistle *Romana
respublica urbi Romae*, in which he resumed the fiction of the personified voice
and image of a speaking Rome. Recalling the splendor of the past, the classical city admonished the modern city, arguing that because she had been
without faithful friends for centuries, it was no wonder that she had fallen
into such a disgraceful state as she was in now. Nevertheless, the Republic
did not need to despair, Barbato wrote, for now *two* men had brought new
life to the city, reviving its fortunes: Petrarch and Cola di Rienzo.[34]
    The remarkable thing about Barbato's text is the author's suggestion
that Petrarch is the mind behind Cola's revolutionary program. Cola carried

out in action what the poet in Avignon had long speculated on. Petrarch's own letter to Cola, *Disperse* 8, probably written in the same weeks that Barbato wrote his epistle, supports this suggestion. In the letter Petrarch appears as just such a poet that the ancient illustrious men had honored and kept with them, so that they might hand down their praises to posterity. The letter, which is a true piece of *ars arengandi*, the medieval art of oration, even known as the most virile and eloquent philippic letter of modern times, opens with a salutation:[35] "I am somewhat undecided, noble soul, whether I should first congratulate you on the achievement of such great glory, or the citizens of your rescued city for your services on their behalf and for the most happy recovery of their liberty. I congratulate both equally. I shall address you both together, nor shall my words distinguish those whom I see linked so inseparably by fate itself."[36]

In these opening lines Petrarch greets Cola, as well as the Roman citizens. When reading the letter more attentively, however, we soon discover that something more important is at stake than a mere polite gesture of salutation. In the very first sentence the poet sets out the course for the ensuing argument of the letter. He celebrates Cola by dubbing him *vir magnanime*, a noble soul or man of high rank, but at the same time he modifies the praise or balances it by way of some qualification. Cola is a *vir magnanime*, but only in the service of liberty. It is the act of rescuing the Roman citizens from tyranny that makes him worthy of this exaltation. Thus, Petrarch evens out his compliment by lowering Cola and extolling the Roman citizens, stressed both by his own indecision about how to greet them and by his acknowledgment in the next sentence: "I congratulate both equally." He explains that he will make no distinction but address the parts on the same level, because their fates are inseparably bound—and that is what he actually does: throughout the letter he shifts in a steady rhythm between turning to the Romans, turning to Cola, and turning to both parties simultaneously.

The central conceptions are liberty and servitude, and throughout the first part of the letter there are clarifications and elaborations on the two terms. According to Petrarch, the whole revolution is about liberty. "Liberty," he writes, "stands in your midst. There is nothing dearer, nothing more earnestly to be desired; and never are these facts more clearly understood than when liberty is lost."[37] Such a loss is what the Roman citizens have experienced. Alien tyrants have long subjected Rome to violence and shame. "Rome—the capital of the world, the queen of the cities, the seat of empire, the citadel of the Catholic faith, and the source of all remarkable models of virtue," as Petrarch so enthusiastically described the city in a later text, has been desecrated, and its freemen degraded to slaves.[38] With some obscure references to Spoleto and to the Rhine or Rhone, the tyrants he is thinking of are obviously the members of the Orsini and Colonna families. The revealing signs that they are strangers are, however, not so much the tyrants' origins. Actually, the place of birth is not important in Petrarch's philosophy of Rome. What makes them alien is their mentality, their distorted perceptions of their own superiority, and their accompanying disdain of the Roman people. They call themselves princes of the Romans (*Romani principes*), Petrarch explains, while the name of the Roman citizens has become low and base in their eyes, something that turns the classical and the Christian visions of the *romanitas* upside-down: "But I am less indignant at this when I behold that they have lost sight of even their human origin. They have lately reached that stage of insanity that they wish themselves considered gods [*dominos*] and not men [*homines*]. Oh, unutterable shame! In that very city in which Caesar Augustus, the ruler of the world and the lawgiver of the nations, by special edict forbade that he be called a god, in the same city, today, beggarly thieves judge themselves unpardonably offended if they are not addressed as gods. Oh wretched wheel of fortune!"[39]

The burden of this quotation is twofold. On the one hand, Petrarch says that a true Roman prince is not the lord but a servant of his people. On the other hand, he emphasizes the universality of being a Roman citizen, regardless of one's place of birth or nationality. Being Roman is related to the concept of being human and being protected by laws valid for all nations. The first argument recalls not only Suetonius's depiction of the exemplary life of Divus Augustus in *De vita Caesarum*, which Petrarch clearly alludes to. Obliquely, the argument of the humble ruler also echoes Dante's treatise *Monarchia,* of which Cola di Rienzo was an eager reader. Behind the second argument—the claimed universality of the Roman laws—we may glimpse the central ideas of Cicero's oration *Pro Archia,* a text discovered by Petrarch in his youth that came to constitute the ideological core of his speech *Collatio laureationis.* Before returning to Petrarch's coronation speech, we will shortly dwell on Cola's familiarity with Dante's political thought.

Cola knew Dante's *Monarchia* well, even though it was judged heretical, as we have seen in Chapter 2, by Pope John XXII in 1328 and condemned to be burnt. However, Cola must have come into possession of a copy, and his comments on Dante's text are actually the oldest ones we have of *Monarchia.*[40] These comments reveal that Cola shared Dante's enthusiasm for classical Rome, and in particular his admiration for Divus Augustus and Constantine the Great. Like Dante he considered the function of the empire as indispensable for a civilized society, where it was possible for clerics to realize the Christian ideals of poverty, humility, and charity. Further on, the comments condemning the corrupt church (*ecclesia carnalis*) and the vices of the pontiff and his priests, in contrast to the *pastor angelicus* (the angelic pope) and the *ecclesia spiritualis,* celebrated by the reformists, testify to Cola's profound sympathy for the Spiritual *fraticelli* and the Joachimites of his time. However, as Pier Giorgio Ricci has argued, Cola demonstrated little interest in *Monarchia*'s theological and philosophical discussions. He was obviously well acquainted with the Latin classics, though, such as Virgil, Cicero, Ovid, Seneca, Lucan, and Valerio, and he had a particular preference for the historians, such as Livy, Sallust, Suetonius, and Orsio.[41] Finally, the comments convey a continuous exaltation of the old Romans—their virtues, hospitality, justice, loyalty to allied peoples, and conduct toward enemies—as well as an awareness of style and literary beauty. Cola praised Dante as the *dissertimus orator* (eloquent speaker) and he admired his *eloquenti et gravi stilo* (elegant and serious style) through which shone the *sententiarum gravitas* (the gravity of the sentences) and the *sermonis lepos* (the charm or wit of the speech).[42]

As we have already seen in Chapter 1, Dante referred to Divus Augustus as the supreme model of the humble ruler, who created the condition of perfect harmony and tranquility throughout the world (*Mn.* I, 16, 1). Petrarch's allusion to the same passage from Suetonius in his letter to Cola may be understood as a reminder of Dante's hero. In *Disperse* 8 Petrarch depicts the contrast between the humble ruler and the modern tyrants or the barons who had long governed Rome. They were aliens and not Romans, he argued, and the reason for this was their feelings of superiority over the Roman laws. As Petrarch writes, they were "men who deemed it basest slavery to live under the same laws with their fellow citizens, men who esteemed nothing noble unless it were unjust and arrogant."[43] The barons were, in other words, far from being servants of the people, which Dante had set as a precondition for being a just monarch. They had brought nothing but shame to the city, seizing its strongholds, its public revenues, and its regions, creating discord, vandalizing the bridges, and damaging the glorious palaces and monuments of the ancients. According to Petrarch, they were simply traitors to all law, both human and divine, and must therefore be expelled. As he quite imaginatively suggests, "The state must be relieved of these as a body would be freed of his poisonous excretions. Thus the state, though diminished in numbers, will be stronger and healthier."[44]

THE MAN OF ARMS AND HIS POET

This process of dispelling the alien elements, the expulsion of the tyrants, is the opposite of what we can read in the speech Petrarch gave in Rome on the occasion of his coronation on Easter Sunday, 1341, and in which he developed his ideas of *romanitas*. After examination for his intellectual skills by Robert of Anjou, king of Naples and Sicily, Petrarch was solemnly crowned poet laureate atop the Capitoline Hill, an honor that offered an alien, or a foreigner like him, the status of Roman citizen.

Collatio laureationis is perhaps Petrarch's best-known oration and was once described as the "first manifesto of the Renaissance" by the scholar Ernest Hatch Wilkins.[45] The reason for this rather loaded phrase is the way in which Petrarch speaks through literary fragments of the ancient poets. His oration is strewn with broken pieces, as reflected in the very location of his speech. The Capitoline Hill, with its two powerful buildings, the Senators' Palace and the Franciscan church of Aracoeli, was visible from the entire *abitato* of Rome, the area between the triangle of the mausoleum of Augustus in the north, Castel Sant'Angelo to the west, and the Tiber Island to the south. From the top of the hill Petrarch could view the shattered city, the *fracte urbis,* that had made such an impression on him on his first trip to the city in 1337, and that is so dramatically remembered in his letter to Giovanni Colonna (*Fam.* VI, 2).[46] From this vantage point, it is as if Rome itself is given a voice through Petrarch's speech. The poet seems to stage himself as a ventriloquist, as Giuseppe Mazzotta has noted in his compelling reading of the discourse: he has internalized the language of the dead and revived as a living tradition the faded sounds of Rome.[47] Echoes petrified in the city's ruins, as well as fragments of the ancient poets, speak through Petrarch and define his program of cultural renewal that would restore the classical polis in the center of the contemporary Holy Roman Empire. As Petrarch wrote in his letter to Colonna evoking the two friends' wanderings among the Roman ruins a few years earlier, the city would rise again if the citizens began remembering their glorious past: "For who can doubt that Rome would rise again instantly if she began to know herself?"[48] The underlying meaning is that the loss of history involves the loss of identity, and that identity can only be regained through the route of memory, through a mental process of remembering and recollecting.

Petrarch's main argument is that the poets play a pivotal role in this process of remembering. Although reinterpreted and reinforced by the Christians as the city of the vicar of Christ, the idea of Rome's eternity, as well as its status as *caput mundi,* drew basically on the ancient city's own authoritative texts, such as Cicero, Varro, Seneca, and of course the imperial scripture itself, Virgil's *Aeneid.* In *Collatio laureationis* Petrarch launches himself as a poet who would bring fame and glory to a future Rome, just like the ancient poets once had. He opens the speech with a passage, not from the *Aeneid,* but from Virgil's *Georgics* (III, 291–292): "Sed me Parnasi deserta per ardua dulcis / raptat amor" ("But a sweet longing urges me upward over the lonely slopes of Parnassus").[49] With these words he offers Virgil the role of the guide for his speech, followed, of course, by quotations from and references to a series of other poets and historians from classical antiquity. At a certain point, however, Petrarch takes the torch and proposes himself as the director on the new route to Rome's future glory: "Boldly, therefore, perhaps, but—to the best of my belief—with no unworthy intention, since others are holding back, I am venturing to offer myself as guide for this toilsome and dangerous path; and I trust that there may be many followers."[50] This quotation suggests that Petrarch is the new Virgil, the Virgil of modern times, a role for which the poet had already fashioned himself, with his ambitious epic *Africa*, about the Roman hero Scipio Africanus.

There is no doubt about Virgil's importance in *Collatio laureationis*. Yet there is another person with whom Petrarch creates subtle bonds of familiarity as well, namely Archias, the poet whom Cicero so strongly defended in his oration *Pro Archia*. Petrarch had retrieved the text during a trip to Liège in 1333, and his use of it in *Collatio laureationis* was a way of demonstrating his humanistic skills.[51] As Dennis Looney has noted, it was in fact Petrarch's activities as a philologist and humanistic scholar, devoted to the recovery, study, and promulgation of texts in the classical tradition, for which he was recognized when he received the crown of laurels, more than for his writings thus far in his poetic career.[52] But how could *Pro Archia* be of especial importance to Petrarch, and how is the text related to his letter to Cola di Rienzo?

Pro Archia is an oration given by Cicero in 62 BCE in defense of the Syrian poet Archias, who had lived in the Greek cities of southern Italy, where he had been widely acclaimed. He gained citizenship of the *municipium* of Heraclea, and, according to the Roman laws *Lex Julia* and *Lex Plautia Papiria*, he should have been eligible for Roman citizenship as well.[53] After many years spent in Rome, he was, however, by virtue of a special law known as *Lex Papia de peregrinis*, accused of possessing citizenship under false premises, and his prosecutors wanted to banish him. Cicero, however, took up the case to defend his friend and teacher and easily proved his rights to citizenship. The charges were empty, according to Roman laws. What seem even more urgent for Cicero were the reflections on poetry and poetry's role in the economy of the city. Should the poet be expelled, and was the fate of the poetry, like that of the poet, to be thought of as alien by the legal and political fabric of Rome?

Behind the discussions of Archias's status, we may glimpse Socrates's arguments in book X of Plato's *Republic* and his harsh critique of Homer. Cicero, however, reverses the Platonic expulsion of the poets from the ideal republic. Based on the Roman idea of universality, which Petrarch also alludes to in his letter to Cola—confirmed by Sulla's free offering of citizenship to the Spaniards and the Gauls (*Pro Archia* X)—all were members of the same city. Archias thus deserved the citizenship of Rome, according to Cicero, and he deserved it above all because he was a poet. As Homer testified, as well as the Greek cities' fight with one another for the honor of being his birthplace, poets were always strangers (*Pro Archia* IXX). Yet it was due to Homer's merit that Greek poetry was read by every nation, whereas Latin was constrained by its own natural borders:

> For if anyone thinks that the glory won by the writing of Greek verse is naturally less than that accorded to the poet who writes in Latin, he is entirely in the wrong. Greek literature is read in nearly every nation under heaven, while the vogue of Latin is confined to its own boundaries, and they are, we must grant, narrow. Seeing, therefore, that the activities of our race know no barrier save the limits of the round earth, we ought to be ambitious that whithersoever our arms have penetrated there also our fame and glory should extend; for the reason that literature exalts the nation whose high deeds it sings, and at the same time there can be no doubt that those who stake their lives to fight in honour's cause find therein a lofty incentive to peril and endeavor.[54]

In short, Cicero's argument was that if Rome were to conquer the world, as it had already done militarily and with arms, and if it was going to extend fame and glory to posterity, it had to praise its poets.

Petrarch obviously thought that he was giving his oration in the very same hall where Cicero had once spoken, and he let his speech resonate with the same concerns that the classical orator expressed in *Pro Archia*.[55] As with Cicero, who was anxious to demonstrate that the poets had defined and sharpened his language, Petrarch too spoke with and through the words of others. And in the wake of Cicero, he claimed that the renewal of Rome depended greatly on its capacity to assimilate poets, even alien poets like himself, into the social fabric of the city. The man of arms and the man of letters belonged to one another like the body to the soul, he claimed: "As we consist of both body and spirit, two ways of seeking glory are set before us, namely the way of the body and the way of the spirit—though in this life each needs the help of the other."[56] Virtuous actions needed the poets' songs in order to be remembered. Only the abundance of the poetic imagination would lay the foundation for the hegemony of Rome as the center of the world and extend its glory to future generations—the myth of Rome's *Urbs et Orbis*. In other words, literature rendered the poets immortal, as well as the virtuous men of whom they sang: "There have indeed been many men who in their lifetime were glorious and memorable for what they wrought in writings or in arms, whose names have nevertheless fallen into oblivion for this one reason, that they did not succeed in expressing in the stable and enduring style of a true man of letters what it was that they really had in their minds and spirits. . . . Certain illustrious men, foreseeing such a possibility, have kept poets with them and held them in high honor, so that there might be someone who would hand down their praises to posterity."[57]

Petrarch offered himself the status of just such a poet as was defended by Cicero. He is not only Archias but even Virgil reborn, who long ago started to write about Rome's glory. Two years after he spoke at the Capitoline Hill, the poet met his man of arms, and they developed a profound friendship based on mutual respect and admiration.

THE NEW BRUTUS

We do not know whether Cola was present at the crowning at the Capitol, but he may have been. Like Petrarch, Cola was a passionate reader of the classics, and after their first encounter in Avignon in 1343 their discussions revolved around the question of Rome. Barbato da Sulmona was probably therefore not exaggerating in depicting Petrarch as the ideologue for or the intellectual constructor of Cola's revolution in Rome in 1347. But how did Petrarch configure Cola? How did the poet sing of his hero? In the passage from *Disperse* 8, after the description of the tyrants as alien, he returns to Cola:

> But evil fortune must come to an end as well as good fortune. The restorer of the early Roman's liberty and the restorer of your liberty were both unexpected. Each age produced its Brutus. There are now three named Bruti celebrated in history. The first exiled the proud Tarquin; the second slew Julius Caesar; the third has brought exile and death to the tyrants of our age. Our third Brutus, then, equals both the others because in his own person he has united the causes of the double glory that the other two divided between them. He is, however, more like the earlier Brutus in disguising his nature and in concealing his purpose. Like him he is young but of a far different temperament; and if he assumed the false exterior of that other Brutus, it was so that, biding his time beneath this false veil, he might at last reveal himself in his true character—the liberator of the Roman people.[58]

Like in the opening of the letter, Petrarch reiterates the fate that had linked the Roman people and Cola. As Machiavelli would later do, he brings the classical goddess Fortuna within the realm of history—the blindfolded goddess who randomly whirls her wheel around, changing the fate of human beings. Some suffer great misfortune, while others gain windfalls. As he depicts it, fortune has once again spun her wheel and offered a liberator to the Roman people. Petrarch calls him the third Brutus, and portrays him as the successor to Lucius Junius Brutus, the founder of the Roman republic in 509 BCE, and of Marcus Junius Brutus, who once had a leading role in the assassination of Julius Caesar in 44 BCE.

It is rather surprising that Brutus the second is mentioned after the severe punishment meted out to him in Dante's *Comedy*. Dante placed him in the bottommost depths of the Inferno, where he is chewed, with Cassius and Judas, by the three-headed Lucifer (*Inf.* XXXIV). As a parody of the Holy Trinity, the three traitors of the two holy institutions, the church and the empire, are punished with the most treacherous of traitors in the universe, Lucifer himself, who wanted to take God's place. Petrarch, however, is cautious in his comparison. It is Brutus the first with whom Cola is associated above all. Like him, he had disguised his nature and concealed his purpose. By keeping his cards close to his chest, he had been waiting for a favorable opportunity, and when one emerged, he was quick to take advantage of it, thus revealing his true character—the liberator of the Roman people.

Within the folds of the story of Brutus we find some subtle details that not only link the two heroes in accidental similarities but also appear to be a warning to the contemporary liberator. Who was this Brutus who lived almost two thousand years before Cola? The story is told by Livy in his first book of *Ab urbe condita,* following the lineage from Aeneas's landing in Italy and the founding of Rome by Romulus and Remus, to Brutus and his fight against King Tarquinius. In Avignon, Petrarch had recovered the first and fourth decade, and worked eagerly on assembling the manuscript, transcribing it, editing it, and enriching it by adding variants from other authoritative witnesses.[59] The allusion to Livy's story in the *Disperse* 8 is, in other words, once again a way to demonstrate the efforts of the humanist's studies, not that different from how the reference to *Pro Archia* worked in Petrarch's *Collatio laureationis.*

As Livy depicts him, Brutus played a pivotal role in the history of Rome.[60] He was the nephew of Rome's seventh king, Tarquinius Superbus, with whom he had a most difficult relationship. The king was a brutal tyrant and had executed a number of leading men in Rome, including Brutus's own brother. However, under the mask of stupidity—the meaning of the Latin *brutus* is "fool" or "dullard"—Brutus saved himself. One day he accompanied the king's son and his cousin Sextus Tarquinius on a trip to the Oracle of Delphi. To the two cousins' question as to which of them would be the next king of Rome, from the depths of the cavern the Oracle responded that the highest power would be his who would be the first of them to kiss his mother. According to Livy, Brutus, who understood "mother" to mean Earth—evidently regarding her as the common mother of all mortals—left the temple and kissed the ground.

Petrarch often connected the word "homo" (man) to "humilitas" (humility), and again to "humus" (earth). In one of the fictive dialogues between Reason and Sorrow (II, 19) in his vast treatise *De remediis utrisuque fortune* (Remedies for fortune fair and foul), Petrarch argues that the word "human" derives from "humus" ("homo ex humo"), a notion partly taken from Genesis 2:7: "formavit igitur Dominus Deus hominem de limo terrae" (And the Lord God formed man of the dust of the ground).[61] A long medieval tradition, however, conveyed above all by Lactantius's expositions in *Divinarum Institutionum* (II, 10), and later by Isidore's *Etymologiae* (XI, 1, 4), etymologically connected "homo" to "humus," and, as we may assume, Petrarch was most familiar with this tradition.[62] In the letter to Cola he recalls Brutus's humility or earthliness as his sign of being a just king: the humility made Brutus as divine as Divus Augustus, who refused to be called a god. Belonging to the Christian record of virtues, humility reflected and reversed Lucifer's sin of pride, or *superbia,* an idea that brings forth an elegant wordplay in Petrarch's text: King Tarquinius was called nothing but Tarquinius Superbus. Brutus, the fool and the humble servant of his people, lifted himself and the Roman citizens to the pinnacle of freedom, whereas the proud king and his family were deposed and had to flee Rome.

The revolution as described by Livy took place as follows: After returning from the Oracle, Brutus and three other Romans were summoned by Lucretia, a Roman noblewoman, to Collatia, a few kilometers northeast of Rome. Here Lucretia told them that she had been raped by Sextus Tarquinius, the son of the king. Believing that the rape had dishonored her and her family, she took a dagger that she had concealed beneath her dress and plunged it into her heart. According to Livy's story, to which Petrarch also refers, Brutus drew out the knife from Lucretia's wound and held it up, dripping with gore, and shouted for the overthrow of the Tarquins. The four men gathered the young men of Collatia and set out for Rome, where Brutus called the people to the Forum by the foot of the Capitoline Hill and urged them to rise up against the king. The people voted for the deposition of the king and the banishment of the royal family. Thus, after the expulsion of the tyrants, defined as alien, Brutus founded the first Roman Republic.

TRAPS OF THE LOFTY HEIGHTS

In the letter to Cola, Petrarch spins delicate threads between Lucretia and the city of Rome. Like Lucretia, Rome has been violated and fallen into disgrace. But the abuse is even worse in this modern case. As he writes, "There is this difference, however: the patience of the early Romans was taxed by one shameful crime, whereas yours has yielded only after countless deeds of shame and countless intolerable wrongs."[63] Nevertheless, Rome seems to have awakened at last after a long and heavy sleep, and Petrarch admonishes the citizens and urges them to support their liberator, the new Brutus:

> But you, citizens, now for the first time truly deserving the name of citizens, be fully convinced that this man has been sent to you from heaven. Cherish him as one of the rare gifts of God. Hazard your lives in his defense. For he too could have lived his life in slavery together with the rest. He too could have submitted to the yoke that so great a people was enduring without a murmur. If such an existence had seemed too burdensome to him, he could have fled far from the sight of the unhappy city and could have escaped the shower of abuse and insults by voluntary exile, as we know was the case with certain prominent citizens. It was only love for his country that kept him back. He considered it sacrilege to abandon it in such condition. In this city he resolved to live; for this city to die. He took pity on your misfortunes. You see to what dangerous heights he has risen. Now give him your support lest he fall.[64]

Leaving aside Petrarch's exalted rhetoric, which may sound quite abhorrent to modern ears, we can see how the poet emphasizes the bonds between Cola and the Roman citizens. Cola is one of them. He too could have lived a life in servitude, as his low birth, the son of a tavern keeper and a cleaning woman, implied. By humility, by love of his country—and here we catch an echo of Brutus's kiss—he has brought himself as well as his fellows out of slavery, from the tyranny of the few toward freedom for all. Success, however, depends on the citizens' support. With their assistance, the revolution may avoid ending in failure.

Cola, on the other hand, is encouraged always to keep his classical model in mind. "You, younger Brutus," Petrarch advises, "always keep the example of the first Brutus before you."[65] Indeed, Cola is even more closely connected to the people than Brutus was. As Petrarch writes, "He was a Consul, you are a Tribune. If we compared the two offices we would find that the consuls performed many acts hostile to the welfare of the Roman plebs; indeed—and I will speak out bravely—they often treated it harshly and cruelly. But the tribunes were always and constantly the defenders of the people."[66] As a tribune, and as a plebeian, Cola must not distance himself from his fellow citizens. The heights of the Capitoline Hill hide many traps, and the abysses are nearby, as Petrarch has already made clear. One of them is the Tarpeian Rock, the steep cliff of the southern summit. During the Roman Republic, the cliff was used as an execution site from which murderers, traitors, and fraudsters were flung to their deaths. In his letter Petrarch warns Cola and the Roman citizens not to flinch in punishing the enemies of the republic: "Wield the arms handed down to you by your fathers only against the enemies of the commonwealth."[67] Like his model, Brutus, Cola must have a courageous heart and not fall for the temptation of being bound by family bonds or bonds of affection. In other words, one way down from the hill involved ignoring the distinctions between private and public affairs. Another temptation was forgetting his humble origins and his office as a servant. As Petrarch discusses so often in his works, the borders between humility and pride are dangerously close to each other. So, if Cola started regarding himself as standing above the people, he would transform himself into a tyrant.

This last temptation was probably the reason for Cola's fall. Fortuna spun her wheel and, when Cola thought of himself as master, he was flung to the ground. Not many months after the revolution, rumors reached Avignon about Cola's misgovernment and Petrarch became deeply disappointed. For several months he had defended Cola's case to friends and the papal curia, and he had encouraged and advised his idol in Rome. Now a tyrant was slowly emerging before him, and in November Petrarch wrote him a letter, asking, "What is this great and sad sound that hurts my ears?"[68] He warns him frankly and directly, "And also help me avoid the very troublesome necessity of being forced to terminate in satire the lyrical foundations of your praises in which I have been heavily engaged (as my pen itself can attest)."[69] It has been suggested that the poem Petrarch is referring to is "Spirto gentil"—one of his most impressive *canzoni* from his collection *Rerum vulgarium fragmenta*—although this is uncertain.[70] In any case, *Disperse* 8 ends with a hyperbolic declaration that Cola may expect such a mighty composition from his poet friend:

> But I fear that my words have detained you longer than is fitting, especially at a time when there is far greater need of action. Neither my calling, alas, nor my lot permit me to assist you in action. Therefore, I send you words, the only means of assistance at my disposal.... Moreover, this subject that I have now treated in loose prose, I may attempt in the near future in different meters, provided that you will not

deceive my hopes and wishes and will not deny my perseverance in your glorious undertaking. Crowned with Apollo's wreath [the laurel], I shall ascend lofty and inspiring Helicon. There, at the brim of the Castilian font, I shall recall the Muses from their exile and sing resounding words in abiding memory of your glory, words that will ring throughout the ages. Farewell, bravest men! Farewell, best of citizens! Farewell most glorious City of the Seven Hills![71]

Petrarch thus states here that he will follow Cola's actions with his pen. If the man of arms does not delude him, the poet will accompany him to the lofty hills from where he will hand down his praises to the world and to posterity. They will, in other words, share the wreath of Apollo—one for his actions, the other for his song. Six months later, however, the poet's song started to appear ridiculous.

THE END

Giuseppe Mazzotta may be right in saying that Petrarch dismissed Cola's revolutionary ideas as denials of time and historical changes. According to Petrarch, he argues, Cola did not grasp the sense of history as a process of endless making and unmaking.[72] Indeed, there is no doubt that Petrarch reflected continually on the impossibility of completely retrieving the ancient glory to which the Roman ruins and the ancient poets testified. On the one hand, Petrarch's philological restoration of texts, his praise and circulation of classical poets and historians, his eager hunt for books and manuscripts, and his attempt to reintroduce the classical genres and style foreshadowed the humanists' enterprise of the coming century.[73] On the other hand, a recurrent theme in Petrarch's vast literary production is the complaint about the devastation of time and the impossibility of reconstructing history. Nowhere is this feeling that the past is out of reach more clearly expressed than in the letter to Giovanni Colonna (*Fam.* VI, 2), where the poet remembered his first visit to Rome. As Mazzotta has convincingly described it, walking among the Roman ruins, Petrarch "perceives the discontinuities at the heart of the tradition, which someone like Dante would still view as a uniform reality; he recognizes the pastness of the past in the sense that the monuments of the past appear to him as taciturn shadows of a shattered historical discourse."[74] Yet when it comes to Cola's antiquarianism, Petrarch seems to throw all such earlier hesitation overboard.

Disperse 8, in which he praises Cola's reestablishment of the Roman Republic, glows with a rare enthusiasm, and the failure of Cola's government had consequences for Petrarch as well. Nevertheless, he never forgot his young idol. Up until the very last days of his life, Petrarch remembered Cola's endeavors in Rome, the tribune's magnificent aim, with a deep nostalgia, as we can read in his polemical text *Invectiva contra eum qui maledixit Italie*, written as late as in 1371 or 1372, just a few years before he died in 1374:

> If only omnipotent God would grant peace and brotherly harmony to her [Rome's] sons—her oldest sons, I mean—how quickly and easily Rome would reduce the rebellious barbarians to their ancient yoke, aided as of old by Italian forces! If this was unclear before, it recently took shape when one man—a person of obscure origin, without wealth, and possessing (as events showed) more courage than constancy—dared to support the state on his weak shoulders and to proclaim the defense of the tottering empire. How suddenly all of Italy was aroused! What great terror and rumors, inspired by the name of Rome, spread to the ends of the earth! And how much greater the effect would have been, if preserving his plan had been as easy as undertaking it![75]

The quotation gives us a clear picture of Petrarch's ambiguity toward Cola. On the one hand he is configured as the savior of Rome and Italy, while on the other his weakness and lack of capacity to fulfill his brave undertakings are stressed. Yet one thing is clear—the old poet still recalled admiringly the long-deceased tribune's courage and plans. As for Petrarch, he continued to try to persuade the pope to restore the Papal See to Rome, and when Pope Urban V did return to the city in 1368, thanks to Birgitta of Sweden's insistence as well, Petrarch congratulated him in a book-length letter (*Sen.* VII, 1). As we shall see in Chapter 5, though, the return was short-lived, and not long thereafter the pope once again was back in Avignon.

In Rome there was increasing pressure on the tribune, both from the local barons and from Pope Clement VI, while Cola's own government swelled in the violence it meted out and in extravagance, more suited to a medieval tyrant. Clement was initially in favor of the revolution. According to Anonimo Romano, the tribune won sympathy throughout Italy and even outside it.[76] The major cities and kings and princes of Christendom sent ambassadors to Cola. Petrarch continued to celebrate his friend. In a letter from July (*Disperse* 9), he says that he writes to him daily, although none of these letters have survived. In August he composed an eclogue in honor of the tribune, the so-called *Pietas pastoralis* (*Bucolicum carmen* V), in which resounds the strong polemic against the feudal Roman families, followed by a letter (*Disperse* 11) providing the keys to interpreting the complex allegories of the eclogue. In yet another letter (*Disperse* 10), the poet informs the tribune about the threats planned against him and his deep anxieties for the fate of the tribune and the Roman Republic.

One of the main ambitions of Cola's political program was to unify Rome and Italy, an ambition that of course went against all interests of the papacy in Avignon. The papacy's final break with Rome became clear when Cola's couriers, bringing a letter to the pope about his coronation ceremonies, were beaten up at the gateways of Avignon and the letter destroyed. After this assault, Petrarch, who had already expressed his increasing anger and bitterness against the papal curia, both in the three "Babylonian sonnets" (*Rerum vulgarium fragmenta* 136–138) and in his sixth and seven eclogues, now wrote one of his harshest outbursts against the Avignon papacy (*Sine nomine* 2). A consequence of this increasingly tense situation was Petrarch's own break with his patron and friend for several years, Cardinal Giovanni Colonna. In *Divortium,* the eighth eclogue of *Bucolicum carmen,* the separation is movingly described, and here Petrarch also announces his plans to leave Avignon and move to Italy. He had by then received invitations from Azzo da Correggio to become a resident at his court in Parma, and we may assume that he also wanted to come closer to Cola in case he needed him in Rome.

Petrarch's loyalty to Cola was challenged, however, when he heard about Cola's abuse of power and the increasing brutality and violence in Rome, and especially when the tribune started to make agreements with King Louis of Hungary, who threatened the kingdom of Naples with invasion, and consequently with abolishing the liberty of Rome and Italy. Petrarch left Avignon on November 20, and from Genoa he wrote his last letter to Cola, in which he furiously warns him against betraying his people. The tribune must remember his role and play it well, he says: "Consider with great zeal, carefully, I beg you, what you may be doing, shake yourself sharply, examine yourself without deceit to see who you are, who you have been, whence you came and where you go, where you are permitted to proceed with unobstructed liberty, what kind of person you have been, what title you have assumed, what hope of yours you have realized, and what you professed to be. You will see yourself not as the master of a state but as its servant."[77]

Like a true melodrama—one that inspired poets and composers such as Lord Byron, Richard Wagner, and Giuseppe Verdi—Cola's story ended most tragically. The pressure against the tribune weakened him. Threatened by excommunication, he attempted reconciliation with the church, while the nobility built up its army. On December 15, Cola abdicated after a revolt led by the Colonna family. Despite his waning popularity among the citizens because of his despotism, his eccentric behavior, his luxurious way of life, and the city's diplomatic and political isolation in the wake of the alliance with the king of Hungary, both he and the Romans wept, according to Anonimo Romano, when he had to descend the Capitoline Hill and was accompanied to Castel Sant'Angelo.[78] Thereafter, Cola fled the city and joined a group of Franciscan Spirituals who had taken refuge in the mountains of Abruzzi. Already heavily influenced by Joachimite prophetic eschatology, to which the enormous frescoes in Rome testified, he now became even more fervent in his convictions about his own unique role in history. As he later told Emperor Charles IV in Prague, the friars in Abruzzi opened to him a divine revelation about the apocalyptic events: that God was finally preparing for the universal reform already foretold by the Joachim and the Spirituals.[79] After a couple of years in hiding at a monastery in the mountains, he traveled in the summer of 1350 to the emperor of the Holy Roman Empire in Prague, whom he thought would be the Emperor of the Last Days, to seek his protection. However, Charles IV, who, after the death of his predecessor, Emperor Ludwig of Bavaria, was in a process of reconciliation with the church, imprisoned him. In 1352, the emperor sent him to Avignon, where he was jailed.

In this period, Petrarch had his last sojourn in Provence. When he heard about Cola's return to Avignon, he wrote a letter to his friend Francesco Nelli (*Fam.* XIII, 6) in which he rather contemptuously ridiculed Cola's attempts as a poet and repudiated his Joachimite convictions, obviously in order to distance himself from the events. Cola, "once a truly feared tribune of the city of Rome, yet now the most miserable of men,"[80] deserved punishment, Petrarch wrote, but, with a certain degree of surprise, he disagreed with the papacy's accusations against the tribune:

> He is not being blamed for what good men dislike in him; and he is considered guilty not for the outcome of his endeavors but for their initiation. Nor is he accused of favoring evildoers, or forsaking liberty, fleeing the Capitoline when nowhere else could he have lived more nobly or have died more gloriously. What is it then? Only one charge is directed against him, and if he is condemned for it, he will, at least for me, be not infamous but worthy of eternal glory. The crime is that he dared to have wanted the republic safe and free, and to have all matters dealing with the Roman Empire and Roman power dealt with in Rome.[81]

Petrarch thus accuses Cola of having been too weak. He was not able to crush his enemies, he argues, and instead of suffering a glorious death on the Capitoline Hill, he yielded to his foes. In other words, Petrarch was still of the same opinion as in 1347 regarding the revolution. Almost nostalgically he recalls his old hero: "I loved his virtue, praised his aims, I admired his spirit. I rejoiced with Italy,"[82] and he then expresses his deep affection: "I had allowed myself to cherish and admire him above all others. Therefore, the more I had hoped in him, the more I now grieve for my last hope, and I confess that, however this may all end, I cannot but marvel at the way it began."[83] As is typical of Petrarch, he once again turns to himself and his own responses to the events rather than to Cola's fate. Still, he demonstrates loyalty to their common vision of Rome, and a little later he writes to the Roman citizens (*Sine nomine* 4), deploring Cola's difficult situation and asking them to plead with the Avignon papacy for the return of the tribune.

Petrarch's letter apparently had an effect. After Pope Clement's death in December 1352, a fresh tumult broke out in Rome.[84] Pope Innocent VI, Clement's successor, was eager to vanquish the city's barons, and he found an excellent tool for this purpose in the former tribune. In September 1353 Cola was released and sent back to Rome, this time as a senator. But now his government went awry as well. Acting more brutally than ever, he soon lost the favor of the people, and on 8 October 1354, the mob caught him in a revolt, according to Anonimo Romano, and took him to the Place of Lions on the Capitoline Hill—the place where the stairs are divided into two directions, one leading to Aracoeli, the other to the Senators' Palace.[85] Here the crowd surrounded him, and, like Lucretia, the new Brutus was pierced, not by one dagger, but by several wounds until his body was entirely maltreated.

CHAPTER 5

THE PROPHETIC WIDOW: BIRGITTA OF SWEDEN AND THE *REVELACIONES*

y the end of 1349, just before the opening of the Holy Year of the Jubilee, as Cola di Rienzo, after his failed revolution, was fleeing northward to Prague to seek the protection of Emperor Charles IV, a widow of high rank and great ambition was entering Rome. She left Sweden in the fall of 1349 and traveled through Europe, where she had a longish stay in Milan as a guest of the archbishop and *signore* Giovanni Visconti, the current ruler of Milan, and son of Matteo Visconti, to whom both Dante and Marsilius once had been linked.[1] A few years later, in 1353, when Petrarch had left Avignon for good, he would also seek the archbishop's hospitality.[2] However, in contrast to Petrarch, Birgitta of Sweden was most critical of the bishop in Milan, as the revelations from her stay testify (*Rev.* III, 5–7).[3] In an ardent vocabulary she rebukes the head of the mighty family, who had once created a strong alliance with Emperor Ludwig of Bavaria in the fight against the pope. In fact, the antipope, Nicholas V, elected by the emperor and his counselor Marsilius of Padua in Rome in 1328, had ordained Giovanni Visconti cardinal, a title that, of course, was not valid after Nicholas's fall in 1330, and that was never approved by the pope in Avignon.

The first traces of the disappointment that came to dominate Birgitta's revelations from her years in Rome may be discovered in her visions from Milan (*Rev.* III, 5–9). In a revelation, the church father, Saint Ambrose, whose shrine Birgitta visited in Milan, tells her how the city's archbishop preferred worldly pleasures and affairs rather than caring for the church (*Rev.* III, 6).[4] Giovanni Visconti is compared to an adulterous husband who spends nine out of ten hours with his housemaid instead of his wife. Before she left Sweden, though, Birgitta had obviously been full of expectations for her forthcoming encounter with Rome, the city of Saint Peter and Saint Paul, and the holy, institutional center of Christianity. As her presence in Rome had supposedly been foretold in one of her revelations only a year before, in that great city she would experience a shorter road between heaven and earth. "Vade Romam," Christ had supposedly told her: "Go to Rome, where the streets are paved with gold and reddened with the blood of saints and where there is a short cut, that is, a shorter way, to heaven because of the indulgences that the holy pontiffs have merited because of their prayers. Moreover, you are to stay there until you see the supreme pontiff and the emperor there at the same time in Rome, and you shall announce my words to them."[5] According to Christ, Rome was a sanctified place where the course of time had been able to create a shortcut—a *brevior via*—between heaven and earth, and the aim of Birgitta's journey is made clear: in Rome, Christ tells her, she could expect the return of both the pope and the emperor.

The meeting with Rome, however, turned out to be not as foreshadowed by her vision in Sweden. By the end of the year, when she finally arrived, the wretched state of the city affected her deeply.[6] Rather than finding a shorter way to heaven, Birgitta discovered a city in ruins, not unlike the *fracte urbis,* about which Petrarch, as we have seen in Chapter 4, wrote so melancholically after his first visit to Rome only a few years earlier. However, the miserable, abandoned city seems to furnish Birgitta with a new energy. In the coming two decades, no one fought with more steadfastness than Birgitta did, both for the return of the pope to Rome and for a reform of the *Ecclesia Romana.* Obviously, as Birgitta saw it and as will be explored in this chapter, the two issues were closely connected. Gifted with an extraordinary vitality and strong will, she never gave up the battle to unite the pope and the emperor in Rome. Likewise, she waited in Italy until that moment happened, as promised in her vision in Sweden, while writing to popes and cardinals, priests, friars, monarchs, and secular magistrates in order to influence the situation.

With her burning commitment, Birgitta came to model her activities on the figure of the widowed Rome who was speaking for the sake of the city, so it might "be heard throughout all of Christendom," as she wrote in a letter from 1350.[7] Before we turn to that letter, though, it may be helpful to provide a brief biography of this unusual woman, who is far less well known to modern readers than the contemporary male figures explored in this book. Birgitta is not just the only woman who was canonized in the fourteenth century (in 1391); she is also, as her modern biographer Bridget Morris has emphasized, the only woman to have founded a monastic order of her own devising, the Ordo Sanctissimi Salvatoris, which still exists today.[8] What is of greater interest in our context, though, is Birgitta's authorship—her voluminous *Liber celestis revelaciones* (Celestial book of revelations)—which, with Catherine of Siena's collection of letters and her book *Dialogo della divina provvidenza* (Dialogue of divine providence), is the most extensive literary production by any female writer in the late Middle Ages. As we will see, both Birgitta and Catherine, the one following the other, also came to play major roles in the political and ecclesiastical debates of the Italian *trecento*.

"A POWERFUL, PRAYERFUL AND PRACTICAL WOMAN"

The main sources about Birgitta's life besides her own *Revelaciones* are the *vita,* written by her two Swedish confessors—Peter Olafsson of Alvastra, usually referred to as Prior Peter, and Peter Olafsson of Skänninge, or Magister Peter, as he is called—and the materials gathered in connection with her process of canonization—the *Acta et processus canonicacionis beate Birgitte*.[9] She was born in 1302/1303, and, as the daughter of the Swedish knight and lawman (*lagman*) Birger Persson and his wife, Ingeborg Bengtsdotter, from the powerful Folkung dynasty, she belonged to the nobility with close links to the Swedish Norwegian royal family. The sources therefore sometimes call her *principessa*, "a princess from the Kingdom of Sweden," and throughout her long life she associated with noble families in Europe.[10] At the age of thirteen, she married Ulf Gudmarsson, who was a lawman too and five years older than her. According to the somewhat conventional portrayal of him in the canonization materials, he was a powerful, wealthy, and prudent nobleman, a handsome knight, and a leader at the king's court.[11]

Birgitta gave birth to eight children, and the couple seemed to have a happy marriage, sharing an interest in books and the devout life. As Morris remarks, beneath the stereotypical surface of the hagiographic conventions, the sources reveal her to be a "powerful, prayerful and practical woman."[12] In 1339 Birgitta and Ulf undertook a pilgrimage on foot to Nidaros in Norway,[13] and two years later, in the summer of 1341, they both set out for their second pilgrimage, this time to Santiago de Compostela in Spain.[14] This was a trip that many of their Swedish ancestors, including Birgitta's father, had made before them, but for Birgitta it turned out to be of decisive significance. Accompanied by a number of clerics and laymen, the married couple traveled across Europe, probably over the Baltic Sea to Germany, and then through France and northern Spain.

The sources do not tell us anything about the veneration of the holy shrines in Santiago, but during their return, they probably visited the Abbey of Saint-Denis, to which the convent of Argenteuil belonged.[15] Argenteuil was an important pilgrimage site because it was said to be in possession of Christ's seamless tunic, which came to play a major role in one of Birgitta's last defenses of the papacy. A general feature of Birgitta's visions is that their content, as well as the figures that emerge to her inner eyes, are often closely connected to the places where she received the visions themselves, such as the appearance of Saint Ambrose in Milan. Also in France she seems to have had an experience connected to a specific place, which later was to reappear in other visions—strengthened and provided with further details.

Whether Birgitta visited the Abbey of Saint-Denis or not, the centrality of the French saint was soon confirmed: During the couple's return to Sweden, Ulf suddenly fell ill in Arras in northern France, which at that time was part of the county of Flanders. Birgitta then received a vision from the local Saint Denis, who told her not to worry. Because of her ardent devotion, she has been chosen by God to do his will. According to Saint Denis, she was entrusted with his protection, and as a sign of his aid, her husband would not die yet.[16]

Nonetheless, shortly after their arrival in Sweden, Ulf died, and Birgitta entered widowhood, which she soon turned into a state of extraordinary activity and authority within the social and political spheres. As Renate Blumenfeld-Kosinski has described it, Birgitta began a "second career" after her husband's death.[17] Despite her grief for the loss of her husband, widowhood offered Birgitta, as it did many other medieval women, newly found authority and respect. A sign of the change in her life is the vision she reportedly received more or less immediately after Ulf's death, which her readers today usually dub her "calling vision":

> After some days, when the bride of Christ was worried about the change in her status and its bearing on her service of God, and while she was praying about this in her chapel, she became rapt in spirit; and while she was in ecstasy, she saw a bright cloud from which she heard a voice saying to her: "Woman, hear me." . . . "Fear me not," he said, "for I am the Creator of all, and not a deceiver. I do not speak to you for your sake alone, but for the sake of the salvation of others. Hear the things that I speak; and go to master Mathias, your confessor, who has the experience of discerning the two types of spirit. Say to him on my behalf what I now say to you: you shall be my bride and my channel, and you shall hear and see spiritual things, and my Spirit shall remain with you even until your death."[18]

As many readers have claimed, it is more correct to label Birgitta a "visionary" or a "prophet" in the biblical sense of the words, rather than a "mystic," which tended to be more commonly used to describe religious women in the later Middle Ages.[19] It is, of course, almost impossible to discern the difference, and Birgitta's visions obviously had both mystical and prophetic aspects. The remarkable aspect of her calling vision, however, is its retrieval of the vocation of the prophets from the Old Testament. Instead of an inner, spiritual journey, which would end in a mystical union with God, the calling vision emphasizes Birgitta's activeness in the salvation of the world. As God tells her, he is not speaking for her sake, but for the salvation of others, and she shall be his bride and channel ("sponsa et canale"). In their *vita*, Birgitta's confessors, the two Peters, confirmed her status as a prophet, saying that she prophesied not only the future but also the present and even the past.[20] The confessors' arguments thus echoed the mission of the prophets from the Old Testament, which was to comment on present and future events by recalling events from the past.

Birgitta's vocation as a prophet also appears in one of her earliest visions from her widowhood. In a revelation from the mid-1340s (*Rev.* VI, 88), Birgitta describes how on Christmas Eve she experienced "such a great and wonderful feeling of exultation ... in [her] heart that she could scarcely contain herself for joy." This tremendous joy was accompanied by "a wonderful sensible movement in her heart like that of a living child turning and turning around."[21] Soon after, the Virgin Mary came to her, explaining that the motion, which resembled the conception of the child Jesus in her own womb, was a sign of Birgitta's calling as an instrument for divine revelation. Mary said that from then on Birgitta was to be considered her "daughter-in-law," entrusted with the mission of proclaiming God's will throughout the world. As Claire L. Sahlin has argued in her compelling reading of this vision, similar identifications with Mary run like a thread throughout the *Revelaciones,* conveying in different ways the idea that God's mother offered Birgitta the authority of a prophet, supporting her power to teach, write, and speak on behalf of God.[22] In other words, the idea is that Birgitta's mystical pregnancy turned her heart, like Mary's womb, into a vessel filled with the word of God. Just as Saint Francis's and later Catherine of Siena's profound acts of *imitatio Christi* resulted in stigmata—in physical signs on their bodies that rendered their words and deeds of visionary proportions—Birgitta's *imitatio Mariae* authorized her pneumatic, prophetic speech.[23] As such, Mary functions as a paradigm for her role as God's mouthpiece, and in the coming years Birgitta offered herself as a spiritual guide who, obediently, transmitted the will of God in the world.

The calling vision marked a shift in Birgitta's life, and in the coming years she was said to have received numerous visions, many of them of a political character. As the calling vision reveals, she obviously enjoyed close collaboration with Magister Mathias Övidi (ca. 1300–ca. 1350), canon of Linköping Cathedral, who, besides the charismatic Birgitta herself, is usually considered to be the other major author in medieval Swedish literature. He was a prolific writer, and of special interest in our context is the strong influence of Franciscan spirituality on his thinking.[24] Mathias spent several years at the University of Paris, from which he probably also visited Avignon, and during these years he developed a deep familiarity with the theology of Bonaventure, whom he frequently cited in his three major theological works—*Alphabetum distinccionum, Exposicio super Apocalypsim,* and *Homo conditus.* The Franciscan traces are particularly recognizable in the *Exposicio super Apocalypsim,* where Mathias, offering a strong critique of the contemporary clergy, insisted on thorough reform of the church.

When he returned to Sweden, Mathias became Birgitta's confessor probably before her husband died, and he and Birgitta built up a close, affectionate friendship that encompassed many dimensions of their personalities. As the calling vision also made clear, he was an expert in *discretio spirituum* (the discernment of spirits), which means that he knew how to distinguish between good and evil spirits.[25] After assembling a collection of the early visions of Birgitta, he submitted them to a commission to have their authenticity verified. The meeting, probably held in Uppsala in 1346, and in which Mathias himself took part, accepted the visions as divine, and soon after a selection of them was sent to Avignon. According to Morris, the purpose of the mission, in addition to seeking papal authorization for Birgitta's visions, was twofold: to propose a solution for a truce in the ongoing battles between England and France during the Hundred Years' War, and to convince the pope to return to Rome for the Holy Year of the Jubilee in 1350.[26] Hence, this seems to testify to the status Birgitta enjoyed at that moment in her home country, and her profound engagement in foreign and national political concerns.

Mathias was involved in the emergence of Birgitta's revelations, and he strongly defended their truthfulness. He also wrote the enthusiastic prologue that precedes book I of Birgitta's *Revelaciones,* where he acknowledges her role as a prophet and visionary. Despite their close contact, however, Birgitta and Mathias's friendship seems to have declined by the end of the 1340s. Mathias died soon after Birgitta left Sweden in 1349, possibly of the Black Death.[27]

THE CELESTIAL REVELATIONS

As a member of the Swedish nobility, Birgitta probably learned to read and write as a child. She reportedly owned a number of books, such as *Speculum virginum, Liber de modo bene vivendi,* the Pseudo-Bonaventurian *Meditationes vitae Christi,* and Henry Suso's *Book of the Eternal Wisdom.*[28] According to the sources, she could read Swedish and Latin, and, later in life, after her arrival in Rome, she probably learned to speak Italian as well. She wrote down many of her revelations in Swedish before having them translated by her male spiritual advisers into the language of the church. However, as the famous passage from the canonization materials explains, she supervised these translations from Swedish to Latin most attentively:

> The words that were given her from God she wrote down in her mother tongue with her own hand when she was well and she had us, her father confessors, make a very faithful translation of them into Latin. She then listened to the translation together with her own writing, which she herself had written, to make sure that not one word was added or subtracted, but was exactly what she had heard and seen in the divine vision. But if she was ill she would call her confessor and a scribe, especially appointed as secretary for this, whereupon with great devotion and fear of God and sometimes in tears, she spoke the words to him in her native language in a kind of attentive mental elevation, as if she was reading them in a book; and he wrote them down there in her presence. When the words had been written down she wished to hear them and she listened very carefully and attentively.[29]

The first to translate Birgitta's revelations was Magister Mathias. After Mathias's death, the two Peters, who accompanied Birgitta to Rome, then became the main translators and transcribers of her revelations; as we have seen, they were also the authors of her *vita,* which later constituted a part of the canonization process of the acts of Birgitta.[30] However, it was Alfonso Pecha da Vadaterra (ca. 1327–1389) who came to be the most important translator and later the general editor of Birgitta's *Revelaciones.* The former bishop of Jaén in Andalucia was reportedly deeply impressed by Birgitta when he came to Rome in the late 1360s. As Morris has explained, Alfonso and Birgitta had much in common, sharing a noble background and an interest in secular and political affairs. Equally, they both conducted "a spiritually pure and elitist form of life" as they searched for new models of monasticism.[31] Of importance is that, due to his profound knowledge of canon law and his connections within the papal curia, Alfonso came to play a key role in Birgitta's attempts to gain papal authorization for her order—the Ordo Sanctissimi Salvatoris—and the monastery she was planning to establish at her castle in Vadstena.[32] In the years after her death, Alfonso was also a key figure in her canonization process; it was he—her Spanish confessor—who at Birgitta's request copied and organized her visions into the form known to us today, the eight books of her *Liber celestis revelaciones.*

Birgitta's revelations may perhaps be regarded as a product of negotiations and compromises between her scribes, her translators, and her confessors. Above all, the influence of Alfonso Pecha, as the final editor of the books, is undeniable. Still, Alfonso and the two Peters mostly served as Birgitta's evangelists. As André Vauchez has argued, they remained in the shadows of the authority of the inspired woman, acting more as her collaborators than as her directors.[33] Many of the visions, we may add, bear the clear hallmark of a most deliberative *auctor,* and some of them are striking in their beauty and depth, revealing an extraordinary rhetorical talent.

In general, the literary style of the *Revelaciones* is characterized by a rare realism and a passionate and appealing diction. A notion that readers are often confronted with throughout the books is that true wisdom may be achieved only by following—with humility and sensitive attention—the curve that runs through the deepness of the experienced world. This may be seen, for instance, in Mary's message to the monk whom Birgitta sees in the famous vision that constitutes the fifth book of her *Revelaciones.* The book, which is called *Liber questionum* (Book of questions), includes Birgitta's longest vision. It was written around the same time that she received the call to go to Rome (around 1349), and it is usually considered to be one of her most lucid philosophical works. From the vantage point of horseback on her way toward her castle in Vadstena, Birgitta sees a man midway on a ladder, the top of which touches the sky. At the top sits Christ on a throne, surrounded by an army of angels and saints, with the Blessed Virgin Mary at his feet. The climber is described as "a learned scholar in the science of theology but full of guile and devilish wickedness."[34] He is restless and obviously eager to reach the top, behaving like an inquisitor who confronts Christ and Mary with a series of questions, as if the mysteries of life could be solved by academic disputation and scholastic methods of inquiry alone. Christ and Mary are patient, though, and answer him by continually reminding him of the weight of his body. At a certain point Mary says, "A person who longs for sweetness should not run away from things that are bitter."[35] The meaning is clear: to reach the summit, the monk, and humans in general, must descend by tasting the bitterness of the world.

Mary's answer in *Liber questionum,* her emphasis on the humility necessary to obtain salvation, corresponds to the keen eye for the ordinary events of life that characterize Birgitta's visions. In her important study, Birgit

Klockars has explored the rich use of metaphors in Birgitta's texts, metaphors taken from every aspect of human experience; there are metaphors taken from many professions and categories of life, such as those of the mother, the bleacher, the bride, the jester, the charcoal-burner, the king, the doctor, the sailor, and the stone mason; there are also metaphors from various houses, such as a castle, a church, and a jail, in addition to furniture, walls, and windows; there are various tools from agricultural life, weapons, and musical instruments; there are also metaphors concerning the human body, such as clothes, food, and drinks; finally, there is the extensive use of images from nature, such as animals, plants, flowers, and minerals.[36] Likewise, Janken Myrdal has discussed how the prolific use of parables in the *Revelaciones,* taken from the reality that surrounded Birgitta, gives modern readers important information about everyday life in both Sweden and Italy in the fourteenth century.[37]

In short, Birgitta's literary style seems to be closely connected to her political and theological convictions as she fashioned them in her *Revelaciones.* Her stylistic expression testifies to a desire to be understood by her readers, whom she addresses. It also testifies to an involvement in the *vita activa* and an ethical and social attention to all social classes, from ordinary humans' daily activities to the way in which clerics and statesmen should act and behave. As such, aesthetics, politics, and theology are inextricably interwoven in Birgitta's revelations.

THE STATE OF THE CHURCH

When Birgitta left Sweden, she had already established herself as the influential, prophetic channel that the calling vision had invited her to become. She had reportedly received about half of her more than seven hundred revelations by then. In many of them, we can witness strong condemnations of the priestly lust for secular power, a critique of the spiritual drought, and appeals for church reform. But the state of the secular world also interested her, for instance the political circumstances in the kingdom of Sweden and later the situation in Rome, Naples, and Cyprus. Above all, the political instability of Europe caused by persistent wars between France and England, as well as the papacy's residency in Avignon, worried her deeply. After her arrival in Rome, her immersion in political as well as ecclesiastical affairs only deepened, and an eagerness to reform the church and return the pope and the emperor to Rome came to constitute the crux of her visions.

In a letter rather than a revelation (*Rev.* IV, 78), addressed to a prelate and dated 1350, just after her arrival in Rome, Birgitta opens with a most unusual salutation:

> Honorable Father, I, a widow, declare that many, very amazing revelations were made to a certain woman while she resided in her homeland. After having been submitted to the diligent examination of bishops and learned religious priests, these revelations were shown to have come from the holy and miraculous enlightenment of the Holy Spirit and from no other source. Even the king and queen of the realm acknowledged this on the basis of credible proof. Moreover, the same woman journeyed abroad to the city of Rome, where, when praying one day in the church of Santa Maria Maggiore, she was caught up in a spiritual vision, while her body seemed to fall into a torpor, though not the torpor of sleep.[38]

Described here is a fundamental feature of Birgitta's visions, their reception in a state of rapture but while still awake. Moreover, the quotation underlines the reliability of Birgitta's revelations. By referring to the process of *discretio spirituum,* which she went through in the 1340s in Sweden, with the eager support of Magister Mathias, she emphasizes the truthfulness of her visions in general, and of the specific revelation she is now going to describe to the reader.

The following revelation takes place in the church of Santa Maria Maggiore in Rome, in which the Virgin comes to Birgitta, commanding her to send a message to the prelate. The Virgin powerfully describes the poor state of the church:

> I would have him [the prelate] know that the foundation of the Holy Church is so heavily deteriorated on its right side that its vaulted roof has many cracks at the top, and that this causes the stones to fall so dangerously that many of those who pass beneath it lose their lives. Several of the columns that should be standing erect are almost level with the ground, and even the floor is so full of holes that blind people entering there take dangerous falls. Sometimes it even happens that, along with the blind, people with good eyesight have bad falls because of dangerous holes in the floor. Because of all this, the church of God is tottering dangerously. The result of this will shortly be seen. I assure you that she will suffer a downfall if she does not receive the help of repairs. And her downfall will be so great that it will be heard throughout all of Christendom. All this is to be taken in a spiritual sense.[39]

The portrayal of the church in which Birgitta finds herself is consistent, as we have seen, with other descriptions of the city of Rome.[40] The discrepancy between the glorious past and the miserable present is now made even more glaring by the fact that the vision is received in Santa Maria Maggiore, the majestic church on the top of the Esquiline Hill. As one of the major basilicas in Rome, and the only one dedicated to the Virgin, the church has played a pivotal role in Rome's history. Birgitta was probably able to admire the astonishing mosaics, which are among the oldest representations of Mary as the mother of God from Christian late antiquity, as well as Jacopo Torriti's apse mosaics of the coronation of the Virgin, completed in 1295. We may assume that the many traces of the church's original beauty may have rendered the current state even more miserable in Birgitta's eyes. As Birgitta describes it, the basilica is now more or less in ruins, with toppled columns, cracks in the roof, and dangerous holes in the floor where visitors can easily stumble and fall.

But it is not only Santa Maria Maggiore that is in such terrible shape. The Virgin Mary emphasizes that she is speaking spiritually, which turns the actual basilica into an image of the Catholic Church in general. As Santa Maria Maggiore has become a most dangerous place for visitors, the Catholic Church in its current state leads people astray, yes, even into the abyss of perdition, configured by the many holes in the ground, rather than saving souls. Birgitta's prophetic voice, conveyed by Mary, subsequently breaks through: the current negligence may be fatal if the church does not receive the restoration needed, she says, and the collapse will resound throughout the Christian world. The physical and spiritual forms of corruption, in other words, reflect one another, and in the subsequent passage Mary hurls out her critique of the contemporary church and its depraved moral state. The church is in need of profound restoration, including the removal of the wicked priests who "lead a life of carnal debauchery," and who are "as insatiable as the ocean chasm in their greed for money":[41] "Such men should not be promoted but rejected in God's church."[42]

I, A WIDOW

The conclusion of the vision from Santa Maria Maggiore reveals its epistolary form.[43] Rather than being an ordinary revelation, the text is written as a formal letter—and once again it is the widow from the introduction who speaks: "The glorious Virgin, who appeared to the woman, commanded that all this be sent to you, Reverend Father. I who have sent this letter to you, swear by Jesus, true and almighty God, and by most worthy Mother Mary, that I have not sent this letter for the sake of any worldly honor or favour, so help me body and soul! I have sent it because that same woman, to whom many other words have been spoken in spiritual revelation, was commanded to make all this known to your Excellency."[44]

The letter is exceptional in the way Birgitta refers to herself as a widow. In accordance with the calling vision, she usually presented herself as a bride of Christ, which was common for holy women in the late Middle Ages. But in the letter from Santa Maria Maggiore, Birgitta does not move within the bridal metaphor. Instead, she presents herself as a widow, which is quite unusual even in her revelations.[45] The letter exhibits a strange emphasis on female voices and female figures: The widow speaks of a woman—both refer to Birgitta, of course—who has received a revelation from the Virgin about the current state of the church, which is also portrayed as a woman. It is as if all the feminine roles on the social spectrum—the virgin, the mother, and the widow—are raising their voices within the trembling shelter of the basilica dedicated to the divine *Theotokos,* the Mother of God.

Birgitta's self-presentation as a widow may be modeled on earlier saintly women who were married, such as the Beguine Marie D'Oignies (1177–1213) and Elizabeth of Hungary (1207–1231).[46] The Beguines consisted of groups of laywomen in the Low Countries and the German Rhineland who, from the beginning of the thirteenth century, lived a devotional, religious life outside the monasteries and in contact with the community that surrounded them. As Dyan Elliott has discussed, the dramatic emergence of female spirituality in this period was part of a clerically sponsored program.[47] Even Pope Gregory IX supported the Beguines, or the *mulieres sanctae* (holy women), as they were often called, and the *vitae* of Marie D'Oignies and her follower, Elizabeth of Hungary, became fairly well known in the thirteenth and fourteenth centuries. However, along with a series of other modes of female religious life, the Beguines gradually came under attack in the fourteenth century and were placed under the control of orthodox powers, which would affect the reputation of Birgitta and Catherine of Siena as well.[48]

As some readers have suggested, Birgitta should have been familiar with the lives of Marie D'Oignies and Elizabeth of Hungary.[49] She knew Elizabeth well from the *Old Swedish Legendary,* a collection of saints' lives and church history based on Jacobus de Voragine's popular *Legenda aurea* (from 1260), which was of great importance to Birgitta, even in her youth.[50] She probably became acquainted with Marie through Magister Mathias, who referred to her exemplary life, described in Jacques de Vitry's hagiography from around 1215.[51] As Päivi Salmesvuori has convincingly argued, both

Marie and Elizabeth offered models to Birgitta in terms of how to live a religious life and strive for sanctity, despite not being a virgin: they legitimated ways of performing piety in practice, so, by imitating them, Birgitta could easily fashion her saintly widowhood and achieve similar authority.[52] However, in addition to Marie D'Oignies and Elizabeth of Hungary, there were other saintly, unmarried women as well, such as Hildegard of Bingen (1098–1179) and the Beguine Mechtild of Magdeburg (1208–1289 / 1294), both of whom produced substantial literary works.[53]

But far less explored, and possibly of great importance to Birgitta, especially after her arrival in Italy, was the figure of the widowed Rome. Birgitta came to Rome not long after Cola di Rienzo's revolution in 1347, and this was still a period of intermezzo before Cola returned and his government was reestablished. Although Birgitta never comments on the many polemical frescoes of the widowed Rome that Cola had commissioned, it is difficult to imagine that they did not make an impact on her. In fact, she never mentions Cola, who was probably a subject for discussion and gossip all over Rome. Nor does she mention Petrarch.[54] If they did meet, it may have been through the Colonna family, with whom both Birgitta and Petrarch were closely connected, but the sources do not tell us this.

Despite the absence of Cola and Petrarch from Birgitta's oeuvre, they may have had some influence. The pictures commissioned by Cola of the widowed Rome must have been striking to the newly arrived Swedish widow in their size, their vivid colors, and their theatricality. The most conspicuous of them were probably the frescos at the Senators' Palace at the Capitoline Hill, where Rome was depicted as a mourning widow, dressed in black, kneeling, with the inscription "Questa ène Roma" (This is Rome). Like this figure, and like Petrarch's metrical epistle (*Epystole* II, 5) that preceded it, where Petrarch retrieved the widow's words from the book of Lamentations, Birgitta uses the rhetorical doctrine of the *personificatio:* "I, a widow" (*ego vidua*), and this in one of her earliest letters from the Roman period that may show it made a certain impression on her.[55]

Similar to Cola's and Petrarch's metaphorical programs, Birgitta spins subtle threads between Rome and the New Jerusalem. In one of her most famous visions (*Rev.* III, 27), also from the period just after her arrival, Birgitta clearly vents her frustration through the voice of Mary: "If all the gardens of the whole world were to be brought alongside Rome, Rome would certainly be as great as to the number of martyrs (I am speaking materially), because it is the place chosen for the love of God. . . . Today I can say of Rome what the prophet said of Jerusalem: 'Once righteousness lodged in her and her princes were princes of peace. Now she has turned to dross and her princes have become murderers.'"[56]

In the quotation, she retrieves the words of the prophet Isaiah's strong condemnation of Jerusalem (1:21):

> See how the faithful city
> has become a prostitute!
> She once was full of justice;
> righteousness used to dwell in her—
> but now murderers!

In Birgitta's vocabulary, however, like Petrarch's and Cola's apocalyptic configurations, the condemnation of Jerusalem transforms into the blaming of Rome. Cola's and Petrarch's depictions of the suffering of Rome widowed also have much in common with Birgitta's desperate cry that soon follows:

> O Rome, if you knew your days, you would surely weep and not rejoice. Rome was in olden days like a tapestry dyed in beautiful colors and woven with noble threads. Its soil was dyed in red, that is, in the blood of the martyrs, and woven, that is, mixed with the bones of the saints. Now her gates are abandoned, in that their defenders and guardians have turned to avarice. Her walls are thrown down and left unguarded, in that no one cares that the souls are being lost. Rather the clergy and the people, who are the walls of God, have scattered away to work for carnal advantage. The sacred vessels are sold with scorn, in that God's sacraments are administered for money and worldly favors.[57]

The notion that this quotation conveys is the sacredness of Rome: The birth, life, and suffering of the martyrs, their blood and bones, have consecrated the city's ground. Rome has literally become a reliquary and is therefore a holy place. However, the city that she encountered by the end of 1349, and that the quoted passage describes, is a vandalized city far from the glorious picture she painted in her vision in Sweden. Rome is abandoned and it has been usurped by fraudsters and criminals.[58] As Mary concludes the vision, the decline started already with Pope Boniface VIII: "Such is Rome, as you have seen it physically. Many altars are abandoned, the collection is spent in taverns, and the people who give to it have more time for the world than of God. But you should know that countless souls ascended into heaven from the time of humble Peter until Boniface ascended the throne of pride."[59] The throne of pride, which Boniface once climbed and where the popes in Avignon still linger, is the seat of Antichrist, an image that once again reveals the prophetic aspect of Birgitta's speech. It connects her to the apocalyptic images of Cola and Petrarch, as well as to the contemporary Franciscan Spirituals.

CONVINCING THE POPE

The letter from Santa Maria Maggiore is written to a cleric of high rank—"Honorable Father," as Birgitta calls him. Who this cleric actually was is unsure, but he is usually referred to as the papal legate in Rome, Cardinal Annibaldo Ceccano. What is of importance, though, is that the letter was composed during the reign of Pope Clement VI, who, as we have seen in Chapter 4, appreciated the matrimonial motifs of widowed sorrow and nuptial joy, as well as of the bridegroom who comes to rescue his bride, the city of Rome. Thus, applying the metaphor of the widow, Birgitta is using a language already favored by the Avignon papacy, and her intention may well have been that the letter should be forwarded to the pope. Indeed, Birgitta's connection to Clement was well established when she wrote this letter. During her first four years in Rome, she lived in a house owned by the cardinal of San Damaso, the brother of Pope Clement, a house that was adjoined to the church of San Lorenzo in Damaso, where we today may find the Palazzo della Cancelleria.[60]

In Sweden, Birgitta had already sent a message to Pope Clement. Among the visions that were brought to Avignon in order to obtain papal approval was a letter addressed to Pope Clement VI in which Birgitta writes as follows (*Rev.* VI, 63): "The Son speaks to the bride: 'Write the following words on my part to Pope Clement: I exalted you and let you ascend through all the ranks of honor. Rise up and establish peace between the kings of France and England, who are like dangerous beasts, betrayers of souls. Then come to Italy and preach the word there and proclaim a year of salvation [the Jubilee] and divine love! Look on the streets paved with the blood of my saints, and I shall give you an everlasting reward.' "[61]

In the revelation, Birgitta strongly condemns Clement for being partisan in supporting the French side in the conflict with England; this may be partly true, since Clement had previously been a papal legate to King Philip the Fair. Indeed, despite the pope's many attempts to create peace between the two fighting kingdoms, Birgitta is harsh: If he does not take heed of what Christ had told her, the punishment will be severe, she prophesies. Christ will castigate him for his lukewarmness in the reestablishment of peace, and it will not be forgotten how greed and ambition flourished and increased in the church during his papacy.

The central idea in the letter from Rome to Pope Clement (*Rev.* IV, 78) is that the reform of the Catholic Church and the return of the pope to Rome are two sides of the same coin. The one question could not be divided from the other. As Vauchez has described it, "From the start, Birgitta's prophetic mission was directed at the reform of the church, beginning with the papacy, which was conditioned on its return to Rome."[62] What became pressing after her arrival in Rome, however, were the tensions between her ideal city—the Rome that she expected to see when she left Sweden, the sacred city, where there was a *brevior via* between heaven and earth—and the reality of Rome, the *fracte urbis,* "with its buildings tumbling in ruin, its unworthy and greedy prelates, and its restless populace always ready to riot."[63] In other words, the reform of the church depended on the restoration of the city—and vice versa. The legitimacy of papal power and of the Catholic Church was simply inseparable from Rome.

The question of Rome came to dominate Birgitta's letters to the Avignon popes in the years to come. Several of these letters are collected at the end of book IV of her *Revelaciones,* a compilation often called *Tractatus de summis pontificibus.* This group of letters did not appear in Alfonso Pecha's first redaction (from 1377–1378) of the revelations, perhaps because of their sensitive content, which could harm the future saint's reputation.[64] Another theory, proposed by Arne Jönsson, is that Alfonso compiled the letters with the intention of gaining support for Pope Urban VI in his conflict with the antipope, Clement VII, during the Great Western Schism. As the letters show, Birgitta's will was that the pope should reside in Rome. According to Jönsson, then, Birgitta's "insistence on Rome as home of the popes, the vilification of everything connected with Avignon, the call for reform, the violent protest against simony and a clear anti-cardinalism, were messages with renewed relevancy after the outbreak of the Great Schism, and was particularly applicable after Clement's departure for Avignon in the summer of 1379, when the anti-Avignon revelations gained relevance in a new context."[65]

Whatever may be correct regarding the compilation of *Tractatus de summis pontificibus,* the group of letters gathered in the last part of book IV gives us a clear picture of Birgitta's commitment to the question of Rome. The first four letters (*Rev.* IV, 132–135) discuss the contemporary priesthood. As Christ tells Birgitta in the first of these letters (*Rev.* IV, 132), the priests teach love of the world rather than speaking about Christ's miracles. They have lost the key to heaven, but have kept the one that leads to hell. They make a wicked man out of a righteous one, a devil out of a simple-hearted one, and a wounded man out of a healthy one. They are even worse than Judas, and they treat Christ as the Jews once did, by crucifying him. In the letter that follows (*Rev.* IV, 133), Christ compares himself to Moses, who liberated the Christian people. The modern-day priests, however, neglect him and love a golden calf instead. They treat him like an idol, and have locked up their liberator so he cannot leave. The next letter (*Rev.* IV, 134), ends with a sigh: "My bride, see how priests treat me! I chose them from among all the angels and other men, and honored them above them all. However, they provoke me more than all the Jews and Gentiles and more than all the demons."[66] Finally, the nuptial metaphors are taken up again in the last of this group of letters (*Rev.* IV, 135): "I am like a bridegroom who leads his bride lovingly into his home. Thus did I join priests to myself with my own body, so that they might be in me and I in them. However, they respond to me like an adulteress to her bridegroom: 'Your words displease me. Your wealth is meaningless. Your desire is like poison. There are three others I prefer to love and follow.' "[67]

Despite the fierce tone in Birgitta's rebukes of contemporary priests, her criticism never targets the church as a historical institution. Rather the opposite: the miserable state of the papal city required the immediate return of the pope. After these reprimands of clerics, there follows a group of letters addressed to the four successive popes—to Clement VI, Innocent VI, Urban V, and finally Gregory XI—in which she persistently tries to convince them to return to Rome. Strongly believing in reconciliation rather than in a rupture between the emperor and the pope, Birgitta attempted to persuade Emperor Charles IV to come to Rome as well. Like Dante and Petrarch before her, she embraced the traditional unity of the two authorities, in which the emperor's role was to protect the church rather than being a purely secular leader. In 1368, then, Birgitta's vision in Sweden, in which she was required to stay in Italy until she could see the supreme pontiff and the emperor there at the same time, appeared for a short moment to be fulfilled: on 21 October, Pope Urban V and Emperor Charles IV made their ceremonial entry into Rome—the pope riding a palfrey, whose bridle was held by the emperor.[68] A few days later, on All Saints' Day, Charles's young wife, Elizabeth of Pomerania, was crowned empress in the church of Saint Peter.

In the canonization materials, the general confessor at Vadstena, Magnus Petri, confirmed that he was present when the pope and emperor entered Rome.[69] Birgitta reportedly met the emperor in person, to appeal both for help in reforming the church and for reconciling Europe. Moreover, of great interest is that Emperor Charles IV was one of those who signed the application for her canonization in 1377. Likewise, as an owner of one of the earliest copies of Birgitta's *Revelaciones,* the book should have been one of his favorite works for reading.[70]

Birgitta also met Pope Urban V, who, soon after his arrival, came to show his continuous preference for France rather than for Rome and the neighboring states. In the summer of 1370, Urban escaped the city and moved to his splendid castle of Montefiascone, where the magnificent view of the Apennines is still reflected in the deep waters of Lake Bolsena, as Guillaume Mollat once so poetically put it.[71] In the summer of 1370 Birgitta, obviously furious, traveled to Montefiascone to convince the pope to return to Rome. In a revelation (*Rev.* IV, 138) she urged Urban to "go back to Rome and Italy for no other purpose than to carry out mercy and justice, strengthen the catholic faith, re-establish the peace and, in this way, renew the Holy Church."[72] After these instructions, a severe threat follows, and once again it is Mary who speaks, testifying to the figure from whom Birgitta drew her authority. If the pope returned to Avignon, a cruel fate awaited him: "As a mother carries her child to the place she likes before uncovering her breasts for him, so I led Pope Urban by my prayer and the work of the Holy Spirit from Avignon to Rome without any physical danger whatever. What did he do to me? . . . If it does happen that he returns to the country where he was elected pope, within a short time he shall be struck with a blow that will knock his teeth out. His sight will become cloudy and darkened, and he will tremble in every limb of his body."[73]

A few weeks later, in September 1370, Urban set sail from Corneto to Marseille. The kings of France and Aragon, Queen Joanna of Naples, and the inhabitants of Avignon and Provence supported the cortege of thirty-four ships, and on 27 September the court entered Avignon. In November, however, the pope fell ill, and on Thursday, 19 December, he died, an event that only strengthened Birgitta's position as a saintly prophet. Her prophecies were, in other words, deemed to have been fulfilled.

THE FLIGHT TO JERUSALEM

Whether it was because of her disappointment about failing to convince Pope Urban to return to Rome, or because of a wish to realize an old dream, we do not know, but soon after her return from Montefiascone, Birgitta once again received a call to go to Jerusalem, a pilgrimage that turned out to be her last, frantic attempt to save the *Ecclesia Romana.* She had received similar calling visions before, both in Arras on her and her husband's return from Santiago de Compostela in 1341,[74] and in Sweden in 1349. By the end of *Liber questionum,* the long revelation that Birgitta received just before she left for Italy and that constitutes the fifth book of her *Revelaciones,* Christ suggests that she would travel to the Holy Land in person to see the five places associated with his humanity—Jerusalem, Bethlehem, Calvary, the Garden of the Sepulchre, and the Mount of Olives (*Rev.* V, 13). In May 1371 Christ reportedly appeared to her again, saying that she should prepare for a pilgrimage to the Holy Sepulchre (*Rev.* VII, 6).

Her experiences from this final pilgrimage are gathered in the seventh book of the *Revelaciones*. It is a remarkable book, partly because of the dense biographical details, such as meetings with friars, knights, and courtiers, encounters with Queen Joanna I of Naples and Queen Eleanor of Aragon in Cyprus, and the descriptions of the dangers and challenges that such a long journey entailed. Another reason that makes the seventh book unique is the beauty, the high aesthetic standard of some of the revelations she received during the trip, such as the two famous visions of the Crucifixion and the Nativity (*Rev.* VII, 15 and 21), which reveal an author at the peak of her intellectual and imaginative capacity. Perhaps the most striking aspect of the seventh book, however, is the intense political implications of some of the visions. Throughout the book we find revelations about purely secular matters, which reveal both the authority and the reputation that Birgitta had now gained. As Morris has argued, "By this point in her life she had gained an authority and could command an audience which enabled her to issue her messages more forcefully than before, having them read from pulpits and in public places, gathering high-ranking audiences to attend."[75] This is what happened both in Cyprus and in Naples, where she had longish stopovers, and where she was involved in political events of both local and international dimensions. However, the overriding question in the seventh book is the Roman one—the return of the papacy and the reformation of the church. As such, the pilgrimage bears witness to aspects that transcend Birgitta's personal salvation.

Before she left Rome, Birgitta had already written to the newly elected Pope Gregory XI, whom she had met in Montefiascone, but then as Cardinal Pierre Roger de Beaufort. In 1370 she received a revelation in which Pope Gregory was compared to a little child lying naked and cold on the ground. But as Birgitta prophesies, Mary will lift him up like a true mother, caress him gently, warm him with her bosom, and feed him with her milk, if only he returns to Rome (*Rev.* IV, 139). In the following letter, also from 1370, she once again instructs the pope to return, but now threatening that if he does not obey, "the lands of the church, which now obey him in united obedience and submission, will be divided in many parts at the hands of the tyrants."[76] It is difficult not to understand this threat as warning of a possible schism. As Birgitta saw it, and as she clearly expresses it here, the pope's stay in Avignon fundamentally jeopardized the church and the papal supporters in the form of a split of the Catholic Church and the loss of papal territories to other lords, above all to the Visconti family in northern Italy. The Viscontis were often called tyrants, and the papacy had been in conflict with them more or less since the very beginning of the stay in Avignon.

Birgitta's support for the papacy is most carefully negotiated in book VII of her *Revelaciones*. On the one hand, she reiterates her call for reform of the church. On the other, she defends the terrestrial and juridical power of the papacy. The danger of a schism and, simultaneously, a justification of the pope's terrestrial authority are repeated in a vision written in the same period as the letter to Pope Gregory (*Rev.* VII, 8). Just before she set out for her long journey to Jerusalem, she received a vision in the mighty Santa Maria Rotunda (Pantheon) in Rome. The vision is written as an answer to a Franciscan friar, and Mary recounts that Pope John XXII's constitution *Cum inter nonnullos* contained no error or heresy regarding the Catholic faith. As discussed in Chapter 3, this constitution from 1323 rejected the doctrine that Jesus and the Apostles owned nothing either individually or as a group, a central notion in the Franciscans' ideal of Christian poverty. The constitution brought about harsh inquisitorial processes against the Spirituals, which were met with strong opposition even among the more moderate Franciscans. However, as Mary tells Birgitta, "Indeed I, who gave birth to the true God himself, bear witness that my son Jesus Christ had *one* personal possession, and that he was its sole owner. This was his tunic that I made with my own hands. The prophet testifies to this saying in the person of my Son: 'For my garment they cast lots.'"[77]

This represents a careful but precise intervention in the contemporary Franciscan controversy. Birgitta argues that Christ did have ownership, although in the modest form of the tunic that his mother made when he was a boy. The tunic has long traditions in the history of Christianity, which will not be repeated here.[78] However, of importance in our context is that the tunic was an image often used to represent the church. In the biblical story, which Birgitta also refers to, the tunic was described as seamless, and therefore indivisible. According to the Gospel of John, the soldiers did not divide Christ's tunic after crucifying him. They instead cast lots to decide who would keep it, because the tunic was woven in one piece and was seamless and could thus not be torn (Jn 19:23–24). However, the Schism in the 1380s when the church split into two, and for a short period even into three factions, with three contemporaneous popes, was often described by contemporary authors as a division of the seamless tunic.

Pope Boniface VIII had used the biblical story of the seamless tunic as an image of the profound unity of the church in his bull *Unam Sanctam* in 1302. As emphasized in the introduction of this book, the bull paved the way for the Avignon papacy: "We venerate this Church as one. . . . He [the Lord] has prayed for his soul, that is for himself, heart and body; and this body, that is to say, the Church, He has called one because of the unity of the Spouse, of the faith, of the sacraments, and of the charity of the Church. This is the tunic of the Lord, the seamless tunic, which was not rent but which was cast by lot."[79]

Another contemporary source for the image of the seamless tunic is the French soldier and author Philippe de Mézières's poem *Le songe du vieil pèlerin* (Song of the old pilgrim) from 1388. As an image of the church, Philippe describes how the institution is torn into two halves, and divided into two pieces.[80] In Birgitta's vision we find a similar meaning as in Philippe's later text, with the consequence that the tunic becomes a key to criticizing the secular power and wealth of the church. The image of the tunic, in all its simplicity, calls for a reform of the current situation, but at the same time it defends the *Ecclesia Romana* as a physical, historical institution, which could not be divided as the schismatics intended, nor abolished, as the most eager Spirituals maintained.

A similar complex balance between critique and defense appears in one of Birgitta's last visions from her trip to the Holy Land. Placed between the two majestic visions of the Passion and the Nativity, where Christ's clothing reappears as a principal topic—both the textile that Mother Mary prepared, in which she swaddled her newborn son, and the strips of fabric she later used to shroud the dead Christ—there is a vision of far more profane character (*Rev.* VII, 20). Its form is that of a letter addressed to a Franciscan friar, Martin of Aragon, who was a secretary to Queen Eleanor of Cyprus. During Birgitta's stay at Queen Eleanor's court on her way to Jerusalem, Martin asked for her advice about doubts regarding the observance of the rule of his order. In Jerusalem, Christ gave her an answer, explaining that friars who violated the vow of poverty wounded the entire Franciscan order, and as an example he recounts the tale of a cleric who, tempted by the devil, entered the order of the spiritual and devoted brothers. His motivation was to gain worldly honor, bodily pleasure, and wealth, and the way to obtain these things was to disguise himself as humble and obedient. "With this intention and desire," Birgitta writes, "he entered the order and the devil immediately entered his heart."[81]

A striking aspect about Birgitta's journey to Jerusalem is that it seems to strengthen the political intensity of her revelations, as if the *axis mundi*, the holy center of the world, where the incarnation and the resurrection once took place, provides her with new power. Her pilgrimage to the Holy Land subtly brings the worldly and the celestial perspectives together, reflected in the many shifts between political and religious revelations, culminating

in the vision of the false friar placed between the two visions of the Passion
and the Nativity. As such, the expedition resembles one of the richest and
most beautiful descriptions of human pilgrimages from the contemporary
literature, namely Dante's *Divine Comedy*, where the traveler never loses
sight of the world during his spiritual journey. When he ascends to the heavenly Jerusalem, the wanderer in the *Divine Comedy* keeps turning his head
back to look at the globe, which should perhaps appear more insignificant
the greater the distance becomes. But when Dante turns around, he relapses
into the violent conflicts of his time. From the top of Purgatory Mountain,
rising on the other pole of the earthly Jerusalem, as well as from the peace
of Paradise, readers are repeatedly hurled back to contemporary historical
and political events, seemingly more urgent than ever before. In *Paradiso*
XXVII, for instance, he bitterly renounces Pope Clement V's and John
XXII's thirst for Christian blood (*Par.* XXVII, 58–59). The point is clear—the
pilgrim's divine perspective offers a more profound understanding of
the ongoing battles in Italy and Europe. And Dante's aim, as with all medieval pilgrims, is to return home with his newly gained divine insight. As
such, the pilgrimage is not a flight from the world—rather the opposite:
the experiences from the journey provide the traveler with a new responsibility to discern the abuses, violence, and injustices of the world and react
against them.

The same might be said about Birgitta's pilgrimage to the Holy Land. Indeed, the two perspectives, both political and religious, more or less converge
when she finally reaches her goal, condensed in the vision of the unfaithful
friar who heralds the vision of the Nativity. The two visions underscore the
desperation of her final pilgrimage: aged almost seventy, Birgitta is not
only about to come to her life's end—the Western Church is also suffering
from one of its most profound crises. In general, the visions gathered in
the seventh book reflect the widow's will to save the *Ecclesia Romana*, even
more than her own soul, as one might expect to be the overall aim of a
medieval pilgrimage. This is confirmed by one of Birgitta's last revelations,
dated to 1373 in Naples, on her return from Jerusalem to Rome (*Rev.* VII,
30): "Hear ye, all my enemies living in the world, for I am not speaking to my
friends who obey my will. Hear ye, all priests, archbishops, bishops, and all
those of lower rank in the church! Hear ye, kings and princes and judges of
the earth and all servants! Hear ye, women, princesses and all ladies and
maid-servants! Everyone of any condition and rank, all those great and small
who inhabit the earth, all of you, hear the words that I, your Creator, address
to you now."[82]

The passage shows Birgitta's tremendous impatience: she now turns to
all ranks of people, irrespective of sex or social class, and the Creator him-

self provides her the authority required—"nunc loquor ad vos!" (now I speak to you!). To a certain extent, Birgitta's political activity confirms Vauchez's assertion that the new stream of fourteenth-century women prophets and visionaries, for whom Birgitta was the "fountainhead," did not promote any subversion of the established order.[83] Birgitta's desire for reform usually started with an attempt to persuade the top of the ecclesiastical hierarchy. Nonetheless, there is something profoundly rebellious about the quoted passage. A laywoman, and even a widow, addresses the broad spectrum of people, and the vision openly calls for a reform of all the members of the church, not only its leaders. Hence, fortified by her newly gained experiences in Jerusalem, Birgitta now returns to her ordinary life in Italy in order to fight her last battle—that of bringing the pope back to Rome.

THE LAST DAYS

From the picture of Birgitta painted by the sources, it is easy to imagine her love for Rome. According to several witnesses during her canonization process, she had become a familiar face in the city. Every day and in all kinds of weather this energetic woman would run along the streets and into the churches and the many holy shrines of Rome.[84] She visited the hospitals to care for patients and she helped the poor, sometimes by begging in the streets herself, since she had handed over all her belongings to Magister Peter, in accordance with her vow of poverty.[85] And Margery Kempe (ca. 1373–1438), the later English mystic who was a great admirer of the Swedish saint, wrote that she was told by one of the servants in Birgitta's household in Rome, when she visited the room in which Birgitta died, that Birgitta "was kind and meek to every creature and that she had a laughing face."[86]

Notwithstanding her vitality, Birgitta was probably tired after her long trip, mostly on foot, to Jerusalem. Not long after her return, she died, but before she did she managed to write at least two letters to Pope Gregory XI, both dated February 1373. In the first one (*Rev.* IV, 142), she once again links the return of the pope and the reformation of the church. Come to Rome as soon as you can, she writes, and as soon as you have come, start the process of reform: "Come, then, and do not delay! Come not with our customary pride and worldly pomp, but with all humility and ardent love! As soon as you have thus come, uproot, pluck out and destroy all the vices of our court. . . . Start to reform the church that I purchased with my own blood in order that it may be reformed and led back spiritually to its pristine state of holiness, for nowadays more veneration is shown to a brothel than my Holy Church."[87]

In the following letter (*Rev.* IV, 143), she acts as a counselor, but this time she intervenes in questions of a more profane character. In this, probably one of her final letters before leaving this world, it is as though she cannot resist trying to save it, for the very last time: "Concerning the dispute between the pope and Barnabò," she writes, "I answer that it is loathsome to me beyond measure, for numberless souls are in peril because of it. It is therefore my will that they should reach an agreement."[88] Birgitta refers here to the conflict that had recently escalated between the pope and the Visconti family. Bernabò was the ambitious and ruthless nephew of Giovanni Visconti, whom Birgitta met in Milan on her way to Rome in 1349. On his uncle's death in 1354, Bernabò and his brothers, Matteo and Galeazzo, inherited his power just when Pope Innocent VI was trying to create order in the Papal States and reestablish the authority of the Holy See in Italy. In this task Pope Innocent received, as discussed in the introduction, help from an experienced warrior, the grand *signore* Cardinal Gil Álvarez Carrillo de Albornoz. Cardinal Albornoz was even offered the tiara after Innocent's death, but he refused it, resulting in Urban V's election.

Although Albornoz's campaign was highly successful, his trickiest enemy was Bernabò Visconti. He was given precious support from Emperor Charles IV, who, as we have seen, was on excellent terms with the pope, unlike his predecessor, Ludwig of Bavaria. As Yves Renouard has described it, "Charles IV might treat papal authority over the Empire cavalierly in Germany, but in Italy his attitude was an enormous assistance to Albornoz's reconquest: a friendly Emperor who would raise no difficulties made it much easier for the pope to go home."[89] It was this alliance that had once made an encounter possible between the pope and the emperor in Rome in 1368, which Birgitta had experienced. For a while the Visconti family seemed under control. But soon after the meeting in Rome, the conflict broke out again, and in 1372 Pope Gregory XI renewed the papal attack on the Viscontis, whose head was Bernabò.

Birgitta's last letter to Gregory reveals how politically well informed she was, and also her desire to support the papal party in the feud. Still, as she admits, the pope's return to Rome was hindered by the conflicts. An agreement was essential, although it would require a humiliation of the pope. As she writes, "Even if the pope were to be expelled from his papacy, it would be better for him to humble himself and come to an agreement, should the occasion present itself, than to allow so many souls to perish in eternal damnation."[90]

In short, these letters from the last years of Birgitta's life indicate both an active correspondence between her and the pope's court in Avignon, and Birgitta's increasing frustration with the pope's hesitation. What effect these letters had, and how decisive Birgitta's voice was for the pope's final return, we do not know. But according to a note written by her youngest daughter, Katherina Ulfsdotter, who stayed with her in Rome, Gregory must have held Birgitta in high esteem. In a letter from 1378 addressed to the Swedish archbishop, Katherina wrote that the pope reportedly had a picture of Birgitta in his papal chamber in Avignon, and she expresses her surprise that her mother was better known in Italy than in her native land.[91]

Birgitta never experienced the final return of the pope, and her rule was not ratified until after her death. She died one summer's day in Rome, on 23 July 1373, and she was buried a few days later, in accordance with her own wish, at the monastery of San Lorenzo in Panisperna. Many of the sisters there, whom Birgitta had befriended during her long stay in the city, came from the Roman nobility, such the Colonna and Orsini families. Immediately after her death, however, the process of canonization started, in which Alfonso came to play a central role. Simultaneously, preparations were made to bring her body back to Sweden. After a long and tiring journey through Europe, the cortege arrived the next summer at Vadstena, where her remains still are buried today.

CHAPTER 6

CATHERINE OF SIENA AND THE MYSTICAL BODY OF THE CHURCH

he letter of February 1373 to Pope Gregory XI in which Birgitta of Sweden called for reform of the Church and the immediate return of the papacy to Rome was based on one of
her final revelations. At Birgitta's request, the letter was taken
to Avignon in person by her confessor, Alfonso Pecha da Vadaterra.[1] During
his visit to Avignon, however, Birgitta died, and shortly afterward Alfonso
was sent by Gregory to Siena to meet Caterina Benincasa. Despite her
young age—she was only twenty-six years old—and despite her being a
laywoman from the Sienese *popolo grasso,* Catherine had already gained a
wide reputation. According to Suzanne Noffke, the pope looked to her as
a potential source of continuing wisdom, for which he had earlier counted
on Birgitta.[2] Alfonso's visit to Siena is reflected in one of Catherine's earliest letters (Letter 127), probably written on March 26 (Palm Sunday) in
1374 and addressed to Bartolomeo Dominici and Tommaso d'Antonio,
usually referred to as Caffarini, in Pisa: "I'll tell you something else. The
pope sent his representative here, the one who was spiritual father to that
countess [Birgitta] who died in Rome. He is the one who for love of virtue
renounced the episcopate, and he came to me in the holy father's name to
say that I should offer special prayer for him and for holy Church, in token
of which he brought me the holy indulgence. Be glad and rejoice, for the
holy father has begun to turn his attention to God's honor and that of holy
Church."[3]

Catherine obeyed the pope's request. In the following years she was im-
mersed in prayers for the Church, as well as for the pope. Perhaps Alfonso's
visit also created a desire for her to imitate Birgitta's authority, as Jane
Tylus has suggested?[4] In any case, Catherine's political engagement, her
attempts to establish peace on the war-ridden Italian peninsula, and her

146

persistent fight for the return of the papacy to Rome increased with an extraordinary fervor in the years to come. In the spring of 1376, she was sent to Avignon by the Florentines to plead the cause of the city that Gregory had placed under an interdict due to serious antipapal revolts. While unsuccessful in this task—Catherine was betrayed by her principals—she achieved something that nobody before her had ever managed: she convinced the pope to return to Rome.

The year after, in the summer and fall of 1377, Catherine stayed at Rocca d'Orcia, about twenty miles from Siena, where she once again worked as a peacemaker in the midst of a fierce political conflict. From there she wrote the famous letter (Letter 272) to her confessor, Raymond of Capua, who had followed Pope Gregory to Rome and who was appointed prior of Santa Maria sopra Minerva, the church where Catherine was to be buried three years later after months of sickness and starvation. The importance of this long letter is reflected in several ways.[5] Toward the end of it, Catherine claims to have received the gift of writing:

> This letter and another I sent you I've written with my own hand on the Isola della Rocca, with so many sights and tears that I couldn't see even when I was seeing. But I was filled with wonder at myself and God's goodness when I thought of his mercy toward his human creatures and his overflowing providence toward me. He provided for my refreshment by giving me the ability to write—a consolation I've never known because of my ignorance—so that when I come down from the heights I might have a little something to vent my heart, lest it burst. Because he didn't want to take me yet from this dark life, he fixed it in my mind in a marvelous manner, the way a teacher does when he gives his pupil a model. Shortly after you left me, I began to learn in my sleep, with the glorious evangelist John and Thomas Aquinas. Forgive me for writing so much, but my hands and tongue run along with my heart.[6]

In addition to her claim of newly gained literacy, this passage makes clear, although more discreetly, that Catherine has a mission to perform sent from above. The mission is symbolically represented by the name Rocca (the rock), and elaborated on in conversations with John the Evangelist, the Gospel writer who thought that the word (*logos*) "enlightens all men" (Jn 1:9), and Thomas Aquinas, the recently canonized theologian of the Dominican order.[7] The letter consists of a long dialogue between a woman (Catherine herself) and Christ. Hence, the letter serves as a draft for her forthcoming book, the *Dialogo della divina provvidenza*. In the book Catherine would explore the disputes about power and justice, recalling both the imagery of the biblical Apocalypse and contemporary discussions of the role of the church. However, in both the letter from Rocca d'Orcia and in the *Dialogo,* the question of the church—Christ's bride—is of superior significance.

Implicitly evoking Thomas Aquinas's notions of Corpus Christi, the gift of the sacraments, which remains uncorrupted even though offered by corrupt priests, she opens the letter to Raymond as follows: "Take heart, dearest father, where Christ's dear bride is concerned, for the more bitter troubles she experiences, the more divine Truth promises to make her overflow with sweet consolation. And this will be her sweetness: reform by means of good holy pastors who are flowers of glory, who give God glory and the fragrance of virtue. This reform concerns the flowers [only], her ministers and pastors. The fruit of this bride has no need of reform, because this is never diminished or spoiled by the sins of her ministers."[8] Here Catherine touches on the problematic but still most fundamental ecclesiastical question at the time—the dual aspect of the church. On the one hand, the church is regarded in the Aristotelian tradition of the body politics as a hierarchical, juridical institution subject to change and reform; on the other hand, the Pauline aspects of the church—the eternal and uncorrupted body of Christ—are accentuated.

This chapter will investigate how Catherine of Siena masterfully came to negotiate these questions in her book *Dialogo.* Like Birgitta, she worked eagerly to persuade the pope to return to Rome, which she argued would involve comprehensive reform of the church. However, Catherine's highly original contribution to the debates about the legitimacy of power was to remind the pope about what she considered to be the sacred core of the church. The foundation of the pope's authority was the Eucharist or the *corpus verum,* consecrated and shared by the vicar of Christ and by the many priests spread throughout Christendom—the "anointed christs on earth," as she called them. In her *Dialogo,* as well as in several letters both to Pope Gregory XI and to Urban VI, she recurrently warns of the *corpus verum* being ignored in the constantly growing fabric of the *corpus mysticum.* The result is a cracking church, a body threatened by discord and splits.

Catherine emphasized the urgency of the question with her own physical suffering. As we shall see toward the end of this chapter, the spectacle of Catherine's bodily renunciation and pain may be understood as a response to the contemporary ecclesiastical crisis, a subject already fully developed in her book *Dialogo.* Before returning to the *Dialogo,* though, we will briefly summarize how Catherine came to establish herself as a leading authority in the years during the Great Western Schism, and in which ways she displayed this authority in her texts.

THE RISE OF A WOOL DYER'S DAUGHTER

What we know about Catherine's life—her childhood and upbringing in Siena, her political activities as a young woman, and her final sufferings in Rome—is mainly based on the hagiographical sources, above all the Dominican friar Raymond of Capua's *Legenda maior*.[9] Catherine and her twin sister, who died shortly after birth, were born as the twenty-third and twenty-fourth children of Lapa and Giacomo di Benincasa in the year the Black Death attacked Italy—an event that came to leave its mark on Catherine as well. She grew up in a family of notaries, merchants, and artisans—her father was a successful wool dyer, and her mother the daughter of a poet.[10] Despite these safe family surroundings, Catherine's childhood and youth took place in a city deeply scarred by pestilence, turmoil, and political tensions. Like with many other citizens of Europe in that period, the terrifying experiences of the Black Death probably spurred on Catherine's religious aspirations. She took a vow of perpetual virginity even as a little girl, she embraced severe regimes such as fasting, self-scourging, and vigils, and as a young woman she joined the group of *mantellate*—a Sienese gathering of female penitents who lived an ascetic, independent life, devoted to serving and nursing the poor and sick in the various hospitals of Siena, without entering a convent or order.[11]

As Raymond depicts it, there is a direct line from Catherine's first vision—supposedly received at the age of six when she saw the Lord, clothed in a pontifical habit, sitting on a throne and surrounded by the apostles Peter, Paul, and John—to what Raymond describes as her mystical marriage to Christ in 1368, shortly after her father's death.[12] Even though Raymond first met Catherine only after she had entered public, political life, it is primarily the young, local saint he depicts, secluded at home or in the neighborhood in the shadows of the Dominican church in Siena. The main part of the *Legenda maior* focuses on her family life or on her life in her hometown, rather than on the events that took place in Avignon, Lucca, Florence, or Rome, which transformed Catherine into the mighty figure she soon became. Raymond does not leave out Catherine's "call" to return to the world after her mystical espousal, but he emphasizes the intensification of her asceticism and humility after she entered the public stage until her death in 1380. Despite her moving around in the word, he stresses how she lived remotely from it through the building of an inner cell, a portrayal that was probably meant to strengthen the image of her saintliness. Thus, as Sofia Boesch Gajano and Odile Redon have argued, Raymond focuses more on Catherine's reluctance to take up a public life than on her actual political activities.[13]

Obviously attempting to compete with the Franciscans' popular saint, who was described by Bonaventure as the Apocalyptic "angel who ascends from the rising sun" (Apoc. 7:2), Raymond portrays Catherine as an angel "descended from the heavens." According to his biography, she experienced a mystical death, received stigmata, and had several Eucharistic visions. In humility and with great patience she reportedly performed miraculous cures, converted sinners and repenting criminals, established peace in Italy, and effected Church reforms. Catherine herself, however, never mentions the mystical espousal in her letters, nor her miraculous cures or her stigmata. In fact, there is, as Karen Scott has convincingly argued, a general discrepancy between her male hagiographers, who emphasize the visionary aspects of Catherine's *vita*—her mission as a mystic—and Catherine's textual self-presentation, where the active and practical aspects of her life are the focus.[14]

According to Raymond, Catherine entered public life after her mystical marriage in 1368. Whether this marriage took place or not, perhaps of greater importance in our context are the events that were unfolding contemporaneously in Rome. In the same period, more correctly in October 1368, Pope Urban V and Emperor Charles IV made their entry to the city. As we have seen in Chapter 5, Birgitta is said to have witnessed their meeting. Because of the Romans' uprisings, though, Urban had to flee to Montefiascone, and shortly after his return to Avignon he died. By the end of 1370, Gregory XI was elected the new pope. About the same time as all these dramatic events took place, Catherine's political activities, as well as her letter writing, were initiated. In the beginning, she worked in her hometown of Siena, but soon the stage was broadened to include the politics of Tuscany, Italy, and even Europe. She was obviously well equipped for this task, as scholars have noted, both by her brothers' connections with Siena's powerful political faction known as the *Dodici*, recently excluded from the government by the *Riformatori*, and by her influential circle of followers or disciples, her *famiglia*, as she preferred to call them, which consisted of an increasing number of laymen and laywomen from Siena's leading families.[15] Furthermore, her emergence in a public role was probably also due to a general cultural climate that privileged female spirituality and prophetic speech.[16] Despite these facts, though, it is still astonishing that an unschooled young woman such as Catherine could win such authority among her contemporaries. From the end of the 1360s, she spent her life as a peacemaker, more or less constantly traveling; as a spiritual adviser; and as an industrious letter writer.

Before she received the letter from Pope Gregory XI, brought to her by Alfonso Pecha, Catherine's activities had mainly been connected to events in her native city. She had, however, earned a wide reputation as a *santa,* a holy woman, and the pope probably contacted her intending to find a new prophetic authority who could bolster his political ambitions, as Birgitta of Sweden had passed away. Shortly after the visit of the Spanish bishop, though, Catherine was summoned to attend the Dominican general chapter in Florence in the summer of 1374. It was probably here that she was assigned the influential Raymond of Capua as her confessor, which resulted in a new turn in her letter writing, as well as her involvement in political and ecclesiastical affairs.

From the perspective of Pope Gregory, Catherine was a useful ally for several reasons. Not only was she intelligent and blessed with rare rhetorical talents, she also contested the corruption of contemporary priests, while strongly defending the papacy and its return to Rome. This combination, in Gregory's view, probably strengthened her authenticity, as was also the case with Birgitta. Pope Gregory had been eager to return to Rome from the very beginning of his government. Despite being Pope Clement VI's nephew and thus well rooted in the culture of Langue d'Oc, he knew Italy well. As a young man he had studied with Baldo degli Ubaldi, a famous lawyer and pupil of Bartolo di Sassoferato in Perugia, and, during Pope Urban V's stay in Rome between 1367 and 1370, he was among his most important cardinals, entrusted with responsibility for the city.[17] For these reasons Gregory XI was clear in his decision to return the Holy See to Rome. This return was delayed, however, because of a series of obstacles, such as the economic challenges arising from the heavy expenses incurred in the building of the papal palace in Avignon, Cardinal Gil Álvarez Carrillo de Albornoz's expensive war with the Visconti, and the resistance of French cardinals, who constituted the majority of the curia. Another reason was the increasing pressure from Florence.

The ruling Guelph party in Florence had been firm in their support for the papacy, and Florentine traders and banking houses enjoyed great success in Avignon. However, the idea of the return of the papacy to Rome was not unequivocally positive from the perspective of the Florentine citizens, and especially not from that of the growing group of *gente nuova,* which challenged the position of the mighty *popolo grasso* of the Guelphs. A return of the papacy represented a threat to Florentine hegemonic ambitions in Tuscany and Italy. With Siena, now governed by the *Riformatori,* who had assumed power after the traditional allies of the pope, the *Dodici,* Florence created a league to which even the Visconti of Milan were extended an invitation. In 1375 the conflict between the papacy and the Florentine league broke out, known as the War of the Eight Saints.

This is the backdrop for Catherine's mission and her interventions on the political battlefields.[18] In the coming years she would work as a peacemaker, attempting both to calm the tempers of the enemies of the papacy and to convince the pope to act more prudently and peacefully in Italy. In addition to the return of the pope to Rome and ecclesiastical reforms, a third point in her political program, intrinsically linked to the two others, was a new crusade. According to Catherine, a crusade, which Pope Gregory had also proclaimed, would put an end to the escalating movement against the church in central Italy by uniting the conflicting parties in a shared undertaking—a common task and agreement that would also make it possible for the pope to return to Rome. Moreover, a crusade would occupy the mercenary troops led by the English condottiere John Hawkwood, who had been engaged on both sides of the wars between the papacy and the Visconti. Because of a short truce between the parties, however, the mercenaries were suddenly left unemployed, which was in itself a threat to potential peace in Italy.

As her letters show, Catherine displayed a remarkable level of engagement in these questions. In early 1375 she traveled to Pisa, and somewhat later to Lucca, to exhort the cities not to enter into an alliance with the antipapal league. In June that same summer she sent her confessor Raymond to Hawkwood's camp with a letter (Letter 140) in which she ardently tried to persuade him and his army to volunteer for the crusade, which Pope Gregory had recently announced. Immediately afterward she wrote to Bernabò Visconti (Letter 28) to gain support for the crusade, and to his wife, Regina della Scala (Letter 29), to encourage her to keep her husband loyal to the papacy. The same summer she wrote her first of several letters to Queen Joanna of Naples, the formal queen of Jerusalem, encouraging her to contribute to the planned crusade as well (Letter 133).

POWERFUL DISCOURSES

More than 380 of Catherine's letters have been preserved—the earliest were written around 1370, while the majority are from 1374, after her meeting with Raymond, until her death. They are addressed to a great variety of people—to secular and ecclesiastical authorities, to kings and queens, to prelates and cardinals, to mendicants, to laywomen and laymen, and even to prostitutes.[19] As Carolyn Muessig has maintained, all these epistles indicate that Catherine had her finger on the pulse of the religious and political world of late medieval Italy.[20] This also applies to her book *Dialogo*.

As for Catherine's literary style, Tylus has carved out a new direction by considering her with the founding figures such as Dante, Petrarch, and

Boccaccio, often labeled *le tre corone* (the three crowns) of Italian literature. By analyzing the interweaving of oral and textual elements in Catherine's work, Tylus presents her as a most self-conscious and dedicated vernacular author. Catherine raised her voice, she explains, armed with the *trecento*'s many connotations—literary and political, as well as religious—of the term *donna,* stemming from the Latin *domina.*[21] In fact, Catherine never played on the supposed inferiority of the female sex in promoting her identity as a prophetic vessel, as earlier mystics like Hildegard von Bingen or even Birgitta of Sweden had done. She is instead reminiscent of Beatrice, who emerges as a *donna* when the wanderer Dante meets her for the first time on his journey: "Donna m'apparve" (*Purg.* XXX, 32: "a woman appeared to me"), one who speaks with authority and wisdom. It is this figure of the Beatrice-like *donna,* and not the weak *femmina,* that Catherine continually returns to, according to Tylus.

Moreover, Catherine's choice of language, the preference for the *volgare* in letters even to addressees who did not know Italian at all, underscores the urgency of her message. She was surrounded by members of the religious elite who knew Latin well and who could easily have translated her spoken or written words, but still she insisted on using the vernacular language. This may be interpreted as a deliberate challenge to the Latinity of the church, as well as to the growing class of humanists who enthusiastically strove for a revival of the classical language of ancient Rome. But what is of equal importance is that with the *volgare,* Catherine draws the attention of her readers and interlocutors to the literal geographical and institutional center of Christianity. As Tylus has argued, Catherine "may well have seen her words as representing Italian vernacular authority in the 'writerly' and Latinate (as well as French) culture of the Avignon papacy, the Dominican order, and more generally, late medieval Europe."[22] Consequently, the use of Italian only underlined the gravity of Catherine's message to reform the church and restore the papacy to its only rightful place, namely, Rome. Her speech was the speech of Rome. And, as we know from history, Catherine's speech was a powerful one.

SERVUS SERVORUM DEI

Catherine's collection of letters contains fifteen epistles to Pope Gregory XI and eight to Pope Urban VI. Together they reflect Catherine's commitment following her call from the end of the 1360s until her death in 1380. In order to grasp the profound anxiety conveyed in her book *Dialogo,* to which we will soon return, it may be useful to dwell briefly on these letters.

The recurrent subjects in the papal letters are the three pillars in Catherine's political program—the planned crusade, the papacy's return to Rome, and the plea for ecclesiastical reforms—all discussed with a prophetic authority. The very first epistle addressed to Pope Gregory XI (Letter 185) sets the tone. It was written shortly after Catherine's visit to Pisa and Lucca and before these cities joined the antipapal league, as becomes clear toward the end of the letter, where she asks the pope to intervene in the conflict by offering his help. The remarkable thing about this epistle is the way she addresses the pope as "her sweetest daddy" (oimè, oimè, dolcissimo Babbo mio).[23] In general, this personal and intimate style characterizes her papal correspondence, despite the fact that her tone in her writing to Urban VI is somewhat more reserved than in that to Gregory XI. The letters often take the form of a personalized homily, as Blake Beattie has noted, which combines the style of humility with a clear expression of what she expects from the pope.[24] Moreover, she persistently uses the rhetorical figures of the humble servant or the poor, foolish girl. The letter to Gregory opens, for instance, with the following phrase: "Your unworthy, poor, and wretched daughter Caterina, servant and slave of Jesus Christ, is writing to you in his precious blood."[25] This humble salutation, however, must be read with care. There is no reason to doubt Catherine's affection and respect for the pope, but to a certain degree this self-presentation only reflects the usual beginnings of papal bulls, where the pope is entitled *servus servorum Dei* (servant of the servants of God). As such, Catherine positions herself, most sophisticatedly, as an infallible source and a prophet to whom it is worth listening. Not unlike the vicar of Christ, she is armed with an authority that originates in God.

In the following letters to Gregory XI, she defends the idea of a crusade by arguing that rather than fighting each other, whether it is the conflict between France and England or between the Italian city-states and the papacy, the different parts of Christendom would be better off turning their military ambitions to the Holy Land. Likewise, she continually underscores that an ecclesiastical reform is closely connected to the papacy's return to Rome, and both of them are essential. As the conflict between the antipapal league and the papacy escalated, Catherine was sent by the Florentines to Avignon in order to moderate Pope Gregory, who had excommunicated thirty-six Florentines and placed the city under interdict. Catherine sent Raymond in advance with a letter to the pope appealing for the cause of peace in Italy and for the pope to be merciful toward the rebellions, and once again we can see how the crusade, the return of the pope, and the ecclesiastical reforms are interlinked (Letter 206):

Oimè! My dear father! I am begging you, I am *telling* you: come! Conquer our enemies with the same gentle hand. In the name of Christ crucified I am telling you! Don't choose to listen to the devil's advisors. They would like to lock your holy and good resolution. Be a courageous man for me, not a coward. Respond to God, who is calling you to come and take possession of the place of the glorious shepherd, Saint Peter, whose vicar you still are. And there raise the standard of the holy cross. For as we were freed through the cross (as said our dear Paul), so by raising this standard (which I see as relief for Christians) we shall be freed—we from war and divisions and many sins, and the unbelievers from their unbelief.[26]

Catherine herself left for Avignon in May 1376, where she arrived a few weeks later, and where she had several encounters with the pope, according to Raymond of Capua. A number of her letters addressed to Gregory were also written in Avignon. Her Florentine mission failed, though, with the consequence that she became even more focused on the need for reformation of the church and the return of the pope and his curia to Rome—and in this last matter she seems to have been successful.

In September 1376 the pope left for Rome, while Catherine stayed in Avignon until November. Thereafter she returned to Siena, only to be sent on a new mission, this time concerning the local government of Siena. In order to negotiate between her native city and the powerful Salimbeni family, she went to Rocca d'Orcia in the province of Siena. In Rome, the conflicts surrounding Pope Gregory's return escalated, and the pope probably blamed Catherine for his decision to leave Avignon. Catherine, for her part, claims in a letter to Raymond, who had followed the pope to Rome, that it was the pope who was responsible for the crisis (Letter 267). He should have listened to her from the very beginning and done what she had told him when he came to Rome. In other words, he should have implemented the ecclesiastical reforms. At the same time, Catherine strongly blames herself for the chaos in Rome. She asks Raymond to convey the following message to the pope: "To his holiness I confess that I have been guilty of great foolishness and negligence against God. I have disobeyed my Creator, who invited me to cry out in restless desire, to cry out before him in prayer, and to be near his vicar with my presence and my words. In every possible way I have sinned outrageously. And I believe it is because of my great wickedness that he and holy Church have suffered these persecutions. So if he complains about me, he has reason to do so, and to punish me for my sins."[27]

Catherine blames herself for not being clear enough in her message. She should have cried out louder, and she should have stayed with the pope in Rome. Her self-accusation is so strong that toward the end of the letter she even writes that she is willing to sacrifice herself for the sake of the church: "In fact, we shall stand in your place to fight courageously for Christ's dear bride [the church], armed with virtue. In her, I want to end my life with tears and sweat and sighs, and give my blood and marrow of my bones for her."[28]

It is during the conflicts in Rome—the Schism was now under way, while Catherine herself was still at Rocca d'Orcia—that she claims to have received the gift of writing. Perhaps she hoped that her book *Dialogo* would have a more powerful impact on the crisis than her own *grida*, her cry, which apparently had not been effective enough. In any case, in the book she would develop more systematically her ideas about legitimacy and reforms, which so far had been conveyed in letters or in conversations.

THE BODY OF CHRIST

Catherine's book *Dialogo della divina providenza,* or simply *il libro* (the book), as she preferred to call it, is written in Italian in the form of a dialogue between her and God. She probably started to compose it immediately after she learned to write in the fall of 1377, and she continued working on it for about a year, until October 1378, when she was summoned to Rome to fight for the recognition of the newly elected pope Urban VI.[29] With her letters and prayers—the twenty-six *orazioni* that she also composed—the book represents a starting point for female literature in Italy. Catherine is in fact the first woman whose work in Italian has survived, and her texts paved the way for prolific production in the decades to come by women connected to monasteries and by secular women, which in itself is a reason to take her authorship seriously. However, the content of the *Dialogo* is also of great importance, especially from the broader perspective of the intellectual debates of fourteenth-century Europe. The text encompasses the central questions of Catherine's theology: the human path to perfection, the gift of the redemptive blood of Christ, the function of tears in the salvation of man, and finally the image of Christ as a bridge to redemption, which is usually considered the central and most important part of the book.[30] However, when we come to the chapters that specifically treat the mystical body of the church (chapters 110–135), we find ourselves at the center of Catherine's speculations, and this is arguably where the true aim of the book is revealed. It is also here that Catherine presents her ideas about ecclesiastical reforms.

Like the letter from Rocca d'Orcia, the book is designed as a conversation with God, who, as we can read in the prologue, "showed her [Catherine] the world's need and how storm-tossed and offensive to God it is."[31] However, in the chapters that treat the question of the mystical body of the church, it becomes clear that the text is primarily addressed to contemporary ecclesiastical authorities. Cloaked in the words of God, Catherine relentlessly thunders against the depraved clergy of her times. "Because things can be better understood by looking at the opposites, I want to show you the dignity of those who use virtuously the treasure I have put into their hands, so that you may better see the wretchedness of those who today are feeding at the breast of this bride."[32] With these words we are placed at the center of Catherine's speculations: by reminding her readers of God's original plan for the church, she presents herself as a prophet, in the biblical sense of the word, who recalls God's promises rather than presenting vague conjecture about the future.

The chapters that discuss the mystical body of the church start with a majestic image of the uncorrupted Corpus Christi, the body of Christ, and Catherine moves swiftly between the body of the Eucharist, the body of the church, and the body of the universal community of Christians, a mixture that was rather common in the Middle Ages.[33] These different aspects of the body, however, are maintained in the image of the sun. As we can read, it is the sun that God has entrusted to the priests: "It is the sun I have given them to administer, for I have given them the light of learning, the heat of divine charity, and the color that is fused with the heat and the light, the blood and body of my Son. His body is indeed the sun, for it is one thing with me, the true Sun. Such is the unity that the one can neither be separated nor cut off from the other, any more than the sun can be divided—neither its heat from its light nor its light from its color, so perfect is its unity."[34]

While the Franciscans focused on the gift of the sun, the light that freely gives itself in abundance to the creation, as expressed in Saint Francis's Canticle of the Sun (*Laudes creaturarum*), Catherine, who moves within the boundaries of the Dominican tradition, stresses its quality as a unifying, unbroken entity. Just as the sun gathers the spectrum of all colors, divine light has in it the color of humanity. The sun is, in other words, an image for the communion, the Christian society of *fideles*. Moreover, like the body of Christ, the sun reflects the whiteness of the bread offered in the Eucharist.[35]

There are two strong traditions for the depiction of the church as a body, which Catherine alternates neatly between in her *Dialogo*. As we have seen in Chapter 2, concerning the body politics of Marsilius of Padua, the associations between the human body and the organization of society are old ones. In Aristotle's *Politics* we encounter the analogies, although the two components were still quite vaguely connected.[36] Likewise, the anthropomorphic idea of the state and the bodily analogy reappeared many times and in different guises in classical literature, from Plato to Seneca and others. Important sources within this tradition are the Aesopic fables (206 and 286) about the members of the body that rebelled against the belly, arguing that they did all the work while the belly just lazily received the food. As already noted, the fables reappeared in *Ab urbe condita* (II, 32, 2–3), where Livy tells the story of Consul Menenius Agrippa and the secession of the plebeians to the Monte Sacro in 494 BCE. In Livy's version, however, the primacy of the belly is replaced by the head, and he thereby established a strong, hierarchical model: as Agrippa explains to the plebeians, the cooperation between the head (the Roman Senate) and the limbs (the plebeians) was essential, and the limbs were necessarily subordinate to the head.

The French historian Jacques Le Goff has discussed the importance of the head (*caput*) in Roman culture. The head, the seat of the brain, he argues, was for the Romans—and for most peoples—the organ that contained the soul (a person's vital force), and that performs the directing function within the body.[37] It was also this model that medieval Christianity adopted from Greco-Roman antiquity. The heart was of course highly important in Christianity as a moral seat and a center for the mystical encounter between man and God. But the value of the head became remarkably strong in the Christian political use of bodily metaphors, reaching its classic definition in the treatise *Policraticus* (1159), by John of Salisbury. In this treatise John suggested that the state (*res publica*) is a body (*corpus quoddam*), and that within that state, the prince occupies the place of the head.[38] In short, John's bodily metaphors defined the functional attributes of various parts of the body politics and underlined the cooperative relationship between them.

The other, and unquestionably the main, source for Catherine's discussion of Corpus Christi is the New Testament. Influenced by Hellenistic culture, Saint Paul described the gathering of believers as multiple limbs connected through Christ to the unity of a single body. As we can read in Saint Paul's epistle to the Corinthians (1 Cor 12:12–14), the body is associated with the church: "For as the body is one, and hath many members, and all the members of that one body, being many, are one body: so also is Christ."[39] Leonard Barkan has noted that there is a rare physicality in this Christian analogy, which did not exist in Greco-Roman culture.[40] The body of Christ is not just an image of the gathering of believers: the Eucharist, reenacting the Last Supper, transforms the host into reality. As the priest declares, holding up the host or the bread, "This is my body which is given for you" (Lk 22:19–22). Although broken and shared, the sacramental host, the real body of Christ, unifies the human and the divine, as well as the congregation of believers, into the mystical body of Christ, which is the church. There is thus a fundamental link between the body politic and the body natural of Christ: indeed, the body politic is not only compared to the physical body of Christ—it is the body of Christ.

These two traditions merge in Catherine's discussions of the church and her call for ecclesiastical reforms. What is equally important, however, is that with her strong insistence on the body of Christ, she proceeds directly to the center of the theology of the Dominican order as well. In their battles with the spiritual and discordant tendencies of the heretical movements, the presence of Christ in the consecrated host and the universal, unifying quality of Christ's body had from the very beginning been imperatives for the Dominicans, and their influence became even stronger with the institutionalization of the feast of Corpus Christi. The feast was declared as late as 1264, probably in the wake of the church's increasing claims of primacy and universality over regional political powers and local liturgical customs, and as the composer of the new liturgy, Pope Urban IV appointed the influential Dominican friar and theologian Thomas Aquinas.[41] What characterizes Thomas's office is that it clearly refutes the heretical trends in certain Eucharistic interpretations that stressed the symbolic and hidden nature of the Eucharist. Miri Rubin has described Thomas's new liturgy as "an office strong in Eucharistic statements articulated in Aristotelian terms, offering a corporeal understanding of a sacramental substance, not veiled but real, which the senses cannot perceive, but faith can recognise."[42] In other words, in contrast to the many heretical movements that the Dominicans aimed to defeat, and that were especially strong in southern France, Thomas powerfully emphasized the real presence of Christ in the Eucharist.

PIOUS AND WICKED SHEPHERDS

In her discussion of the body of Christ, Catherine follows the tradition of the Dominicans, and, as we have already seen, Thomas played a pivotal role in the self-presentation of her own intellectual growth. According to the letter to Raymond quoted at the beginning of this chapter (Letter 272), it was Thomas and the evangelist John who were her teachers. And what is clear from the very beginning of God's discourse on the mystical body of the church in Catherine's Dialogo is that at the center of the image, whether it touches on ecclesiastical, juridical, or spiritual questions, is the consecrated host, administered by the priesthood and divided between all congregations of believers. From God's discourse we may understand that it is this sacrament that makes the priests unique: "They are my anointed ones and I call them my 'christs,' because I have appointed them to be my ministers to you and have sent them like fragrant flowers into the mystic body of holy Church. No angel has this dignity, but I have given it to those men whom I have chosen to be my ministers. I have sent them like angels, and they ought to be earthly angels in this life."[43] Catherine thus acknowledges priestly authority based on their being "christs" on earth, or, as she explains a little later, ministers who ought to provide and nourish people with grace and spiritual gifts.[44] Through God's voice, she recalls the shepherds' original mission: the shepherds, or the priests, derive their power from their gift of being able to administer and share the holy sacrament.

Good priests would do this service in perfect humility, according to Catherine. As God tells her, they are stewards of the sun that give "brightness of supernatural learning, the color of a holy and honorable life in following the teaching of my Truth, and the warmth of blazing charity."[45] As examples of such good priests she mentions Augustine, Jerome, Sylvester, Gregory the Great, and Thomas, who all bore fruit in the church thanks to their virtues and teachings. They celebrated the Mass with a bodily purity and a spiritual sincerity, and as gardeners "with care and holy fear they rooted out the brambles of deadly sin and put in their place the fragrant plants of virtue."[46] Above all, they were good doctors who were not afraid of cutting off "rotten" members from the congregation that could infect the whole body with the filth of deadly sin.[47]

This praise for the good priest functions as a backdrop to Catherine's critique of the present condition of the priesthood. As God says, "I have told you all this so that you may better know how I have dignified my ministers, and thus grieve more over their wickedness."[48] But what has gone awry, according to Catherine? On the contemporary situation she writes that wherever she turns, to the secular or religious, to the clerics or prelates, to the lowly or great, to the young or old, she can see nothing but sin.[49] Nothing, however, displeases God more than sin in the priesthood: "You cannot imagine how much more I despise this sin in these celibates—even more than in ordinary people of the world."[50] Such "wretched priests" disturb the order of creation by turning vices into virtues. They have based their principles and foundation in their own selfish self-centeredness, from which nothing but pride, impurity, and avarice are born. Due to a lack of discernment, they have assumed honor and glory for themselves by seeking higher offices and adornments and delicacies for their bodies. They are stingy, greedy, and avaricious toward the poor, and they have abandoned caring for souls for temporal possessions. They commit simony and usury and they "lustfully" spend the goods of the church on clothes, magnificent steeds, gold and silver vessels, lavish homes, and feasting.[51]

As we have seen from the previous chapters, these images are not particularly innovative or exceptional. Rather, they are part of the fairly common political language of the fourteenth century, especially among critics of the Avignon papacy. We can recognize them from Birgitta's *Revelaciones,* and we have encountered the same dark rhetoric in Dante's *Monarchia,* in Marsilius's *Defensor pacis,* in Petrarch's *Sine nomine,* and in the many Franciscan polemics from the same period. But the important thing is Catherine's strong insistence: Her accusations seem never-ending, even though God restrains himself in his long list of vices: "They [the wretched priests] hound me constantly with so many villainous sins that your tongue could never describe them, and you would faint if you heard them."[52] The worst sin, however, and one on which Catherine dwells especially, is the maltreatment of the Eucharist: "They do not so much as know what the Divine Office is, and even if they say it from time to time they are saying it with their tongue while their heart is far away from me."[53] The vile priests come to the mystery of the sacrament wholly impurely, she continues, and some of them not only do not revere the sacrament but even resort to diabolical incantations, whereupon there follows a long passage of several paragraphs where Catherine, through the voice of God, addresses her speech directly to the priests.

According to Catherine, the clergy and ministers, even the pope himself, are concerned only with the grandeur of rank, nobility, and wealth. Like Lucifer, they have fallen from the light of heaven to the darkness of the abyss. So great has their darkness and wickedness become that they often pretend to consecrate the Eucharist while not doing so at all, which is the greatest of all sins, according to Catherine, because they make idolaters of people by letting them adore a host that is nothing but bread rather than the body of Christ.[54] In this way they lead themselves *and* their children to the brink of deadly sin. As Christ tells her, "O dearest daughter, I set them [the priests] on the bridge of my Truth's teaching to serve you pilgrims with the sacraments of holy Church, and they are instead in the wretched river beneath the bridge, and there in the river of worldly pleasures and baseness they exercise their ministry."[55] As we may grasp from the quotation, contemporary priests were neglecting their original mission. Their attention was turned to secular matters rather than to the salvation of souls through the Eucharistic office. Such neglect is grave and its consequences are fatal, according to Catherine.

THE FRACTURED BODY

Catherine's critique is based on the conviction that only properly ordained priests—the anointed "christs"—have the authority to celebrate the sacrament and consecrate the body of Christ. The legitimacy of their power was founded on the possession of this privilege, which, with the weapon of excommunication—"to cut off rotten members from the congregation"[56]—was the secret of empire by which the church tried to govern a tempestuous world. However, by accentuating the centrality of the Eucharist, Catherine does not only recall the feast of Corpus Christi and the authority of her teacher, Thomas Aquinas, who was in fact canonized by the Avignonese pope John XXII in 1323. She goes directly to the heart of the political and theological debate that had dominated the entire Avignon period, namely, the question of the secular power of the church.

In his now classic study *Corpus Mysticum: The Eucharist and the Church in the Middle Ages*, Henri Lubac has explored how the concept of the mystical body of the church was radically transformed in the late thirteenth and early fourteenth centuries.[57] He describes how the transformations were connected to the increasing jurisdiction and temporal influence of the church, and how this resulted in the bizarre detachment of the concept from any liturgical connotations. "It would be common," he argues, "to speak of 'mystical body' without any references to the Eucharist, to the same extent that theories concerning the Church, whether in its visible form or in its hidden life, would develop outside the sacramental framework."[58] Although Catherine plays no role in Lubac's account, nor in Ernst Kantorowicz's chapter on *Corpus Ecclesia mysticum* in his book *The King's Two Bodies,* a chapter that is largely based on Lubac's research, Catherine's discussions of the mystical body of the church may fruitfully be read within this context.[59]

The events that Lubac analyzes and that he calls both strange and perplexing start with Boniface VIII's notorious bull, *Unam Sanctam* (1302). In fact, the first chronological instance of the appearance of the expression *corpus mysticum* is, according to Lubac, in the opening of this bull, a decree that strongly emphasized the political and juridical sovereignty of the pope, and that, as such, represented an important prelude to the Avignon papacy and the popes' claim to secular power:[60] "Urged by faith, we are obliged to believe and to maintain that the Church is one, holy, catholic, and also apostolic. We believe in her firmly and we confess with simplicity that outside of her there is neither salvation nor the remission of sins . . . and she represents one sole *mystical body* whose Head is Christ and the head of Christ is God."[61]

As already discussed in the introduction of this book, Boniface obviously mobilized the analogy of *corpus mysticum* as a weapon—a claim of the unification of Christendom under the domain of the Catholic Church—against King Philip the Fair of France and his ambitions of national sovereignty. The concept of *corpus mysticum*, however, was older than Boniface's bull, although it was not based on any biblical evidence: it had its origin in the Carolingian period, but only in the sense of the meaning of the Eucharist. However, in the wake of the Lateran council in 1215 and the dogma of transubstantiation, the concept was increasingly applied to the church in its institutional and ecclesiological aspects, while the term *corpus verum* was used for the Eucharist due to the need to emphasize the real presence of Christ in the host. As Kantorowicz has explained, the very same tendencies were occurring in the secular world: The term *corpus mysticum* placed the church as a body politic within the horizon of the Aristotelian anthropomorphic image of the body as a representation of society, as a political and legal organism on the same level as the secular bodies politic. In contrast, the secular world proclaimed itself the holy empire, indicating "the activity of indeed interrelated impulses and ambitions by which the spiritual *corpus mysticum* and the secular *sacrum imperium* happened to emerge simultaneously."[62] In other words, disguised in a strong rhetoric of the sacred, the institutional power of both the church and the state increased considerably in the period before and during the Avignon papacy.

Both Lubac and Kantorowicz have described the development comprehensively, and they emphasize a gradual secularization of the church, discernible chiefly in the construction of the term *corpus mysticum*. When Thomas Aquinas used the term, he emphasized the Aristotelian aspects of the notion by replacing the expression *Corpus Christi mysticum*—the gathering of *fideles* in the Eucharist—with *Corpus Ecclesiae mysticum*—an institution in its own right. However, the term "mystical body" was never completely detached from the sacramental sphere and continued to have sacred or spiritual associations because it recalled the host and the original consecrated sacrifice. However, with Pope Boniface VIII, this changed. In accordance with the bull *Unam Sanctam,* the theologians surrounding the pope, such as Giles of Rome and others who were eager to claim power, would apply only corporational senses to the term, which soon led things astray. As Lubac writes, "But in thus applying to the juridical and social order a word whose resonances were entirely 'mystical' and spiritual, their doctrine would mark a sort of degeneration of the mystical body, exposing ecclesiastical power to the resentment of secular rulers and to the polemics of their theologians."[63]

In the wake of this secularization process of the church, the idea of the pope's plenitude of power was set, while previous thoughts about the kingdom and priesthood as "the two swords" of the world—an idea that, as we previously have discussed, was rooted in the Gelasian theory from the fifth century and repeated later by influential theologians such as Peter Damian and Thomas Aquinas—were now universally condemned. The papal theologians started to proclaim that due to the fear of creating a monster, a single body could only have a single head. This claim was of course modified, rejected, or even turned upside-down by the royal theologians and the defenders of the emperor such as Dante, or, more drastically, by Marsilius of Padua. Dante suggested that there were two heads—the monarch and the pope—but that they were both subject to a superior power, the almightiness of God. For his part, Marsilius, who configured society as a healthy organism in Aristotelian and Galenic terms, localized the legitimacy of power in the human legislator. He even stressed the ruling part of society (*pars principans*) as the heart, and not the head: "For from the soul of the universal body of the citizens or its prevailing part, one part is or should be formed first within it which is analogous to the *heart*. In this the soul instituted a certain virtue or form with the active potential or authority to institute the remaining parts of the city. And this part is the principate, the virtue of which is the authority to judge, command and execute sentences of what is advantageous or just in civil terms."[64]

Thanks to his comparison of the heart and government, Marsilius opposed the traditional Roman-Christian configuration of the ruling part, the prince or the monarch, as the head. As Takashi Shogimen has noted, the intriguing thing about the metaphor of the heart is its possible centralization, which takes place around the civil government or the *pars principans*, and not the vertical hierarchy expressed by the head.[65] However, to a certain degree Marsilius retained the hierarchical structure, but reversed it: the universal body of the citizens possessed plenitude of power, he argued, and the prestige of the priesthood originated wholly from the authority of secular rulers.

REFORMING THE BRIDE

Catherine's discussion of the mystical body of the church must be read within the framework of the conflicts that had raged throughout the century. She seems to be able to discern the potential cost of the disagreements, the threat of schism, while attempting to find a way out of the impasse. The medicine she prescribes is to reclaim the interpretation of the term that was valid before the Avignon papacy. She recalls the understanding of *corpus mysticum* that prevailed before the time of the ambitious theologians surrounding Boniface VIII, and returned it to the folds of the sacramental sphere of the church.

Over a number of paragraphs in her *Dialogo* (from chapter 126 to chapter 129), she writes about "the three pillars of vice" that characterize the "wretched" priests: impurity, avarice, and pride. But at the base of all of them are selfishness and self-centeredness, their total ignorance of their original mission as administrators of the holy sacraments and their striving for power and ecclesiastical rank. The required purity, poverty, and humility of the anointed "christs on earth" are transformed into filth, greed, and arrogance because of their utter selfishness. As she explained some chapters earlier, the priests have lost the right perspective from which to judge things and have made themselves the center of the world, leading to profound injustice from which the entire church is suffering: "I want you, therefore, to know that nothing causes as much darkness and division in the world among laypeople and religious, clergy and shepherds of holy Church, as does the lack of the light of justice and the invasion of the darkness of injustice."[66] This lack of justice is accompanied by the risk that "the whole body [will] become fetid and corrupt."[67] Thus, the problem consists of a secularization of the institution in the *etymological* sense of the word, making earthly success the foundation and the benchmark of power. As she writes, "You have made the world and yourself your god and lord."[68] The "wretched" priests are "blinded by their selfish self-centeredness."[69] They have turned away from the perspective of God, from which one realizes that one is nothing—"by yourselves you are nothing at all"[70]—to a self-sufficiency and a judgment of the church as a body in its own right, independent of its sacramental heart.

According to Catherine, the church is tormented by this selfishness, by the priesthood's profound ignorance of their spiritual mission and the divine origin of their authority. The priests do not do what they ought. They should humbly serve the church and the people by administering the holy sacrament, but instead they seek power, earthly possessions, and pleasure.[71] Because of this confusion, or this loss of true measure, they avoid correcting authorities or persons of importance, even though they may be guilty of greater sins than more lowly people, as they fear that such bigwigs will deprive them of their rank and their way of living. They do, however, correct the little people because they are innocuous.[72] This selfishness has poisoned the entire world and the mystic body of the holy church.

Like so many other critical voices in the Italian *trecento*, Catherine depicts an institution writhing in agony, and the spectacle of her own forthcoming suffering during the Great Schism in Rome would make manifest most tragically what she describes as the pallor of death that had come over the church:

> Indeed, the whole world is corrupt, and they [the wretched priests] behave much more badly than their worldly peers. With their filthiness they defile the face of their own souls and corrupt their subjects and suck the blood of my bride, holy Church. By their sins they have left her pallid. The loving charity they ought to have had for this bride they lavished on themselves, thinking of nothing but snitching her grapes one by one, taking her high offices and lucrative positions when they should have been seeking after souls. Thus their evil lives lead the laity (though these are not thereby excused) to irreverence and disobedience toward the Church.[73]

Catherine calls for a reform of the church, a renovation that would restore the dignity of the priesthood and redirect the secularizing tendencies of the institution. As such, Catherine arguably falls under the category of what James Hankins has described as those who believe in reforming individuals through institutional reforms, rather than reforming institutions by reforming individuals, although Hankins applies these categories in his analyses of the political theories of the early humanists rather than of "holy women" such as Catherine.[74]

Which reforms would Catherine propose then? In addition to regaining the sacred core of the mystical body, she offers some very specific advice, for instance a better policy to bring priests to the vocation. Because of their greed and lust for power, she explains, pastors are entrapped in vicious circles where sins circulate from one generation of God's servants to the next: "Those who were foolish and proud as subjects are even more foolish and proud as superiors. So great is their foolishness that like blind men they give the office of priesthood to idiots who scarcely know how to read and could never pray the Divine office. . . . They are blind recruiters of the blind."[75]

Catherine's proposal for reform is thus twofold: On the one hand, she would restore Thomas's and the pre-Avignonese theologians' interpretation of the term *corpus mysticum* by reinstating its status within the orbit of the sacramental sphere of the church. On the other hand, she demands organizational changes within the institution itself, ones that would restore the sacred authority of the church, but that nevertheless would reduce its secular power. Catherine thus defended the visible church and the historical role of the institution: the mystical body of the church was by no means an entity independent of the body of Christ, and was not therefore an easy part to reject, according to Catherine. Such a rejection was obviously the inherent effect of the claimed secular power articulated by the papal theologians during the Avignon papacy: by reducing the concept of the mystical body to pertain only to corporational senses—to pertain to only secular and juridical parts of the church separate from any liturgical connotations—they indirectly strengthened the Spirituals' critique of the *ecclesia carnalis.*

Despite applying much of the same dark rhetoric, Catherine's solution is very different from those we encounter among the contemporary Spirituals, such as Ubertino da Casale and others. The Spirituals' rejection of the historical institution was clearly rooted in the secularization of the body of the church. By detaching its sacred bonds, which, according to Catherine, the "wicked" priests promoted, the church easily appeared as a mere conventional expression of power and greed. However, as Catherine depicts it in the *Dialogo,* the *corpus mysticum* was inseparably linked to the *corpus verum*—the uncorrupted, consecrated host that was wholly divine and wholly human, both spiritual and flesh, visible and invisible at the same time. Only these subtle bonds would make reform possible, a reformation that is expressed in her final plea to God: "You created us out of nothing. So, now that we exist, be merciful and remake the vessels you created and formed in your image and likeness; re-form them to grace in the mercy and blood of your Son."[76]

The important aspect to Catherine's ideas about a reformation of the church is that the sacraments always remain unaffected. The sacraments and the church are something greater than and above the pope and clerics. Just as no uncleanness can defile the sun, she argues, the priests' sinfulness cannot infect the sacraments: "Their sin cannot injure the sacraments of holy Church or lessen their power. But grace is lessened and sin increased in those who administer or receive them unworthily."[77] Or, as she explains a little later, "You receive grace through these sacraments no matter how sinful the bearers may be when you receive them worthily, for love for me."[78] Thus, Catherine's appeal for ecclesiastical reforms was founded on trust in the uncorrupted and unifying center of the church, the Communion or the Eucharist, from which the authority of the vicar of Christ and the priesthood originated and from which grace flowed to all its members. This does not mean, however, that one should ignore the faults of the priesthood, she argues. Rather the opposite: "You ought to despise and hate the ministers' sin," she writes.[79] But her solution is unlike what we have seen in a critic such as Marsilius of Padua, who wanted to place priests under the jurisdiction of civil law. As Catherine writes, civil law has no power to punish the priests.[80] You are not to judge them, God explains to Catherine, but leave the judging to me, the supreme Judge, who knows how to punish them.[81]

Unlike the most radical critics of her time, Catherine chose a standpoint similar to the pre-Avignonese idea of the two swords, or the two spheres that could be kept separate; this makes her more akin to a contemporary figure like Dante. As she writes before the final praise, "Now I repeat that, in spite of all their sins and even if they were worse yet, I do not want any secular powers meddling in the business of punishing them. . . . Both the one and the other are devils incarnate: In divine justice the one devil punishes the other, but both are guilty of sin. The secular has no excuse in the sin of the cleric, nor the cleric in the sin of the secular."[82] Catherine articulated, in other words, a harsh critique of the increasing secular power of the church, though without arriving at the radicalism of those who required the complete subordination or even the abolition of the institution. Rather, she strongly defended the visible church and the providential role of the *Ecclesia Romana* in history. While trusting the institutional role of the church in the economy of salvation, her solution was an appeal for a reform that would break the circle of violence, greed, and ignorance that had burdened the church for almost a century.

A MARTYR'S SELF-SACRIFICE

When Catherine wrote her letter from Rocca d'Orcia and her *Dialogo,* Pope Gregory XI was already in Rome. However, in March 1378 Gregory died. The election of Urban VI took place a few weeks later against the background of the threat from the Roman mob that had descended on the Vatican palace, demanding the election of a Roman or Italian.[83] What they feared was a new Gallic pope who would immediately flee to Avignon, leaving the city in the misery that had afflicted it for seven decades. Still, the discord within the papal court only increased, and in September the French flank of the old cardinals that Urban had replaced with twenty-four new cardinals chose Clement VII as the new pope, claiming that the election of Urban VI was invalid.

The reason for the Great Western Schism involved some profound nationalistic aspects, although the political picture was far more complex than that. Catherine's defense of Rome, however, was not only motivated by nationalism. It was primarily a justification of the historical role of the church. Rome represented a constant reminder of the historical roots of the church, the works of Saint Peter and Saint Paul—who adorned the banners of Cola di Rienzo when he marched through Rome early in the morning on Pentecost Sunday in 1347—and the profound providential role of the institution. As such, Catherine's fight for the return of the papacy could be understood as a correction of the Joachimites' and the radical Franciscans' reduction of the church to a purely spiritual society of believers. In addition, she strongly rebuked the secularizing tendencies that had been present throughout the period of the Avignon papacy.

Raymond in his biography depicts Catherine's prophesy of the schism several years before it took place, during her stay in Pisa in 1375. In a conversation with her confessor about the current state of the church, she declared, according to Raymond, "You will soon see what happens . . . when the Pope tries to do something to reform the scandalous way they live. They will cause a scandal throughout the whole of God's Church, and the consequent schism will split the Church, and torment it like a plague of heresy. . . . So be prepared to have to suffer this, for you will find yourself witnessing what I have said."[84] To a modern reader, the remarkable thing about this quotation is perhaps not the prophesy in itself, which may be explained by the text's genesis from a retrospective perspective. What is interesting, though, is the link it creates between the torments of the church and its members, thus clearly touching on Catherine's forthcoming suffering in Rome.

At Pope Urban's invitation, Catherine left for Rome in November 1378. From Rome she resumed the role of a diplomat writing to regents, such as Queen Joanna of Naples and King Charles V of France, and to politicians, friars, cardinals, and princes in order to defend the pope and put an end to the schism that was quickly unfolding. In a storm of letters, all written in Rome—she produced 125 letters during Pope Urban's papacy—she tried in harsh and passionate terms to detach influential people from the antipope by repeating, as she had also done in her *Dialogo* (chapter 154), that outside the church, there was no salvation.

Her letters and her cry (*grida*) became more and more desperate as her own body decayed. In her compelling reading of Catherine's letters from the last months in Rome, Tylus has examined how this also is reflected in her writing: by creating subtle bonds between the words *pena* (pain) and *penna* (pen), Catherine increasingly compared her decaying body with her gradually increasing inability to write, something that once again reveals Catherine as a most cautious author.[85] As we recurrently see in her oeuvre, there is a deep affinity between content and style, an affinity that during her final days in Rome only stressed the importance of her message.

Catherine has long been famous for her Eucharistic piety—her obsessive fasting and bodily renunciations—and in Raymond's account, even more than in Catherine's own letters, there is a strong emphasis on her inability to eat, as Caroline Walker Bynum has observed.[86] However, in the context of the ecclesiastical crisis, Catherine's fasting has clear political connotations, as it dramatically places the focus on the sacramental host, the *corpus verum,* as the true remedy for the *corpus mysticum.* Beginning in January 1380, though, Catherine was no longer able to eat at all, not even to swallow water, as she wrote to Raymond (Letter 373). In this final letter, written as a companion to the previous letter (Letter 371), in which she describes a mystical experience, she recounts how she went in great pain to Saint Peter's Church. With a handful of her *famiglia,* she lived in a house on the road once called Via Papae, between Santa Maria sopra Minerva and Campo di Fiori, and every day she dragged herself through the streets of Rome to the afternoon service at Saint Peter's.[87] Here, she says, she prayed beneath Giotto's now lost mosaic, *Navicella* (the little ship), a picture that was supposedly the model for the grandiose fresco that Cola di Rienzo commissioned on the Capitoline Hill (Letter 373):[88] "At the hour of Tierce I get up from Mass, and you would see a dead woman walking to Saint Peter's, and I enter once more to work on board the little ship of holy Church. There I stay until close to the hour of Vespers. I don't want to leave that place, day or night, until I see this people a bit stabilized and settled with their father. This body [of mine] is living without food—not even a drop of water—with such sweet physical torment as I've never endured. So my life is hanging by a hair!"[89]

Catherine clearly expresses here that she wishes to remain in Saint Peter's, the very center of the Catholic institution, until the schism is over and the Roman citizens have come to an agreement with the pope. Moreover, she connects the ecclesiastical institution with its sacramental heart, symbolically represented in her inability to eat or drink. The letter to Raymond is full of bitterness and despair, and, as with the letter that goes with it (Letter 371), her pain takes the form of a political strike, indeed a hunger strike. In the previous letter she describes a vision in which God recommends her to sacrifice herself for the sake of the unified church. "What can I do?" Catherine cries out, and God answers her, "You can once again offer your life, and never give yourself rest. This is the assignment I gave you and now give you again—you and all who are or will be your followers."[90] By the end of the letter, Catherine calls out, "Oh eternal God, accept the sacrifice of my life within this mystic body [*corpo mistico*], holy Church! I have nothing to give except what you have given me. Take my heart and squeeze it out over the face of this bride."[91]

Configuring herself as a martyr, this final expression cannot be understood other than as a clear political reaction. As with Birgitta of Sweden, who staged herself as the widowed Rome, Catherine dramatized, with her own body, what had occupied her for a long time—the corruption of the mystical body of Christ. Not unlike the widow from Sweden who was often seen in the streets of Rome, Catherine's agony was a spectacle that the Roman citizens took part in on her daily trip to Saint Peter's. Finally, after weeks of suffering, she succumbed beneath Giotto's *Navicella*. As Noffke has described it, referring to the deposition in the canonization sources, "While praying in Saint Peter's on the Third Sunday of Lent, 26 February, she suffered an attack in which it seemed to her that the ship of the Church (*la navicella*) weighed so heavily on her shoulders that it pressed her to the floor. Her disciples had to carry her home, where she lay paralyzed until her death two months later."[92] Before she left the world, though, she witnessed a twofold victory. In April 1379, one year before the very day she died, according to Raymond, Pope Urban's army took control of Castel Sant'Angelo, which until then had been in the hands of the schismatics, and the antipope's forces were suppressed, their leaders taken prisoner and many put to death.[93] The antipope Clement soon left Italy for good and Urban could take up residency for the first time at Saint Peter's. On Catherine's advice, the pope went barefoot to the church, followed by a crowd of people; and, according to Raymond, the "Church and Pontiff began to breathe a little more freely, to the no small satisfaction of the holy virgin."[94]

CONCLUSION

he papacy's residence in Avignon in the fourteenth century represents the zenith of papal power in Europe. Over the approximately seven decades during which the pope and his curia sojourned in southern France, the church was subjected to an ambitious process of centralization. The institutional bureaucracy swelled out, and the Avignonese popes could increasingly exercise their power more straightforwardly than ever before. It was a stable period for the curia, in contrast to its itinerant character in the previous century, and the city of Avignon itself had several advantages, such as a more peaceful population and a better climate than Rome, in addition to its central location on the trading routes between southern and northern Europe.

The papacy's revenues relied on taxation and a comprehensive reorganization of the financial system, which was especially effective under the government of Pope John XXII. Another issue that came to bolster papal authority was the concentration of ecclesiastical affairs in the curia, effectuated in particular through the appointment of clergy to ecclesiastical offices. The church could thus develop into an absolute monarchy where its head, the pope, claimed fullness of power in religious as well as in secular matters, as first articulated in Pope Boniface VIII's bull *Unam Sanctam* from 1302. The papal court, keen as it was to exhibit its wealth and prestige, soon came to surpass all other courts in Europe. As Guillaume Mollat has ironically remarked, more accounts of civil feasts—dinners, tournaments, weddings, dances, and suchlike—have been preserved than of religious banquets during the Avignon papacy.[1] It was undoubtedly a glorious period for the city, which was soon turned into an economic, political, and cultural center—a truly cosmopolitan place that gathered notaries, lawyers, physicians, architects, artists, traders, and merchants from all over Europe. As such, the Avignon papacy set the standard for the future Renaissance popes. Surrounded by a rich and magnificent court, supported by a well-organized bureaucracy, and governing a still undivided church, the Renaissance popes came to function like their predecessors in Avignon as important patrons of and benefactors for the flourishing culture in Rome.

Notably, the ecclesiastical changes that took place in the Avignonese period coincide with similar ambitions among European kingdoms and secular rulers. Emperors, kings, barons, and princes strove for supremacy in national or local affairs, and politically they moved toward absolutism like the church did. The papacy thus had to struggle with national monarchies, with the Holy Roman Empire, and above all with the communes, the *signorie,* and the Papal States in Italy. Although there were several good reasons to remain in Avignon, residency there was initially regarded as only temporary. During the first decades, the plan was to return to Rome as soon as the upheavals there were put to an end and peace was established in the Papal States. These attempts, however, had to be repeatedly postponed, resulting in the stay in Avignon at a certain point appearing to be permanent. Avignon had become the *altera Roma,* the other Rome, a situation that distressed the considerable group of Italian immigrants in Avignon. Conditions also became increasingly more difficult for Rome, whose economic and political power was strongly diminished because of the long absence of the city's two rightful lords—the pope and the emperor.

The papacy had to fight with other groups as well, such as the mendicant orders, and especially the Spiritual Franciscans, who, despite their earlier strong bonds with the papacy, were condemned as heretics after bitter disputes over apostolic poverty. Another group that contested the Avignon papacy was the growing crowds of educated laity in the cities, which often sympathized with their secular rulers. As we have seen in this book, what may be labeled as a literary war broke out. It engaged a series of critics and intellectuals from different traditions and cultures, and from every corner of Europe. Indeed, the fights were far more hostile and long lasting than any earlier conflict between secular rulers and the papacy in the Middle Ages, and at the heart of the debate was the question of the legitimacy of the Avignon popes.

What happened when the papacy finally returned to Rome? Rather than solving the problems caused by Avignon, Gregory XI's move in January 1377 threw Italy and Europe into new conflicts. In fact, because of the turbulence in Rome, Gregory prepared to go back to Avignon, but he died at the end of March 1378, before he realized these plans. On 7 April the sixteen cardinals gathered to elect a new pope. The story goes that during the conclave in the Vatican palace, which was not at all a silent and secure place for the cardinals, the Roman populace was shouting from the outside: "We want a Roman pope—or at least an Italian. If not, we'll cut you to pieces!" This is at least what the French cardinals, the disaffected majority of the Sacred College, later recounted. The conclave elected Bartolomeo Prignano, archbishop of Bari, the new pope, and he took the name Urban VI. He was old and frail, and the cardinals obviously expected him to follow the Avignon system. As princely co-governors of the church, they had so far been given both substantial authority and income. Moreover, the cardinals hoped that Urban would bring them in safety back to Avignon. Yet, Urban appeared to be hard as nails. He reduced the cardinals' power and share of papal revenues, and required a severe moral lifestyle of them. This happened along with a series of Italian appointments, which probably spurred the fear and anger of the French wing of the Sacred College of Cardinals, because the appointments demonstrated that Urban did not have any intention to return to Avignon.

Catherine of Siena was summoned to Rome to fight for the recognition of the newly elected pope, a fight that appeared to be a tough task. The rebellious cardinals, on their side, fled to Anagni, the city where Boniface VIII once was caught, and from here they denounced the election as invalid because, as they argued, it was decided under pressure from the Roman mob. On 20 September they elected Cardinal Robert of Geneva as Pope Clement VII. In Rome Pope Urban refused to withdraw and substituted the old college with twenty-five new cardinals. With these events, the Great Western Schism was initiated, and soon Christendom was split between the Urbanists and the Clementists, as the rival factions came to be labeled in the following years, indeed even long after the deaths of the respective popes. Clement VII brought his cardinals and officials back to Avignon, strongly supported by King Charles V of France and his brother Louis of Anjou. Other supporters of Pope Clement in Avignon were Naples, Burgundy, Savoy, and Scotland, and, later on, Castile, Aragon, and Navarre. Around Urban assembled Portugal, England, the Holy Roman Empire, Poland, Scandinavia, Hungary, the Italian city-states, and Sicily.

The schism stretched out in time. In Rome Boniface IX (1389–1404), Innocent VII (1404–1406), and Gregory XII (1406–1415) followed Urban VI, while in Avignon Benedict XIII was elected after Clement VII's death. At the Council of Pisa (1409) a delegation of cardinals and prelates from both sides assembled, though without the two popes, and they elected a new pope, Alexander V. As both Gregory XII in Rome and Benedict XIII in Avignon refused to abdicate, the church thus had for a moment three sitting popes, who all excommunicated each other. Only after long and tiring negotiations did a new council, the Council of Constance (1414–1418), succeed in deposing the three popes. On 11 November 1417 the council elected Cardinal Odo Colonna, who took the name Pope Martin V, and a new era for the city of Rome began.

In contrast to earlier schisms, which were the results of tensions between popes and secular rulers, the Western Schism was in the beginning a question about election. And, like most historians have stressed, as a rivalry about legitimacy, the conflicts were politically rather than theologically motivated. Yet, the conflicts, stretching over a period of forty years, after the seven unstable decades of the Avignon papacy, effected a deep trembling of the church, in both spiritual and institutional regards. The schism seriously threatened the authority of the pope and fed the growing resentment in different parts of Europe, among groups such as the Lollards, the Hussites, and the Waldensians. Moreover, Pope Martin V and the following Renaissance popes had to struggle with the conciliar movement, which argued that a general council, consisting of the whole body of Christians, was superior to the pope, and, as such, represented the highest authority in the church. The conciliarism was condemned at the Fifth Lateran Council (1512–1517), but by then the final split of the Catholic Church was already under way. In short, once the Great Western Schism was over, another and far more fatal schism was awaiting—the Protestant Reformation. There is, in other words, a direct connection between the Avignon papacy and the subsequent failure of papal leadership during the schism, and the Protestant Reformation in the early sixteenth century, in which many of the arguments of the six authors studied in this book once again were revitalized.

The aim of this book has been to explore some of the most significant critics of the Avignon papacy, critics who in many ways came to prepare the ground for the harsh disputes in the coming two centuries in Europe. The critics have been selected because of the strength and originality of their arguments, their authorial voices in the contemporary debates, and the general impact of their work on later generations. Dante Alighieri, Marsilius of Padua, William of Ockham, Francis Petrarch, Birgitta of Sweden, and Catherine of Siena are towering protagonists in European intellectual history. The reception of their work, however, has not been a topic per se in this book, but their undeniable centrality for future political and theological discourses has been a vital criterion for the study of their texts. Other criteria have been the different social, political, and national backgrounds of these six figures. Despite their striking dissimilarities—an expelled Florentine poet, a physician trained at the University of Padua and later a rector at the University of Paris, a Franciscan friar and theologian from England, a humanist at the papal court in Avignon, a princess from Sweden, and an uneducated young woman from the Sienese *popolo grasso*— these thinkers shared a series of factors. Primarily, their works were produced during the era of the Avignon papacy, which they all profoundly despised. As we have seen, each of them challenged in specific ways papal power and the papacy's stay in southern France, and they all played key roles in contemporary public debates. Moreover, a network of people and events links them together, and some of them probably even met each other in person as well. Finally, together they offer us a rich and detailed glimpse of the bitter and multifaceted conflicts over the legitimacy of the Avignon papacy from 1309, when the pope settled in Provence, to Pope Gregory XI's final return to Rome in 1377.

What have the main discoveries been? The findings are closely connected to the method that has been employed. By analyzing the individual texts against the backdrop of actual historical events, we have learned how the works by these six figures were composed in order to intervene in concrete situations. These aspects are often ignored by traditional histories of political thought, where the complex interactions between modes of thinking and historical context are frequently downplayed for the benefit of original and outstanding ideas. Read within the framework of the Avignon papacy, the texts reveal a sense of urgency. Such a reading uncovers how my protagonists were thrown, sometimes even against their will, onto contemporary battlefields, and how these conflicts left significant marks on their ideas and proposed solutions. Of equal importance is that the two major female voices during the Avignon papacy, Birgitta and Catherine, are brought back to the realm of the political debates of the fourteenth century along with their male colleagues. Any attempt to eliminate them from histories of political thought is the result of either limited explorations or anachronistic judgments. Of course, as women, both Birgitta and Catherine were excluded from the traditional institutions, such as the universities or the ecclesiastic hierarchies, which usually lent their members authority. However, as this book has demonstrated, Birgitta and Catherine cloaked their authority in spiritual and mystical discourses, which nonetheless were concerned with political and ecclesiastical questions. As such, their discourses came to be highly effective weapons in disputes about the legitimacy of the power and reform of the church.

My hope is that this book will spur on further interest. There is still much to explore, such as the influence of Marsilius's and Ockham's writings on the conciliar movement during the Great Western Schism, or the effect of Dante, Petrarch, and Cola di Rienzo on later humanists' political ideas. Perhaps the most surprising discovery in the work involved in this book has been the force of Birgitta of Sweden and Catherine of Siena, whose political and literary receptions are more or less uncharted territory. What impact did these two formidable women have on later political discourses? Although highly important research has been carried out during the last few decades to explore female writers in the Renaissance, the next step might be to explore the legacy of Birgitta and Catherine. Did Birgitta and Catherine have any influence on the reform movements or the coming generations of female humanists, poets, and letter writers in the fifteenth and sixteenth centuries? If so, it would be a groundbreaking task to explore how women intellectuals in the flourishing culture of the European Renaissance and Counter-Reformation came to fashion themselves on the model of the two female masters from the Italian *trecento*.

CHRONOLOGY

NOTES

BIBLIOGRAPHY

ACKNOWLEDGMENTS

INDEX

CHRONOLOGY

THE AVIGNON POPES

Clement V	(1305–1315)
John XXII	(1316–1334)
Benedict XII	(1334–1342)
Clement VI	(1342–1352)
Innocent VI	(1352–1362)
Urban V	(1362–1370)
Gregory XI	(1370–1378)

THE BOOK'S PROTAGONISTS

Dante Alighieri	(1265–1321)
Marsilius of Padua	(ca. 1275–ca. 1342)
William of Ockham	(ca. 1287–ca. 1347)
Francis Petrarch	(1304–1374)
Birgitta of Sweden	(1303–1373)
Catherine of Siena	(1347–1380)

KEY DATES

1302   Pope Boniface VIII issues the bull *Unam Sanctam* in November. Some months earlier in the same year, Dante is condemned to perpetual exile from Florence.

1303   The Outrage at Anagni and the captivity of Pope Boniface VIII take place in September.

1309   In March Pope Clement V settles in Avignon.

1312   Henry VII is crowned in Rome as the emperor of the Holy Roman Empire.

1313   Emperor Henry VII dies in August. Ludwig IV of Bavaria is elected as the successor to Henry VII.

1317– 1318	Dante probably writes his treatise *Monarchia* and the sixth canto of *Paradiso*.
1322– 1323	Pope John XXII issues the bulls *Ad conditorem* (1322) and *Cum inter nonnullos* (1323), which challenge the Franciscan friars' claim to apostolic poverty. The conflict between the Franciscans and the papacy escalates.
1324	Marsilius of Padua composes his *Defensor pacis*. William of Ockham is summoned to Avignon.
1328	Ludwig of Bavaria is crowned as emperor of the Holy Roman Empire in Rome. Among his court are Marsilius of Padua and Ubertino da Casale. He enters Rome in January and leaves the city in August. In May, the group of Franciscans, including William of Ockham, flees from Avignon and meets Ludwig and his court in Pisa in September.
1336– 1337	Petrarch first visits Rome.
1341	Petrarch receives his laurel crown on the Capitoline Hill in Rome on 8 April and gives his speech, the *Collatio laureationis*.
1342	William of Ockham writes his *Breviloquium*. A Roman delegation, led by Stefano Colonna the Younger, is sent to Avignon in order to plead with Pope Clement VI to return to Rome.
1343	A new delegation from Rome, called the Thirteen Good Men, led by Cola di Rienzo, is sent from Rome to the pope in Avignon. Cola is sent back to Rome the year after, appointed by the pope as the new notary of the Chamber of Rome. During the stay in Avignon, Petrarch and Cola begin their friendship.
1347	Cola di Rienzo's revolution in Rome takes place during Pentecost in May. On the Capitoline Hill, Cola is declared tribune of the revived Roman Republic. Petrarch writes his letter (*Disperse* 8) to Cola and the Roman citizens. In December, Cola abdicates and flees from Rome.
1348	The Black Death spreads rapidly in Europe.
1349	Birgitta leaves Sweden for Rome. She has a longish stay in Milan as the guest of the archbishop and the current ruler of Milan, Giovanni Visconti.
1350	The Papal Jubilee takes place in Rome. Both Petrarch and Birgitta of Sweden travel to Rome. Birgitta writes the letter (*Rev.* IV, 78) in which she presents herself as a widow.

1353   Cola di Rienzo is liberated in Avignon and in September sent by Pope Innocent VI to Rome as senator of the city. Concurrently, the pope sends Cardinal Gil Álvarez Carrillo Albornoz as a legate to Italy with a mercenary army to establish peace in the Papal States and reestablish the authority of the pope. Albornoz starts his campaign in Rome and makes his way northward, where he receives support from Milan, Pisa, Florence, and Siena.

1368   Pope Urban V and Emperor Charles IV enter Rome.

1370   Pope Urban V leaves for Avignon. Birgitta visits him in Montefiascone, where she urges him to return to Rome. Pope Urban prefers to return to Avignon, and soon after he dies.

1371   Petrarch writes his *Invectiva contra eum qui maledixit Italie,* where he once again expresses his admiration for Cola di Rienzo and complains about the brutal end of his revolution.

1371–   Birgitta undertakes her pilgrimage to Jerusalem. In 1373 she
1373   writes her final letters to Pope Gregory XI. She dies in Rome on 23 July.

1374   Petrarch dies in Arquà in July. Catherine of Siena writes Letter 127, in which she refers to Birgitta of Sweden, explaining that she was invited by Pope Gregory XI to pray for the church. In the summer, she is summoned to the Dominican General Chapter in Florence.

1375   The conflict between the papacy and the coalition of Italian city-states led by Florence breaks out, known as the War of the Eight Saints. The war ends in 1378. Catherine comes to play a key role as a peacemaker in the conflict.

1376   Catherine of Siena is sent in May to Avignon by the city of Florence. In September, Pope Gregory XI leaves Avignon for Rome, and Catherine leaves in November for Siena.

1377   In January, Pope Gregory arrives in Rome. During the summer, Catherine stays at Rocca d'Oro, outside Siena, where she probably composes her *Dialogo della divina providenza.*

1378   In October, Catherine is summoned to Rome in order to defend the newly elected pope, Urban VI.

1380   On 29 April, Catherine dies in Rome.

NOTES

INTRODUCTION

1. The story is told in the *Chronicle of Nicolas the Minorite,* a collection of documents with contextual introductions, probably first assembled, according to Patrick Nold, in dossier form by Bonagrazia da Bergamo. Patrick Nold, "Pope John XXII, the Franciscan Order and Its *Rule,*" in *The Cambridge Companion to Francis of Assisi,* ed. Michael J. P. Robson (New York: Cambridge University Press, 2012), 653–673; 265. Nicolas's text can be found in G. Gál and D. Flood, eds., *Nicolaus Minorita: Chronica* (Saint Bonaventure, NY: Franciscan Institute, 1996), 227–424. See also Patrick Nold, *Pope John XXII and His Franciscan Cardinal Bertrand de la Tour and the Apostolic Poverty Controversy* (Oxford: Clarendon, 2004). The story of the flight is also conveyed by the German historian Jürgen Miethke in his book *Ai confini del potere: Il dibattito sulla* potestas *papale da Tommaso d'Aquino a Guglielmo d'Ockham* (Padua: Editrici Francescane, 2005 [2000]), 277–279. Furthermore, David Burr describes the flight in his extensive study of the late medieval Franciscans, *The Spiritual Franciscans: From Protest to Prosecution in the Century after Saint Francis* (University Park: Pennsylvania State University Press, 2001), 277.
2. A classic study of the development of the monarchical structure of the church is Walter Ullmann, *The Growth of Papal Government in the Middle Ages* (London: Methuen, 1955). Other useful studies are Michael Wilks, *The Problem of Sovereignty in the Later Middle Ages* (Cambridge: Cambridge University Press, 1964), and Brian Tierney, *The Crisis of Church and State, 1050–1300* (Englewood Cliffs, NJ: Prentice-Hall, 1964). A short and informative study is Joseph Canning, *The Ideas of Power in the Late Middle Ages, 1296–1417* (Cambridge: Cambridge University Press, 2011). An informative survey with a particular focus on the Avignon papacy is to be found in Yves Renouard, *The Avignon Papacy: The Popes in Exile 1305–1403* (New York: Barnes and Noble Books, 1994 [1954]).
3. Renouard, *Avignon Papacy,* 14.
4. Barbara H. Rosenwein, *A Short History of the Middle Ages* (Toronto: University of Toronto Press, 2014), 258.
5. Quoted from "Unam Sanctam: Bull of Pope Boniface VIII Promulgated November 18, 1302," Papal Encyclicals Online, accessed 10 February 2017, http://www.papalencyclicals.net/Bon08/B8unam.htm. For Latin text with notes, see "Unam Sanctam," Catholic Planet, notes and translation by Ronald L. Conte Jr., accessed 10 Feburary 2017, http://www.catholicplanet

.com/TSM/Unam-Sanctam-Latin.htm: "Unam Sanctam Ecclesiam Catholicam et ipsam Apostolicam urgente fide credere cogimur et tenere. Nosque
hanc firmiter credimus et simpliciter confitemur: extra quam nec salus est,
nec remissio peccatorum . . . quae unum corpus mysticum repraesentat,
cujus caput Christus, Christi vero Deus. . . . Igitur Ecclesiae unius et unicae
unum corpus, unum caput, non duo capita quasi monstrum, Christus videlicet, et Christi vicarius Petrus Petrique successor. . . . In hac ejusque potestate duos esse gladios, spiritualem videlicet et temporalem, Evangelicis dictis
instruimur. . . . Certe qui in potestate Petri temporalem gladium esse negat,
male verbum attendit Domini proferentes, 'Converte gladium tuum in vag-
inam.' [Mt 26:52] Uterque ergo est in potestate Ecclesiae, spiritualis scilicet
gladius et materialis. Sed is quidem pro Ecclesia, ille vero ab Ecclesia exer-
cendus. Ille sacerdotis, is manu regum et militum, sed ad nutum et patien-
tiam sacerdotis."

6. Joëlle Rollo-Koster, *Avignon and Its Papacy, 1309–1417* (Lanham, MD: Rowman
   and Littlefield, 2015), 27.
7. Henry Lubac has presented a thorough and often quoted analysis of the transformation of the concept of *corpus mysticum* in the late Middle Ages: Henri
   Lubac, *Corpus Mysticum: The Eucharist and the Church in the Middle Ages,* ed. Laurence Paul Hemming and Susan Frank Parsons, trans. Gemma Simmonds with
   Richard Price and Christopher Stephens (London: SCM Press, 2006); first
   published as *L'Eucharistie et l'Église au moyen âge,* 1944. For a brief explanation
   and analyses of the content of *Unam Sanctam,* see, for instance, Canning, *Ideas
   of Power,* 11–18. The concept of *corpus mysticum* and Catherine of Siena's discussion of it will be explored in Chapter 6 of this book.
8. Arthur Stephen McGrade, *The Political Thought of William of Ockham: Personal and
   Institutional Principles* (Cambridge: Cambridge University Press, 2002 [1974]), 1.
9. Rollo-Koster, *Avignon and Its Papacy,* 3.
10. Ibid., 1–22; Patrick N. R. Zutshi, "The Avignon Papacy," in *The New Cambridge
    Medieval History,* vol. 6, *C. 1300–c. 1415,* ed. Michael Jones (Cambridge: Cam-
    bridge University Press, 2000), 653–674.
11. Guillaume Mollat, *The Popes at Avignon, 1305–1378* (London: Thomas Nelson,
    1963).
12. Renouard, *Avignon Papacy.*
13. Edwin Mullin, *The Popes of Avignon: A Century in Exile* (New York: BlueBridge,
    2008).
14. Diana Wood, *Clement VI: The Pontificate and Ideas of an Avignon Pope* (Cambridge:
    Cambridge University Press, 1989). A recent study on Pope Clement VI is
    Étienne Anheim, *Clément VI au travail: Lire, écrire, prêcher au XIVe siècle* (Paris:
    Publications de la Sorbonne, 2014).
15. Diego Quaglioni, ed., *Storia della chiesa,* vol. 11, *La crisi del trecento e il papato avi-
    gnonese (1274–1378)* (Milan: San Paolo, 1994).
16. Quentin Skinner, *The Foundation of Modern Political Thought,* vol. 1, *The Renais-
    sance* (Cambridge: Cambridge University Press, 2004 [1978]); Janet Coleman, *A*

History of Political Thought: From the Middle Ages to the Renaissance (Oxford: Blackwell, 2000); Canning, *Ideas of Power.*

17. Jürgen Miethke, *De potestate papæ: Die päpstliche Amtskompetenz im Widerstreit der politischen Theorie von Thomas von Aquin bis Wilhelm von Ockham,* Spätmittelater und Reformation 16 (Tübingen, Germany: Mohr Siebeck, 2000); Italian trans., *Ai confini del potere.*

18. Two important sources guiding this chapter are the works by Giuseppe Mazzotta and Albert Russell Ascoli. The first offers thought-provoking analyses of *Paradiso* VI to which the readings in this present book are particularly indebted; the second provides significant discussions of how Dante transformed and challenged the traditional medieval concepts of authorship and authority. See Giuseppe Mazzotta, *Dante, Poet of the Desert* (Princeton, NJ: Princeton University Press, 1979); Giuseppe Mazzotta, *Dante's Vision and the Circle of Knowledge* (Princeton, NJ: Princeton University Press, 1993); and Albert Russell Ascoli, *Dante and the Making of a Modern Author* (Cambridge: Cambridge University Press, 2008). For the examinations of Dante's political thought, the most important studies are Alexander Passerin d'Entrèves, *Dante as a Political Thinker* (Oxford: Clarendon, 1952); Ernst H. Kantorowicz, "Man-Centered Kingship: Dante," in *The King's Two Bodies: A Study in Mediaeval Political Theology* (Princeton, NJ: Princeton University Press, 1997 [1957]), 451–495; Charles T. Davis, *Dante and the Idea of Rome* (Oxford: Clarendon, 1957); Joan Ferrante, *The Political Vision of the "Divine Comedy"* (Princeton, NJ: Princeton University Press, 1984); John Woodhouse, ed., *Dante and Governance* (Oxford: Clarendon, 1997); and John M. Najemy, "Dante and Florence," in *The Cambridge Companion to Dante,* ed. Rachel Jacoff (Cambridge: Cambridge University Press, 2007 [1991]), 236–256. Najemy's book *A History of Florence, 1200–1575* (Malden, MA: Blackwell, 2007) contains important information on Dante's political context as well. A good study of Dante and the legal structures in the *Commedia* is Justin Steinberg, *Dante and the Limits of the Law* (Chicago: University of Chicago Press, 2014). Finally, Anthony K. Cassell has offered rich comments and an informative introduction in his translation of Dante's *Monarchia.* See Anthony K. Cassell, *The "Monarchia" Controversy: An Historical Study with Accompanying Translations of Dante Alighieri's "Monarchia," Guido Vernani's "Refutation of the 'Monarchia' Composed by Dante," and Pope John XXII's Bull "Si fratrum"* (Washington, DC: Catholic University of America Press, 2004).

19. The document was famously exposed as a forgery by Lorenzo Valla in his tractate *De falso credita et ementita Constantini donatione* (1440).

20. An important study on *Inferno* VI, which is discussed in this chapter, is Simone Marchesi, "'Epicuri de grege porcus': Ciacco, Epicurus and Isidore of Seville," *Dante Studies, with the Annual Report of the Dante Society* 117 (1999): 117–131. Marjorie Reeves has offered an insightful comparative reading of Dante and Marsilius in her now classic article "Marsiglio of Padua and Dante Alighieri," in *Trends in Mediaeval Political Thought,* ed. Beryl Smalley (Oxford: Basil Blackwell, 1965), 86–105. As for Marsilian scholarship, the seminal work by Alan Gewirth is still

of great significance; Alan Gewirth, *Marsilius of Padua and Medieval Political Philosophy* (New York: Columbia University Press, 1951). Key studies within the tradition of the historical and pro-imperial interpretation of Marsilius are Georges de Lagarde, *Le Defensor pacis* (Leuven, Belgium: Nauwelaerts, 1970); Jeannine Quillet, *Le philosophie politique de Marsile de Padoue* (Paris: J. Vrin, 1970); Annabel Brett, "Introduction," in *Marsilius of Padua: The Defender of the Peace,* ed. and trans. Annabel Brett, Cambridge Texts in the History of Political Thought (Cambridge: Cambridge University Press, 2005); and Annabel Brett, "Political Right(s) and Human Freedom in Marsilius of Padua," in *Transformations in Medieval and Early-Modern Rights Discourse,* ed. Virpi Mäkinen and Petter Korkman (Dordrecht, Netherlands: Springer, 2006), 95–116. Other important studies for this chapter are Cary J. Nederman, *Community and Consent: The Secular Political Theory of Marsiglio of Padua's "Defensor Pacis"* (Lanham, MD: Rowman and Littlefield, 1995); George Garnett, *Marsilius of Padua and "The Truth of History"* (Oxford: Oxford University Press, 2006); and Gerson Moreno-Riano and Cary J. Nederman, eds., *A Companion to Marsilius of Padua* (Leiden: Brill, 2012). Of special importance is the chapter by Takashi Shogimen, "Medicine and the Body Politic in Marsilius of Padua's *Defensor pacis,*" in Moreno-Riano and Nederman, *Companion to Marsilius of Padua,* 71–117; Joel Kaye, "The New Model of Equilibrium in Medieval Political Thought, Part 1: The *Defensor pacis* of Marsilius of Padua," in *A History of Balance, 1250–1475: The Emergence of a New Model of Equilibrium and Its Impact on Thought* (Cambridge: Cambridge University Press, 2014), 299–344.

21. A significant study on William of Ockham's political writings is McGrade, *Political Thought of William of Ockham.* See also McGrade's chapter "Right(s) in Ockham," in Mäkinen and Korkman, *Transformations in Medieval and Early-Modern Rights Discourse,* 63–94. Another useful survey is John Kilcullen, "The Political Writings," in *The Cambridge Companion to Ockham,* ed. Paul Vincent Spade (Cambridge: Cambridge University Press, 1999), 302–326. The latest study on Ockham's political writings, which has been invaluable for this chapter, is Takashi Shogimen, *Ockham and Political Discourse in the Late Middle Ages* (Cambridge: Cambridge University Press, 2007). Other important texts are three studies by Brian Tierney: the two chapters "John XXII and the Franciscans" and "William of Ockham" in his book *Origins of Papal Infallibility, 1150–1350* (Leiden: Brill, 1972); and "Villey, Ockham and the Origin of Individual Rights," chap. 1 in *The Idea of Natural Rights* (Grand Rapids, MI: William B. Eerdmans, 1997). Other significant surveys are also the chapters on Ockham in Coleman, *History of Political Thought,* 169–198; in Canning, *Ideas of Power,* 107–133; and in Miethke, *Ai confini del potere,* 277–329.

22. Pierre de Nolhac, *Petrarque et l'humanisme,* 2nd ed. (Paris: H. Champion, 1907), 1:1.

23. Useful surveys of Petrarch's life and works, with updated bibliographies on modern scholarship, are Victoria Kirkham and Armando Maggi, eds., *Petrarch: A Critical Guide to the Complete Works* (Chicago: University of Chicago Press, 2009), and Albert Russell Ascoli and Unn Falkeid, eds., *The Cambridge*

Companion to Petrarch (Cambridge: Cambridge University Press, 2015). The classic and still-valid biography of Petrarch is Ernest Hatch Wilkins, *Life of Petrarch* (Chicago: University of Chicago Press, 1961). Important works of scholarship that have challenged the romantic view of Petrarch as "the first modern man" in the tradition from Jacob Burckhardt and Theodore Mommsens to Paul Oskar Kristeller and Hans Blumenberg are, for instance, John Freccero, "The Fig Tree and the Laurel: Petrarch's Poetics," *Diacretics* 5, no. 1 (Spring 1975): 34–40; Bartolo Martinelli, *Petrarca e il Ventoso* (Bergamo, Italy: Minerva Italiana, 1977); Thomas Greene, "Petrarch Viator: The Displacements of Heroism," *Yearbook of English Studies* 12 (1982): 35–57; Carol Everhart Quillen, *Rereading the Renaissance: Petrarch, Augustine, and the Language of Humanism* (Ann Arbor: University of Michigan Press, 1998); Albert Russell Ascoli, "Petrarch's Middle Age: Memory, Imagination, History, and the 'Ascent of Mt. Ventoux,'" in *"A Local Habitation and a Name": Imagining Histories in the Italian Renaissance* (New York: Fordham University Press, 2011; first published 1991), 21–58; and Albert Russell Ascoli, "Petrarch's Private Politics," in *"A Local Habitation and a Name,"* 118–158. See also Unn Falkeid, "Style, the Muscle of the Souls: Theories on Reading and Writing in Petrarch's Texts," *Quaderni d'Italianistica* 29, no. 1 (2008): 21–38; and Unn Falkeid, "Petrarch, Mont Ventoux and the Modern Self," *Forum Italicum* 43, no. 1 (2009): 5–29. The most important works of scholarship from the last two decades on early humanism are the impressive studies by Ronald G. Witt, *"In the Footsteps of the Ancients": The Origins of Humanism from Lovato to Bruni* (Leiden: Brill, 2000), and Ronald G. Witt, *The Two Latin Cultures and the Foundation of Renaissance Humanism in Medieval Italy* (Cambridge: Cambridge University Press, 2012). A significant study for the chapter on Petrarch and Cola di Rienzo in this book is Ronald G. Musto, *Apocalypse in Rome: Cola di Rienzo and the Politics of the New Age* (Berkeley: University of California Press, 2003).

24. *Epystole* III, 19, 15–16: "Nullaque iam tellus, nullus michi permanet aer;/incola ceu nusquam, sic sum peregrinus ubique" (I have now no permanent land or sky. I am nowhere a citizen and a wanderer everywhere). Francesco Petrarca, "Epistole metriche," ed. Enrico Bianchi, in idem, *Rime, trionfi e poesie latine*, ed. Ferdinando Neri, Guido Martellotti, Enrico Bianchi, and Natalino Sapegno (Milano-Napoli: Ricciardo Ricciardi editore, 1951), 798.

25. Bridget Morris's explorations of the corpus of Birgitta's oeuvre have resulted in some of the most important studies on Birgitta of Sweden. Her biography is seminal: *St. Birgitta of Sweden* (Woodbridge, UK: Boydell, 1999); likewise, Morris's introductions to and comments in the English translations of Birgitta's *Revelaciones*. See *The Revelations of St. Birgitta of Sweden,* vols. 1–4, trans. Denis Searby, introductions and notes by Bridget Morris (Oxford: Oxford University Press, 2006–2015). Other important studies on Birgitta are Ingvar Fogelqvist, *Apostasy and Reform in the Revelations of St. Birgitta,* Bibliotheca Theologiae Practicae 51 (Stockholm: Almqvist and Wiksell International, 1993); Claire L. Sahlin, *Birgitta of Sweden and the Voice of Prophecy* (Woodbridge, UK: Boydell,

2001); Birgit Klockars, *Birgitta och böckerna: En undersökning av den heliga Birgittas källor,* Historiska serien (Stockholm: Kungliga Vitterhets Historie och Antikvitets Akademien [KVHAA], 1966); and Birger Bergh, *Heliga Birgitta: Åttabarnsmor och profet* (Lund, Sweden: Historiska media, 2002). Several anthologies and proceedings from conferences have been published, such as Olle Ferm, Alessandro Perriccioli Saggese, and Marcello Rotili, eds., *Santa Brigida, Napoli, l'Italia,* Atti del Convegno di studi italo-svedese Santa Maria Capua Vetere, 10–11 maggio 2006 (Naples: Tipografica Editrice, 2009); Claes Gejrot, Sara Risberg, and Mia Åkestam, eds., *Saint Birgitta, Syon and Vadstena: Papers from a Symposium in Stockholm, 4–6 October 2007* (Stockholm: KVHAA, 2010); and Claes Gejrot, Mia Åkestam, and Roger Andersson, eds., *The Birgittine Experience: Papers from the Birgitta Conference in Stockholm 2011* (Stockholm: KVHAA, 2013). Studies on Birgitta's political work are rather scarce, although there are some of importance, such as Arne Jönsson, *St. Bridget's Revelations to the Popes: An Edition of the So-Called "Tractatus de summis pontificibus"* (Lund, Sweden: Lund University Press, 1997), and, more recently, Päivi Salmesvuori, *Power and Sainthood: The Case of Birgitta of Sweden* (New York: Palgrave Macmillan, 2014). Finally, a fresh study that has been significant for the chapter in this book is Mary Dzon, "Birgitta of Sweden and Christ's Clothing," in *The Christ Child in Medieval Culture: Alpha es et O!,* ed. Mary Dzon and Theresa M. Kenney (Toronto: University of Toronto Press, 2012), 117–145.

26. There has been increasing interest in Catherine of Siena in the last decades, and especially since the translations of Catherine's letters into English by Suzanne Noffke. See *The Letters of Catherine of Siena,* ed. and trans. with introduction and notes by Suzanne Noffke, vols. 1–4 (Tempe, AZ: Arizona Center for Medieval and Renaissance Studies, 2000–2008). An important introduction to Catherine's work, studies of her reception, and a survey of the scholarship since the beginning of the nineteenth century are to be found in Carolyn Muessig, George Ferzoco, and Beverly Mayne Kienzle, eds., *A Companion to Catherine of Siena* (Leiden: Brill, 2012). Another good anthology is Jeffrey F. Hamburger and Gabriela Signori, eds., *Catherine of Siena: The Creation of a Cult* (Turnhout, Belgium: Brepols, 2013). A useful introduction to Catherine is the book by Giulia Cavallini, *Catherine of Siena* (London: Geoffrey Chapman, 1998). Another much quoted study is Caroline Walker Bynum, *Holy Feast and Holy Fast: The Religious Significance of Food to Medieval Women* (Berkeley: University of California Press, 1987), of which pp. 165–180 in particular treat Catherine of Siena. The most important studies on Catherine's political activity are Karen Scott, *"Io Caterina:* Ecclesiastical Politics and Oral Culture in the Letters of Catherine of Siena," in *Dear Sister: Medieval Women and the Epistolary Genre,* ed. Karen Cherewatuk and Ulrike Wiethaus (Philadelphia: University of Pennsylvania Press, 1993), 87–121. See also Karen Scott, "Urban Spaces, Women's Network, and the Lay Apostolate in the Siena of Catherine Benincasa," in *Creative Women in Medieval and Early Modern Italy,* ed. E. Ann Matter and John Cloakely (Philadelphia: University of Pennsylvania Press, 1994), 105–119; F. Thomas Luongo, *Saintly*

Politics of Catherine of Siena (Ithaca, NY: Cornell University Press, 2006); and Gerald Parson, *The Cult of Saint Catherine of Siena: A Study in Civil Religion* (Aldershot, UK: Ashgate, 2008). In her rich and important study, Jane Tylus reconsidered Catherine as an author by situating her in a broader context of Italian culture, alongside key authors such as Dante and Petrarch. See Jane Tylus, *Reclaiming Catherine of Siena: Literacy, Literature, and the Signs of Others* (Chicago: University of Chicago Press, 2009).

27. Dante Alighieri, *Commedia,* con il commento di Anna Maria Chiavacci Leonardi, 3 vols. (Milan: Mondadori, 1991), trans., with commentary, by Charles S. Singleton as *The Divine Comedy,* Bollington LXXX (Princeton, NJ: Princeton University Press, 1970). Throughout this volume, Dante's *Commedia* will be quoted from these editions.

28. Renouard, *Avignon Papacy,* 36.

29. Emmanuel Le Roy Ladurie, *Montaillou: Village occitan de 1294 à 1324* (Paris: Gallimard, 1975); English trans., *Montaillou: The Promised Land of Error,* trans. Barbara Bray (New York: George Braziller, 1978 [1975]).

30. Rollo-Koster, *Avignon and Its Papacy,* 57.

31. "Predecessores nostri nesciverunt esse papa." See Mollat, *Popes at Avignon,* 38; Renouard, *Avignon Papacy,* 46; and Rollo-Koster, *Avignon and Its Papacy,* 70.

32. In his revisionist study of the Chambre du Cerf, Etienne Anheim refutes the traditional description of this Gothic style as "naturalism." See Etienne Anheim, "La Chambre du Cerf: Image, savoir et nature à Avignon au milieu du XIVe siècle," *Micrologus* 16 (2008): 57–124.

33. Musto, *Apocalypse in Rome,* 62. See also Wood, *Clement VI.*

34. Renouard, *Avignon Papacy,* 50.

35. Rollo-Koster, *Avignon and Its Papacy,* 121.

36. Ibid., 123.

37. See Unn Falkeid, "*De vita solitaria* and *De otio religioso:* The Perspective of the Guest," in Ascoli and Falkeid, *Cambridge Companion to Petrarch,* 111–120; 111–112.

38. Mollat, *Popes at Avignon,* 59.

39. Luongo, *Saintly Politics of Catherine of Siena.*

40. Renouard, *Avignon Papacy,* 63–64.

41. Rollo-Koster, *Avignon and Its Papacy,* 141–146.

42. Renouard, *Avignon Papacy,* 98–100. See also Mollat, *Popes at Avignon,* 335–342.

43. Renouard, *Avignon Papacy,* 106–108.

44. Mollat, *Popes at Avignon,* 310.

45. Ibid., 311.

46. See, for instance, Beryl Smalley, ed., *English Friars and Antiquity in the Early Fourteenth Century* (Oxford: Basil Blackwell, 1960); Giuseppe Billanovich, *Petrarca letterato,* vol. 1, *Lo scrittoio del Petrarca* (Rome: Edizioni di storia e letteratura, 1947); Giuseppe Billanovich, *La tradizione del testo di Livio e le origini dell'umanesimo: Tradizione e fortuna di Livio tra Medioevo e Umanesimo,* vol. 2, *Il Livio del Petrarca e del Valla* (Padua: Antenore, 1981); Daniel Williman, Marie-Henriette Jullien de Pommerol, and Jacques Monfrin, *Bibliothèques ecclésiastiques au temps de la papauté*

d'Avignon (Paris: Editions du CNRS, 1980); Birger Munk Olsen, "L'étude des classiques à Avignon au XIVe siècle," in *Avignon and Naples: Italy in France— France in Italy in the Fourteenth Century,* ed. Lene Waage Petersen, Marianne Pade, and Hannemarie Ragn Jensen, Analecta Romana Instituti Danici Supplementum 25 (Rome: "L'Erma" di Bretschneider, 1997); Witt, *"In the Footsteps of the Ancients";* Cathleen Fleck, "Seeking Legitimacy: Art and Manuscripts for the Popes in Avignon from 1378 to 1417," in *A Companion to the Great Western Schism (1378–1417),* ed. Joëlle Rollo-Koster and Thomas Izbicki (Leiden: Brill, 2009), 239–302. For an insightful study of the humanism at the papal court in the following century, see Christopher Celenza, *Renaissance Humanism and the Papal Curia: Lapo da Castiglionchio the Younger's "De Curiae Commodis"* (Ann Arbor: University of Michigan Press, 2000).

47. The portrait is famously echoed in Petrarch's sonnets 77 and 78 in his collection of poetry, *Rerum vulgarium fragmenta.*

48. Nino Pirotta, *Music and Culture in Italy from the Middle Ages to the Baroque* (Cambridge, MA: Harvard University Press, 1984), 29; see also Gunther Morche, "L'ars nova et la musique liturgique au temps des papes d'Avignon," *Annuaire de la Société des amos du Palais des papes et des monuments d'Avignon* 77 (2000): 131–141.

1. THE EAGLE'S FLIGHT

1. For a detailed historical presentation of Pope Gelasius I and the emergence of caesaropapism in the fifth century, see Walter Ullmann, *The Growth of Papal Government in the Middle Ages* (London: Methuen, 1955), 14–28. For the long-standing influence of the Gelasian theory in shaping the theoretical foundations of the returning political crisis in the Middle Ages, see, for instance, Ernst H. Kantorowicz, *The King's Two Bodies: A Study in Mediaeval Political Theology* (Princeton, NJ: Princeton University Press, 1997 [1957]), 456–457; and Michael Wilks, *The Problem of Sovereignty in the Later Middle Ages* (Cambridge: Cambridge University Press, 1964), 303–309. A good historical survey is given by Sophia Menache in her article "The Gelasian Theory from a Communication Perspective: Development and Decline," *Revista de Historia* 13 (2012): 57–76.

2. Menache, "Gelasian Theory from a Communication Perspective," 68.

3. Yves Renouard, *The Avignon Papacy: The Popes in Exile, 1305–1403* (New York: Barnes and Noble Books, 1994 [1954]), 15.

4. Menache, "Gelasian Theory from a Communication Perspective," 71. For a survey of the political implications of *Unam Sanctam* and the escalating debates about the legitimacy of power in the wake of the bull, see Joseph Canning, *The Ideas of Power in the Middle Ages, 1296–1417* (Cambridge: Cambridge University Press, 2011), 18–59.

5. For a detailed and useful survey of the intricate discussions of the time of composition of *Monarchia,* see Albert Russell Ascoli, *Dante and the Making of a Modern Author* (Cambridge: Cambridge University Press, 2008), 230n2.

6. Alexander Passerin d'Entrèves, *Dante as a Political Thinker* (Oxford: Clarendon, 1952).

7. Bruno Nardi, *Dal "Convivio" alla "Commedia," Studi Storici*, fasc. 35–39 (Rome: Istituto Storico Italiano, 1960).

8. See, for instance, Charles T. Davis, *Dante and the Idea of Rome* (Oxford: Clarendon, 1957).

9. Ernst H. Kantorowicz, "Man-Centered Kingship: Dante," in *King's Two Bodies*, 465.

10. See Albert Russell Ascoli, "'No Judgements among Equals': Dividing Authority in Dante's *Monarchia*," in *Dante and the Making of a Modern Author*, 229–274; 238.

11. John M. Najemy, "Dante and Florence," in *The Cambridge Companion to Dante*, ed. Rachel Jacoff (Cambridge: Cambridge University Press, 2007), 236. For a good introduction to Dante's life, see Giuseppe Mazzotta, "Life of Dante," in Jacoff, *Cambridge Companion to Dante*, 1–13. A more extensive biography is Giorgio Petrocchi, *Vita di Dante* (Rome: Editori Laterza, 1984).

12. Philip Henry Wicksteed, ed., *The Early Lives of Dante: Primary Source Edition* (London: Alexander Moring, 1904), 121.

13. Najemy, "Dante and Florence," 237.

14. Ibid., 238.

15. Dante Alighieri, *Epistola* VII, 1, in *Dantis Alagherii Epistolae: The Letters of Dante*, trans. Paget Toynbee (Oxford: Clarendon Press, 1966), 101; Latin text: *Epistole*, ed. Arsenio Frugoni and Giorgio Brugnoli, in *Opere minori*, vol. 2, ed. Pier Vincenzo Mengaldo et al. (Milan: Riccardo Ricciardi, 1979), 562–564: "et, ceu Titan, praeoptatus exoriens, nova spes Latio seculi melioris effulsit."

16. See also *Inf.* XIX, 104–117, and *Purg.* XVI, 103–111, for similar attacks on the papacy.

17. As Ascoli has made clear, scholars today generally maintain that the work on *Monarchia* overlapped with the composition of the last canticle of the *Commedia*, including *Paradiso* VI. See Ascoli, *Dante and the Making of a Modern Author*, 230, 230n2.

18. Dante Alighieri, *Monarchia* III, 16, 14: "Unde fit quod aliquando patiantur dissidium quibus denuntiandi dignitas est indulta." Latin text: *Monarchia*, ed. Bruno Nardi, in Mengaldo et al., *Opere minori*, 2:500, translated by Anthony K. Cassell as *The "Monarchia" Controversy* (Washington, DC: Catholic University of America Press, 2004), 173. Throughout this volume, Dante's *Monarchia* will be quoted from these two editions.

19. Ascoli, *Dante and the Making of a Modern Author*, 238–239.

20. Among others, Cassell has argued for this. See the discussion in Cassell, *"Monarchia" Controversy*, 3, 23, 230n3.

21. Nick Havely, *Dante and the Franciscans: Poverty and the Papacy in the "Commedia"* (Cambridge: Cambridge University Press, 2004), 159–175.

22. Ibid., 161n101.

23. See Chapter 3 for a more detailed presentation of the controversies between the Franciscans and the papacy about the question of apostolic poverty.

24. Augustine, *De civitate Dei,* XIV, 28: "Fecerunt itaque civitates duas amores duo, terrenam scilicet amor sui usque ad contemptum Dei, caelestem vero amor Dei usque ad contemptum sui. . . . Illi in principibus ejus, vel in eis quas subjugat nationibus dominandi libido dominator: in hac serviuunt invicem in charitate, et praepositi consulendo, et subditi obtemperando." Latin text quoted from Jacques-Paul Migne, ed., *Patrologiae cursus completus,* Series Latina (Paris, 1841–1866), 41:436; English trans., Augustine, *Concerning the City of God against the Pagans,* trans. Henry Bettenson (London: Penguin Books, 1984), 593.

25. I am indebted to Giuseppe Mazzotta's reading of *Paradiso* VI, in both his volume *Dante, Poet of the Desert* (Princeton, NJ: Princeton University Press, 1979), 180–184, and *Dante's Vision and the Circle of Knowledge* (Princeton, NJ: Princeton University Press, 1993), 103–109. A recent study of the legal structures of Dante's *Comedy* is Justin Steinberg's book *Dante and the Limits of the Law* (Chicago: University of Chicago Press, 2014). Steinberg's argument is that Dante sought to address the gap between the universality of Roman law and the lack of a sovereign power to enforce it, which in many ways is related to the argument that is developed in this chapter. Emperor Justinian and *Paradiso* VI, however, play a minor role in Steinberg's analysis.

26. This is also discussed in *Inferno* XIX, where Pope Nicolas III is waiting in the tomb for Pope Boniface VIII, who is not yet dead.

27. Marcus Tullius Cicero, *De natura deorum* III, 56, in *De natura deorum: Libri secundus et tertius,* ed. Arthur Stanley Pease (Cambridge, MA: Harvard University Press, 1958), 1111–1112: "Quintus quem colunt Pheneata, qui Argum dicitur interemisse ob eamque causam Aegyptum profugisse atque Aegyptiis leges et litteras tradidisse"; English trans., *The Nature of Gods,* trans. Horace C. P. McGregor (Harmondsworth, UK: Penguin Books, 1972), 216: "This is the Mercury who is said to have slain Argus and for this reason to have fled to Egypt and given laws and the art of writing to the Egyptians."

28. Dante Alighieri, *Convivio* II, 13, 11–12, in *Opere minori,* vol. 1, pt. 2, ed. Cesare Vasoli and Domenico De Robertis (Milan: Riccardo Ricciardi, 1988), 224–227: "E lo cielo di Mercurio si può comparare a la Dialettica per due proprietadi: che Mercurio è la più picciola stella del cielo, ché la quantitade del suo diametro non è più che di dugento trentadue miglia, secondo che pone Alfagrano, che dice quello essere de le ventotto parti una del diametro de la terra, lo quale è sei milia cinquecento miglia. L'altra proprietade si è che più va velata de li raggi del Sole che null'altra stella. E queste due proprietadi sono ne la Dialettica: ché la Dialettica è minore in suo corpo che null'altra scienza, ché perfettamente è compilata e terminata in quello tanto testo che ne l'Arte vecchia e ne la Nuova si truova; e va più velata che nulla scienza, in quanto procede con più sofistici e probabili argomenti più che altra"; English trans., *The Convivio,* trans. Richard Lansing (New York: Columbia University, Center for Digital

Research and Scholarship, 1998), http://digitaldante.columbia.edu/library/dantes-works/the-convivio/.

29. Isidore of Seville, *Etymologiarum Libri Vingti,* bk. II, xxii, "Dialectica est disciplina ad disserendas rerum causas inventa. Ipsa est philosophiae species, quae Logica dicitur, id est rationalis definiendi, quaerendi et disserendi potens. Docet enim in pluribus generibus questionum quemadmodum disputando vera et falsa diiudicentur." Latin text quoted from Migne, *Patrologiae cursus completus,* 82:140; English trans., Isidore of Seville, *The Etymologies of Isidore of Seville,* trans., with introduction and notes, by Stephen A. Barney, W. J. Lewis, J. A. Beach, and Oliver Berghof (Cambridge: Cambridge University Press, 2006), 79.

30. Peter of Spain, *Summulae logicales,* tractatus V, 31. Quoted from Cassell, *"Monarchia" Controversy,* 316n239.

31. Dante, *Monarchia* II, 10, 4: "Dico ergo quod, si romanum Imperium de iure non fuit, Cristus nascendo persuasit iniustum; consequens est falsum: ergo contradictorium antecedentis est verum. Inferunt enim se contradictoria invicem a contrario sensu." Latin text, 426; English trans., 147.

32. Canning, *Ideas of Power,* 75.

33. Dante, *Convivio* II, 13, 11–12: "più velata che nulla scienza, in quanto procede con più sofistici e probabili argomenti più che altra."

34. Monophysites, who rejected the Council of Chalcedon (451) and the doctrine of Christ's two natures united in one person, held that Christ's body, the flesh that God had assumed in the incarnation, was not human but divine. See, for instance, Barbara H. Rosenwein, *A Short History of the Middle Ages* (Toronto: University of Toronto Press, 2014), 8.

35. By exploring Justinian's Monophysitism and the effect of his conversion on his work on *Corpus iuris civilis,* Steven Grossvogel has convincingly argued that Justinian's autobiographical sketch is also an account of his *justificatio,* or justification in the eyes of God. Steven Grossvogel, "Justinian's Jus and Justificatio: Paradiso 6.10–27," Italian issue supplement, *Modern Language Notes* 127, no. 1 (2012): 130–137.

36. As Mazzotta has discussed, later on, in the heaven of Jupiter (*Par.* XVIII–XX), Dante is confronted with the pressing question of the borders of Europe and the experience of "otherness" in the heart of the Christian world. See Giuseppe Mazzotta, "Spettacolo e geometria della giustizia (*Paradiso* XVIII–XX): L'Europa e l'universalità di Roma," in *Confine quasi orizzonte: Saggi su Dante* (Rome: Edizioni di storia e letteratura, 2014), 81–97.

37. Dante, *Monarchia* I, 2, 2: "Est ergo temporalis Monarchia, quam dicunt 'Imperium,' unicus principatus et super omnes in tempore vel in hiis et super hiis que tempore mensurantur." Latin text, 284–286; English trans., 112.

38. Ascoli, *Dante and the Making of a Modern Author,* 234.

39. Mazzotta, *Dante's Vision and the Circle of Knowledge,* 107.

40. Dante, *Monarchia* I, 2, 3: "Maxime autem de hac tria dubitata queruntur: primo nanque dubitatur et queritur an ad bene esse mundi necessaria sit; secundo an romanus populus de iure Monarche offitium sibi asciverit; et tertio

an auctoritas Monarche dependeat a Deo immediate vel ab alio, Dei ministro seu vicario." Latin text, 286; English trans., 112.

41. Dante, *Monarchia* I, 4, 2: "patet quod genus humanum in quiete sive tranquillitate pacis ad proprium suum opus, quod fere divinum est iuxta illud.... Unde manifestum est quod pax universalis est optimum eorum que ad nostram beatitudinem ordinantur." Latin text, 302–304; English trans., 114–115.

42. A good discussion of Dante's political vision of this meaning of universality—the *universitas humana*—is to be found in Kantorowicz, *King's Two Bodies*, 451–496, see esp. 471–475.

43. Suetonius, *Divus Augustus*, 53, edited, with introduction and commentary, by John M. Carter (Bristol: Bristol Classical Press, 1982), 62: "Domini appellationem ut maledictum et obprobrium semper exhorruit ... dominumque se posthac appellari ne a liberis quidem aut nepotibus suis vel serio vel ioco passus est, atque eius modi blanditias etiam inter ipsos prohibuit." English trans.: *The Twelve Caesars*, trans. Robert Graves (Harmondsworth, UK: Penguin Books, 1979), 84.

44. Dante, *Monarchia* I, 11, 11: "Ubi ergo non est quod possit optari, inpossibile est ibi cupiditatem esse: destructis enim obiectis, passiones esse non possunt." Latin text, 338; English trans., 120.

45. Cassell, *"Monarchia" Controversy*, 294n70. For a valuable examination of the connections between the Franciscans and the papacy as they appear in Dante's *Comedy*, see also Havely, *Dante and the Franciscans*.

46. Dante, *Convivio* IV, xii, 15–17.

47. Dante, *Monarchia* I, 11, 12: "Sed Monarcha non habet quod possit optare: sua nanque iurisdictio terminatur Occeano solum." Latin text, 338–340; English trans., 120.

48. Virgil, *Aeneid* 6, 847–853; Dante, *Monarchia* II, 6, 9: "Excudent alii spirantia mollius era,/credo equidem; vivos ducent de marmore vultus,/orabunt causas melius, celique meatus/describent radio, et surgentia sidera dicent:/tu regere imperio populos, Romane, memento./Hae tibi erunt artes, pacique imponere morem,/parcere subiectis et debellare superbos." Latin text, 404; English trans., 139.

49. Dante, *Monarchia* I, 16, 4: "O genus humanum, quantis procellis atque iacturis quantisque naufragiis agitari te necesse est dum, bellua multorum capitum factum, in diversa conaris!" Latin text, 364; English trans., 127–128.

50. For Dante's apocalyptic images and their connections to the Spirituals' discourse, see Havely, *Dante and the Franciscans*, 159–175. Charles T. Davis has also explored the apocalyptic rhetoric and its links to the Franciscans in his chapter "Rome and Babylon in Dante," in *Dante: The Critical Complex*, vol. 5, *Dante and History: From Florence and Rome to the Heavenly Jerusalem*, edited with introduction by Richard Lansing (New York: Routledge, 2003).

51. Cassell, "Monarchia" *Controversy*, 9.

52. Dante, *Monarchia* III, 10, 7: "Imperii vero fundamentum ius humanum est." Latin text, 476; English trans., 164.

53. Dante, *Monarchia* III, 15, 7: "beatitudinem silicet huius vite . . . ; et beatitudinem vite ecterne." Latin text, 498; English trans. 172.

54. Dante, *Monarchia* III, 16, 10: "Propter quod opus fuit homini duplici directivo secundum dublicem finem: scilicet summo Pontifice, qui secundum revelata humanum genus perduceret ad vitam ecternam, et Imperatore, qui secundum phylosophica documenta genus humanum ad temporalem felicitatem dirigeret." Latin text, 498; English trans., 172.

55. See Erich Auerbach, *Dante, Poet of the Secular World* (Chicago: University of Chicago Press, 1961); Davis, *Dante and the Idea of Rome;* Joan Ferrante, *The Political Vision of the "Divine Comedy"* (Princeton, NJ: Princeton University Press, 1984).

56. Charles T. Davis, "Dante and the Empire," in Jacoff, *Cambridge Companion to Dante,* 257–270; 263.

57. Mazzotta, *Dante, Poet of the Desert,* 180–185.

58. Dante, *Monarchia* III, 4, 14: "sunt ergo huiusmodi regimina remedia contra infirmitatem peccati." Latin text, 450–452; English trans., 156.

59. A fundamental notion in Bonaventure's theology is that Christ is at the center of history, and not at the end, as Augustine maintained. In his *Collationes in Hexaemeron* (Collations on the seven gifts of the Holy Spirit), Bonaventure replaced the old scheme of seven ages of history with Joachim's double scheme. Rather than being the *telos,* the endpoint or the purpose into which all things flowed together and in which the world was concluded and overcome, Christ came in Bonaventure's scheme to represent the *axis mundi,* firmly rooted in history. After the Passion of Christ, history continued in seven new stages. During these ages, the truth, which in many cases still belonged to the dark future for Augustine and the church fathers, was gradually unfolding, like a fruit or a tree that carries seeds within itself (*Hexameron* XIII, 2; XV, 10). The present time, thus, was not a time of perfect fulfillment, according to Bonaventure. There was more to expect: there was still hope for a future immanent or inner-historical transformation, also of the church, and the figure who heralded this coming transformation was Saint Francis. See Joseph Ratzinger's study on Bonaventure's appropriation of Joachim's theology, *The Theology of History in St. Bonaventure,* trans. Zachary Hayes (Chicago: Franciscan Herald, 1971; originally published in Germany in 1961). See also Zachary Hayes, "Bonaventure: Mystery of the Triune God," in *The History of Franciscan Theology,* ed. Kenan B. Osborne (New York: Franciscan Institute, 2007 [1994]), 39–127.

60. In his classic study *Music and Culture in Italy from the Middle Ages to the Baroque* (Cambridge, MA: Harvard University Press, 1984), Nino Pirotta has explored the links between Ars Nova and its influence on the *trecento* culture in Italy.

61. Cassell distinguishes between "decretists" and "decretalists." The latter he describes as theocratic commentators on collections of pontifical letters containing a *decretum,* rescript, or decision of a date later than Gratian's *Decretum.* This is in contrast to the decretists who made commentaries on Gratian's original *Concordantia discordantium Canonum* or *Decretum Gratinai.* It was above all against

the decretalists, the strong supporters of the pope's plenitude of power, that Dante directed his attack. Cassell, "Monarchia" Controversy, 211–212.

62. Dante, Monarchia III, 3, 9–10: "Sunt etiam tertii—quos decretalistas vocant—qui, theologie ac phylosophie cuiuslibet inscii et expertes, suis decretalibus—quas profecto venerandas existimo—tota intentione innixi, de illarum prevalentia—credo—sperantes, Imperio derogant. Nec mirum, cum iam audiverim quendam de illis dicentem et procaciter asserentem traditiones Ecclesie fidei fundamentum." Latin text, 440; English trans., 152.

63. See, for instance, the comments by Chiavacci Leonardi in Dante, Commedia.

2. MARSILIUS OF PADUA AND THE QUESTION OF LEGITIMACY

1. Giovanni Boccaccio, Trattatello in laude di Dante, ed. Pier Giorgio Ricci, in Tutte le opere di Giovanni Boccaccio, ed. Vittore Branca (Milan: Aldo Mondadori, 1974), 3:638–639: "Questo libro più anni dopo la morte dell'auttore fu dannato da messer Beltrando cardinal del Poggetto e legato di papa nelle parti di Lombardia, sedente Giovanni papa XXII. E la cagione fu perciò che Lodovico, duca di Baviera, dagli elettori della Magna eletto in re de' Romani, e venendo per la sua coronazione a Roma, contra il piacere del detto Giovanni papa, essendo in Roma, fece, contra gli ordinamenti ecclesiastici, uno frate minore, chiamato frate Pietro della Corvara, papa, e molti cardinali e vescovi; e quivi a questo papa si fece coronare. E, nata poi in molti casi della sua autorità quistione, egli e' suoi seguaci, trovato questo libro, a difensione di quella e di sé molti degli argomenti in esso posti cominciarono ad usare; per la qual cosa il libro, il quale infino allora appena era saputo, divenne molto famoso. Ma poi, tornatosi il detto Ludovico nella Magna, e li suoi seguaci, e massimamente i chierici, venuti al dichino e disperse, il detto cardinal, non essendo chi a ciò s'opponesse, avuto il soprascrito libro, quello in publico, sì come cose eretiche contenente, dannò al fuoco." English trans., Life of Dante, trans. Philip H. Wicksteed, ed. William Chamberlain (London: Oneworld Classics, 2011), 63.

2. Enciclopedia Dantesca (Roma: Istituto della enciclopedia italiana, 1971), 3:1002.

3. For a rich and updated version of Marsilius's biography, see Frank Godthardt, "The Life of Marsilius of Padua," in A Companion to Marsilius of Padua, ed. Gerson Moreno-Riano and Cary J. Nederman (Leiden: Brill, 2012), 13–57.

4. Joan Ferrante, The Political Vision of the "Divine Comedy" (Princeton, NJ: Princeton University Press, 1984), 37.

5. Alan Gewirth, Marsilius of Padua and Medieval Political Philosophy (New York: Columbia University Press, 1951), 51.

6. Dante Alighieri, Epistola VII, 23–26: "Et Florentia, forte nescis?, dira hec pernicies nuncupatur. Hec est vipera versa in viscera genitricis; hec est languida pecus gregem domini sui sua contagione commaculans.... Vere matrem viperea feritate dilaniare contendit, dum contra Romam cornua rebellionis exacuit, que ad ymaginem suam atque similitudinem fecit illam." Latin text

quoted from Dante Alighieri, *Epistole,* ed. Arsenio Frugoni and Giorgio Brugnoli, in *Opere minori,* vol. 2, ed. Pier Vincenzo Mengaldo et al. (Milan: Riccardo Ricciardi, 1979), 570; English trans., *Dante Alighieri: Four Political Letters,* trans. and ed. Claire E. Honess, MHRA Critical Texts, vol. 6 (London: Modern Humanities Research Association, 2007), 78–79.

7. The event was described by Giovanni Villani in his *Nuova cronica* III, 2.

8. Simone Marchesi, "'Epicuri de grege porcus': Ciacco, Epicurus and Isidore of Seville," *Dante Studies, with the Annual Report of the Dante Society* 117 (1999): 117–131.

9. Isidore of Seville, *Etymologiae,* bk. 8, vi, 15–17: "Epicurei dicti ab Epicuro, quodam philosopho amatore vanitatis, non sapientiae, quem etiam ipsi philosophi *porcum* nominaverunt, quia se volutans in caeno carnali, voluptatem corporis summum bonum asseruit, qui etiam dixit nulla providentia divina instructum esse aut regi mundum.... Asseruit autem Deum nihil agree, omnia constare corporibus, animam nihil aliud esse quam corpus. Unde et dixit: 'Non ero postea quam mortuus fuero.'" Latin text quoted from Jacques-Paul Migne, ed., *Patrologiae cursus completus,* Series Latina (Paris, 1841–1866), 82:306–307; English trans., Marchesi, "'Epicuri de grege porcus,'" 118.

10. Giuseppe Mazzotta, "Dante's Poetics of Births and Foundations," in *Dante: A Critical Reappraisal,* ed. Unn Falkeid (Oslo: Unipub, 2008), 7–27. For a good historical survey of the use of the fable of the belly in medieval and Renaissance literature, see David G. Hale, "Intestine Sedition: The Fable of the Belly," in *Comparative Literature Studies* 5, no. 4 (December 1968): 377–388.

11. Quentin Skinner, *The Foundation of Modern Political Thought,* vol. 1, *The Renaissance* (Cambridge: Cambridge University Press, 2004 [1978]), 45.

12. Marsilius of Padua, *Defensor Pacis* [hereafter *DP*] I, 12, 3: "Nos autem dicamus secundum veritatem atque consilium Aristotelis III *Politicae,* capitulo 6*, *legislatorem* seu causam legis effectivam primam et propriam esse populum seu civium universitatem, aut eius valentior partem per suam electionem seu voluntatem in generali civium congregatione per sermonem expressam.... Et dico consequenter huic, quod eadem auctoritate prima, non alia, debent leges et aliud quodlibet per electionem institutum approbationem necessariam suscipere." Latin text, *The Defensor Pacis of Marsilius of Padua,* ed. C. W. Previté-Orton (Cambridge: Cambridge University Press, 1928), 49; ed. and trans. by Annabel Brett as *Marsilius of Padua: The Defender of the Peace,* Cambridge Texts in the History of Political Thought (Cambridge: Cambridge University Press, 2005), 66–67. Throughout this volume, Marsilius's *Defensor pacis* will be quoted from these two editions.

13. Gewirth, *Marsilius of Padua,* 184.

14. Marsilius, *DP* I, 12, 3: "in generali civium congregatione per sermonem expressam." Latin text, 49; English trans., 66.

15. Marsilius, *DP* I, 8, 3: "*Politia* vero, licet in una significatione sit commune quiddam ad omne genus vel speciem regiminis seu principatus, in una tamen ipsius significatione importat speciem quandam principatus temperati, in quo civis

quilibet participat aliqualiter principatu vel consiliativo vicissim iuxta gradum et facultatem seu conditionem ipsius, ad commune etiam conferens et civium voluntatem sive consensum." Latin text, 29; English trans., 41–42.

16. Marsilius, *DP* I, 15, 6: "Nam ab anima universitatis civium aut eius valentioris partis formatur aut formari debet in ea pars una primum proportionata cordi, in qua siquidem virtutem, quandam seu formam statuit cum activa potentia seu auctoritate instituendi partes reliquas civitatis. Haec autem pars est principatus, cuius quidem virtus causalitate universalis lex est, et cuius activa potentia est auctoritas iudicandi, praecipiendi, et exequendi sententias conferentium et iustorum civilium." Latin text, 70; English trans., 92.

17. Marsilius, *DP* I, 17, 2: "Hunc autem solummodo principatum, supremum silicet, dico unum numero ex necessitate fore, non plures, si debeat regnum aut civitas recte disponi." Latin text, 89; English trans., 115.

18. Gewirth, *Marsilius of Padua,* 310; Nicolai Rubenstein, "Marsilius of Padua and Italian Political Thought of His Time," in *Europe in the Late Middle Ages,* ed. John Hale, Roger Highfield and Beryl Smalley (London: Faber, 1965), 44–75; Skinner, *Foundations,* 1:60–65; Cary J. Nederman, *Community and Consent: The Secular Political Theory of Marsiglio of Padua's "Defensor Pacis"* (Lanham, MD: Rowman and Littlefield, 1995).

19. Gewirth, *Marsilius of Padua,* 315.

20. Skinner, *Foundations,* 1:65.

21. Nederman, *Community and Consent,* 147.

22. Joseph Canning, *The Ideas of Power in the Late Middle Ages, 1296–1417* (Cambridge: Cambridge University Press, 2011), 93.

23. Janet Coleman, *A History of Political Thought: From the Middle Ages to the Renaissance* (Oxford: Blackwell, 2000), 154.

24. Key scholars in the tradition of the more historical and pro-imperial interpretation of Marsilius are Georges de Lagarde, Jeannine Quillet, and Annabel Brett. See Georges de Lagarde, *Le Defensor pacis* (Leuven, Belgium: Nauwelaerts, 1970); Georges de Lagarde, *La naissance de l'esprit laïque au decline du moyen âge,* vol. 5 (Leuven, Belgium: Nauwelaerts, 1956); Jeannine Quillet, *La philosophie politique de Marsile de Padoue* (Paris: J. Vrin, 1970); and Annabel Brett, "Politics, Right(s) and Human Freedom in Marsilius of Padua," in *Transformations in Medieval and Early-Modern Rights Discourse,* ed. Virpi Mäkinen and Petter Korkman (Dordrecht, Netherlands: Springer, 2006), 95–116.

25. Annabel Brett, "Introduction," in Brett, *Marsilius of Padua: The Defender of the Peace,* xxx–xxxi.

26. Marsilius, *DP* I, 1, 6: "Antenorides ego quidam . . . oppressorum siquidem misericordiam et reservationem, opprimentium vero ab erroris devio revocationem, eaque permittentium, hiis tamen obviare debentium atque potentium, excitationem; in te quoque respiciens singulariter tamquam Dei ministrum huic operi finem daturum, quem extrinsecus optat inesse, inclitissime Ludovice, Romanorum Imperator." Latin text, 5; English trans., 8.

27. Marsilius, *DP* III, 3: "Amplius, per ipsum comprehendere potest tam principans quam subiectum quae sunt elementa prima civilitatis cuiuslibet, quid
observare oporteat propter conservationem pacis et propriae libertatis." Latin
text, 500; English trans., 557.

28. Marsilius, *DP* I, 19, 12: "Haec itaque Romanorum quorundam episcoporum
extimatio non recta et perversa fortassis affectio principatus, quem sibi de-
beri asserunt ex eisdem (ut dicunt) per Christum tradita plenitudine potestatis, causa est singularis illa quam intranquillitatis seu discordiae civitatis
aut regni factivam diximus. Ipsa enim in omnia regna serpere prona, quemadmodum prooemialiter dicebatur, infesta sui actione dudum vexavit Italicum
regnum, et a sui tranquillitate seu pace prohibuit prohibetque continuo, princi-
pantis, scilicet imperatoris Romani, promotionem seu institutionem, ipsiusque
actionem in dicto imperio, sui toto conanime prohibendo." Latin text, 107–108;
English trans., 135.

29. Marsilius, *DP* II, 4, 1: "et quod Christi consilio et exemplo, praesertim in com-
munitatibus fidelium, talem principatum, si eisdem offeratur aut conferatur
per auctoritatem eius habentem, debeant recusare." Latin text, 128; English
trans., 159.

30. Marsilius, *DP* II, 4, 3: "sed magis subici secundum statum praesentis saeculi."
Latin text, 129; English trans., 161.

31. George Garnett, *Marsilius of Padua and "The Truth of History"* (Oxford: Oxford
University Press, 2006), 77.

32. Dante Alighieri, *Monarchia* III, 15, 17–18: "Que quidem veritas ultime ques-
tionis non sic stricte recipienda est, ut romanus Princeps in aliquo romano
Pontifici non subiaceat, cum mortalis ista felicitas quodammodo ad inmor-
talem felicitatem ordinetur. Illa igitur reverentia Cesar utatur ad Petrum qua
primogenitus filius debet uti ad patrem: ut luce paterne gratie illustratus vir-
tuosius orbem terre irradiet, cui ab Illo solo profectus est, qui est omnium
spiritualium et temporalium gubernator." Latin text, 502; English trans., 173.

33. Marsilius, *DP* I, 19, 12: "Non enim Romano vel alteri episcopo, sacerdoti, aut cui-
quam spirituali ministro, inquantum huiusmodi, in quemquam cuiuscumque
conditionis singularem personam, communitatem, vel collegium aliquod cnvenit
officium principatus coactivi." Latin text, 108; English trans., 135.

34. On Marsilius's legal positivism, see Ewart Lewis, "The 'Positivism' of Marsilius of Padua," *Speculum* 38 (1963): 541–582.

35. Marsilius, *DP* II, 2, 3: "nomen *ecclesia* . . . de universitate fidelium credentium
et invocantium nomen Christi." Latin text, 117; English trans., 145.

36. As Brett has also argued in the footnotes of her translation, this definition of
universitas or *congregatio fidelium* was widespread as one of the senses of the *ecclesia* in polemics against the canonists' legal analysis of the church and its
actions. See Marsilius of Padua, *Defender of the Peace,* 145n7.

37. "The Three of the Crucified Life of Jesus: Book Five (Excerpts) by Ubertino
da Casale," in *Francis of Assisi: Early Documents,* vol. 3, *The Prophet,* ed. Regis J.

Armstrong, J. A. Wayne Hellmann, and William J. Short (New York: New City Press, 1998), 149.

38. For a profound description of the influence of Joachimism on the Spirituals, see Marjorie Reeves, *The Influence of Prophecy in the Later Middle Ages: A Study in Joachimism* (Notre Dame, IN: University of Notre Dame Press, 2011 [1969]), 191–228.

39. See Garnett, *Marsilius of Padua,* 29. See also David Burr, *The Spiritual Franciscans: From Protest to Prosecution in the Century after Saint Francis* (University Park: Pennsylvania State University Press, 2001), 267–277. The main source of Marsilius's and Ubertino's activities in the deposition of John XXII is Albertino Mussato's historical work "Ludovicus Bavarus," which is to be found in Johann Friedrich Böhmer, ed., *Fontes rerum Germanicarum* (Stuttgart, 1843; repr. Aalen, Germany: Scientia Verlag, 1969), 1:170–189.

40. This has already been suggested by Previté-Orton. See Previté-Orton, *Defensor pacis,* 380n3. See also Garnett, *Marsilius of Padua,* 154.

41. Some of the scholars who have discussed the relationship with the conciliarists are Paul E. Sigmund Jr., "The Influence of Marsilius of Padua on XVth Century Conciliarism," *Journal of the History of Ideas* 23 (1962): 392–402; Jeannine Quillet, "Le *Defensor pacis* de Marsile e Padoue et le *De concordantia catholica* de Nicolas de Cues," in *Niccolò Cusano agli inizi del mondo moderno: Atti del congresso internazinale in occasione del V centenario della morte di Niccolò Cusano, Bressanone, 6–10 settembre 1964* (Florence: G. C. Sansoni, 1970), 485–506; and Jürgen Miethke, "Marsilius und Ockham: Publikum und Leser ihrer politischen Schriften im späteren Mittelalter," *Medioevo* 6 (1980): 534–558. See also Jürgen Miethke, *Ai confini del potere: Il dibattito sulla* potestas *papale da Tommaso d'Aquino a Guglielmo d'Ockham* (Padua: Editrici Francescane, 2005 [2000]), 244–246.

42. Marjorie Reeves, "Marsiglio of Padua and Dante Alighieri," in *Trends in Mediaeval Political Thought,* ed. Beryl Smalley (Oxford: Basil Blackwell, 1965), 86–105; 100.

43. Takashi Shogimen, "Medicine and the Body Politic in Marsilius of Padua's *Defensor pacis,*" in Moreno-Riano and Nederman, *Companion to Marsilius of Padua,* 71–117; Joel Kaye, "The New Model of Equilibrium in Medieval Political Thought, Part 1: The *Defensor pacis* of Marsilius of Padua," in *A History of Balance, 1250–1475: The Emergence of a New Model of Equilibrium and Its Impact on Thought* (Cambridge: Cambridge University Press, 2014), 299–344.

44. Kaye, "New Model of Equilibrium," 315.

45. David George Hale, *The Body Politic: A Political Metaphor in Renaissance English Literature* (The Hague: Mouton, 1971), 38.

46. Marsilius, *DP* I, 2, 3: "Debentes itaque describere tranquillitatem et suum oppositum, suscipiamus cum Aristotele I et V *Politicae* suae, capitulis 2 et 3, civitatem esse velut animatam seu animalem naturam quandam. Nam sicuti animali bene dispositum secundum naturam componitur ex quibusdam proportionatis partibus invicem ordinatis, suaque opera sibi mutuo communicantibus et ad totum, sic civitas ex quibusdam talibus constituitur

cum bene disposita et instituta fuerit secundum rationem. Qualis est igitur comparatio animalis et suarum partium ad sanitatem, talis videbitur civitatis sive regni et suarum partium ad tranquillitatem." Latin text, 7–8; English trans., 12.

47. Kaye, "New Model of Equilibrium," 316.

48. This is also noted by Brett in *Marsilius of Padua: The Defender of the Peace*, 12n4.

49. In an interesting passage in his study, Kaye discusses the paucity of Galenic citations compared to quotations from Aristotle in *Defensor pacis*. As he argues, theology had already long been integrated with Aristotelianism at the University of Paris when Marsilius wrote his treatise, whereas Galenic naturalism had not gained such integration. Furthermore, as the dominant intellectual mode in Paris, Aristotelianism gave more weight and textual authority to Marsilius's radical arguments. See Kaye, "New Model of Equilibrium," 309–310.

50. Marsilius, *DP* I, 2, 3: "Extimant enim sanitatem esse dispositionem animalis optimam secundum naturam, sic quoque tranquillitatem dispositionem optimam civitatis secundum rationem institutae. Sanitas autem, ut aiunt peritiores physicorum describentes ipsam, est bona dispositio animalis, qua potest unaquaeque suarum partium perfecte facere operationes convenientes suae naturae; secundum quam siquidem analogiam erit tranquillitas bona dispositio civitatis aut regni, qua poterit unaquaeque suarum partium facere perfecte operationes convenientes sibi secundum rationem et suam institutionem." Latin text, 8; English trans., 12–13.

51. Marsilius, *DP* I, 1, 3: "In has ergo miseri praecipitis feruntur tenebras propter discordiam seu litem ipsorum invicem, quae, velut animalis aegritudo, sic prava civilis regiminis dispositio fore dignoscitur." Latin text, 3; English trans., 5.

52. Canning, *Ideas of Power*, 94–95.

53. Marsilius, *DP* I, 4, 2: "Hoc ergo statuamus tamquam demonstrandorum omnium principium naturaliter habitum, creditum, et ab omnibus sponte concessum: omnes scilicet homines, non orbatos aut aliter impeditos, naturaliter sufficientem vitam appetere, hinc quoque nociva refugere et declinare; quod etiam nec solum de homine confessum est, verum de omni animalium genere." Latin text, 12; English trans., 18–19.

54. In her comments to *Inf.* VI, Chiavacci Leonardi makes several references both to Dino Compagni's *Cronica* and to Giovanni Villani's *Nuova Cronica*. See Dante Alighieri, *Commedia*, con il commento di Anna Maria Chiavacci Leonardi, vol. 1, *Inferno* (Milan: Mondadori, 1991).

55. Gewirth, *Marsilius of Padua*, 61.

56. Marsilius, *DP* I, 12, 8: "Quia enim lege debent omnes cives mensuari secundum proportionem debitam, et nemo sibi scienter nocet aut vult iniustum, ideoque volunt omnes aut plurimi legem convenientem communi civium conferenti." Latin text, 53; English trans., 71.

57. See Shogimen's discussion of Marsilius's concept of justice in "Medicine and the Body Politic in *Defensor pacis*," 93–94.

58. Garnett, among others, is of a different opinion. He has argued that, according to Marsilius, "true cognisance" of justice was only possible among Christians. See Garnett, *Marsilius of Padua,* 66.

59. Canning, *Ideas of Power,* 101.

60. Albertino Mussato, "Ludovicus Bavarus," 175, lines 36–176: "Protinus vehementissimis populi Romani caloribus, ignitique ad has res novas animis, Iohannes XXII papa excommunicationibus propinatis, in personam at actus eius, prout iam dicti Marsilius et Ubertinus consultores ac etiam processuum dictatores conscribere atque componere multo studio scriverunt, edicta a senatu populoque Romano promulgata sunt." English trans. quoted from Godthardt, "Life of Marsilius of Padua," 46.

61. Leonardo Bruni, *History of the Florentine People,* ed. and trans. James Hankins, I Tatti Renaissance Library (Cambridge, MA: Harvard University Press, 2001–2004), vol. 2, lib. V, ch. 137, 126.

62. Giovanni Villani, *Cronica* (Florence, 1823), vol. 5, lib. X, ch. 9, 71.

63. One of Petrarch's best friends from his youth was Giacomo Colonna, the son of Cardinal Stefano the Elder. After Stefano's death Petrarch was in the service of Stefano's other son and brother of Giacomo, Cardinal Giovanni Colonna, and he was hosted by the Colonna family during his first trip to Rome in 1336. However, as we shall see in Chapter 4, Petrarch turned against his old supporters when Cola di Rienzo ascended the Capitoline Hill in Rome in 1347.

64. Godthardt, "Life of Marsilius of Padua," 43–44.

65. See the quotation from *Constitutiones* in Godthardt, "Life of Marsilius of Padua," 44–45.

66. Godthardt, "Life of Marsilius of Padua," 43.

67. Ibid., 50–51.

3. INDIVIDUAL FREEDOM IN WILLIAM OF OCKHAM'S *BREVILOQUIUM*

1. William of Ockham, *Breviloquium,* Prologus: "Audite hec omnes gentes, auribus percipite omnes, qui habitatis orbem, quoniam de rebus magnis et vobis necessariis locuturus sum. Doleo enim et gemo super iniquitatibus et iniuriis, que universitati vestre in totius orbi dispendium per illum, qui super cathedram Petri sedere se iactat, et nonnullos, qui ipsum in tyrannico principatu et nequitia precesserunt, et malignissime, sunt illate. Non minor autem affligor angustia, quia, quam sit divino honori contrarius, fidei periculosus catholice, iuribus et libertatibus a Deo et a natura vobis concessis adversus huiusmodi tyrannicus principatus, super vos nequiter usurpatus, vana sollicitudine inquirere non curatis, et, quod deterius est, vos de veritate informare volentes abicitis, confunditis et ipsos iudicatis." Latin text: *Wilhelm von Ockham als politischer Denker und sein Breviloquium de principatu tyrannico,* ed. Richard Scholz (Leipzig: Verlag Karl H. Hiersemann, 1944), 39; trans. by John Kilcullen as *A Short Dis-*

course on the Tyrannical Government, ed. Arthur Stephen McGrade (Cambridge: Cambridge University Press, 1992), 3. Throughout this chapter, Ockham's *Breviloquium* will be quoted from these two editions.

2. Ockham, *Breviloquium,* Prologus: "Ne tamen illorum numero, qui humanam amittere gratiam formidantes loqui libere pertimescunt, merito debeam aggregari, libera voce illorum in hoc opusculo impugnare conabor errores, qui propiis iuribus non contenti, ad aliena, tam divina quam humana, temporali confisi potentia et favore, manus extendere non pavescunt." Latin text, 39; English trans., 3.

3. Arthur Stephen McGrade, *The Political Thought of William of Ockham: Personal and Institutional Principles* (Cambridge: Cambridge University Press, 2002 [1974]), 7.

4. George Knysh, "Biographical Rectifications concerning Ockham's Avignon Period," *Franciscan Studies* 46 (1986): 61–91.

5. Volker Leppin, *Wilhelm von Ockham: Gelehrter, Streiter, Bettelmönch* (Darmstadt, Germany: Primus Verlag, 2003), 122. For a summary of the different opinions regarding Ockham's trip to and stay in Avignon, see Takashi Shogimen, *Ockham and Political Discourse in the Late Middle Ages* (Cambridge: Cambridge University Press, 2007), 2–3.

6. McGrade, *Political Thought of William of Ockham,* 8.

7. Much of the historical account in the following is based on the thorough studies by Jürgen Miethke and David Burr. See Jürgen Miethke, *Ai confini del potere: Il dibattito sulla* potestas *papale da Tommaso d'Aquino a Guglielmo d'Ockham* (Padua: Editrici Francescane, 2005 [2000]), and David Burr, *The Spiritual Franciscans: From Protest to Prosecution in the Century after Saint Francis* (University Park: Pennsylvania State University Press, 2001).

8. Francis of Assisi, "The Rule of 1223," chap. 6 in *St. Francis of Assisi: Writings and Early Biographies; English Omnibus of the Sources for the Life of St. Francis,* ed. Marion A. Habig (Quincy, IL: Franciscan Press, Quincy University, 1991), 61. See also William J. Short, "The Rule and Life of the Friars Minor," in *The Cambridge Companion to Francis of Assisi,* ed. Michael J. P. Robson (Cambridge: Cambridge University Press, 2012), 50–68.

9. Miethke, *Ai confini del potere,* 301–302; Burr, *Spiritual Franciscans,* 4.

10. André Vauchez, *Francis of Assisi: The Life and Afterlife of a Medieval Saint,* trans. Michael F. Cusato (New Haven, CT: Yale University Press, 2012), 200.

11. As for the Franciscans' hypocrisy and the reactions it provoked, see Burr, *Spiritual Franciscans,* 262–267.

12. Ibid., 213.

13. Umberto Eco, *The Name of the Rose,* trans. William Weaver (San Diego: Jovanovich, 1983). Originally published in Italian in 1980.

14. Burr, *Spiritual Franciscans,* 275–277.

15. According to Brian Tierney, these reactions to Pope John's review of the earlier papal bull *Exiit qui seminat* came ironically enough to represent an important

step toward the notion of papal infallibility. See Brian Tierney, *Origins of Papal Infallibility, 1150–1350* (Leiden: Brill, 1972), 171–237. On the discussion of this, see also McGrade, *Political Thought of William of Ockham*, 9–10.

16. Patrick Nold, "Pope John XXII, the Franciscan Order and Its *Rule*," in Robson, *Cambridge Companion to Francis of Assisi*, 258–272; 267.

17. Ibid., 272.

18. John Kilcullen, "The Political Writings," in *The Cambridge Companion to Ockham,* ed. Paul Vincent Spade (Cambridge: Cambridge University Press, 1999), 302–326; 306.

19. McGrade, *Political Thought of William of Ockham*, 11.

20. William of Ockham, *Epistola ad frates minores*, in *Guillelmi de Ockham Opera politica*, vol. 3, ed. H. S. Offler et al. (Manchester: Manchester University Press, 1956), 6–17; 6.

21. Ibid., 3–4: "In quibus quamplura haereticalia, erronea, stulta, ridiculosa, fantastica, insana et diffamatoria, fidei orthodoxae, bonis moribus, rationi naturali, exerientiae certae et caritati fraternae contraria pariter et adversa patenter inveni." English trans., *A Letter to the Minor Friars and Other Writings,* trans. John Kilcullen, ed. Arthur Stephen McGrade and John Kilcullen (Cambridge: Cambridge University Press, 1995), 3–15; 3.

22. Miethke, *Ai confini del potere*, 303.

23. Arthur Stephen McGrade and John Kilcullen, "Introduction," in Ockham, *Short Discourse*, xviii.

24. McGrade, *Political Thought of William of Ockham*, 23.

25. Ibid., 4. McGrade quotes Conrad of Megenberg, *Tractatus contra Wilhelmum Occam,* in *Unbekannte kirchenpolitische Streitschriften aus der Zeit Ludwigs des Bayern (1327–1354),* ed. Richard Scholz (Rome: Bibliothek des Königlich-Presussischen Historischen Institutes in Rom, 1914), 2:364.

26. Ockham, *Breviloquium*, I, 9: "Nam quod quis pro se inducit, etiam contra se inductum reprobare non debet dist. 19. *Si Romanorum.* Sic etiam qui inducit tesem pro se, tenetur eum contra se repicere, extra de testibus, *Presentium,* 4.q.3. *Si quis testibus.* Si igitur papa decretales pro se induxerit, debet ipsas contra se repicere; et similiter de imperatore, si pro se leges induxerit, est dicendum." Latin text, 50; English trans., 14.

27. Ockham, *Breviloquium,* Prologus: "Que autem per scripturas sacras vel per rationem evidentem aut quocumque modo sunt certa, nulliua correctioni subicio, quia illa approbanda sunt et nullatenus corrigenda." Latin text, 40; English trans., 4.

28. See Kilcullen's footnote on the manuscript tradition and this sudden interruption in the text in Ockham, *Short Discourse*, 169.

29. Shogimen, *Ockham and Political Discourse*, 235.

30. Ockham, *Breviloquium* II, 1: "Sane, sicut interdum ex uno principio vero sane intellecto veritates concluduntur innumere, ita nonnumquam ex uno falso vel etiam vero male intellecto innumerabiles inferuntur errores; quodam sapiente testante, quod uno inconvenienti dato multa sequuntur, et alibi dicitur, quod

parvus error in principio magnus est in fine, quod circa potestatem papalem estimo accidisse. Quia enim in quibusdam scripturis, quas multi tamquam autenticas venerantur, assertive scriptum habetur, quod papa habet in terris plenitudinem potestatis, quidam summi pontifices appellati, verum intellectum verborum huiusmodi ignorantes, non solum ad errores, sed etiam ad iniurias et iniquitates patentissimas processerunt." Latin text, 54; English trans., 17–18.

31. Joseph Canning, *The Ideas of Power in the Late Middle Ages, 1296–1417* (Cambridge: Cambridge University Press, 2011), 119.

32. Ockham, *Breviloquium* II, 3: "Istam assertionem non solum falsam et periculosam toti communitati fidelium, sed etiam hereticalem existimo." Latin text, 56; English trans., 21.

33. Ockham, *Breviloquium* II, 3: "Lex autem Mosayca propter importabilitatem servitutis ipsius secundum sententiam beati Petri, ut habetur Actis 15, non erat fidelibus imponenda." Latin text, 56; English trans., 22.

34. Ockham, *Breviloquium* II, 3: "Sed si papa per preceptum et ordinationem Christi talem haberet plenitudinem potestatis, ut omnia tam in temporalibus, quam in spiritualibus sine omni exceptione posset de iure, que non obviant legi divine neque iuri naturali, lex Christi esset horrendissime servitutis et incomparabiliter maioris, quam fuerit lex vetus." Latin text, 57; English trans., 23.

35. Ockham, *Breviloquium* II, 15: "quia in quampluribus nec filii parentibus, cum non sint servi, sed liberi, nec uxores viris, cum non sint ancille, sed ad paria iudicentur in multis." Latin text, 83; English trans., 47.

36. Ockham, *Breviloquium* III, 7: "Domine commune toti generi humano est illud, quod Deus dedit Ade et uxori sue pro se et omnibus posteris suis, quod fuit potestas disponendi et utenti temporalibus rebus ad utilitatem suam; et ista potestas fuisset in statu innocentie absque potestate appropriandi rem aliquam temporalem alicui uni persone vel alicui collegio speciali aut aliquibus certis personis; sed post lapsum est cum tali potestate appropriandi res temporales. Aliud est dominium proprium, quod in scientiis legalibus et scripturis modum loquendi scientiarium legalium imitantibus vocatur 'proprietas.'" Latin text, 125–126; English trans., 88.

37. See Kilcullen's commentary in *Short Discourse*, 91n38.

38. Janet Coleman, *A History of Political Thought: From the Middle Ages to the Renaissance* (Oxford: Blackwell, 2000), 173.

39. Duns Scotus, *Quaestiones Quodlibetales* VII, 8. Quoted from *God and Creatures: The Quodlibetal Questions,* trans., with an introduction, notes, and glossary, by Felix Alluntis and Allan B. Wolter (Princeton, NJ: Princeton University Press, 1975), 162.

40. Ockham, *Breviloquium* V, 2: "Dicendum est ergo, quod licet papa sit vicarius Christi, tamen nequaquam, sicut aliqui papalatre adulatorie et hereticaliter fabulantur, tota potestas Christi neque secundum divinitatem neque secundum humanitatem concessa est pape, sed, sicut dictum est prius, a potestate pape

excepta sunt iura et libertates aliorum a Deo et a natura concessa et concesse, ut innocentes et iustos ultra illa, que de necessitate facienda sunt et ad que per legem divinam et ius naturale tenentur, premere nequeat nolentes et invitos onerosis et gravibus ordinationibus, statius, legibus vel preceptis." Latin text, 170; English trans., 133.

41. Ockham, *Breviloquium* V, 3: "Sed sensus misticus, qui non est expressus in scriptura sacra, allegari taliter minime potest, nisi in quantum alii scripture vel rationi evidenti innititur." Latin text, 171; English trans., 134.

42. Tierney, who has studied what he calls Ockham's "anti-papal infallibility," has argued that through his critique of the popes in Avignon, Ockham was implicitly affirming a new doctrine of papal infallibility because his aim was to save the contemporary church from heresy. As Tierney writes, Ockham's "paradoxes always arise from [his] conviction that the true church had to be infallible while the existing, institutional church was in error." See Tierney, *Origins of Papal Infallibility,* 227.

43. Ockham, *Breviloquium* V, 4: "Certius est enim quilibet orthodoxus, papam posse peccare contra bonos mores et errare contra fidem, et ideo doctrina sua inter doctrinas illorum episcoporum, qui secundum Augustinum possunt iusto iudicio et nulla temeritate culpari, est omnimode computanda.... Quantecumque enim auctoritatis fuerit papa, semper est sibi veritas preferenda, precipue que ad ius divinum dinoscitur pertinere." Latin text, 175; English trans., 137.

44. Ockham, *Breviloquium* V, 4: "Huic respondeo, quod iudicare de hoc per modum simplicis cognitionis et exteritoris assertionis, quomodo medicus iudicat de medicinalibus et quilibet artifex de hiis, que spectant ad artem suam, pertinet ad quemlibet certitudinaliter cognoscentem veritatem, sive cognoscat eam per solam fidem, si sit talis veritas, quod ad fidem spectat, sive per rationem evidentem vel experientiam certam, si sit cognoscibilis tali modo. Unde si papa diffiniret aliquid vel assereret aut etiam opinaretur contra illa, que quilibet christianus credere tenetur explicite, quilibet haberet iudicare isto modo, papam errare in hoc casu." Latin text, 175–176; English trans., 137.

45. Canning, *Ideas of Power,* 130.

46. A rich study on Valla's radical reform of Aristotelian scholasticism is the book by Lodi Nauta, *In Defense of Common Sense: Lorenzo Valla's Humanist Critique of Scholastic Philosophy* (Cambridge, MA: Harvard University Press, 2009).

47. Ockham, *Breviloquium* V, 4: "Sic etiam error Iohannis 22, quod in rebus usu consumptibilibus usus facti non potest a dominio seu proprietate separari, est tam apertus etiam simplicibus, quod etiam simplices debent iudicare, ipsum errare." Latin text, 176; English trans., 138.

48. Ockham, *Breviloquium* III, 8: "Duplex potestas predicta, scilicet appropriandi res temporales et instituendi rectores iurisdictionem habentes, data est a Deo immediate non tantum fidelibus, sed etiam infidelibus sic, quod cadit sub precepto et inter pure moralia computatur, propter quod omnes obligat tam fideles, quam etiam infideles." Latin text, 128; English trans., 91.

49. Ockham, *Breviloquium* III, 1: "Sacra scriptura dicit contrarium evidenter, scilicet quod ymmo iure divino, non humano fuerit dominium introductum." Latin text, 108; English trans., 73.

50. Ockham, *Breviloquium* III, 1: "ergo extra ecclesiam nullum est verum dominium temporalium nec aliqua potestas ordinata vel concessa, sed permissa tantummodo." Latin text, 109; English trans., 73.

51. This is above all suggested by McGrade and Kilcullen, who in their introduction to *Breviloquium* write as follows: "While exponents of unlimited papal power such as Giles of Rome and Augustinus Triumphus provide impressive medieval models for later absolutist conceptions of sovereignty, the whole thrust of Ockham's thought is against absolutism, both ecclesiastical and secular. His work is a contribution to political thought in the constitutionalist tradition." McGrade and Kilcullen, "Introduction," xx.

52. See Shogimen, *Ockham and Political Discourse*, 6–10.

53. While earlier scholars such as Charles Howard McIlwan and the Carlyle brothers—R. W. Carlyle and A. J. Carlyle—presented Ockham as a political thinker, the scholars who have emphasized the difficulties with this label are Walter Ullmann, Anthony Black, and Joseph Canning. See Charles Howard McIlwain, *The Growth of Political Thought in the West from the Greeks to the End of the Middle Ages* (New York: Macmillan, 1932); R. W. Carlyle and A. J. Carlyle, *A History of Medieval Political Theory in the West*, 6 vols. (Edinburgh: W. Blackwood and Sons, 1970 [1903–1936]); Walter Ullmann, *A History of Political Thought: The Middle Ages* (Harmondsworth, UK: Penguin, 1965); Anthony Black, *Political Thought in Europe, 1250–1450* (Cambridge: Cambridge University Press, 1992); Joseph Canning, *A History of Medieval Political Thought, 300–1450* (London: Routledge, 1996); and Canning, *Ideas of Power*.

54. Coleman, *History of Political Thought*, 169.

55. Canning, *Ideas of Power*, 118–119.

56. Egidius Romanus [Giles of Rome], *De ecclesiastica potestate*, ed. Richard Scholtz (Weimar, Germany: H. Böhlaus Nachfolger, 1929), 206. Quoted from McGrade, *Political Thought of William of Ockham*, 82.

57. McGrade, *Political Thought of William of Ockham*, 84–85.

58. See Shogimen's analysis of free will in Ockham's work in *Ockham and Political Discourse*, 246–250.

59. Francis Petrarch, *De sui ipsius et multorum ignorantia* IV, 107, in *Invectives*, ed. and trans. David Marsh, I Tatti Renaissance Library (Cambridge, MA: Harvard University Press, 2003): "Video nempe uirtutem ab illo egregie diffiniri et distingui tractatarique acriter, et cuique sunt propria, seu uitio, seu uirtuti. Que cum didici, scio plusculum quam sciebam; idem tamen est animus qui fuerat, uoluntasque eadem, *idem ego*." Latin text, 314; English trans., 315.

60. Petrarch, *De sui ipsius*, IV, 108: "Aliud est enim scire atque aliud amare, aliud intelligere atque aliud uelle. Docet ille, non infitior, quid est uirtus; at stimulus ac uerborum faces, quibus ad amorem uirtutis uitiique odium mens urgetur atque incenditur, lectio illa uel non habet, uel paucissimos habet. . . .

Quid profuerit autem nosse quid est uirtus, si cognita non ametur?" Latin
text, 314; English trans., 315.

61. Petrarch, *De sui ipsius,* II, 28, 248.

62. Petrarch, *De sui ipsius,* III, 31: "Nam et ego ipse recogitans quam multa michi
desint ad id quo sciendi auida mens suspirat, ignorantiam meam dolens ac
tacitus recognosco." Latin text, 250; English trans., 251.

63. For a further reading of Petrarch's *De ignorantia* in connection with Petrarch's
discussions of the will, see Unn Falkeid, "Petrarch, Mont Ventoux and the
Modern Self," *Forum Italicum* 43, no. 1 (2009): 5–29.

64. Giovanni Boccaccio, *Epistole* II, "Mavortis milex extrenue," dated 1339 and
probably addressed to Petrarch, in *Epistole e lettere,* ed. Ginetta Auzzas, vol. 5.1
of *Tutte le opere di Giovanni Boccaccio,* ed. Vittore Branca (Milan: Aldo Mondadori, 1992), 514: "estque in artibus per excellentiam hiis monarcha: in gram-
aticha Aristarcus, Occam in logica."

4. PETRARCH, COLA DI RIENZO, AND
THE BATTLE OF ROME

1. Francis Petrarch, *Lettere disperse: Varie e miscellanee,* ed. Alessandro Pancheri
(Parma, Italy: Ugo Guandi, 1994). There is no published English translation
of the entire *Lettere disperse.* The English translation cited is this chapter is
taken from the volume *Petrarch: The Revolution of Cola di Rienzo,* ed. Mario
Emilio Cosenza, 3rd ed., with new introduction, notes, and bibliography by
Ronald G. Musto (New York: Italica, 1996), 10–36. All the quotations in this
chapter are taken from these two editions.

2. For a short reading of the letter, see Lynn Lara Westwater, "The Uncollected
Poet," in *Petrarch: A Critical Guide to the Complete Works,* ed. Victoria Kirkham
and Armando Maggi (Chicago: University of Chicago Press, 2009), 301–309.
See also the introductory notes to Cosenza, *Petrarch: The Revolution of Cola di
Rienzo,* 9–10.

3. Francis Petrarch, *Rerum familiarum libri,* ed. Ugo Dotti, 3 vols. (Rome: Archivio
Guido Izzi, 1991); ed. and trans. by Aldo S. Bernardo as *Rerum familiarum libri,
I–VIII* (Albany: State University of New York Press, 1975), *Letters on Familiar
Matters: Rerum familiarum libri, IX–XVI* (Baltimore: John Hopkins University
Press, 1982), and *Letters on Familiar Matters: Rerum familiarum libri, XVII–XXIV*
(Baltimore: John Hopkins University Press, 1985). Throughout the volume, the
work will be quoted from these editions.

4. Francis Petrarch, *Senilium rerum libri* XVIII, 1, in *Epistole di Francesco Petrarca,* ed.
Ugo Dotti (Turin, Italy: Unione Tipografico-Editrice Torinese, 1978), 876; ed.
and trans. by Aldo S. Bernardo, Saul Levin, and Reta A. Benardo as *Letters of Old
Age: Rerum senilium libri, I–XVIII* (Baltimore: Johns Hopkins University Press,
1992), 2:672. For studies of Petrarch's life, see Ernest Hatch Wilkins, *Life of
Petrarch* (Chicago: University of Chicago Press, 1961), and Ugo Dotti, *Vita di Petrarca* (Rome–Bari: Laterza, 1991 [1987]).

5. Petrarch, *Sen.* XVIII, 1, 876: "Avinio urbi nomen—ubi romanus pontifex turpi in exilio Cristi tenet Eccesiam." English trans., 674.

6. Francis Petrarch, *Epystola* I, 2, vv. 90–91: "infames venere proci, qui nostra petentes/coniugia, invitam violarunt corpu inerme." *Epystole metriche*, in *Poemata minora quae exstant omnia/Poesie minori del Petrarca*, ed. Domenico Rossetti, vol. 3 (Milan: Società Tipografica dei Classici Italiani, 1834). There is no complete English translation.

7. Francis Petrarch, *Invectiva contra eum qui maledixit Italie* (Invective against a detractor of Italy), in *Invectives*, edited and translated by David Marsh, 364–475, I Tatti Renaissance Library (Cambridge, MA: Harvard University Press, 2003), 368–369.

8. Augustine, *De civitate Dei*, ed. Bernardus Dombart and Alphonsus Kalb, 1928–1929, Corpus christianorum: Series Latina, vols. 47–48 (Turnhout, Belgium: Brepols, 1955), bk. XVIII, 22. See also Charles T. Davis, *Dante and the Idea of Rome* (Oxford: Clarendon, 1965), esp. 235–243; and Charles T. Davis, "Rome and Babylon in Dante," in *Rome in the Renaissance: The City and the Myth: Papers of the Thirteenth Annual Conference of the Center for Medieval & Early Renaissance Studies*, ed. Paul A. Ramsey (Binghamton, NY: Medieval and Renaissance Texts and Studies, Center for Medieval and Early Renaissance Studies, 1982), 19–40.

9. Davis, "Rome and Babylon in Dante," 29. See also David Burr, *The Spiritual Franciscans: From Protest to Prosecution in the Century after Saint Francis* (University Park: Pennsylvania State University Press, 2001), 272–273.

10. Francis Petrarch, *Liber sine nomine* 18, in *Sine nomine: Lettere polemiche e politiche*, ed. Ugo Dotti (Rome–Bari: Editori Laterza, 1974), 202: "omnis vicus his vermibus scatet." English trans., *Petrarch's Book without a Name*, trans. Norman P. Zacour (Toronto: Pontifical Institute of Medieval Studies, 1973), 110.

11. Petrarch, *Sine nomine* 18, 202: "meretrix fornicata cum regibus terre." Apoc. 17:1–2. English trans., 111.

12. Petrarch, *Sine nomine* 18, 202: "Babilon mater fornicationum et abominationum terre." Apoc. 17:5. English trans., 111.

13. Petrarch, *Sine nomine* 18, 202: "mulierem ebriam de sanguine sanctorum et de sanguine martirium Jesu." Apoc. 17:6. English trans., 111.

14. Anonimo Romano, *Cronica*, ed. Giuseppe Porta (Milan: Adelphi, 1979), trans. by John Wright as *The Life of Cola di Rienzo* (Toronto: Pontifical Institute of Medieval Studies, 1975). Chapter XVIII of *Cronica* treats Cola di Rienzo's biography: "Delli granni fatti li quali fece Cola di Rienzo, lo quale fu tribuno de Roma augusto," 143–211. The following account of the situation in Rome is also much indebted to Ronald G. Musto, the modern biographer of Cola di Rienzo. See Ronald G. Musto, *Apocalypse in Rome: Cola di Rienzo and the Politics of the New Age* (Berkeley: University of California Press, 2003).

15. Anonimo Romano, *Cronica*, cap. XVIII, lines 326–327, Porta, 154; English trans., 41.

16. According to Musto, the fourth conspirator probably came from the church of San Giorgio in Velabro. See Musto, *Apocalypse in Rome*, 139.

17. Anonimo Romano, *Cronica,* cap. XVIII, lines 290–308, Porta, 153: "Fatto questo, la citate de Roma stava in grannissima travaglia. Rettori non aveva. Onne dìe se commatteva. Da onne parte derobava. Dove era luoco, le vergine se detoperavano. Non ce era reparo. Le piccolo zitelle se furavano e menavanose a desonore. La moglie era toita allo marito nello prorio lietto. Li lavoratori, quanno ivano fòra a lavorare, erano derobati, dove? su nella porta de Roma. Li pellegrini, li quali viengo per merito delle loro anime alle sante chiesie, non erano defesi, ma erano scannati e derobati. Li prieti staiavano per male fare. Onne lascivia, onne male, nulla iustizia, nullo freno. Non ce era più remedio. Onne perzona periva. Quello più avea rascione, lo quale più poteva colla spade. Non ce era aitra salvezza se non che ciascheuno se defenneva con parienti e con amici. Onne dìe se faceva adunanza de armati." English trans., 40.

18. Musto, *Apocalypse in Rome,* 57.

19. I am most grateful to Ronald L. Martinez, who has let me read the unpublished article "The Widow Writes to the Whore: Petrarch Laments the Avignon Papacy," in which he offers a rich and convincing reading of Petrarch's *Epystole* II, 5, as well as tracing the medieval genealogy of the representation of Rome as the widowed Jerusalem. See also Nancy J. Vickers, "Widowed Words: Dante, Petrarch, and the Metaphors of Mourning," in *Discourses of Authority in Medieval and Renaissance Literature,* ed. Kevin Brownlee and Walter Stephens (Hanover, NH: University Press of New England, 1989), 97–108; and Cristelle L. Baskins, "Trecento Rome: The Poetics and Politics of Widowhood," in *Widowhood and Visual Culture in Early Modern Europe,* ed. Allison Levy (Aldershot, UK: Ashgate, 2003), 197–209.

20. Line Cecilie Engh has offered an insightful reading of the letter in her chapter "Embodying the Female Body Politic: Pro-Papal Reception of Ephesians 5 in the Later Middle Ages," in *Bodies, Borders, Believers: Ancient Texts and Present Conversations,* ed. Anne Hege Grung, Marianne Bjelland Kartzow, and Anna Rebecca Solevåg (Eugene, OR: Pickwick, 2015), 164–197.

21. Bernard of Clairvaux, *Epistola* 243, in *Patrologiae cursus completus,* ed. Jacques-Paul Migne, Series Latina, 182:437–440; 439: "Aperi, gens misera, aperi oculos tuos, et vide desolationem tuam jamjamque imminentem. Quomodo in brevi mutatus est color optimus [Thren. IV.1], facta est quasi vidua domina gentium, princeps provinciarum [Thren. I.1]?" English trans.: *The Letters of Saint Bernard of Clairvaux,* ed. and trans. Bruno S. James (Chicago: Regnery, 1953), 391–394.

22. Bible, New International Version, https://www.biblegateway.com.

23. *Vitis mystica seu tractatus de Passione Domini* [The true vine: A treatise on the Passion of Our Lord], in Migne, *Patrologiae cursus completus,* 184:638. For a profound study of this literature in both Latin and the vernacular languages, see Thomas Bestul, *Texts of the Passion: Latin Devotional Literature and Medieval Society* (Philadelphia: University of Pennsylvania Press, 1996).

24. See Engh, "Embodying the Female Body Politic," 174.

25. For a rich reading of Dante's use of the biblical image of the bride and the widow, see Olivia Holmes, "Jerusalem and Babylon: Brides, Widows, and

Whores," in *Dante's Two Beloveds* (New Haven, CT: Yale University Press, 2008), 119–157.

26. See Musto, *Apocalypse in Rome*, 67. See also Diana Wood, *Clement VI: The Pontificate and Ideas of an Avignon Pope* (Cambridge: Cambridge University Press, 1989), 46.

27. Petrarch, *Epystola* II, 5, 277–279, in *Poemata minora quae exstant omnia / Poesie minori del Petrarca*, 3:30; English translation by Ronald L. Martinez in his unpublished article "The Widow Writes to the Whore: Petrarch Laments the Avignon Papacy."

28. Anonimo Romano, *Cronica*, cap. XVIII, lines 7–20, Porta, 134: "Fu da soa ioventutine nutricato de latte de eloquenzia, buono gramatico, megliore rettorico, autorista buono. Deh, como e quanto era veloce elitore! Moito usava Tito Livio, Seneca e Tulio e Valerio Massimo. Moito li delettava le magnificenze de Iulio Cesari raccontare. Tutta dìe se speculava nelli intagli de marmo li quali iaccio intorno a Roma. Non era aitri che esso, che sapessi leiere li antiqui pataffii. Tutte scritture antiche vulgarizzava. Queste figure de marmo iustamente interpretava. Deh, como spesso diceva: 'Dove soco questi buoni Romani? Dove ène loro summa iustizia? Pòterame trovare in tiempo che questi fussino!'" English trans., 31.

29. Cola di Rienzo, Letter 1, to the Roman people (Avignon, 28–31 January 1343), in *Die Briefwechsel des Cola di Rienzo*, ed. Konrad Burdach and Paul Pier, Vom Mittelater zur Reformation, vols. 2.1–5 (Berlin: Wedimann, 1913–1929), vol. 2.3. See also Musto, *Apocalypse in Rome*, 73.

30. Musto, *Apocalypse in Rome*, 76.

31. Anonimo Romano, *Cronica*, cap. XVIII, lines 29–32, Porta, 144; English trans., 32.

32. Musto, *Apocalypse in Rome*, 76–82.

33. Anonimo Romano, *Cronica*, cap. XVIII, lines 64–132, Porta, 145–146: "Anco secunnario lo preditto Cola ammonìo li rettori e'llo puopolo allo bene fare per una similitudine la quale fece pegnare nello palazzo de Campituoglio 'nanti lo mercato. Nello parete fòra sopra la Cammora penze una similitudine in questa forma. Era pento uno grannissimo mare, le onne orribile, forte turvato. In mieso de questo mare stava una nave poco meno che soffocata, senza tomone, senza vela. In questa nave, la quale per pericolare stava, stava una femina vedova vestuta de nero, centa de cengolo de tristezze, sfessa la gonnella da pietto, sciliati li capelli, como volessi piagnere. Stava inninocciata, incrociava le mano piecate allo pietto per pietate, in forma de precare che sio pericolo non fussi. Lo soprascritto diceva; 'Questa ène Roma'. Attorno a questa nave, dalla parte de sotto, nell'acqua stavano quattro nave affonnate, loro vele cadute, rotti li arbori, perduti li tomoni. In ciascheuna stava una femina affoncata e morta. La prima avea nome Babillonia, la secunna Cartaine, la terza Troia, la quarta Irusalem. Lo soprascritto diceva: 'Queste citati per la iniustizia pericolaro e vennero meno'. Una lettera iessiva fra queste morte femine e diceva così: 'Sopra onne signoria fosti in aitura./Ora aspettamo qui la toa rottura.'" English trans., 33–34.

34. Roberto Weiss, "Barbato da Sulmona, il Petrarca e la rivoluzione di Cola di Rienzo," in *Studi Petrarcheschi,* ed. Carlo Calcaterra (Bologna: Minerva, 1950), 13–22.

35. Cosenza, *Petrarch: The Revolution of Cola di Rienzo,* 10.

36. Petrarch, *Disperse* 8, 38: "Primum tibi, vir magnanime, pro tantarum rerum gloria an libertatis per te civibus pro tuis erga illos meritis et felicissimo successu restitute libertatis gratuler, incertus sum. Utriusque pariter gratulabor, utrosque simul alloquar, neque quos tam coniunctos rebus ipsis video, sermone disiungam." English trans., 10.

37. Petrarch, *Disperse* 8, 40: "Libertas in medio vestrum est, qua nichil dulcius, nichil optabilius nunquam certius quam perdendo cognoscitur." English trans., 10.

38. Petrarch, *Invectiva contra eum qui maledixit Italie,* 368: "Roma, vero, mundi caput, urbium regina, sedes imperii, arx fidei catholice, fons omnium memorabilium exemplorum." English trans., 369.

39. Petrarch, *Disperse* 8, 44–46: "Sed minus indignor, dum eos etiam humanitatis oblitos video: nonne enim iampridem eo vesanie perventum est, ut non 'homines' sed 'dominos' dici velint? Proh nefas! In qua Urbe divus Cesar Augustus, mundi rector ac regnorum omnium moderator, edicto vetuit se dominum dici, in ea nunc menidci fures gravi iniuria se affectos putant, nisi domini vocitentur. O miserabilem fortune vertiginem, o mutationem temporis inauditam!" English trans., 12.

40. Pier Giorgio Ricci, "Il commeno di Cola di Rienzo alla 'Monarchia' di Dante," *Studi medievali,* ser. 3, vol. 6, no. 2 (1965): 665–708; 678.

41. Ibid., 672–673.

42. Ibid., 677.

43. Petrarch, *Disperse* 8, 50: "quibus equo iure vivere cum civibus extrema servitus, quibus nichil nisi iniustum atque insolens videtur esse posse magnificum." English trans., 14.

44. Petrarch, *Disperse* 8, 60: "qui enim contra sentiunt, non de populi, sed de hostium numero sunt habendi, quibus velut pravis humoribus exoneratum reipublice corpus quo tenuius eo expeditius validiusque remanebit." English trans., 17–18.

45. Ernest Hatch Wilkins, "Petrarch's *Coronation Oration,*" in *Studies in the Life of Petrarch* (Cambridge, MA: Mediaeval Academy of America, 1955), 300–313; 300. For readings of *Collatio laureationis,* see also Giuseppe Mazzotta, "Petrarca e il Discorso di Roma," in *Petrarca: Canoni, esemplarità,* ed. Valeria Fenucci (Rome: Bulzoni editore, 2006), 259–273; and Dennis Looney, "The Beginnings of Humanistic Oratory. Petrarch's *Coronation Oration, Collatio laureationis,*" in Kirkham and Maggi, *Petrarch: A Critical Guide to the Complete Works,* 131–141.

46. For readings of this letter, see, for instance, Giuseppe Mazzotta, "Antiquity and the New Arts," in *The Worlds of Petrarch* (Durham, NC: Duke University Press, 1993), 14–32; David Galbraith, "Petrarch and the Broken City," in *Antiquity and Its Interpreters,* ed. Alina Payne, Ann Kuttner, and Rebekah Smick (Cambridge: Cambridge University Press, 2000), 17–20; and Unn Falkeid, "Pe-

trarch and the Vision of Rome," *Acta Ad Archeologiam et Artium Historiam Pertinentia* 25 (n.s. 11) (2012): 195–207.

47. Mazzotta, "Petrarca e il Discorso di Roma," 262–263.

48. Petrarch, *Fam.* VI, 2, 14: "Quis enim dubitare potest quin illico surrectura sit, si ceperit se Roma cognoscere?"

49. Francis Petrarch, *Collatio laureationis,* in Bufano, *Opere Latine di Francesco Petrarca,* 2:1256–1283; 1256. The English trans. is to be found in Wilkins, "Petrarch's *Coronation Oration,*" 300.

50. Petrarch, *Collatio laureationis,* 1268: "Audacter itaque fortassis, sed non, ut michi videor, maligno propsito, ceteris cessantibus, me in tam laborioso et michi quidem periculoso calle ducem prebere non expavi, multos posthac, ut arbitror, secuturos." English trans., 306.

51. The discovery is remembered in a letter to Petrarch's friend Francesco Nelli (*Fam.* XIII, 6), and in a letter to the papal secretary, Luca da Penna (*Sen.* XVI, 1).

52. Looney, "Beginnings of Humanistic Oratory," 134.

53. See the introduction by N. H. Watts to his translation of *Pro Archia* in Marcus Tullius Cicero, *The Speeches,* with an English translation by N. H. Watts (London: William Heinemann; New York: G. P. Putnam's Son, 1923), 4.

54. Cicero, *Pro Archia* XXIII, 30–32: "Nam si quis minorem gloriae frucum putat ex Graecis versibus percipi quam ex Latinis, vehementer errat, propterea quod Graeca leguntur in omnibus fere gentibus, Latina suis finibus, exiguis sane, continentur. Qua re si res eae, quas gessimus, orbis terrae regionibus definiuntur, cupere debemus, quo manuum nostrarum tela pervenerint, eodem gloriam famamque penetrare, quod quum ipsis populis, de quorum rebus scribitur, haec ampla sunt, tum iis certe, qui de vita gloriae causa dimicant, hoc maximum et periculorum incitamentum est et laborum." English trans., 31–33.

55. This is wrong, according to Dennis Looney. See Looney, "Beginnings of Humanistic Oratory," 136.

56. Petrarch, *Collatio laureationis,* 1276: "sicut ex anima et corpore constamus, sic duplex querende glorie via nobis parata est, corporis scilicet atque animi, licet, dum in hac vita sumus, alter alterius egeat auxilio." English trans., 309.

57. Petrarch, *Collatio laureationis,* 1272: "Et profecto multi fuerunt in vita gloriosi et memorabiles viri, tam in scripturis quam in re bellica, et quorum tamen nomina, lapsu temporum, contexit oblivio nullam ob aliam causam nisi quia literati hominis que in animo habuerunt stilo mansuro et stabili committere nesciverunt.... Fortes autem et bellicosi, vel alias eternitatem nominis promeriti, in oblivionem abierunt, quia non contigit eis scriptor ydoneus. Ideo simul cum corporibus talium fama sepulta est." English trans., 308.

58. Petrarch, *Disperse* 8, 48: "Verum ut prospera sic adversa futuna suum finem habet, et illorum et vestre libertati defensor insperatus adfuit, et suum Brutum utraque tulit etas. Tres iam hinc ex prdine celebrantur Bruti: primus qui Superbum regem expulit; secundus qui Iulium Cesarem interfecit; tertius qui nostri temporis tyrannos et exilio et morte persequitur: in hoc ambobus similis, quod

gemine laudis materiam, quam inter se alii duo unitam dividunt, iste totam occupat, priori tamen quadam morum ac propositi occultatione similor: 'iuvenis' uterque 'longe alius ingenio quam cuius simulationem induerat, ut sub hoc obtentu liberator ille Populi Romani animus latens aperiretur tempore suo.'" English trans., 13–14. The text Petrarch is quoting here is Livy, *Ab urbe condita*, I, 56, 7–9.

59. The manuscript, now the MS Harley 2493 in the British Library, later came into the possession of Lorenzo Valla, who enriched it further. See Giuseppe Billanovich, *La tradizione del testo di Livio e le origini dell'umanesimo*, vol. 2, *Il Livio del Petrarca e del Valla* (Padua: Antenore, 1981).

60. See the history of Brutus in Livy, *Ab urbe condita*, I, 56–60, in *Livy in Fourteen Volumes*, vol. 1, bks. 1–2, trans. B. O. Foster (Cambridge, MA: Harvard University Press / Loeb, 1919).

61. Francis Petrarch, *De remediis utrusque fortunae*, II, 19, trans. by Conrad H. Rawski as *Petrarch's Remedies for Fortune Fair and Foul: A Modern English Translation of "De remediis utriusque fortune," with a Commentary* (Bloomington: Indiana University Press, 1991), 3:244.

62. For a more thorough investigation of the concepts of *humilitas* in Petrarch's works, see Unn Falkeid, "'Thorn in the Flesh': Pain and Poetry in Petrarch's *Secretum*," in *Pangs of Love and Longing: Configurations of Desire in Premodern Literature*, ed. Anders Cullhed et al. (Cambridge: Cambridge Scholars, 2013), 74–89.

63. Petrarch, *Disperse* 8, 50: "Hoc interfuit, quod illorum patientia unius indignitate sceleris, vestra innumerabilibus flagitiis atque intollerabilibus iniuriis victa est." English trans., 14.

64. Petrarch, *Disperse* 8, 66–68: "Vos vero, nunc primum veri cives, hunc virum celitus vobis missum credite, hunc ut rarum aliquod Dei munus colite, pro salute eius animas vestras exponite! Licuit et sibi cum reliquis in servito degere, et quod tam magnus populus sponte subierat iugum pati; licuit, si id molestum videretur, procul a conspectu miserrime Urbis effugere, et, quod quosdam summos viro fecisse novimus, spontaneo exilio suum caput contumeliis eripere. Retraxit eum solus amor patrie, quam cum in eo statu deserere sacrilegium putaret, in hac sibi vivendum esse pro hac moriendum statuit fortunas vestras miseratus. In quam precipitem locum venerit, videtis: opem ferte, ne corruat!" English trans., 20–21.

65. Petrarch, *Disperse* 8, 58: "Iunior Brute, senioris imaginem ante oculos semper habe." English trans., 17.

66. Petrarch, *Disperse* 8, 58: "ille consul erat, tu Tribunus. Si conferimus dignitates, multa quidem a consulibus adversus plebem Romanam animose dicta, multa etiam atrociter facta sunt, cuius tribunos constantissimos defensores semper accepimus." English trans., 17.

67. Petrarch, *Disperse* 8, 74: "et tradita vobis a patribus vestris non nisi in hostes publicos arma converite." English trans., 23.

68. Petrarch, *Fam.* VII, 7, 2: "Quis est hic qui vulnerat aures meas, tantus et tam tristis fragor?" English trans., *Letters on Familiar Matters, I–VIII*, 349.

69. Petrarch, *Fam.* VII, 7, 6: "et hanc michi quoque durissimam necessitatem exime, ne lyricus apparatus tuarum laudum, in quo—teste quidem hoc calamo—multus eram, desinere cogatur in satyram." English trans. *Letters on Familiar Matters, I–VIII,* 350.

70. For a fuller discussion about this, see Cosenza, *Petrarch: The Revolution of Cola di Rienzo,* 32–33n33.

71. Petrarch, *Disperse* 8, 74–76: "Sed iam vereor ne plus equo vos in verbis detineam, hoc presertim tempore cum factis potius opus est. Que quoniam neque professioni neque fortune mee suppetunt, quod unum auxilii genus habeo, verba transmitto. . . . Ceterum quod soluta oratione nunc attigi, attingam fortasse propediem alio dicendi genere, modo michi, quod spero quidem et cupio, gloiosi principii perseverantiam non negetis. Apollinea fronde redimitus desertum atque altum Helicona penetrabo; illic Castalium ad fontem Musis ab exilio revocatis ad mansuram glorie vestre memoriam sonantius aliquid canam quod longius audietur. Vale, vir fortissime! Valete, viri optimi! Vale gloriosissima Septicollis!" English trans., 23–24.

72. Mazzotta, "Petrarca e il Discorso di Roma," 271: "A Cola, che è convinto della possibile identità tra passto e presente, sfugge il senso della storia come differenza, come processo senza posa del fare e disfare."

73. Much has been written about Petrarch's formative role in early humanism since the time of Pierre de Nolhac's study *Pétrarque et l'humanism,* 2 vols. (Paris: E. Bouilon, 1892). A few studies can be mentioned: Giuseppe Billanovich, *Petrarca letterato,* vol. 1, *Lo scrittoio del Petrarca* (Rome: Edizioni di storia e letteratura, 1947); Giuseppe Billanovich, *Petraraca e il primo umanesimo* (Padua: Edizioni Antenore, 1996); Eugenio Garin, *Italian Humanism: Philosophy and Civic Life in Renaissance Italy* (Oxford: Blackwell, 1965 [1952]); Charles Trinkhaus, *The Poet as Philosopher: Petrarch and the Formation of Renaissance Consciousness* (New Haven, CT: Yale University Press, 1979); Mazzotta, *Worlds of Petrarch;* Carol Everhart Quillen, *Rereading the Renaissance: Petrarch, Augustine, and the Language of Humanism* (Ann Arbor: University of Michigan Press, 1998); Riccardo Fubini, *Humanism and Secularization: From Petrarch to Valla* (Durham, NC: Duke University Press, 2003); and Timothy Kircher, *The Poet's Wisdom: The Humanists, the Church, and the Formation of Philosophy in the Early Renaissance* (Leiden: Brill, 2006). For an updated survey, see Timothy Kircher, "Petrarch and the Humanists," in *The Cambridge Companion to Petrarch,* ed. Albert Russell Ascoli and Unn Falkeid (Cambridge: Cambridge University Press, 2015), 179–191; and, finally, Gur Zak, *Petrarch's Humanism and the Care of the Self* (Cambridge: Cambridge University Press, 2010). For broad, solid, and most useful studies on early humanism including Petrarch, see the two books by Ronald G. Witt, *"In the Footsteps of the Ancients": The Origin of Humanism from Lovato to Bruni* (Boston: Brill Academic, 2003), and *The Two Latin Cultures and the Foundation of Renaissance Humanism in Medieval Italy* (Cambridge: Cambridge University Press, 2012).

74. Mazzotta, *Worlds of Petrarch,* 22.

75. Petrarch, *Invectiva contra eum qui maledixit Italie,* 382, 384: "Que, o si filiis suis—
    illis dico maioribus—Deus omnipotens pacem daret fraternamque concordiam,
    quam cito, quam facile rebellantem barbariem iugo illi veteri, italicis ut olim
    viribus adiuta, compesceret! Id si anea fuisset incognitum, nuper apparuit, dum
    vir unus, obscurissime originis et nullarum opum atque, ut res docuit, plus
    animi habens quam constantie, reipublice imbecillos humero subicere ausus
    est et tutelam labentis imperii profiteri. Quam subito erecta omnis Italia!
    Quantus ad extrema terrarum Romani nominis terror ac fama pervenit! Et
    quanto gravior pervenisset, si tam facile esset perserverare quam incipere!" En-
    glish trans., 383, 385.
76. Anonimo Romano, *Cronica,* cap. XVIII, lines 1054–1129, Porta, 178–180; En-
    glish trans., 64–66.
77. Petrarch, *Fam.* VII, 7, 13: "circumpice, oro, summo studio quid agas, excute
    acriter te ipsum, examina tecum, nec te fallas, qui sis, qui fueris, unde, quo
    veneris, quorsum inoffensa libertate progredi fas sit, quam personam indu-
    eris, quod nomen assumpseris, quam spem tui feceris, quid professus fueris:
    videbis te non dominum reipublice, sed ministrum." English trans., *Letters on
    Familiar Matters, I–VIII,* 351–352.
78. Anonimo Romano, *Cronica,* cap. XVIII, lines 1972–1981, Porta, 208–209; En-
    glish trans., 93. See also Guillaume Mollat, *The Popes at Avignon, 1305–1378*
    (London: Thomas Nelson, 1963), 152.
79. Anonimo Romano, *Cronica,* cap. XXVII, lines 1–54, Porta, 237–238; English
    trans., 125–126. See also Musto, *Apocalypse in Rome,* 267, and Mollat, *Popes in
    Avignon,* 153.
80. Petrarch, *Fam.* XIII, 6, 5: "olim late formidatus tribunus urbis Rome, nunc
    omnium hominum miserrimus." English trans., *Letters on Familiar Matters,
    IX–XVI,* 193.
81. Petrarch, *Fam.* XIII, 6, 19–21: "Quod ita esse, ex obiecti criminis qualitate perpen-
    ditur; nichil enim ex his que bonis omnibus in illo viro displicent, arguitur, neque
    omnino finis sed principii reus est; non sibi obicitur quod malis adheserit, quod
    libertatem destituerit, quod e Capitolio fugerit, cum nusquam honestius vivere,
    nusquam gloriosius mori posset. Quid ergo? illud unum sibi crimen opponitur,
    unde si condemnatus fuerit, non michi quidem infamis sed eterna decoratus
    gloria videbitur; quod scilicet cogitare ausus sit ut salvam ac liberam vellet esse
    rempublicam et de Romano imperio deque romanis potestatibus Rome agi." En-
    glish trans., *Letters on Familiar Matters, IX–XVI,* 196.
82. Petrarch, *Fam.* XIII, 6, 6: "Amabam virtutem, laudabam propositum, mira-
    barque animum viri; gratulabar Italie." English trans. *Letters on Familiar Matters,
    IX–XVI,* 193.
83. Petrarch, *Fam.* XIII, 6, 15: "post clarissimum illud opus assumptum colere ante
    alios mirarique permiseram, ideoque quanto magis speravi tanto nunc magis
    doleo spe prerepta, fateorque, qualiscunque sit finis, adhuc non possum princi-
    pium non mirari." English trans., *Letters on Familiar Matters, IX–XVI,* 195.

84. See Musto, *Apocalypse in Rome,* 310.

85. Anonimo Romano, *Cronica,* cap. XXVII, lines 334b–350b, Porta, 264; English trans., 151.

5. THE PROPHETIC WIDOW

1. On Birgitta's stay in Milan, see Margherita Giordano Locranz, "Intorno al viaggio italiano di Birgitta di Svezia: Il soggiorno milanese (autunno 1349)," in *Vestigia: Studi di onore di Giuseppe Billanovich,* ed. Rino Avesani (Rome: Edizione di storia e letteratura, 1984), 387–398.

2. According to Petrarch, he lived close to the Basilica of Saint Ambrose, which Birgitta also visited. See Petrarch, *Fam.* XVI, 11. For Petrarch's early years in Milan, see Ugo Dotti, *Vita di Petrarca* (Rome–Bari: Laterza, 1991 [1987]), 281–288.

3. The Latin texts of the *Revelaciones* are published in Birgitta of Sweden, *Revelaciones,* the second series of Latin writings in the collections of the Svenska fornskriftsällskapet (Uppsala: Almquist and Wiksells Boktryckeri): bk. I, ed. Carl-Gustav Undhagen (1978); bk. II, ed. Carl-Gustav Undhagen and Birger Bergh (2001); bk. III, ed. Ann-Mari Jönsson (1988); bk. IV, ed. Hans Aili (1992); bk. V, ed. Birger Bergh (1971); bk. VI, ed. Birger Bergh (1991); bk. VII, ed. Birger Bergh (1967); bk. VIII, ed. Hans Aili (2002). All the Latin quotations from Birgitta's *Revelaciones* in this chapter are taken from these publications. Trans. by Denis Searby, with an introduction and notes by Bridget Morris, as *The Revelations of St. Birgitta of Sweden* (Oxford: Oxford University Press), vol. 1, *Liber caelestis,* bks. I–III (2006); vol. 2, *Liber caelestis,* bks. IV–V (2008); vol. 3, *Liber caelestis,* bks. VI–VII (2012); vol. 4, *The Heavenly Emperor's Book to Kings, the Rule, and Minor Works* (2015). All English quotations from Birgitta's *Revelaciones* in this chapter are taken from Searby and Morris's publications.

4. Birgitta's visit to Saint Ambrose in Milan is described in the canonization materials gathered in Isak Collijn's edition, *Acta et processus canonizacionis beate Birgitte,* ed. Isak Collijn, Svenska fornskriftsällskapet, ser. 2, Latinska skrifter 1 (Uppsala: Almquist and Wiksells Boktryckeri, 1924–1931), 14, 97, 309, 579.

5. "Vade Romam, vbi platee strate sunt auro et sanguine sanctorum rubricate, vbi compendium, id est brevior via, est ad celum propter indulgencias, quas promeruerunt sancti pontifices oracionibus suis. Stabis autem ibi in Roma, donec summum pontificem et imperatorem videbis ibidem insimul in Roma et eis verba mea nunciabis." Collijn, *Acta et processus,* 94.

6. Birgitta's arrival in Rome is testified to in Collijn, *Acta et processus,* 353, by Latino Orsini, who during the canonization process said that he met her even before the Holy Jubilee. The same is confirmed in Collijn, *Acta et processus,* 580. See also Birger Bergh, *Heliga Birgitta: Åttabarnsmor och profet* (Lund, Sweden: Historiska media, 2002), 92.

7. Birgitta, *Rev.* IV, 78, 12: "quod per totam Christianitatem audietur." English trans., 2:150.

8. Bridget Morris, *St. Birgitta of Sweden* (Woodbridge, UK: Boydell, 1999), 1.

9. Collijn, *Acta et processus.* Yet another important source is the *Diarium Vadstenense,* a memorial book in Vadstena written in Latin, which covers the events from 1336 to 1545. For further information about the sources on Birgitta, see Morris, *St. Birgitta of Sweden,* 3–9.

10. Birgitta's final confessor, Alfonso Pecha da Vadaterra, bishop of Jaén, describes her as a "principessa de regno Suecie," both in his *Informaciones* § 3 and his *Prologus Libri Celestis* § 2. See Arne Jönsson, *St. Bridget's Revelations to the Popes: An Edition of the So-Called "Tractatus de summis pontificibus"* (Lund, Sweden: Lund University Press, 1997), 63.

11. Collijn, *Acta et processus,* 504, 64, 482.

12. Morris, *St. Birgitta of Sweden,* 63.

13. The pilgrimage to Nidaros is referred to in Collijn, *Acta et processus,* 14, 309, 579.

14. On the pilgrimage to Spain, see Vicente Almazán, "Saint Birgitta on the Pilgrimage Route to Santiago," in *Scandinavia, Saint Birgitta and the Pilgrimage Route to Santiago de Compostela: Proceedings of the VIII Spain and Sweden Encounters throughout History, Santiago de Compostela, October, 18–20, 2000* (Santiago de Compostela, Spain: Martìnez Ruiz, Erique, 2002), 13–20. See also Morris, *St. Birgitta of Sweden,* 59–63.

15. This is convincingly argued by Mary Dzon, "Birgitta of Sweden and Christ's Clothing," in *The Christ Child in Medieval Culture: Alpha es et O!,* ed. Mary Dzon and Theresa M. Kenney (Toronto: University of Toronto Press, 2012), 117–145.

16. Collijn, *Acta et processus,* 80, ex. 92. Also, in *Rev.* IV, 103–104, Saint Denis appears to her.

17. Renate Blumenfeld-Kosinski, *Poets, Saints, and Visionaries of the Great Schism, 1378–1417* (University Park: Pennsylvania State University Press, 2004), 7.

18. Collijn, *Acta et processus,* 80–81: "Post aliquos dies cum sponsa Christi solicita esset de mutacione status sui ad seruiendum Deo et super hoc stabat orando in capella sua, tunc rapta fuit in spiritu, et cum esset in extasi vidit nubem lucidam et de nube audiuit vocem dicentem sibi: 'Mulier, audi me.' . . . 'Noli' inquit, 'timere, quia ego sum omnium conditor, non deceptor, non enim loquor tecum propter te solam, sed propter salutem aliorum. Audi loquor et vade magistrum Mathiam, confessorem tuum, qui experus est dorum spirituum secundum discrecionem, dic ei ex parte mea, que dico tibi, quia tu eris sponsa mea et canale meum et audies et videbis spiritualia, et spiritus meus permanebit tecum vsque ad mortem." Trans. by Morris, *St. Birgitta of Sweden,* 64–65.

19. On Birgitta as a prophet, see, for instance, Anders Piltz, "Inspiration, vision, profetia: Birgitta och teorierna om uppenbarelsen," in *Heliga Birgitta—budskapet och förebilden: Föredrag vid Jubileumssymposiet i Vadstena 3–7 oktober 1991,* Konferanser 28, ed. Alf Härdelin and Mereth Lindgren (Stockholm: Kungliga Vitterhets Historie och Antikvitets Akademien [KVHAA], 1993), 67–88; Morris, *St. Birgitta of Sweden,* 64–67; Claire L. Sahlin, *Birgitta of Sweden and the Voice of Prophecy* (Woodbridge, UK: Boydell, 2001); and Alessandra Bartolomei Romagnoli, "Mistica,

profezia femminile, e poteri alla fine del Medioevo," in *Il "Liber" di Angela Foligno e la mistica dei secoli XIII–XIV in rapporto alle nuove culture: Atti del XLV convegno storico internazionale, Todi, 12–15 ottobre, 2008* (Spoleto, Italy: Fondazione centro italiano di studi sull'alto medioevo, 2009), 485–515.

20. Collijn, *Acta et processus*, 86.

21. Birgitta, *Rev.* VI, 88, 1: "Nocte natalis Domini tam mirabilis et magna aduenit spons Christi exultacio cordis, vt vix se pre lectitia tenere posset, et in eodem momento sensit in corde motum sensibilem admirabilem, quasi si in corde esset puer viuus et voluens se et reuoluens." English trans., 3:155.

22. See Claire L. Sahlin, "Mystical Pregnancy and Prophecy in the Revelations: Birgitta's Identification with Virgin Mary," in *Birgitta of Sweden and the Voice of Prophecy*, 78–109.

23. The comparison between Birgitta's mystical pregnancy and stigmata has already been suggested by Aron Andersson, *Guds moder och den heliga Birgitta: En antologi* (Vadstena, Sweden: Vadstena Affärstryck, 1978), 46. In her thought-provoking reading of Birgitta's "mystical pregnancy," Maria Husabø Oen has emphasized how this passage connects Birgitta's task as a visionary to Mary's role when she gave flesh to Christ. Birgitta's mission was to be a vessel to make Christ present in the world. See Maria Husabø Oen, "The Visions of St. Birgitta: A Study of the Making and Reception of Images in the Later Middle Ages" (PhD diss., University of Oslo, 2015), 223–224.

24. Anders Piltz is the scholar who most systematically has studied the works by Mathis of Linköping. See, for instance, "Magister Mathias of Sweden in His Theological Context: A Preliminary Survey," in *The Editing of Philosophical and Theological Texts from the Middle Ages*, ed. Monica Asztalos (Stockholm: Almqvist and Wiksell, 1986), 137–160.

25. For an insightful study of the character of Birgitta's vision and the lay visionary culture of the late Middle Ages, see Oen, "Visions of St. Birgitta." The theological and political aspects of the processes of *discretio spirituum* in the period are thoroughly discussed by Dyan Elliott, *Proving Woman: Female Spirituality and Inquisitional Culture in the Later Middle Ages* (Princeton, NJ: Princeton University Press, 2004).

26. Morris, *St. Birgitta of Sweden*, 79–82.

27. Collijn, *Acta et processus*, 267–268, 324.

28. Birgitta's literary sources have been profoundly studied by Birgit Klockars, *Birgitta och böckerna: En undersökning av den heliga Birgittas källor*, Historiska serien (Stockholm: KVHAA, 1966).

29. Collijn, *Acta et processus*, 84: "verba diuinitus ei data scribebat in lingua sua materna manu sua propria, quando erat sana, et faciebat illa translatari in lingua latina fidelissime a nobis confessoribus suis et postea ascultabat illa cum scriptura sua, quam ipsa scripserat, ne vnum verbum ibi plus adderetur uel deficeret, nisi que ipsa in visione diuinitus audierat et viderat. Si vero erat infirma, vocabat confessorem et scriptorem suum secretarium ad hoc specialiter deputatum, et tunc ipsa cum magna deuocione et timore Dei et aliquando

cum lacrimis referebat ei verba illa in uulgari suo cum quadam attenta eleua-
cione mentali, quasi si legeret in libro, et tunc confessor dicebat illa verba in
lingua latina illi scriptori, et ille scribebat illa ibidem in sua presencia, et
postea cum erant verba conscripta, ipse volebat illa ascultare et ascultabat
valde diligenter et attente." English trans., Bridget Morris, "General Introduction," in *Revelations of St. Birgitta of Sweden,* 1:12.

30. Morris, "General Introduction," 1:13. According to Morris, Prior Peter did not
    follow Birgitta to Rome when she left in 1349, but he traveled regularly be-
    tween Sweden and Rome in the years to come.

31. Ibid., 1:14.

32. In 1346 the Swedish king, Magnus Eriksson, bequeathed his palace in Vad-
    stena to Birgitta for her planned monastery. His desire was that he and his
    wife should be buried at the monastery. See Morris, *St. Birgitta of Sweden,* 86.

33. André Vauchez, *The Laity in the Middle Ages: Religious Beliefs and Devotional Prac-
    tices* (Notre Dame, IN: University of Notre Dame Press, 1993 [1987]), 248.

34. Birgitta, *Rev.* V, Prologus, 7: "religiosum quendam sii notum adhuc corpore
    tunc viuentem magne litterature in sciencia theologie, plenum quoque dolo et
    malicia dyabolica." English trans., 2:271.

35. Birgitta, *Rev.* V, Rev. 2: "Ergo, qui dulcedinem appetit, non refugiat amara."
    English trans., 2:277.

36. Klockars, *Birgitta och böckerna.*

37. Janken Myrdal, "The Revelations of Saint Birgitta and Everyday Life in the
    Fourteenth Century," in *Saint Birgitta, Syon and Vadstena: Papers from a Sympo-
    sium in Stockholm, 4–6 october 2007,* ed. Claes Gejrot, Sara Risberg, and Mia Åke-
    stam (Stockholm: KVHAA, 2010), 231–246.

38. Birgitta, *Rev.* IV, 78, 1–3: "Vestre honorande paternitati ego vidua quedam sig-
    nifico, quod mulieri cuidam in sua patria existenti multa valde miraculosa
    sunt reuelata, que diligenti examinacione episcoporum ac magistrorum claus-
    tralium ac secularium clericorum probata sunt ex pia et mirifica Spiritus
    sancti illustracione et non aliunde processisse, quod eciam illius regni rex et
    regina nouerunt probabili racione. Eadem itaque mulier ad urbem Rome per-
    egre profecta est; que die quadam in ecclesia maiori beate Virginis oracioni
    vacans in spiritualem visionem rapta est corpore tanquam in grauedinem
    ducto set non tamen in sompni grauedinem." English trans., 2:149–150.

39. Birgitta, *Rev.* IV, 78, 10–12: "Ego quidem illi notum facio, quod in parte dextera
    sancte ecclesie fundamentum vehementer dilapsum est in tantum, quod
    summa testudo plures in se rupturas habet dans ex se casus tam periculosos,
    quod multi de subeuntibus perdunt vitam. Plereque eius columpne, que in altum
    tendere deberent, usque ad terram se iam inclinat, totumque pauimentum
    ipsius tam fossum est, quod ceci introeuentes periculose cadunt, et adhuc in-
    terdum contingit clare videntes una cum cecis grauiter cadere causa periculo-
    sarum fossarum eiusdem pauimenti. Et propter has causas stat nimis periculose
    eccesia Dei. Et quid sibi ex hoc eueniet, statim propinquius esse dinoscitur.
    Nam ruinam certissime pacietur, nisi reparacionis iuuamen habuerit. Et ipsius

ruina tam grandis erit, quod per totam Christianitatem audietur; et hec debent spiritualiter intelligi." English trans., 2:150.

40. Long parts of the same vision occur also in *Rev.* III, 10, but not in an epistolary form as here.

41. Birgitta, *Rev.* IV, 78, 18, "qui in carne sua vitam meretricalem habent et sunt insaciabilis ac sine fundo sicut vorago maris ad cupiitatem pecunie." English trans., 2:151.

42. Birgitta, *Rev.* IV, 78, 21. "Et tales in sancta Ecclesia exaltari non deberent set deprimi." English trans., 2:151.

43. The epistolary character of the letter is explored by Jan Öberg, *Kring Birgitta* (Stockholm: KVHAA, 1969), 5–6.

44. Birgitta, *Rev.* IV, 78, 25–27: "Hec omnia vero illa gloriosa virgo, que mulieri apparuit, mitti precepit vobis in scriptis, unde nouerit vestra reuerenda paternitas, quod ego, que hanc litteram vobis misi, iuro per Ihesum verum et omnipotentem Deum et per eius dignissimam Matrem Mariam volens, ut ita me adiuuent ad utrumque, scilicet ad corpus et animam, sicut hanc litteram propter aliquem mundi honorem seu propter cupiditatem aut propter humanum fauorem non misi, set quoniam inter plura alia verba, que eidem mulieri in spirituali reuelacione dicta sunt, omnia que hec cartula in se continent iussa sunt vestre dignitati intimari." English trans., 2:151.

45. See Morris's comment to the revelation in the *Revelations of St. Birgitta of Sweden,* 2:149n1.

46. This has been suggested by several scholars, such as Bengt Strömberg, *Magister Mathias och fransk mendikantpredikan* (Stockholm: Svenska Kyrkans Diakonistyrelses Bokförlag, 1944), 160; Klockars, *Birgitta och böckerna,* 17; Morris, *St. Birgitta of Sweden,* 42; and Sahlin, *Birgitta of Sweden and the Voice of Prophecy,* 42n. However, the links between Birgitta, Elizabeth of Hungary, and Marie D'Oignies are most extensively explored by Päivi Salmesvuori, *Power and Sainthood: The Case of Birgitta of Sweden* (New York: Palgrave Macmillan, 2014), 44–61.

47. Elliott, *Proving Woman,* 47.

48. On the Beguines, see also Bernard McGinn, *The Flowering of Mysticism: Men and Women in the New Mysticism, 1200–1350* (New York: Crossroad, 1998), and Mary A. Suydam, "Beguine Textuality: Sacred Performance," in *Performance and Transformation: New Approaches to Late Medieval Spirituality,* ed. Mary A. Suydam and Joanna E. Ziegler (New York: St. Martin's, 1999), 169–210.

49. Morris, however, has rejected their impact since, as she argues, Birgitta was not attracted to poverty and mendicancy like the eager Beguine women were. Birgitta was rather "an elitist, reforming visionary whose interest lies outside the monastic enclosure," according to Morris. See Bridget Morris, "Birgittines and Beguines in Medieval Sweden," in *New Trends in Feminine Spirituality,* ed. Juliette Dor, Lesley Johnson, and Jocelyn Wogan-Browne (Turnhout, Belgium: Brepols, 1999), 159–175.

50. The impact of the *Old Swedish Legendary* on Birgitta's *Revelaciones* is discussed by Klockars, *Birgitta och böckerna,* 165–176.

51. Salmesvuori, *Power and Sainthood,* 57.

52. Ibid., 60.

53. However, according to Klockars, it is most likely that Birgitta did not read the writings of Hildegard and Mechtild. Klockars, *Birgitta och böckerna,* 227.

54. Petrarch's fifth and last stay in Rome is treated in one of his letters to Boccaccio, *Fam.* XI, 1. The letter describes Petrarch's pilgrimage to Rome in the year of the holy Jubilee (1350). See also Dotti, *Vita di Petrarca,* 220–224.

55. More or less contemporaneously, Fazio degli Uberti (ca. 1305–1367) used the image of the *Roma vidua* in his *Dittamondo,* a long, didactic poem that entails a trip throughout the world, written in *terza rima,* obviously imitating Dante's *Comedy.* In *Ditt.* I, 11, 40–42, the description of the widow is clear: "vidi il suo volto ch'era pien di pianto,/vidi la vesta sua rotta e disfatta/e raso e guasto il suo vedovo manto." Later, in *Ditt.* II, 52–57, he describes how the widowed Rome laments the Pantheon as the burden she must bear in her womb: II, 6, 52–57: "Il Panteon dentro dal grembo mio/allor fu fatto in nome d'una dia,/la qual si disse madre d'ogni dio./Di questa cosí bella profezia/non m'accorsi io allora, ma or ne godo,/ché veggio che s'intese di Maria." For the full Italian text, see http://bepi1949.altervista.org/dittamondo/libro_2_1.html.

56. Birgitta, *Rev.* III, 27, 23–28: "Nam si omnes orti de toto mundo coniuncti essent Rome, certe Roma esset eque magna de martiribus, in carne loquor, quia ille locus electus est ad amorem Dei. . . . Nunc autem ego possum loqui de Roma, sicut propheta loquebatur de Iherusalem: 'Olim', inquiens 'habitauit in ea iusticia et principes eius principes pacis. Nunc autem versa est in scoriam et principes eius homicide.'" English trans., 1:313.

57. Birgitta, *Rev.* III, 27, 23–28: "O, si cognosceres dies tuos, o Roma, fleres utique et non gauderes. Roma quippe in diebus antiquis erat quasi tela colorata omni colore pulcherrimo et contexta nobilissimo filo. Terra quoque eius erat colorata colore rubeo, id est sanguine martirum et contexta, id est commixta ossibus sanctorum. Nunc autem porte eius desolate sunt, quia defensores et custodes earum inclinati sunt ad cupiditatem. Muri eius depressi sunt et sine custodia, quia iam non curant animarum dampna, sed clerus et populus, qui sunt murus Dei, disperguntur ad faciendum utilitatem carnis." English trans., 1:313.

58. As Alessandra Bartolomei Romagnoli has forcefully argued, like Maria Magdalene, who came to the empty tomb of Christ, a similar sorrow overwhelmed Birgitta when she arrived at the empty tomb of the Apostolic See: Where have they put him? And where was the pope? All Birgitta's prophetic activity, Romagnoli suggests, revolved around this feeling of loss. Romagnoli, "Mistica, profezia femminile, e poteri," 488–489.

59. Birgitta, *Rev.* III, 27, 30–32: "Talis est Roma, corporaliter sicut vidisti, nam altaria plura desolata sunt, offertorium expenditur in tabernis, offerentes vacant plus mundo quam Deo. Verumptamen scias, quod a tempore Petri humilis usque dum Bonifacius ascendit sedem superbie, innumerabiles anime ascenderunt in celum." English trans., 1:314.

60. Morris, *St. Birgitta of Sweden,* 99.
61. Birgitta, *Rev.* VI, 63, 1–2: "Filius loquitur ad sponsam: 'Scribe ex parte mea pape Clementi hec verba: Ego exaltaui te et ascendere te feci super omnes gradus honoris. Surge igitur ad faciendum pacem inter reges Francie et Anglie, qui sunt periculose bestie, animarum proditores. Veni deinde in Italiam et predica ibi verbum et annum salutis et dileccionis diuine et vide plateas stratas sanctorum meorum sanguine, et dabo tibi mercedem illam, que non finietur.'" English trans., 3:126.
62. Vauchez, *Laity in the Middle Ages,* 246.
63. Ibid., 246–247.
64. For a useful overview of the redaction of these letters, see Bridget Morris, introduction to bk. IV, in *Revelations of St. Birgitta of Sweden,* 2:16–18. See also Jönsson, *St. Bridget's Revelations to the Popes.*
65. Jönsson, *St. Bridget's Revelations to the Popes,* 65–66.
66. Birgitta, *Rev.* IV, 134, 15: "Ecce, sponsa, quid sacerdotes faciunt michi! Ipsos pre omnibus angelis et hominibus elegi et super omnes honoraui. Ipsi autem pre omnibus Iudeis et gentilibus, pre omnibus demonibus me magis prouocant." English trans., 2:243.
67. Birgitta, *Rev.* IV, 135, 1–2: "Ego sum quasi sponsus, qui sponsam suam cum omni caritate ducit in domum suam. Sic ego coniunxi sacerdotes michi cum corpore meo, ut ipsi essent in me et ego in eis. Set ipsi respondent michi sicut adultera sponso: 'Verba tua non placent michi, diuicie tue vane, voluptas tua quasi venenum. Ego habeo tres, quos magis diligere volo et sequi.'" English trans., 2:244.
68. Guillaume Mollat, *The Popes at Avignon, 1305–1378* (London: Thomas Nelson, 1963), 58.
69. Collijn, *Acta et processus,* 267. About the event, see also Morris, *St. Birgitta of Sweden,* 116.
70. Bridget Morris, introduction to bk. VIII, in *Revelations of St. Birgitta of Sweden,* 4:10.
71. Mollat, *Popes at Avignon,* 58.
72. Birgitta, *Rev.* IV, 138, 12: "Propter precem meam obtinuit ipse Spiritus sancti infusionem, ut deberet ad Romam et Ytaliam declinare ad nichil aliud, nisi ut misericordiam et iusticiam faceret, fidem catholicam roboraret, pacem reformaret et sic sanctam Ecclesiam innouaret." English trans., 2:249.
73. Birgitta, *Rev.* IV, 138, 13–17: "Sicut mater ducit filium suum ad locum, ubi sibi placet, dum ostendit sibi ubera sua, ita duxi ego Vrbanum papam mea prece et opere Spiritus sancti de Awinione ad Romam sine quouis periculo suo corporali. Quid fecerat ipse michi? . . . Si contigerit ipsum redire ad terras, ubi fuit electus papa, ipse habebit in breui tempore unam percussionem siue alapam, quod dentes sui stringentur seu stridebunt: visus caligabit et fuscus erit et tocius corporis sui membra contremiscent." English trans., 2:249.
74. Collijn, *Acta et processus,* 80, 96.
75. Morris, *St. Birgitta of Sweden,* 140.

76. Birgitta, *Rev.* IV, 140, 18: "terre Ecclesie, que sub una eius obediencia et subieccione modo eidem obediunt, diuidentur in plures partes in manus tyrannorum." English trans., 2:252.

77. Birgitta, *Rev.* VII, 8, 4–5: "Ego quidem, que ipsum verum Deum genui, testimonium perhibeo, quod vunum proprium habebat idem Ihesus Christus filius meus, et illud ipse solus possidebat. Hoc enim fuit illa tunica, quam ego propriis manibus meis feci. Et hoc testificatur propheta in persona filii mei sic dicens: 'Super vestem meam miserunt sortem.'" English trans., 3:217.

78. Dzon offers a useful and interesting overview of the interpretations of the tunic in her article "Birgitta of Sweden and Christ's Clothing," 130–137.

79. Quoted from "Unam Sanctam: Bull of Pope Boniface VIII Promulgated November 18, 1302," Papal Encyclicals Online, accessed 10 February 2017, http://www.papalencyclicals.net/Bon08/B8unam.htm. Hierocrats such as Giles of Rome and Henry of Cremona also used the seamless tunic as an image for the indivisible church. For a brief discussion of this, see Michael Wilks, *The Problem of Sovereignty in the Later Middle Ages* (Cambridge: Cambridge University Press, 1964), 20.

80. For a compelling discussion of the typological passages on the seamless tunic in Philippe's poem, and the tunic as an image of the church during the Schism, see Blumenfeld-Kosinski, *Poets, Saints, and Visionaries,* 113. After his own journey to Jerusalem in 1346, Philippe was reportedly connected to the royal court at Cyprus until 1372, before he left for Paris. Whether Birgitta met him there is unclear, but the context made it possible.

81. Birgitta, *Rev.* VII, 20, 15: "Et sic cum ista intencione et voluntate prefatus clericus intrauit dictum ordinem statimque dyabolus intrauit in cor eius." English trans., 3:248.

82. Birgitta, *Rev.* VII, 30, 4–5: "Audite omnes inimici mei in mundo viuentes, quia ad amicos meos non loquor, qui sequuntur voluntatem meam. Audite omnes clerici, archiepiscopi et episcopi et omnes inferiores gradus Ecclesie! Audite omnes religiosi, cuiuscumque ordinis estis! Audite reges et principes et iudices terre et omnes seruientes! Audite mulieres, principisse ac omnes domine et ancille, et omnes, cuiuscumque condicionis et gradus estis, magni et parui, qui habitatis orbem, verba hec, que ego ipse, qui creaui vos, nunc loquor ad vos!" English trans., 3:264.

83. Vauchez, *Laity in the Middle Ages,* 220–224.

84. Collijn, *Acta et processus,* 94; trans. by Morris, *St. Birgitta of Sweden,* 15, 367, 579. See also Morris's chapter about Birgitta's years in Rome, ibid., 93–113, and Birger Bergh's chapter on the same subject in *Heliga Birgitta,* 93–115.

85. Collijn, *Acta et processus,* 262, 316, 367, 478, 498.

86. Sanford Brown Meech, *The Book by Margery Kempe,* Early English Text Society 212 (London: Oxford University Press, 1940), 95.

87. Birgitta, *Rev.* IV, 142, 13–15: "Veni igitur et noli tardare! Veni non cum superbia solita et mundana pompa set cum omni humilitate et ardenti caritate! Et postquam sic veneris, extirpa, euelle et dissipa omnia vicia de curia tua! . . .

Incipe renouare Ecclesiam meam, quam ego acquisiui meo proprio sanguine, ut renouetur et spiritualiter reducatur ad pristinum statum suum sanctum, quia iam nunc magis veneratur lupanar quam sancta mea Ecclesia." English trans., 2:255.

88. Birgitta, *Rev.* IV, 143, 6–7: "De discordia vero inter papam et Bernabonem respondeo, quod ultra modum est michi odiosa, quia infinite anime de illa periclitantur. Ideo placitum est michi, quod concordia fiat." English trans., 2:256.

89. Yves Renouard, *The Avignon Papacy: The Popes in Exile, 1305–1403* (New York: Barnes and Noble Books, 1994 [1954]), 52.

90. Birgitta, *Rev.* IV, 143, 7: "Nam eciam si papa expulsus esset a papatu suo, melius esset quod ipse humiliaret se et faceret concordiam, quacumque occasione posset fieri, antequam tot anime perirent in eternam damnacionem." English trans., 2:256–257.

91. Sara Ekwall, *Vår äldsta Birgittavita och dennas viktigaste varianter* (Stockholm: Almquist and Wiksell, 1965), 99, 129–30. See also Morris, introduction to bk. IV, in *Revelations of St. Birgitta of Sweden*, 2:21n33.

6. CATHERINE OF SIENA AND THE MYSTICAL BODY OF THE CHURCH

1. Arne Jönsson, *Alfonso of Jaén: His Life and Works with Critical Editions of the "Epistola Solitarii," the "Informaciones" and the "Epistola Serui Christi."* Studia Graeca et Latina Lundensia 1 (Lund, Sweden: Lund University Press, 1989), 48–53.

2. This is claimed by Suzanne Noffke. See Suzanne Noffke, ed. and trans., *The Letters of Catherine of Siena*, with an introduction and notes, vols. 1–4 (Tempe, AZ: Arizona Center for Medieval and Renaissance Studies, 2000–2008), 1:40n12.

3. The English translations of Catherine's letters are taken from Noffke, *Letters of Catherine of Siena*. The Italian text is taken from Niccolò Tommaseo, ed., *Le lettere di S. Caterina da Siena, ridotte a miglior lezione, e in ordine nuovo disposte con premio e note di Niccolò Tommaseo*, 4 vols. (Florence, 1860). English text, Letter T127, 1:40; Italian text, Letter CXXVII, 2:315–316: "E per tanto io vi dico che 'l papa mandò di qua uno suo vicario; ciò fue il padre spirituale di quella Contessa che morì a Roma; e è colui che renunziò al vescovo per amore della virtù, e venne a me da parte del Padre santo, dicendo che io dovessi fare special orazione per lui e per la santa Chiesa: e per segno mi recò la santa indulgenza. *Gaudete* dunque, *et exultate*, perocchè il Padre santo ha cominciato ad esercitare l'occhio verso l' onore di Dio e della santa Chiesa."

4. Jane Tylus, "Mystical Literacy: Writing and Religious Women in Late Medieval Italy," in *A Companion to Catherine of Siena*, ed. Carolyn Muessig, George Ferzoco, and Beverly Mayne Kienzle (Leiden: Brill, 2012), 155–185; 178–179.

5. In Tylus's comprehensive study of Catherine's literacy, in which Catherine's literary production is brought into the fold of the history of European

humanism, as well as the language and literature of Italy, this letter plays a pivotal role. See Jane Tylus, *Reclaiming Catherine of Siena: Literacy, Literature, and the Signs of Others* (Chicago: University of Chicago Press, 2009).

6. Catherine of Siena, English text, Letter T272, 2:505; Italian text, Letter CCLXXII, 3:481: "Questa lettera, e un' altra ch'io vi mandai, ho scritto di mia mano in su l'Isola della Rocca, con molti sospiri e abondanzia di lagrime; in tanto che l'occhio, vedendo, non vedeva: ma piena d'ammirazione ero di me medesima, e della bontà di Dio, considerando la sua misericordia verso le creature che hanno in loro ragione, e la sua Providenzia; la quale abondava verso di me, che per refrigerio, essendo private della consolazione, la quale per mia ignoranzia io non cognobbi, m'aveva dato, e proveduto con darmi l'attitudine dello scrivere; acciocché discendendo dall'altezza, avessi un poco con chi sfogare 'l cuore, perché non scoppiasse."

7. Thomas Aquinas was canonized in 1323 by Pope John XXII.

8. Catherine of Siena, English text, Letter T272, 2:495; Italian text, Letter CCLXXII, 3:466: "Confortatevi, carissimo padre, nella dolce sposa di Cristo; perocché quanto abonda più in tribulazioni e amaritudine, tanto più promette la divina Verità di farla abondare in dolcezza e in consolazioni. E questa sarà la docezza sua: la riformazione de' santi e buoni pastori, i quali sono fiori di gloria, cioè che rendono odore e gloria di virtù a Dio. Questa è la riformazione del fiore de' suoi ministri e pastori. Ma non n'ha bisogno il frutto di questa sposa d'essere riformato, perocché non diminuisce né guasta mai per li difetti de' ministri."

9. Raymond of Capua, *Vita S. Catharina Senensis,* Acta Sanctorum, III Aprili, Dies 30 (Antwerp, 1675), cols. 853A–959B; English trans., *The Life of St. Catherine of Siena,* trans. George Lamb (Charlotte, NC: TAN Books, 2011 [2003]). For a modern account of Catherine's life, see Carolyn Muessig, "Introduction," in Muessig, Ferzoco, and Kienzle, *Companion to Catherine of Siena,* 1–21.

10. Despite Raymond's underlining of Catherine's modest background and family, recent scholarship has presented a far more nuanced picture. According to F. Thomas Luongo, Catherine did not come from such humble circumstances, rather the opposite. See F. Thomas Luongo, *Saintly Politics of Catherine of Siena* (Ithaca, NY: Cornell University Press, 2006), 29–30.

11. Only after Catherine's time were the *mantellate,* which appeared in different places in Italy during the thirteenth century, "domesticated" and included as an official third order of the Dominicans, thanks above all to Raymond's efforts.

12. This is depicted at the end of part 1 of *Legenda maior.*

13. Sofia Boesch Gajano and Odile Redon, "La *Legenda maior* di Raimondo da Capua, costruzione di una santa," in *Atti del simposio internazionale Cateriniano-Bernadiniano,* ed. Domenico Maffei and Paolo Nardi (Siena: Accademia Senese degli Intronati, 1982), 15–36.

14. Karen Scott, "St. Catherine of Siena, *Apostola,*" *Church History* 61, no. 1 (1992): 34–46.

15. Blake Beattie, "Catherine of Siena and the Papacy," in Muessig, Ferzoco, and Kienzle, *Companion to Catherine of Siena,* 73–98; 78; Luongo, *Saintly Politics of Catherine of Siena,* 63–71.

16. Luongo, *Saintly Politics of Catherine of Siena,* 7.

17. Yves Renouard, *The Avignon Papacy: The Popes in Exile, 1305–1403* (New York: Barnes and Noble Books, 1994 [1954]), 62.

18. For Catherine's entry into Tuscan politics, see Luongo, *Saintly Politics of Catherine of Siena,* 80–89.

19. For a good survey of Catherine's letters—the early history of the letters, the first printed editions, the critical editions, and the scholarly studies—see Suzanne Noffke, "Introduction," in *Letters of Catherine of Siena,* 1:xiii–lvi; xvi–xxxix. See also Suzanne Noffke, "The Writings of Catherine of Siena: The Manuscript Tradition," in Muessig, Ferzoco, and Kienzle, *Companion to Catherine of Siena,* 295–339. Although she claimed the ability to write, and the recent scholarship has tended to confirm this, we have no written text in Catherine's own hand. Different scribes in her circle, both female and male, probably wrote down most of the letters, and sometimes she supposedly dictated two or three at the same time to different scribes. See Noffke, "Introduction," xxi.

20. Muessig, "Introduction," 6.

21. Tylus, *Reclaiming Catherine of Siena,* 118.

22. Ibid., 153.

23. Catherine of Siena, English text, Letter T185, 1:246; Italian text, Letter CLXXXV, 3:71.

24. Beattie, "Catherine of Siena and the Papacy," 84.

25. Catherine of Siena, English text, Letter T185, 1:244; Italian text, Letter CLXXXV, 3:69–70: "A Voi, reverendissimo e dilettissimo padre in Cristo Gesù, la vostra indegna, misera, miserabile figliuola Catarina, serva e schiava de' servi di Gesù Cristo, scrive nel prezioso sangue suo."

26. Catherine of Siena, English text, Letter T206, 2:63; Italian text, Letter CCVI, 3:161–162: "Oimè, dolce padre mio, con questa dolce mano vi prego e vi dico, che veniate a sconfiggere li nostri nemici. Da parte di Cristo crocifisso vel dico; non vogliate credere a' consiglieri del dimonio, che volsero impedire il santo e buono proponimento. Siatemi uomo virile, e non timorose. Rispondete a Dio, che vi chiama che veniate a tenere e possedere il luogo del glorioso pastore santo Pietro, di cui vicario sete rimasto. E drizzart il gonfalone della croce santa: ché come per la croce fummo liberati (così disse Paolo), così levando questo gonfalone il quale mi pare refrigerio de' Cristiani, saremo liberati, noi dalla guerra e divisione e molte iniquità, il popolo infedele dalla sua infidelità."

27. Catherine of Siena, English text, Letter T267, 2:474; Italian text, Letter CCLXVII, 3:449: "umilmente me gli raccomandate, redendomi in colpa alla Santità sua di molta ignoranzia e negligenzia che io ho commessa contro Dio, e disobedienzia contra il mio Creatore, il quale m'invitava a gridare con ansietato desiderio, e che con l'orazione gridassi dinanzi da lui, e con la parola e

con la presenzia fussi presso al vicario suo. Per tutti quanti i modi ho com-
messo smisurati difetti; per li quali io credo che egli abbia ricevute molte per-
secuzioni, e la Chiesa santa, per le molte iniquitadi mie. Per la qual cosa, se
egli si lagna di me, egli ha ragione; e di punirmi de' difetti miei."

28. Catherine of Siena, English text, Letter T267, 2:476; Italian text, Letter
CCLXVII, 3:451: "anco, staremo nel luogo nostro a combattere virilmente con
l'arme della virtù per la dolce sposa di Cristo. In lei voglio terminare la vita mia,
con lagrime, con sudori, e con sospiri, e dare il sangue e le mirolla dell'ossa."

29. Giuliana Cavallini, *Catherine of Siena* (London: Geoffrey Chapman, 1998), 3.

30. See Suzanne Noffke, introduction to *The "Dialogue" of Catherine of Siena*, trans.
Suzanne Noffke, preface by Giuliana Cavallini (New York: Paulist, 1980), 17.
Heather Webb has offered a thoughtful reading of the *Dialogo* in the light of
communal piety in the late Middle Ages. By comparing the passages on tears
in the *Dialogo* with Dante's poetry, she discusses how Catherine established
her authority as a prophet. See Heather Webb, *"Lacrime Cordiali:* Catherine of
Siena and the Value of Tears," in Muessig, Ferzoco, and Kienzle, *Companion to
Catherine of Siena*, 99–112.

31. Catherine of Siena, *Il Dialogo*, 2nd ed., ed. Giuliana Cavallini, Testi Cateriniani I (Siena, Cantagalli, 1995), 610; electronic version published by Centro
internazionale di studi cateriniani, http://www.centrostudicateriniani.it/4
/download.html. Proemio, cap. 2: "essendo mostrato dalla prima Verità la ne-
cessità del mondo, ed in quanta tempesta e offesa di Dio egli era." English
translation: Catherine of Siena, *"Dialogue,"* trans. Noffke, 27.

32. Catherine of Siena, *Il Dialogo*, cap. 110: "E perché meglio si cognosce l'uno contrario per l'altro, voglioti mostrare la dignità di coloro che esercitarono in
virtù il tesoro che Io lo' missi nelle mani, e per questo meglio vedrai la miseria
di coloro che oggi si pascono al petto di questa sposa." English trans., 205.

33. See the rich historical account by Miri Rubin, *Corpus Christi: The Eucharist in
Late Medieval Culture* (Cambridge: Cambridge University Press, 1991).

34. Catherine of Siena, *Il Dialogo*, cap. 110: "A costoro ò dato a ministrare il Sole,
dandolo' el lume della scienzia il caldo della divina carità, e'l colore unito col
caldo e col lume, cioè il sangue e'l corpo del mio Figliuolo. Il quale corpo è
uno sole, perché è una cosa con meco, vero Sole. E tanto è unito, che l'uno non
si può separare da l'altro né tagliare, se non come il sole, che non si può dividere, né il caldo suo da la luce né la luce dal suo colore, per la sua perfezione de
l'unione." English trans., 206.

35. The uncorrupted quality of Corpus Christi is also elaborated on in another
image, an image that derives from both speculation on the divine light and the
Pauline figure of the mirror (1 Cor 13:12): *Il Dialogo*, cap. 110: "E sì come il sole
non si può dividere, così non si divide tutto me Dio e uomo in questa bian-
chezza de l'ostia. Poniamo che l'ostia si dividesse: se mille migliaia di minuz-
zoli fusse possibile di farne, in ciascuno è tutto Dio e tutto uomo, come detto
è. Sì come lo specchio che si divide, e non si divide però la imagine che si vede
dentro nello specchio, così dividendo questa ostia non si divide me tutto Dio e

tutto uomo, ma in ciascuna parte è tutto." English trans., 207: "And just as the sun cannot be divided, so neither can my wholeness as God and as human in this white host. Even if the host is divided, even if you could break it into thousands and thousands of tiny bits, in each one I would be there, wholly God and wholly human. It is just as when a mirror is broken, and yet the image one sees reflected in it remains unbroken. So when this host is divided, I am not divided but remain completely in each piece, wholly God, wholly human."

36. For a rich investigation of the human body as an image for the cosmos, for society, and for art, see Leonard Barkan, *Nature's Work of Art: The Human Body as Image of the World* (New Haven, CT: Yale University Press, 1975). See also Michel Feher, ed., *Fragments for a History of the Human Body*, 3 vols. (New York: Zone, 1989).

37. Jacques Le Goff, "Head or Heart? The Political Use of Body Metaphors in the Middle Ages," in Feher, *Fragments for a History of the Human Body*, 1:13–26; 13.

38. Le Goff, "Head or Heart?," 17.

39. Saint Paul, 1 Cor 12:12 (King James Version).

40. Barkan, *Nature's Work of Art*, 68–69.

41. Rubin, *Corpus Christi*, 12.

42. Ibid., 188.

43. Catherine of Siena, *Il Dialogo*, cap. 113: "Essi sono i miei unti e chiamoli i miei cristi, perché l'ò dato a ministrare me a voi, e messili come fiori odoriferi nel corpo mistico della santa Chiesa. Questa dignità non à l'angelo, ed òlla data a l'uomo, a quelli che Io ò eletti per miei ministri, e quelli ò posti come angeli, e debbono essere angeli terrestri in questa vita, però che debbono essere come angeli." English trans., 212.

44. Catherine of Siena, *"Dialogue,"* 213.

45. Catherine of Siena, *Il Dialogo*, cap. 119: "rendendo lume nel corpo mistico della santa Chiesa: lume di scienzia sopranaturale col colore d'onesta e santa vita, cioè seguitando la dottrina della mia Verità, e ministrano il caldo de l'ardentissima carità." English trans., 222.

46. Catherine of Siena, *Il Dialogo*, cap. 119: "con sollicitudine e santo timore divellevano le spine de' peccati mortali e piantavano piante odorifere di virtù." English trans., 223.

47. Catherine of Siena, *Il Dialogo*, cap. 119: "E se'l membro fusse pure ostinato nel suo male fare, el tagliarà dalla congregazione, acciò che non gl' imputridisca con la colpa del peccato mortale." English trans., 224: "And if the members are still obstinate in their evildoing, they will cut them off from the congregation so that they will not infect the whole body with the filth of deadly sin."

48. Catherine of Siena, *Il Dialogo*, cap. 113: "O carissima figliuola, tutto questo t'ò detto acciò che tu meglio cognosca la dignità dove Io ò posti i miei ministri, acciò che più ti doglia delle miserie loro." English trans., 212.

49. Catherine of Siena, *Il Dialogo*, cap. 121; English trans., 231.

50. Catherine of Siena, *Il Dialogo*, cap. 124: "non potresti tanto udire quanto più mi dispiace questo difetto in loro, oltre al dispiacere che Io ricevo dagli uomini

generali del mondo, e dei particulari continenti dei quali Io t'ò detto." English trans., 239.

51. Catherine of Siena, *Il Dialogo,* cap. 121; English trans., 231–232.

52. Catherine of Siena, *Il Dialogo,* cap. 123: "continuamente mi perseguitano in tanti diversi e scellerati peccati che la lingua tua non gli potrebbe narrare, e a udirlo ci verresti meno." English trans., 235.

53. Catherine of Siena, *Il Dialogo,* cap. 123: "E non sanno che si sia officio; e se alcuna volta el dicono, el dicono con la lingua e'l cuore loro è dilonga da me." English trans., 235–236.

54. Catherine of Siena, *Il Dialogo,* cap. 128; English trans., 254.

55. Catherine of Siena, *Il Dialogo,* cap. 130: "O carissima figliuola, Io l'ò posto in sul ponte della dottrina della mia Verità a ministrare a voi peregrini i sacramenti della santa Chiesa, ed egli sta nel miserabile fiume di sotto al ponte, e nel fiume delle delizie e miserie del mondo ve li ministra." English trans., 262.

56. Catherine of Siena, *Il Dialogo,* cap. 119: "E se'l membro fusse pure ostinato nel suo male fare, el tagliarà dalla congregazione, acciò che non gl' imputridisca con la colpa del peccato mortale." English trans., 224.

57. Henri Lubac, *Corpus Mysticum: The Eucharist and the Church in the Middle Ages,* ed. Laurence Paul Hemming and Susan Frank Parsons, trans. Gemma Simmonds with Richard Price and Christopher Stephens (London: SCM Press, 2006); first published as *L'Eucharistie et l'Église au moyen âge,* 1944.

58. Lubac, *Corpus Mysticum,* 114.

59. Ernst H. Kantorowicz, *The King's Two Bodies: A Study in Mediaeval Political Theology* (Princeton, NJ: Princeton University Press, 1997); first published 1957.

60. Lubac, *Corpus Mysticum,* 3.

61. Quoted from "Unam Sanctam: Bull of Pope Boniface VIII Promulgated November 18, 1302," Papal Encyclicals Online, accessed 10 Feburary 2017, http://www.papalencyclicals.net/Bon08/B8unam.htm; Latin text quoted from "Unam Sanctam," Catholic Planet, notes and translation by Ronald L. Conte Jr., accessed 10 Feburary 2017, http://www.catholicplanet.com/TSM /Unam-Sanctam-Latin.htm: "Unam Sanctam Ecclesiam Catholicam et ipsam Apostolicam urgente fide credere cogimur et tenere. Nosque hanc firmiter credimus et simpliciter confitemur: extra quam nec salus est, nec remissio peccatorum, Sponso in Canticis proclamante, 'Una est columba mea, perfecta mea: una est matris suae, electa genitrici suae:' [Canticles 6:8] quae unum *corpus mysticum* repraesentat, cujus caput Christus, Christi vero Deus. [1 Cor 11:3]." My emphases.

62. Kantorowicz, *King's Two Bodies,* 197.

63. Lubac, *Corpus Mysticum,* 115.

64. Marsilius of Padua, *DP* I, 15, 6: "Nam ab anima universitatis civium aut eius valentioris partis formatur aut formari debet in ea pars una primum proportionata *cordi,* in qua siquidem virtute, quendam seu formam statuit cum activa potentia seu auctoritate instituendi partes reliquas civitatis. Haec autem

pars est principatus, cuius quidem virtus causalitate universalis lex est, et cuius activa potentia est auctoritas iudicandi, praecipiendi, et exequendi sententias conferentium et iustorum civilium." My emphasis. Latin text, 70.

65. Takashi Shogimen, "Medicine and the Body Politic in Marsilius of Padua's *Defensor pacis*," in *A Companion to Marsilius of Padua*, ed. Gerson Moreno-Riano and Cary J. Nederman (Leiden: Brill, 2012), 71–117.

66. Catherine of Siena, *Il Dialogo*, cap. 119: "Unde Io voglio che tu sappi che per veruna cosa è venuta tanta tenebre e divisione nel mondo tra secolari e religiosi, cherici e pastori della santa Chiesa, se non solo perché il lume della giustizia è mancato ed è venuta la tenebre della ingiustizia." English trans., 224.

67. Catherine of Siena, *Il Dialogo*, cap. 119: "tutto il corpo imputridiscie e corrompe." English trans., 224.

68. Catherine of Siena, *Il Dialogo*, cap. 29: "Tu t'ài fatto dio e signore el mondo e te medesimo." English trans., 260.

69. Catherine of Siena, *Il Dialogo*, cap. 125: "aciecati da l'amore proprio di loro medesimi." English trans., 240.

70. Catherine of Siena, *Il Dialogo*, cap. 110: "da voi non sete alcuna cosa." English trans., 207.

71. Catherine of Siena, *"Dialogue,"* 229.

72. Ibid., 234.

73. Catherine of Siena, *Il Dialogo*, cap. 132: "Anco tutto il mondo è corrotto, facendo molto peggio eglino che i secolari del grado loro, unde con le loro puzze lordano la faccia de l'anima loro e corrompono i sudditi e succhiano il sangue a la Sposa mia, cioè a la santa Chiesa. Unde per li loro difetti essi la impalidiscono, ciò è che l'amore e l'affetto della carità che debbono avere a questa sposa, l'ànno posto a loro medesimi, e non attendono ad altro che a piluccarla e a trarne le prelazioni e le grandi rendite, dove essi debbono cercare anime. Unde per la loro mala vita vengono i secolari ad inreverenzia e a disobbedienzia della santa Chiesa, benché essi non il debbano fare, né non è scusato il difetto loro per lo difetto de' ministri." English trans., 271.

74. James Hankins, "Humanism and the Origins of Modern Political Thought," in *The Cambridge Companion to Renaissance Humanism*, ed. Jill Kraye (Cambridge: Cambridge University Press, 1996), 118–141; 119.

75. Catherine of Siena, *Il Dialogo*, cap. 129: "Ignorante e superbo era suddito, e molto più è ignorante e superbo ora che è prelato. E tanta è la sua ignoranzia che come cieco darà l'offizio del sacerdote a uomo idioto, che a pena saprà pure leggere e non saprà l'offizio suo. . . . Essi sono ciechi e ragunatori di ciechi." English trans., 256.

76. Catherine of Siena, *Il Dialogo*, cap. 134: "Tu ci creasti di non cavelle, adunque, ora che noi siamo, facci misericordia e rifà i vaselli che tu ài creati e formati a la imagine e similitudine tua, e riformali a grazia nella misericordia e nel sangue del tuo Figliuolo." English trans., 76.

77. Catherine of Siena, *Il Dialogo*, cap. 115: "però che la colpa sua neuna lesione a' sacramenti della santa Chiesa può fare, né diminuire la virtù in loro. Ma bene

diminuisce la grazia, e cresce la colpa in colui che'l ministra e in colui che'l riceve indegnamente." English trans., 215.

78. Catherine of Siena, *Il Dialogo,* cap. 120: "Da' quali sacramenti ricevete la vita della grazia, ricevendoli degnamente, non ostante che essi siano in tanto difetto, per amore di me." English trans., 230.

79. Catherine of Siena, *Il Dialogo,* cap. 120: "Debbanvi dispiacere, e odiare i difetti loro." English trans., 230.

80. Catherine of Siena, *"Dialogue,"* 215.

81. Ibid., 231.

82. Catherine of Siena, *Il Dialogo,* cap. 133: "Ora ti ridico da capo che, con tutti quanti i loro difetti, e se fussero ancora più, Io non voglio che neuno secolare se ne 'mpacci di punirli. . . . Ma l'uno e gli altri sono dimoni incarnati, e per divina giustizia l'uno dimonio punisce l'altro, e l'uno e l'altro offende. Il secolare non è scusato per lo difetto del prelato, né il prelato per lo peccato del secolare." English trans., 272.

83. Beattie, "Catherine of Siena and the Papacy," 87.

84. Raymond of Capua, *Life of St. Catherine of Siena,* II, 10, 232.

85. Tylus, *Reclaiming Catherine of Siena,* 215–269.

86. For a rich study of Catherine's fasting and Eucharistic piety, see Caroline Walker Bynum, *Holy Feast and Holy Fast: The Religious Significance of Food to Medieval Women* (Berkeley: University of California Press, 1987), 158–180.

87. For Catherine's stay in Rome, see A. Odrasso Cartotti, "La dimora di Santa Caterina da Siena," *L'Urbe* 24 (1961): 28–34.

88. As scholars have suggested, the painting on the Capitoline Hill evoked Giotto's mosaic the *Navicella,* which once occupied the main façade of the old Saint Peter's Basilica in Rome. The mosaic was made around 1310, after the pope's settlement in Avignon, and a few decades before Cola's revolution. It was almost entirely destroyed during the construction of the new Saint Peter's Basilica in the seventeenth century. Nicolas Beatrizet's engraving of Christ rescuing Saint Peter on the Sea of Galilee from 1559 is the clearest image of the mosaic before it was reformatted, damaged, and partly dismembered. It shows the composition in reverse, without the original inscription. This image of the storm-tossed ship has many similarities with Anonimo Romano's description of the painting on the Capitoline Hill commissioned by Cola. But, in contrast to Cola's fresco, there is no widow in the engraving of Giotto's mosaic.

89. Catherine of Siena, English text, Letter T373, 4:367–368; Italian text, Letter CCCLXXIII, 4:487–488: "Quando egli è l'ora della terza, e io mi levo dalla messa, e voi vedreste andare una morta a Santo Pietro; ed entro di nuovo a lavorare nella navicella della santa Chiesa. Ine mi sto così infino presso all'ora del vespro; e di quello luogo non vorrei escire né dì né notte, infino che io non veggo un poco fermato e stabilito questo popolo col padre loro. Questo corpo sta senza veruno cibo, eziandio senza la gocciola dell'acqua; con tanti dolci tormenti corporali, quanto io portassi mai per veruno tempo: in tanto che per uno pelo ci sta la vita mia."

90. Catherine of Siena, English text, Letter T371, 4:360; Italian text, Letter CCCLXXI, 4:471: "E crescendo il dolore e il fuoco del desiderio, gridava nel cospettoo di Dio dicendo: 'Che posso fare, o inestimabile fuco?' E la sua benignità rispondeva: 'Chet u di nuovo offeri la vita tua. E mai non dare riposo a te medesima. A questo esercizio t'ho posta e pongo, te e tutti quelli che ti seguitano e segguiteranno.'"

91. Catherine of Siena, English text, Letter T371, 4:362; Italian text, Letter CCCLXXI, 4:474: "O Dio eterno, ricevi il sacrifizio della vita mia in questo corpo mistico della santa Chiesa. Io non ho che dare altro se non quello che tu hai dato a me. Tolli il cuore dunque, e premilo sopra la faccia di questa Sposa."

92. Suzanne Noffke, introduction to Letter T370, 4:354.

93. Raymond of Capua, *Life of St. Catherine of Siena,* III, 2, 287.

94. Ibid., III, 2, 288.

CONCLUSION

1. Guillaume Mollat, *The Popes at Avignon, 1305–1378* (London: Thomas Nelson, 1963), 313.

BIBLIOGRAPHY

PRIMARY SOURCES

Acta et processus canonizacionis beate Birgitte. Edited by Isak Collijn. Svenska fornskriftsällskapet, ser. 2, Latinska skrifter 1. Uppsala: Almquist and Wiksells Boktryckeri, 1924–1931.

Alighieri, Dante. *Commedia.* Con il commento di Anna Maria Chiavacci Leonardi. 3 vols. Milan: Mondadori, 1991. Translated, with commentary, by Charles S. Singleton as *The Divine Comedy,* Bollington LXXX (Princeton, NJ: Princeton University Press, 1970).

——. *Convivio.* In *Opere minori,* vol. 1, pt. 2, edited by Cesare Vasoli and Domenico De Robertis, 3–885. Milan: Riccardo Ricciardi, 1988. Translated by Richard Lansing as *The Convivio* (New York: Columbia University, Center for Digital Research and Scholarship, 1998), http://digitaldante.columbia.edu/library/dantes-works/the-convivio/.

——. *Dante Alighieri: Four Political Letters.* Edited and translated by Claire E. Honess. MHRA Critical Texts, vol. 6. London: Modern Humanities Research Association, 2007.

——. *Epistole.* Edited by Arsenio Frugoni and Giorgio Brugnoli. In *Opere minori,* vol. 2, edited by Pier Vincenzo Mengaldo et al., 507–643. Milan: Riccardo Ricciardi, 1979.

——. *Monarchia.* Edited by Bruno Nardi. In *Opere minori,* vol. 2, edited by Pier Vincenzo Mengaldo et al., 241–503. Milan: Riccardo Ricciardi, 1979. Translated by Anthony K. Cassell as *The "Monarchia" Controversy* (Washington, DC: Catholic University of America Press, 2004).

Anonimo Romano. *Cronica.* Edited by Giuseppe Porta. Milan: Adelphi, 1979. Translated by John Wright as *The Life of Cola di Rienzo* (Toronto: Pontifical Institute of Medieval Studies, 1975).

Augustine. *Concerning the City of God against the Pagans.* Translated by Henry Bettenson. London: Penguin Books, 1984.

——. *De civitate Dei.* Edited by Bernardus Dombart and Alphonsus Kalb.
1928–1929. Corpus christianorum: Series Latina, vols. 47–48.
Turnhout, Belgium: Brepols, 1955.

Birgitta of Sweden. *Birgitta of Sweden: Life and Selected Revelations.* Edited,
with a preface, by Marguerite Tjader Harris. Translation and notes
by Albert Ryle Kezel. Introduction by Tore Nyberg. New York:
Paulist, 1990.

——. *Revelaciones.* The second series of Latin writings in the collections of
the Svenska fornskriftsällskapet. Uppsala: Almquist and Wiksells
Boktryckeri. Bk. I, edited by Carl-Gustav Undhagen (1978). Bk. II,
edited by Carl-Gustav Undhagen and Birger Bergh (2001). Bk. III,
edited by Ann-Mari Jönsson (1988). Bk. IV, edited by Hans Aili
(1992). Bk. V, edited by Birger Bergh (1971). Bk. VI, edited by Birger
Bergh (1991). Bk. VII, edited by Birger Bergh (1967). Bk. VIII, edited
by Hans Aili (2002). Translated by Denis Searby, with introductions
and notes by Bridget Morris, as *The Revelations of St. Birgitta of Sweden*
(Oxford: Oxford University Press), vol. 1, *Liber caelestis,* bks. I–III
(2006); vol. 2, *Liber caelestis,* bks. IV–V (2008); vol. 3, *Liber caelestis,*
bks. VI–VII (2012); vol. 4, *The Heavenly Emperor's Book to Kings, the
Rule, and Minor Works* (2015).

Boccaccio, Giovanni. *Epistole e lettere.* Edited by Ginetta Auzzas. Vol. 5.1 of
Tutte le opere di Giovanni Boccaccio, edited by Vittore Branca. Milan:
Aldo Mondadori, 1992.

——. *Life of Dante.* Translated by Philip H. Wicksteed. Edited by William
Chamberlain. London: Oneworld Classics, 2011.

——. *Trattatello in laude di Dante.* Edited by Pier Giorgio Ricci. In *Tutte le
opere di Giovanni Boccaccio,* edited by Vittore Branca, vol. 3. Milan:
Aldo Mondadori, 1974.

Bruni, Leonardo. *History of the Florentine People.* Edited and translated by
James Hankins. I Tatti Renaissance Library. Cambridge, MA:
Harvard University Press, 2001–2004.

Catherine of Siena. *Il Dialogo.* 2nd ed. Edited by Giuliana Cavallini.
Testi Cateriniani I. Siena: Cantagalli, 1995. Electronic version
published by Centro internazionale di studi cateriniani, http://www
.centrostudicateriniani.it/4/download.html. Translated, with an
introduction, by Suzanne Noffke as *The "Dialogue" of Catherine of
Siena,* preface by Giuliana Cavallini (New York: Paulist, 1980).

———. *Le lettere di S. Caterina da Siena, ridotte a miglior lezione, e in ordine nuovo disposte con premio e note di Niccolò Tommaseo.* Edited by Niccolò Tommaseo. 4 vols. Florence, 1860. Edited and translated, with introduction and notes, by Suzanne Noffke as *The Letters of Catherine of Siena*, vols. 1–4 (Tempe, AZ: Arizona Center for Medieval and Renaissance Studies, 2000–2008).

Cicero, Marcus Tullius. *De natura deorum: Libri secundus et tertius.* Edited by Arthur Stanley Pease. Cambridge, MA: Harvard University Press, 1958. Translated by Horace C. P. McGregor as *The Nature of Gods* (Harmondsworth, UK: Penguin Books, 1972).

———. *The Speeches.* With an English translation by N. H. Watts. London: William Heinemann; New York: G. P. Putnam's Sons, 1923.

Cola di Rienzo. *Die Briefwechsel des Cola di Rienzo.* Edited by Konrad Burdach and Paul Pier. Vom Mittelater zur Reformation, vols. 2.1–5. Berlin: Wedimann, 1913–1929.

Duns Scotus. *God and Creatures: The Quodlibetal Questions.* Translated, with an introduction, notes, and glossary, by Felix Alluntis and Allan B. Wolter. Princeton, NJ: Princeton University Press, 1975.

Egidius Romanus [Giles of Rome]. *De ecclesiastica potestate.* Edited by Richard Scholtz. Weimar, Germany: H. Böhlaus Nachfolger, 1929.

Francis of Assisi: Early Documents. Vol. 3, *The Prophet.* Edited by Regis J. Armstrong, J. A. Wayne Hellmann, and William J. Short. New York: New City Press, 1998.

Francis of Assisi: Writings and Early Biographies; English Omnibus of the Sources for the Life of St. Francis. Edited by Marion A. Habig. Quincy, IL: Franciscan Press, Quincy University, 1991.

Il Processo Castellano: Con appendice di documenti sul culto e la canonizzazione di S. Caterina. Edited by Marie-Hyacinthe Laurent. Fontes vitae S. Catharinae Senensis historici, vol. 9. Milan: Fratelli Bocca, 1942.

Isidore of Seville. *The Etymologies of Isidore of Seville.* Translated, with introduction and notes, by Stephen A. Barney, W. J. Lewis, J. A. Beach, and Oliver Berghof. Cambridge: Cambridge University Press, 2006.

Livy. *Ab urbe condita.* In *Livy in Fourteen Volumes,* vol. 1, bks. 1–2. Translated by B. O. Foster. Cambridge, MA: Harvard University Press / Loeb, 1919.

Marsilius of Padua. *The Defensor Pacis of Marsilius of Padua.* Latin text.
    Edited by C. W. Previté-Orton. Cambridge: Cambridge University
    Press, 1928. Edited and translated by Annabel Brett as *Marsilius
    of Padua: The Defender of the Peace,* Cambridge Texts in the History
    of Political Thought (Cambridge: Cambridge University Press, 2005).

Migne, Jacques-Paul, ed. *Patrologiae cursus completus.* Series Latina, 221
    vols. Paris, 1841–1866.

Mussato, Albertino. "Ludovicus Bavarus." In *Fontes rerum Germanicarum,*
    edited by Johann Friedrich Böhmer, 1:170–189. Stuttgart, 1843; repr.
    Aalen, Germany: Scientia Verlag, 1969.

Petrarch, Francis. *Collatio laureationis.* In *Opere Latine di Francesco Petrarca,*
    vol. 2, edited by Antonietta Bufano, 1256–1283. Turin, Italy: Unione
    Tipografico-Editrice Torinese, 1975. Translated by Ernest Hatch
    Wilkins as "Petrarch's *Coronation Oration,*" in *Studies in the Life of
    Petrarch,* 300–313 (Cambridge, MA: Mediaeval Academy of America,
    1955).

———. *De remediis utrusque fortunae.* Translated by Conrad H. Rawski as
    *Petrarch's Remedies for Fortune Fair and Foul: A Modern English Transla-
    tion of "De remediis utriusque fortune," with a Commentary* (Bloomington:
    Indiana University Press, 1991).

———. *De sui ipsius et multorum ignorantia.* In *Invectives,* edited and translated
    by David Marsh, 222–363. I Tatti Renaissance Library. Cambridge,
    MA: Harvard University Press, 2003.

———. "Epistole metriche." Edited by Enrico Bianchi. In *Francesco Pe-
    trarca. Rime, trionfi e poesie latine,* edited by Ferdinando Neri, Guido
    Martellotti, Enrico Bianchi, and Natalino Sapegno, 706–805.
    Milano-Napoli: Ricciardo Ricciardi editore, 1951.

———. *Invectiva contra eum qui maledixit italie.* In *Invectives,* edited and
    translated by David Marsh, 364–475. I Tatti Renaissance Library.
    Cambridge, MA: Harvard University Press, 2003.

———. *Lettere disperse: Varie e miscellanee.* Edited by Alessandro Pancheri.
    Parma, Italy: Ugo Guandi, 1994.

———. *Liber sine nomine.* In *Sine nomine: Lettere polemiche e politiche,* edited by
    Ugo Dotti. Rome–Bari: Editori Laterza, 1974. Translated by
    Norman P. Zacour as *Petrarch's Book without a Name* (Toronto:
    Pontifical Institute of Medieval Studies, 1973).

——. *Poemata minora quae exstant omnia / Poesie minori del Petrarca.* Edited by Domenico Rossetti. Vols. 2–3. Milan: Società Tipografica dei Classici Italiani, 1831–1834.

——. *Rerum familiarum libri.* Edited by Ugo Dotti. 3 vols. Rome: Archivio Guido Izzo, 1991. Edited and translated by Aldo S. Bernardo as *Rerum familiarum libri, I–VIII* (Albany: State University of New York Press, 1975), *Letters on Familiar Matters: Rerum familiarum libri, IX–XVI* (Baltimore: John Hopkins University Press, 1982), *Letters on Familiar Matters: Rerum familiarum libri, XVII–XXIV* (Baltimore: Johns Hopkins University Press, 1985).

——. *Rime, Trionfi e Poesie Latine.* Edited by F. Neri, G. Martellotti, E. Bianchi, and N. Sapegno. Milan: Riccardo Ricciardi, 1951.

——. *Senilium rerum libri.* Latin text: *Epistole di Francesco Petrarca.* Edited by Ugo Dotti. Turin, Italy: Unione Tipografico-Editrice Torinese, 1978. Edited and translated by Aldo S. Bernardo, Saul Levin, and Reta A. Benardo as *Letters of Old Age: Rerum senilium libri, I–XVIII*, 2 vols. (Baltimore: Johns Hopkins University Press, 1992).

Raymond of Capua. *The Life of St. Catherine of Siena.* Translated by George Lamb. Charlotte, NC: TAN Books, 2011 [2003].

Suetonius. *Divus Augustus.* Edited, with introduction and commentary, by John M. Carter. Bristol: Bristol Classical Press, 1982.

——. *The Twelve Caesars.* Translated by Robert Graves. Harmondsworth, UK: Penguin Books, 1979.

William of Ockham. *Breviloquium de principatu tyrannic.* Latin text: *Wilhelm von Ockham als politischer Denker und sein Breviloquium de principatu tyrannico.* Edited by Richard Scholz. Leipzig: Verlag Karl H. Hiersemann, 1944. Translated by John Kilcullen as *A Short Discourse on the Tyrannical Government,* edited by Arthur Stephen McGrade (Cambridge: Cambridge University Press, 1992).

——. *Epistola ad frates minores.* In *Guillelmi de Ockham Opera politica,* vol. 3, edited by H. S. Offler et al. (Manchester: Manchester University Press, 1956), 6–17. Translated by John Kilcullen as *A Letter to the Minor Friars and Other Writings,* edited by Arthur Stephen Mc-Grade and John Kilcullen (Cambridge: Cambridge University Press, 1995).

SECONDARY SOURCES

Almazán, Vicente. "Saint Birgitta on the Pilgrimage Route to Santiago." In *Scandinavia, Saint Birgitta and the Pilgrimage Route to Santiago de Compostela: Proceedings of the VIII Spain and Sweden Encounters throughout History, Santiago de Compostela, October, 18–20, 2000,* 13–20. Santiago de Compostela, Spain: Martìnez Ruiz, Erique, 2002.

Andersson, Aron. *Guds moder och den heliga Birgitta: En antologi.* Vadstena, Sweden: Vadstena Affärstryck, 1978.

Anheim, Étienne. "La Chambre du Cerf: Image, savoir et nature à Avignon au milieu du XIVe siècle." *Micrologus* 16 (2008): 57–124.

———. *Clément VI au travail: Lire, écrire, prêcher au XIVe siècle.* Paris: Publications de la Sorbonne, 2014.

Armstrong, Regis J., J. A. Wayne Hellmann, and William J. Short, eds. *Francis of Assisi: Early Documents.* Vol. 3, *The Prophet.* New York: New City Press, 1998.

Ascoli, Albert Russell. *Dante and the Making of a Modern Author.* Cambridge: Cambridge University Press, 2008.

———. *"A Local Habitation and a Name": Imagining Histories in the Italian Renaissance.* New York: Fordham University Press, 2011.

———. "Petrarch's Middle Age: Memory, Imagination, History, and the 'Ascent of Mt. Ventoux.'" In *"A Local Habitation and a Name": Imagining Histories in the Italian Renaissance,* 21–58. New York: Fordham University Press, 2011. First published 1991.

———. "Petrarch's Private Politics." In *"A Local Habitation and a Name": Imagining Histories in the Italian Renaissance,* 118–158. New York: Fordham University Press, 2011.

Ascoli, Albert Russell, and Unn Falkeid, eds. *The Cambridge Companion to Petrarch.* Cambridge: Cambridge University Press, 2015.

Auerbach, Erich. *Dante, Poet of the Secular World.* Chicago: University of Chicago Press, 1961.

Barkan, Leonard. *Nature's Work of Art: The Human Body as Image of the World.* New Haven, CT: Yale University Press, 1975.

Baskins, Cristelle L. "Trecento Rome: The Poetics and Politics of Widowhood." In *Widowhood and Visual Culture in Early Modern Europe,* edited by Allison Levy, 197–209. Aldershot, UK: Ashgate, 2003.

Beattie, Blake. "Catherine of Siena and the Papacy." In *A Companion to Catherine of Siena*, edited by Carolyn Muessig, George Ferzoco, and Beverly Mayne Kienzle, 73–98. Leiden: Brill, 2012.

Beckwith, Sarah. *Christ's Body: Identity, Culture and Society in Late Medieval Writings.* London: Routledge, 1993.

Bergh, Birger. *Heliga Birgitta: Åttabarnsmor och profet.* Lund, Sweden: Historiska media, 2002.

Bernard Guillemani. "Il papato ad Avignone." In *Storia della chiesa,* vol. 11, *La crisi del trecento e il papato avignonese (1274–1378),* ed. Diego Quaglioni, 234–281. Milan: San Paolo, 1994.

Billanovich, Giuseppe. *Petrarca letterato.* Vol. 1, *Lo scrittoio del Petrarca.* Rome: Edizioni di storia e letteratura, 1947.

——. *La tradizione del testo di Livio e le origini dell'umanesimo: Tradizione e fortuna di Livio tra Medioevo e Umanesimo.* Vol. 2, *Il Livio del Petrarca e del Valla.* Padua: Antenore, 1981.

Black, Anthony. *Political Thought in Europe, 1250–1450.* Cambridge: Cambridge University Press, 1992.

Blumenfeld-Kosinski, Renate. *Poets, Saints, and Visionaries of the Great Schism, 1378–1417.* University Park: Pennsylvania State University Press, 2004.

Brett, Annabel. "Introduction." In *Marsilius of Padua: The Defender of the Peace,* edited and translated by Annabel Brett, xi–xxxi. Cambridge Texts in the History of Political Thought. Cambridge: Cambridge University Press, 2005.

——. "Politics, Right(s) and Human Freedom in Marsilius of Padua." In *Transformations in Medieval and Early-Modern Rights Discourse,* edited by Virpi Mäkinen and Petter Korkman, 95–116. Dordrecht, Netherlands: Springer, 2006.

Burr, David. *The Spiritual Franciscans: From Protest to Prosecution in the Century after Saint Francis.* University Park: Pennsylvania State University Press, 2001.

Bynum, Caroline Walker. *Holy Feast and Holy Fast: The Religious Significance of Food to Medieval Women.* Berkeley: University of California Press, 1987.

Canning, Joseph. *A History of Medieval Political Thought, 300–1450.* London: Routledge, 1996.

——. *The Ideas of Power in the Late Middle Ages, 1296–1417.* Cambridge: Cambridge University Press, 2011.

Carlyle, R. W., and A. J. Carlyle. *A History of Medieval Political Theory in the West.* 6 vols. Edinburgh: W. Blackwood and Sons, 1970 [1903–1936].

Cartotti, A. Odrasso. "La dimora di Santa Caterina da Siena." *L'Urbe* 24 (1961): 28–34.

Cassell, Anthony K. *The "Monarchia" Controversy: An Historical Study with Accompanying Translations of Dante Alighieri's "Monarchia," Guido Vernani's "Refutation of the 'Monarchia' Composed by Dante," and Pope John XXII's Bull "Si fratrum."* Washington, DC: Catholic University of America Press, 2004.

Cavallini, Giuliana. *Catherine of Siena.* London: Geoffrey Chapman, 1998.

Celenza, Christopher. *Renaissance Humanism and the Papal Curia: Lapo da Castiglionchio the Younger's "De Curiae Commodis."* Ann Arbor: University of Michigan Press, 2000.

Coleman, Janet. *A History of Political Thought: From the Middle Ages to the Renaissance.* Oxford: Blackwell, 2000.

Cosenza, Mario Emilio, ed. *Petrarch: The Revolution of Cola di Rienzo.* 3rd ed. With new introduction, notes, and bibliography by Ronald G. Musto. New York: Italica, 1996.

Davis, Charles T. "Dante and the Empire." In *The Cambridge Companion to Dante,* edited by Rachel Jacoff, 257–270. Cambridge: Cambridge University Press, 2007 [1991].

——. *Dante and the Idea of Rome.* Oxford: Clarendon, 1957.

——. "Rome and Babylon in Dante." In *Rome in the Renaissance: The City and the Myth: Papers of the Thirteenth Annual Conference of the Center for Medieval & Early Renaissance Studies,* edited by Paul A. Ramsey, 19–40. Binghamton, NY: Medieval and Renaissance Texts and Studies, Center for Medieval and Early Renaissance Studies, 1982.

D'Entrèves, Alexander Passerin. *Dante as a Political Thinker.* Oxford: Clarendon, 1952.

Dor, Juliette, Lesley Johnson, and Jocelyn Wogan-Browne, eds. *New Trends in Feminine Spirituality.* Turnhout, Belgium: Brepols, 1999.

Dotti, Ugo. *Vita di Petrarca.* Rome–Bari: Laterza, 1991 [1987].

Durling, Robert M. "The Ascent of Mt. Ventoux and the Crisis of Allegory." *Italian Quarterly* 18 (1974): 7–28.

Dzon, Mary. "Birgitta of Sweden and Christ's Clothing." In *The Christ Child in Medieval Culture: Alpha es et O!,* edited by Mary Dzon and Theresa M. Kenney, 117–145. Toronto: University of Toronto Press, 2012.

Eco, Umberto. *The Name of the Rose.* Translated by William Weaver. San Diego: Jovanovich, 1983. Originally published in Italian in 1980.

Ekwall, Sara. *Vår äldsta Birgittavita och dennas viktigaste varianter.* Stockholm: Almquist and Wiksell, 1965.

Elliott, Dyan. *Proving Woman: Female Spirituality and Inquisitional Culture in the Later Middle Ages.* Princeton, NJ: Princeton University Press, 2004.

Engh, Line Cecilie. "Embodying the Female Body Politic: Pro-papal Reception of Ephesians 5 in the Later Middle Ages." In *Bodies, Borders, Believers: Ancient Texts and Present Conversations,* edited by Anne Hege Grung, Marianne Bjelland Kartzow, and Anna Rebecca Solevåg, 164–197. Eugene, OR: Pickwick, 2015.

Falkeid, Unn, ed. *Dante: A Critical Reappraisal.* Oslo: Unipub, 2008.

———. "*De vita solitaria* and *De otio religioso:* The Perspective of the Guest." In *The Cambridge Companion to Petrarch,* edited by Albert Ascoli and Unn Falkeid, 111–120. Cambridge: Cambridge University Press, 2015.

———. "Petrarch and the Vision of Rome." *Acta Ad Archeologiam et Artium Historiam Pertinentia* 25 (n.s. 11) (2012): 195–207.

———. "Petrarch, Mont Ventoux and the Modern Self." *Forum Italicum* 43, no. 1 (2009): 5–29.

———. "Style, the Muscle of the Souls: Theories on Reading and Writing in Petrarch's Texts." *Quaderni d'Italianistica* 29, no.1 (2008): 21–38.

———. "'Thorn in the Flesh': Pain and Poetry in Petrarch's *Secretum.*" In *Pangs of Love and Longing: Configurations of Desire in Premodern Literature,* edited by Anders Cullhed et al., 74–89. Cambridge: Cambridge Scholars, 2013.

Feher, Michel, ed. *Fragments for a History of the Human Body.* 3 vols. New York: Zone, 1989.

Ferrante, Joan. *The Political Vision of the "Divine Comedy."* Princeton, NJ: Princeton University Press, 1984.

Fleck, Cathleen. "Seeking Legitimacy: Art and Manuscripts for the Popes in Avignon from 1378 to 1417." In *A Companion to the Great Western Schism (1378–1417),* edited by Joëlle Rollo-Koster and Thomas Izbicki, 239–302. Leiden: Brill, 2009.

Fogelqvist, Ingvar. *Apostasy and Reform in the Revelations of St. Birgitta.* Bibliotheca Theologiae Practicae 51. Stockholm: Almqvist and Wiksell International, 1993.

Freccero, John. *Dante: The Poetics of Conversion.* Cambridge, MA: Harvard University Press, 1986.

——. "The Fig Tree and the Laurel: Petrarch's Poetics." *Diacretics* 5, no. 1 (Spring 1975): 34–40.

Gajano, Sofia Boesch, and Odile Redon. "La *Legenda maior* di Raimondo da Capua, costruzione di una santa." In *Atti del simposio internazionale Cateriniano-Bernadiniano,* edited by Domenico Maffei and Paolo Nardi, 15–36. Siena: Accademia Senese degli Intronati, 1982.

Galbraith, David. "Petrarch and the Broken City." In *Antiquity and Its Interpreters,* edited by Alina Payne, Ann Kuttner, and Rebekah Smick, 17–20. Cambridge: Cambridge University Press, 2000.

Garnett, George. *Marsilius of Padua and "The Truth of History."* Oxford: Oxford University Press, 2006.

Gejrot, Claes, Mia Åkestam, and Roger Andersson, eds. *The Birgittine Experience: Papers from the Birgitta Conference in Stockholm 2011.* Stockholm: Kungliga Vitterhets Historie och Antikvitets Akademien, 2013.

Gejrot, Claes, Sara Risberg, and Mia Åkestam, eds. *Saint Birgitta, Syon and Vadstena: Papers from a Symposium in Stockholm, 4–6 October 2007.* Stockholm: Kungliga Vitterhets Historie och Antikvitets Akademien, 2010.

Gewirth, Alan. *Marsilius of Padua and Medieval Political Philosophy.* New York: Columbia University Press, 1951.

Godthardt, Frank. "The Life of Marsilius of Padua." In *A Companion to Marsilius of Padua,* edited by Gerson Moreno-Riano and Cary J. Nederman, 13–57. Leiden: Brill, 2012.

Grossvogel, Steven. "Justinian's Jus and Justificatio: Paradiso 6.10–27." Italian issue supplement, *Modern Language Notes* 127, no. 1 (2012): 130–137.

Habig, Marion A., ed. *St. Francis of Assisi: Writings and Early Biographies; English Omnibus of the Sources for the Life of St. Francis.* Quincy, IL: Franciscan Press, Quincy University, 1991.

Hamburger, Jeffrey F., and Gabriela Signori, eds. *Catherine of Siena: The Creation of a Cult.* Turnhout, Belgium: Brepols, 2013.

Hankins, James. "Humanism and the Origins of Modern Political Thought." In *The Cambridge Companion to Renaissance Humanism,* edited by Jill Kraye, 118–141. Cambridge: Cambridge University Press, 1996.

Härdelin, Alf, and Mereth Lindgren, eds. *Heliga Birgitta–budskapet och förebilden: Föredrag vid Jubileumssymposiet i Vadstena 3–7 oktober 1991.* Konferanser 28. Stockholm: Kungliga Vitterhets Historie och Antikvitets Akademien, 1993.

Havely, Nick. *Dante and the Franciscans: Poverty and the Papacy in the "Commedia."* Cambridge: Cambridge University Press, 2004.

Hayes, Zachary. "Bonaventure: Mystery of the Triune God." In *The History of Franciscan Theology,* edited by Kenan B. Osborne, 39–127. New York: Franciscan Institute, 2007 [1994].

Holmes, Olivia. *Dante's Two Beloveds.* New Haven, CT: Yale University Press, 2008.

Jacoff, Rachel, ed. *The Cambridge Companion to Dante.* Cambridge: Cambridge University Press, 2007 [1991].

Jönsson, Arne. *Alfonso of Jaén: His Life and Works with Critical Editions of the "Epistola Solitarii," the "Informaciones" and the "Epistola Serui Christi."* Studia Graeca et Latina Lundensia 1. Lund, Sweden: Lund University Press, 1989.

———. *St. Bridget's Revelations to the Popes: An Edition of the So-Called "Tractatus de summis pontificibus."* Lund, Sweden: Lund University Press, 1997.

Kantorowicz, Ernst H. *The King's Two Bodies: A Study in Mediaeval Political Theology.* Princeton, NJ: Princeton University Press, 1997. First published 1957.

Kaye, Joel. *A History of Balance, 1250–1475: The Emergence of New Model of Equilibrium and Its Impact on Thought.* Cambridge: Cambridge University Press, 2014.

Kilcullen, John. "The Political Writings." In *The Cambridge Companion to Ockham,* edited by Paul Vincent Spade, 302–326. Cambridge: Cambridge University Press, 1999.

Kircher, Timothy. *The Poet's Wisdom: The Humanists, the Church, and the Formation of Philosophy in the Early Renaissance.* Leiden: Brill, 2006.

Kirkham, Victoria, and Armando Maggi, eds. *Petrarch: A Critical Guide to the Complete Works.* Chicago: University of Chicago Press, 2009.

Klockars, Birgit. *Birgitta och böckerna: En undersökning av den heliga Birgittas källor.* Historiska serien. Stockholm: Kungliga Vitterhets Historie och Antikvitets Akademien, 1966.

Knysh, George. "Biographical Rectifications concerning Ockham's Avignon Period." *Franciscan Studies* 46 (1986): 61–91.

Kraye, Jill, ed. *The Cambridge Companion to Renaissance Humanism.* Cambridge: Cambridge University Press, 1996.

Ladurie, Emmanuel Le Roy. *Montaillou: The Promised Land of Error.* Translated by Barbara Bray. New York: George Braziller, 1978 [1975].

Lagarde, Georges de. *Le Defensor pacis.* Leuven, Belgium: Nauwelaerts, 1970.

Le Goff, Jacques. "Head or Heart? The Political Use of Body Metaphors in the Middle Ages." In *Fragments for a History of the Human Body,* 3 vols., edited by Michel Feher, 1:13–26. New York: Zone, 1989.

Lewis, Ewart. "The 'Positivism' of Marsilius of Padua." *Speculum* 38 (1963): 541–582.

Locranz, Margherita Giordano. "Intorno al viaggio italiano di Birgitta di Svezia: Il soggiorno milanese (autunno 1349)." In *Vestigia: Studi di onore di Giuseppe Billanovich,* edited by Rino Avesani, 387–398. Rome: Edizione di storia e letteratura, 1984.

Looney, Dennis. "The Beginnings of Humanistic Oratory: Petrarch's *Coronation Oration, Collatio laureationis.*" In *Petrarch: A Critical Guide to the Complete Works,* edited by Victoria Kirkham and Armando Maggi, 131–141. Chicago: University of Chicago Press, 2009.

Lubac, Henri. *Corpus Mysticum: The Eucharist and the Church in the Middle Ages.* Edited by Laurence Paul Hemming and Susan Frank Parsons. Translated by Gemma Simmonds with Richard Price and Christopher Stephens. London: SCM Press, 2006. First published as *L'Eucharistie et l'Église au moyen âge,* 1944.

Luongo, F. Thomas. "The Historical Reception of Catherine of Siena." In *A Companion to Catherine of Siena*, edited by Carolyn Muessig, George Ferzoco, and Beverly Mayne Kienzle, 23–47. Leiden: Brill, 2012.

———. *Saintly Politics of Catherine of Siena.* Ithaca, NY: Cornell University Press, 2006.

Maffei, Domenico, and Paolo Nardi, eds. *Atti del simposio internazionale Cateriniano-Bernadiniano.* Siena: Accademia Senese degli Intronati, 1982.

Mäkinen, Virpi, and Petter Korkman, eds. *Transformations in Medieval and Early-Modern Rights Discourse.* Dordrecht, Netherlands: Springer, 2006.

Marchesi, Simone. "'Epicuri de grege porcus': Ciacco, Epicurus and Isidore of Seville." *Dante Studies, with the Annual Report of the Dante Society* 117 (1999): 117–131.

Mazzotta, Giuseppe. *Confine quasi orrizonte: Saggi su Dante.* Rome: Edizioni di storia e letteratura, 2014.

———. *Dante, Poet of the Desert.* Princeton, NJ: Princeton University Press, 1979.

———. "Dante's Poetics of Births and Foundations." In *Dante: A Critical Reappraisal*, edited by Unn Falkeid, 7–27. Oslo: Unipub, 2008.

———. *Dante's Vision and the Circle of Knowledge.* Princeton, NJ: Princeton University Press, 1993.

———. "Petrarca e il Discorso di Roma." In *Petrarca: Canoni, esemplarità*, edited by Valeria Fenucci, 259–273. Rome: Bulzoni editore, 2006.

———. *The Worlds of Petrarch.* Durham, NC: Duke University Press, 1993.

McGinn, Bernard. *The Flowering of Mysticism: Men and Women in the New Mysticism, 1200–1350.* New York: Crossroad, 1998.

McGrade, Arthur Stephen. *The Political Thought of William of Ockham: Personal and Institutional Principles.* Cambridge: Cambridge University Press, 2002 [1974].

———. "Right(s) in Ockham." In *Transformations in Medieval and Early-Modern Rights Discourse*, edited by Virpi Mäkinen and Petter Korkman, 63–94. Dordrecht, Netherlands: Springer, 2006.

Meech, Sanford Brown. *The Book by Margery Kempe.* Early English Text Society 212. London: Oxford University Press, 1940.

Menache, Sophia. "The Gelasian Theory from a Communication Perspective: Development and Decline." *Revista de Historia* 13 (2012): 57–76.

Miethke, Jürgen. *Ai confini del potere: Il dibattito sulla potestas papale da Tommaso d'Aquino a Guglielmo d'Ockham*. Padua: Editrici Francescane, 2005 [2000].

——. "Marsilius und Ockham: Publikum und Leser ihrer politischen Schriften im späteren Mittelalter." *Medioevo* 6 (1980): 534–558.

Mollat, Guillaume. *The Popes at Avignon, 1305–1378*. London: Thomas Nelson, 1963.

Morche, Gunther. "L'ars nova et la musique liturgique au temps des papes d'Avignon." *Annuaire de la Société des amos du Palais des papes et des monuments d'Avignon* 77 (2000): 131–141.

Moreno-Riano, Gerson, ed. *The World of Marsilius of Padua*. Turnhout, Belgium: Brepols, 2006.

Moreno-Riano, Gerson, and Cary J. Nederman, eds. *A Companion to Marsilius of Padua*. Leiden: Brill, 2012.

Morris, Bridget. "Birgittines and Beguines in Medieval Sweden." In *New Trends in Feminine Spirituality*, edited by Juliette Dor, Lesley Johnson, and Jocelyn Wogan-Browne, 159–175. Turnhout, Belgium: Brepols, 1999.

——. *St. Birgitta of Sweden*. Woodbridge, UK: Boydell, 1999.

Muessig, Carolyn, George Ferzoco, and Beverly Mayne Kienzle, eds. *A Companion to Catherine of Siena*. Leiden: Brill, 2012.

Mullin, Edwin. *The Popes of Avignon: A Century in Exile*. New York: Blue-Bridge, 2008.

Musto, Ronald G. *Apocalypse in Rome: Cola di Rienzo and the Politics of the New Age*. Berkeley: University of California Press, 2003.

Myrdal, Janken. "The Revelations of Saint Birgitta and Everyday Life in the Fourteenth Century." In *Saint Birgitta, Syon and Vadstena: Papers from a Symposium in Stockholm, 4–6 October 2007*, edited by Claes Gejrot, Sara Risberg, and Mia Åkestam, 231–246. Stockholm: Kungliga Vitterhets Historie och Antikvitets Akademien, 2010.

Najemy, John M. "Dante and Florence." In *The Cambridge Companion to Dante*, edited by Rachel Jacoff, 236–256. Cambridge: Cambridge University Press, 2007 [1991].

——. *A History of Florence, 1200–1575.* Malden, MA: Blackwell, 2007.

Nardi, Bruno. *Dal "Convivio" alla "Commedia."* Studi Storici, fasc. 35–39. Rome: Istituto Storico Italiano, 1960.

Nederman, Cary J. *Community and Consent: The Secular Political Theory of Marsiglio of Padua's "Defensor Pacis."* Lanham, MD: Rowman and Littlefield, 1995.

Nold, Patrick. *Pope John XXII and His Franciscan Cardinal Bertrand de la Tour and the Apostolic Poverty Controversy.* Oxford: Clarendon, 2004.

——. "Pope John XXII, the Franciscan Order and Its *Rule.*" In *The Cambridge Companion to Francis of Assisi,* edited by Michael J. P. Robson, 258–272. New York: Cambridge University Press, 2012.

Nyberg, Tore, ed. *Birgitta, hendes værk og hendes klostre i Norden.* Odense University Studies in History and Social Sciences 150. Odense, Denmark: Odense University Press, 1991.

Oen, Maria Husabø. "The Visions of St. Birgitta: A Study of Making and Reception of Images in the Later Middle Ages." PhD diss., University of Oslo, 2015.

Olsen, Birger Munk. "L'étude des classiques à Avignon au XIVe siècle." In *Avignon and Naples: Italy in France—France in Italy in the Fourteenth Century,* edited by Lene Waage Petersen, Marianne Pade, and Hannemarie Ragn Jensen, 13–25. Analecta Romana Instituti Danici Supplementum 25. Rome: "L'Erma" di Bretschneider, 1997.

Parson, Gerald. *The Cult of Saint Catherine of Siena: A Study in Civil Religion.* Aldershot, UK: Ashgate, 2008.

Petersen, Lene Waage, Marianne Pade, and Hannemarie Ragn Jensen, eds. *Avignon and Naples: Italy in France—France in Italy in the Fourteenth Century.* Analecta Romana Instituti Danici Supplementum 25. Rome: "L'Erma" di Bretschneider, 1997.

Piltz, Anders. "Magister Mathias of Sweden in His Theological Context: A Preliminary Survey." In *The Editing of Philosophical and Theological Texts from the Middle Ages,* edited by Monica Asztalos, 137–160. Stockholm: Almqvist and Wiksell, 1986.

Pirotta, Nino. *Music and Culture in Italy from the Middle Ages to the Baroque.* Cambridge, MA: Harvard University Press, 1984.

Quaglioni, Diego, ed. *Storia della chiesa*. Vol. 11, *La crisi del trecento e il papato avignonese (1274–1378)*. Milan: San Paolo, 1994.

Quillen, Carol Everhart. *Rereading the Renaissance: Petrarch, Augustine, and the Language of Humanism*. Ann Arbor: University of Michigan Press, 1998.

Quillet, Jeannine. *La philosophie politique de Marsile de Padoue*. Paris: J. Vrin, 1970.

Reeves, Marjorie. *The Influence of Prophecy in the Later Middle Ages: A Study in Joachimism*. Notre Dame, IN: University of Notre Dame Press, 2011 [1969].

——. "Marsiglio of Padua and Dante Alighieri." In *Trends in Mediaeval Political Thought*, edited by Beryl Smalley, 86–105. Oxford: Basil Blackwell, 1965.

Renouard, Yves. *The Avignon Papacy: The Popes in Exile, 1305–1403*. New York: Barnes and Noble Books, 1994 [1954].

Ricci, Pier Giorgio. "Il commeno di Cola di Rienzo alla 'Monarchia' di Dante." *Studi medievali*, ser. 3, vol. 6, no. 2 (1965): 665–708.

Rico, Francisco. *Vida u Obra de Petrarca: Lectura del Secretum*. Vol. 1. Padua: Antenore, 1974.

Robbins, Jill. "Petrarch Reading Augustine: 'The Ascent of Mont Ventoux.'" *Philological Quarterly* 64 (1985): 533–553.

Robson, Michael J. P., ed. *The Cambridge Companion to Francis of Assisi*. Cambridge: Cambridge University Press, 2012.

Rollo-Koster, Joëlle. *Avignon and Its Papacy, 1309–1417*. Lanham, MD: Rowman and Littlefield, 2015.

Rollo-Koster, Joëlle, and Thomas Izbicki, eds. *A Companion to the Great Western Schism (1378–1417)*. Leiden: Brill, 2009.

Romagnoli, Alessandra Bartolomei. "Mistica, profezia femminile, e poteri alla fine del Medioevo." In *Il "Liber" di Angela Foligno e la mistica dei secoli XIII–XIV in rapporto alle nuove culture: Atti del XLV convegno storico internazionale, Todi, 12–15 ottobre, 2008*, 485–515. Spoleto, Italy: Fondazione centro italiano di studi sull'alto medioevo, 2009.

Rosenwein, Barbara H. *A Short History of the Middle Ages*. Toronto: University of Toronto Press, 2014.

Rubenstein, Nicolai. "Marsilius of Padua and Italian Political Thought of His Time." In *Europe in the Late Middle Ages,* edited by John Hale, Roger Highfield, and Beryl Smalley, 44–75. London: Faber, 1965.

Rubin, Miri. *Corpus Christi: The Eucharist in Late Medieval Culture.* Cambridge: Cambridge University Press, 1991.

Sahlin, Claire L. *Birgitta of Sweden and the Voice of Prophecy.* Woodbridge, UK: Boydell, 2001.

Salmesvuori, Päivi. *Power and Sainthood: The Case of Birgitta of Sweden.* New York: Palgrave Macmillan, 2014.

Scott, Karen. "*Io Caterina:* Ecclesiastical Politics and Oral Culture in the Letters of Catherine of Siena." In *Dear Sister: Medieval Women and the Epistolary Genre,* edited by Karen Cherewatuk and Ulrike Wiethaus, 87–121. Philadelphia: University of Pennsylvania Press, 1993.

———. "St. Catherine of Siena, *Apostola.*" *Church History* 61, no.1 (1992): 34–46.

———. "Urban Spaces, Women's Network, and the Lay Apostolate in the Siena of Catherine Benincasa." In *Creative Women in Medieval and Early Modern Italy,* edited by E. Ann Matter and John Cloakely, 105–119. Philadelphia: University of Pennsylvania Press, 1994.

Shogimen, Takashi. "Medicine and the Body Politic in Marsilius of Padua's *Defensor pacis.*" In *A Companion to Marsilius of Padua,* edited by Gerson Moreno-Riano and Cary J. Nederman, 71–117. Leiden: Brill, 2012.

———. *Ockham and Political Discourse in the Late Middle Ages.* Cambridge: Cambridge University Press, 2007.

Sigmund, Paul E., Jr. "The Influence of Marsilius of Padua on XVth Century Conciliarism." *Journal of the History of Ideas* 23 (1962): 392–402.

Skinner, Quentin. *The Foundation of Modern Political Thought.* Vol. 1, *The Renaissance.* Cambridge: Cambridge University Press, 2004 [1978].

Smalley, Beryl, ed. *English Friars and Antiquity in the Early Fourteenth Century.* Oxford: Basil Blackwell, 1960.

———. *Trends in Mediaeval Political Thought.* Oxford: Basil Blackwell, 1965.

Spade, Paul Vincent, ed. *The Cambridge Companion to Ockham.* Cambridge: Cambridge University Press, 1999.

Steinberg, Justin. *Dante and the Limits of the Law.* Chicago: University of Chicago Press, 2014.

Strömberg, Bengt. *Magister Mathias och fransk mendikantpredikan.* Stockholm: Svenska Kyrkans Diakonistyrelses Bokförlag, 1944.

Suydam Mary A., and Joanna E. Ziegler, eds. *Performance and Transformation: New Approaches to Late Medieval Spirituality.* New York: St. Martin's, 1999.

Tierney, Brian. *The Crisis of Church and State, 1050–1300.* Englewood Cliffs, NJ: Prentice-Hall, 1964.

——. *The Idea of Natural Rights.* Grand Rapids, MI: William B. Eerdmans, 1997.

——. "The Idea of Natural Rights—Origins and Persistence." *Northwestern University Journal of International Human Rights* 2, no.1 (2004): 3–13.

——. *Origins of Papal Infallibility, 1150–1350.* Leiden: Brill, 1972.

Tylus, Jane. "Mystical Literacy: Writing and Religious Women in Late Medieval Italy." In *A Companion to Catherine of Siena,* edited by Carolyn Muessig, George Ferzoco, and Beverly Mayne Kienzle, 155–185. Leiden: Brill, 2012.

——. *Reclaiming Catherine of Siena: Literacy, Literature, and the Signs of Others.* Chicago: University of Chicago Press, 2009.

Ullmann, Walter. *The Growth of Papal Government in the Middle Ages.* London: Methuen, 1955.

——. *A History of Political Thought: The Middle Ages.* Harmondsworth, UK: Penguin, 1965.

Vauchez, André. *Francis of Assisi: The Life and Afterlife of a Medieval Saint.* Translated by Michael F. Cusato. New Haven, CT: Yale University Press, 2012.

——. *The Laity in the Middle Ages: Religious Beliefs and Devotional Practices.* Notre Dame, IN: University of Notre Dame Press, 1993 [1987].

Vickers, Nancy J. "Widowed Words: Dante, Petrarch, and the Metaphors of Mourning." In *Discourses of Authority in Medieval and Renaissance Literature,* edited by Kevin Brownlee and Walter Stephens, 97–108. Hanover, NH: University Press of New England, 1989.

Webb, Heather. "*Lacrime Cordiali:* Catherine of Siena and the Value of Tears." In *A Companion to Catherine of Siena,* edited by Carolyn Muessig, George Ferzoco, and Beverly Mayne Kienzle, 99–112. Leiden: Brill, 2012.

Weiss, Roberto. "Barbato da Sulmona, il Petrarca e la rivoluzione di Cola di Rienzo." In *Studi Petrarcheschi,* edited by Carlo Calcaterra, 13–22. Bologna: Minerva, 1950.

Westwater, Lynn Lara. "The Uncollected Poet." In *Petrarch: A Critical Guide to the Complete Works,* edited by Victoria Kirkham and Armando Maggi, 301–309. Chicago: University of Chicago Press, 2009.

Wilkins, Ernest Hatch. *Life of Petrarch.* Chicago: University of Chicago Press, 1961.

——. *Studies in the Life of Petrarch.* Cambridge, MA: Mediaeval Academy of America, 1955.

Wilks, Michael. *The Problem of Sovereignty in the Later Middle Ages.* Cambridge: Cambridge University Press, 1964.

Williman, Daniel, Marie-Henriette Jullien de Pommerol, and Jacques Monfrin. *Bibliothèques ecclésiastiques au temps de la papauté d'Avignon.* Paris: Editions du CNRS, 1980.

Witt, Ronald G. *"In the Footsteps of the Ancients": The Origin of Humanism from Lovato to Bruni.* Leiden: Brill, 2000.

——. *The Two Latin Cultures and the Foundation of Renaissance Humanism in Medieval Italy.* Cambridge: Cambridge University Press, 2012.

Wood, Diana. *Clement VI: The Pontificate and Ideas of an Avignon Pope.* Cambridge: Cambridge University Press, 1989.

Woodhouse, John, ed. *Dante and Governance.* Oxford: Clarendon, 1997.

Zac, Gur. *Petrarch's Humanism and the Care of the Self.* Cambridge: Cambridge University Press, 2010.

Zutshi, Patrick N. R. "The Avignon Papacy." In *The New Cambridge Medieval History,* vol. 6, *C. 1300–c. 1415,* edited by Michael Jones, 653–674. Cambridge: Cambridge University Press, 2000.

ACKNOWLEDGMENTS

This book emerged over a number of years. I am deeply indebted to the two institutions that have financed my research, and to countless colleagues and friends who have contributed constructive criticism and encouraged and inspired me en route.

I would like to express my gratitude to the Faculty of Humanities at the University of Oslo for giving me the opportunity to follow my interests by providing me with a postdoctoral fellowship from 2008 to 2013. Many thanks go to my former colleagues at the Department of Literature, Area Studies, and European Languages, and above all to my supervisor during my PhD, and my later mentor and dear friend, Jon Haarberg. As he once commented, this book is indeed six volumes in one because of its six protagonists, each of them accompanied by an array of scholarly traditions and critical literature. At times when I found my project just too ambitious or altogether insurmountable, Jon put me back on the right track in his affable and gentle manner.

In 2014 I was awarded a five-year fellowship at the Royal Swedish Academy of Letters, History and Antiquities in Stockholm. Warm thanks go to my colleagues and students at the Department of Culture and Aesthetics at Stockholm University, with which I was affiliated, and to the academy. They were truly some fabulous years in Stockholm, and I am immensely grateful for the opportunities that I was given to present and discuss my ongoing research, to organize seminars and conferences, and to discover new fields of interest that I believe will bear fruit in the near future—all this within the vivid, trustful, and intellectually stimulating atmosphere that surrounded me. Heartfelt thanks as well to Anders Cullhed, professor in the department and director of the academy. The precious combination of mentorship and friendship over the last decade has been invaluable to me. Also, I would like to express my gratitude to the network of friends and colleagues that followed in the wake of the collaboration with Anders, such as (in alphabetic order) Carin Franzén, Peter Gillgren, Sofie Kluge, Mats Malm, Elisabeth Wåghäll Nivre, Erland Sellberg, Inga Elmqvist Söderlund, and my two PhD students, Håkan Trygger and Johanna Vernqvist.

When I was only halfway through the fellowship in Stockholm, I accepted a position as associate professor in Oslo and had to leave Sweden. Warm and sincere thanks, then, go to all my current colleagues at the Department of Philosophy, Classics, History of Art and Ideas at the University of Oslo.

I owe a tremendous debt of gratitude to Giuseppe Mazzotta at Yale University. In spring 2007 he invited me to give two talks on Petrarch at the Italian Department. When I first mentioned to him the idea of a book about intellectual debates during the Avignon papacy, an idea that stemmed from my many years of studying Petrarch, he responded enthusiastically. I am deeply grateful to him for his interest in my work, for his generosity, and for the many stimulating conversations we have enjoyed. Mazzotta's outstanding works on Dante and Petrarch, his broad intellectual and imaginative orientation, and his familiarity with the theological, philosophical, and literary questions of the *trecento* set the course for my research. Already in the spring of 2008 he invited me back to Yale to give a series of four seminars, the so-called Spring Seminar, based on my preliminary steps on the Avignon project. Later I spent the entire academic year 2010–2011 at Yale as a Fulbright Visiting Scholar. I am also indebted to Maria Rosa Menocal, now sadly passed away, who openhandedly invited me to be a fellow at the Whitney Humanities Center at Yale the very same year. Many thanks to the students and colleagues at Yale, who responded to my work, raised vital questions, and offered comments and advice, thus fundamentally shaping the form of the project. Warmest thanks go to Angela Capodivacca, whom I first met at Yale, and who since then has become a dear friend.

I have discussed this book with a number of people, and many of them have read parts of it and provided me with valuable comments and viewpoints. In alphabetical order I extend my thanks to Roger Andersson, Erminia Ardessino, Albert Russell Ascoli, Zygmunt Baranski, Susanna Barsella, Renate Blumenfeld-Kosinski, Theodore J. Cachey Jr., Christopher S. Celenza, Virginia Cox, Line Cecilie Engh, Aileen Astorga Feng, Else Marie Lingaas, F. Thomas Luongo, Lodi Nauta, Maria Husabø Oen, Marianne Pade, Jennifer Rushworth, Päivi Salmesvuori, Federico Schneider, Jane Tylus, Anna Fay Wainwright, and Christopher Wood. Particular thanks go to Albert Russell Ascoli for his precious friendship and for our long collaboration on Petrarch; to Aileen Astorga Feng, who roused my interest in women writers of the Renaissance, and with whom I enjoyed cheerful collaboration on the *cinquecento* poet Gaspara Stampa; to Jane Tylus, whose work on Catherine of Siena was a true discovery that had a profound impact on me, and who has given me invaluable comments during our strolls in Stockholm, Berlin, and Rome; and finally to Maria Husabø Oen, whose ongoing research on Birgitta of Sweden has been a great inspiration to me, and whose friendship has enriched my life.

Warm thanks to Kate Lowe, the editor of the I Tatti Studies in Italian Renaissance History, who received my book proposal enthusiastically; to the two anonymous readers from Harvard University Press, whose comments, objections, and notes improved my book considerably; to Peter Glen, who has been my superb copyeditor for many years; and to my excellent editor at Harvard University Press, Andrew Kinney. I would also like to extend my thanks to two special colleagues in Oslo whose work I admire and whose friendship has been essential to me: Kristin Bliksrud Aavitsland and Victor Plahte Tschudi. Thanks for our many inspiring and always uplifting conversations about all kinds of things, and for making studies within the fields of European medieval and Renaissance culture such a pleasurable activity—even in Norway, despite the limited traditions we have at hand for this in our country.

Last but not least, words cannot express my gratitude to my family, to my beloved husband, Hans Butenschøn, and our three children: Emma, Therese, and Bernhard. I cannot repeat this enough: you are simply my everything!

This book is dedicated to my parents, Sigrid and Kolbein Falkeid. I thank you for bringing me up in such an emotionally and intellectually stimulating home, with bookshelves from floor to ceiling. From early childhood my parents taught my siblings and me that there was literature for every occasion, every shifting mood, and every new turn in life. Books became our extended family; we lived with them, we cried or laughed with them, and we discussed scenes and episodes around the dinner table or late into the evening. My parents' open-mindedness and incessant curiosity have taught me the value of being on a continuous journey, an experience Petrarch once captured in the expression *peregrinus ubique*. To put it another way: if you think you have finished learning, you are not learned, but finished!

INDEX

usus (use): *dominium* vs., 11, 78, 89–90; Ockham on right of minimal use, 76; in prelapsarian state, 85

Valla, Lorenzo, 89, 187n19
Vatican Council, 88
Vauchez, André, 78, 128, 136, 143
Verdi, Giuseppe, 118
Villani, Giovanni, 69, 73
Virgil, 109, 111; *Aeneid,* 42; *Eclogues,* 102–103; *Georgics,* 108–109
Visconti, Bernabò, 18, 144, 152
Visconti, Galeazzo, 144
Visconti, Giovanni, 121
Visconti, Matteo, 53, 121, 144
Visconti family, 15, 18, 140, 144, 151
Vitry, Jacques de, 132
Vitry, Philippe de, 22

volgare (vernacular language), 153
Voragine, Jacobus de, *Legenda aurea,* 132

Wagner, Richard, 118
Waldensians, 176
War of the Eight Saints, 19, 151
Webb, Heather, 230n30
White Guelphs, 29, 96
widow metaphor: Birgitta's use of, 12, 135; in book of Lamentations, 100–101; Dante's use of, 101; Petrarch's use of, 100, 102, 133; Rome characterized by, 100–102, 104, 122, 133–134
Wilkins, Ernest Hatch, 108
will, 92–94
William of Moerbeke, 58
Wood, Diana, 7, 17